WILLIAM MARSHAL

David Crouch's *William Marshal*, now in its third edition, depicts this intriguing medieval figure as a ruthless opportunist, astute courtier, manipulative politician and a brutal but efficient soldier. Born the fourth son of a minor baron, he ended his days as Earl of Pembroke and Regent of England, and was the only medieval knight to have a contemporary biography written about him. Using this biography, in addition to the many other primary sources dedicated to him, the author provides a narrative of William Marshal and a survey of the times in which he lived, and also considers the problems and questions posed by the *History*.

The third edition has been extensively updated and revised, and now includes:

- expanded sections on the reality of medieval tournaments and warfare as it is described in the biography;
- an in-depth study of Marshal's family life and children based on the latest research, including material from the new edition of the Marshal family acts and letters; and
- more on Marshal's royal patrons and contemporaries, in particular the relationship between Marshal and his nemesis, King John.

William Marshal explores the world of medieval knighthood and the the aristocratic life of the times in engaging, readable prose, and is a unique resource for students of medieval history.

David Crouch is Professor of Medieval History at the University of Hull and a Fellow of the British Academy. His recent publications include *The English Aristocracy, 1070–1272* (2013) and *The Acts an* ... *of Pembroke 1145–124{* ... *dieval Life* ... *and Earls*

WILLIAM MARSHAL

Third edition

David Crouch

Routledge
Taylor & Francis Group

LONDON AND NEW YORK

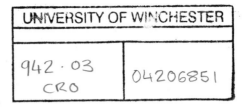

This edition published 2016
by Routledge
2 Park Square, Milton Park, Abingdon, Oxon OX14 4RN

and by Routledge
711 Third Avenue, New York, NY 10017

Routledge is an imprint of the Taylor & Francis Group, an informa business

© 2016 David Crouch

The right of David Crouch to be identified as author of this work
has been asserted by him in accordance with sections 77 and 78
of the Copyright, Designs and Patents Act 1988.

First edition published 1990 by Pearson Education Limited

Second edition published 2002 by Routledge

British Library Cataloguing-in-Publication Data
A catalogue record for this book is available from the British Library

Library of Congress Cataloging-in-Publication Data
Names: Crouch, David.Title: William Marshal / David Crouch.
   Description: Third edition. | London : Routledge, 2016. | "First edition published 1990 by
   Pearson Education Limited; second edition published 2002"--Title page verso. | Includes
   bibliographical references and index.
   Identifiers: LCCN 2015034082| ISBN 9781138939325 (hardback : alkaline paper) | ISBN
   9781138939332 (paperback : alkaline paper) | ISBN 9781315642468 (ebook)
   Subjects: LCSH: Pembroke, William Marshal, Earl of, 1144?-1219. | Great Britain--History--
   Angevin period, 1154-1216. | Knights and knighthood--Great Britain--Biography. | Regents--
   Great Britain--Biography. | Chivalry--Great Britain--History--To 1500.
   Classification: LCC DA209.P4 C73 2016 | DDC 942.03/4092--dc23LC record available at
   http://lccn.loc.gov/2015034082

ISBN: 978-1-138-93932-5 (hbk)
ISBN: 978-1-138-93933-2 (pbk)
ISBN: 978-1-315-64246-8 (ebk)

Typeset in Bembo and Stone Sans
by Florence Production Ltd, Stoodleigh, Devon, UK
Printed in Great Britain by
Ashford Colour Press Ltd, Gosport, Hants

CONTENTS

Contents

MAPS, GENEALOGICAL TABLES AND FIGURES

Maps

Tables

Figures

PREFACE TO FIRST EDITION

In writing this book, I have incurred a number of debts. I must acknowledge first the help of David Bates, who came to me with the idea for the book, and neatly shepherded the resulting flock of words into several well-ordered folds. Thanks are also due to others who have contributed ideas and suggestions: Adrian Ailes, David Carpenter, Steve Church, Lindy Grant, Sandy Heslop, Tom Keefe, Derek Keene, Chris Lewis, Tom McNeill and Jeffrey West. Any remaining errors and obscurities are my own doing. Eric Hemming's endeavours while my research assistant must be warmly acknowledged. The forbearance of my wife while I was writing this book was constant and generous.

The staff of a number of record repositories and libraries gave me material assistance: notably the British Library, the Public Record Office at Chancery Lane, the Archives Nationales in Paris, Somerset and Wiltshire Record Offices, and Birmingham Central Reference Library. Of a wholly different order has been the contribution of the Institute of Historical Research, which hosted for four years the research project from which the material for this book has been drawn. I gratefully acknowledge the immense debt owed to Professor Michael Thompson, Dr Alice Prochaska and their staff in the Institute's administration and library in furthering my research. The Economic and Social Research Council provided the funds for computer support of the project. Lastly, I must thank the Leverhulme Trust, whose remarkable generosity has principally funded the research out of which this book has resulted, and without which it would not have been possible.

PREFACE TO SECOND EDITION

It was a great privilege and pleasure to be asked to revise and extend this book for a second edition. The study of the twelfth and thirteenth centuries has – I'm glad to say – not stood still since it was written in 1989. When I revised the bibliography, I was impressed with the depth and range of the works published in the field in the past 13 years. In all these debates, the Marshal has been in the thick of things, as he was in the thick of things in his own lifetime. Another reason for a revision is the fact that his biography, the *History*, is about to appear in a new edition, and in its first English translation, in a special publication of the Anglo-Norman Text Society, under the general editorship of Ian Short. I would like to acknowledge the generosity of the Society in allowing me to quote from the new translation. This will be a major event in the study of both Angevin history and medieval French literature. The new edition has made advances in the analysis of the text and its construction, and its findings and voice need to be taken into account in this revision. In rewriting this book, I can also put right some errors, not least the absence in the first edition of a text reference to Meyer's monumental edition of the *History*, an omission commented upon humorously by several reviewers.

I did not end up liking the Marshal any more after finishing this edition than I did in 1989, but at least, having advanced further down the path of life, I think I understand the older Marshal a little better. I take pleasure in recording yet again my thanks to other scholars in producing this book, not least to the wisdom and expertise of my colleagues in editing the *History*, Tony Holden and Stewart Gregory, who were very tolerant of a historian trampling all over their text. A younger generation of medievalists has arisen to make their contribution, too. Rick Barton, Kieran O'Conor, Daniel Power and Kathleen Thompson all contributed insights I could not have otherwise found. A mighty debt is owed to Nicholas Vincent, whose Herculean labours in the archives of Western Europe have been so fruitful and so generously shared with fellow scholars.

Scarborough
June 2002

PREFACE TO THIRD EDITION

When the famous French medievalist Georges Duby first presented his views on William Marshal in the early 1980s, it was on a French radio series called 'History's Unknowns' (*Les inconnus de l'histoire*). That is no longer a description that could be applied to the Marshal, who has now a solid bibliography of works, both academic and general, to his credit. He has also acquired quite a profile in the world of film and fiction and, indeed, a Facebook page. Just as the second edition of this book was inspired by the publication of the three-volume academic edition of the previously inaccessible biography the *History of William Marshal*, so this edition is inspired by another new academic work, my edition of the Marshal family's surviving literary remains: *The Acts and Letters of the Marshal Family, Marshals of England and Earls of Pembroke 1145–1248* (Camden Society, 5th series, 47, 2015). Work on editing this has turned up much that was new on William Marshal (and quite a bit of necessary correction to my earlier work). Other academic work has since opened up new avenues in Marshal studies: not least the works of historians of medieval Ireland, Marie Therese Flanagan and Colin Veach, who have provided new material and insights into relations between the Marshal and his nemesis, King John. I acknowledge here the particular help of Elizabeth Chadwick and Colin Veach in readying the manuscript for publication.

Scorborough Hall
August 2015

ACKNOWLEDGEMENTS

The publishers would like to thank St Bartholomew's Hospital Archives, Durham Cathedral Archives, the National Library of Ireland, the Pierpont Morgan Library and the Royal Library of Belgium for their permission to reproduce copyright material.

ABBREVIATIONS

Acts and Letters	*The Acts and Letters of the Marshal Family, Marshals of England and Earls of Pembroke 1145–1248*, ed. D. Crouch (Camden Society, 5th series, 47, 2015).
Anonymous	*Histoire des ducs de Normandie et des rois d'Angleterre*, ed. F. Michel (Société de l'Histoire de France, Paris, 1840).
Barnwell	*Memoriale Walteri de Coventria*, ed. W. Stubbs (2 vols, Rolls Series, 1872–1873).
Complete Peerage	*Complete Peerage of England, Scotland, Ireland and Great Britain*, ed. V. Gibbs (13 vols in 14, London, 1919–1959).
Curia Regis Rolls	*Curia Regis Rolls preserved in the Public Record Office* (20 vols, London, HMSO, 1922–2007).
Diceto	*Ymagines Historiarum*, in *Radulfi de Diceto Decani Lundoniensis Opera Historica*, ed. W. Stubbs (2 vols, Rolls Series, 1876).
History	*History of William Marshal*, ed. A.J. Holden and D. Crouch, trans. S. Gregory (3 vols, Anglo-Norman Text Society, Occasional Publications, 3–5, 2002–2007).
Howden, *Chronica*	Roger of Howden, *Chronica*, ed. W. Stubbs (4 vols, Rolls Series, 1868–1871).
Howden, *Gesta*	[Roger of Howden], *Gesta Henrici Secundi*, ed. W. Stubbs (2 vols, Rolls Series, 1867).
Monasticon	*Monasticon Anglicanum*, ed. J. Caley and others (8 vols, Record Commission, 1817–1830).
Newburgh	William of Newburgh, Historia Rerum Anglicarum, in *Chronicles and Memorials of the Reigns of Stephen, Henry II and Richard I*, ed. R. Howlett (4 vols, Rolls Series, 1884–1890).
Rot. Chartarum	*Rotuli Chartarum, 1199–1216*, ed. T.D. Hardy (London, 1837).
Rot. Clausarum	*Rotuli Litterarum Clausarum, 1204–1227* i, ed. T.D. Hardy (Record Commission, 1833).

Rot. Patentium	*Rotuli Litterarum Patentium*, ed. T.D. Hardy (Record Commission, 1835).
Royal Letters	*Royal and Other Historical Letters Illustrative of the Reign of Henry III*, ed. W.W. Shirley (2 vols, Rolls Series, 1862–1866).
TNA: PRO	The National Archives (Public Record Office).
Torigny	*Chronica*, in *Chronicles of the Reigns of Stephen, Henry II and Richard*, ed. R. Howlett, IV (Rolls Series, 1889).

INTRODUCTION

William Marshal, Earl of Pembroke (or 'the Marshal' as he was generally known in his own lifetime),[1] was born some time around 1147 in Wiltshire, or perhaps Berkshire, in the reign of King Stephen. We do not know precisely when or where because his family was not then important enough for the fact to be thought worth mentioning by anyone. He was the fourth son (the second by his second marriage) of John Marshal, a court officer and minor baron, a man well connected but not overly wealthy. From these small beginnings, William rose in his 72 or so years of life to be a great earl and marcher lord in Wales and Ireland, a man of European celebrity and, until his final illness, Regent of England for the boy king Henry III.

The biography and its author

The Marshal lived a life that resembled an epic, and nothing was more suitable after his death in 1219 than that his sons and followers should commission a poem in the vein of a romance epic to celebrate it. The *History* – as the one surviving text calls it – is an astonishing survival, even in the imperfect copy that has come down to the twenty-first century. It is a Middle French poem of 19,214 lines in rhyming couplets all celebrating the life of one remarkable man. Its author gives his name as John, and that is about all that he tells us of himself, other than the fact that he composed verses for a living. Other than that, we can only work out that he was a young man when he wrote and that he was a Frenchman from the lost Angevin lands of the Plantagenet dynasty.

The original editor of the text, the great French scholar Paul Meyer, worked out that John the poet began writing in the summer of 1224. His chief patron,

---

1 The various names by which William Marshal was known are treated fully in Appendix II.

the younger Earl William Marshal (eldest son of the biography's hero) had sailed for Ireland as royal governor in June of that year. We can work out that his poet was left behind in south-east Wales to complete the poem before the earl returned. It may be that Earl William had set the poet to work as part of the process of settling his affairs before he left for Ireland. The younger Marshal knew that many people believed that his dead father had been a man of compromised loyalties, far too friendly with the Capetian kings of France.

The biography would set the record straight, once and for all, and Young William would discharge the debt to his father's memory. John the poet tells us that he was being supported by the earl's money while he worked, and also that of the Marshal's old friend and executor, John of Earley. Indications in the text tell us that the author had already composed over three-quarters of the text we have now by February 1225. He seems then to have set the poem aside until he had news of his patron's return, and enjoyed perhaps a quiet life in South Wales for a year, or went off elsewhere on his own business. He only got back to work again in the spring of 1226, and finally reached the end of the poem after the second Earl William's return in the autumn of that year.

The poem was perhaps finished in a rush. The only text that survives from the Middle Ages is a mid-thirteenth-century copy of what may have been the author's original and unrevised draft. There were once, perhaps, more finished drafts in circulation. We do know that several manuscripts of the *History* existed in the Middle Ages, for two medieval library catalogues mention copies that cannot be the one that survives today. One was at Canterbury in the abbey of St Augustine, another in the Worcestershire Cistercian abbey of Bordesley (which had it from a fourteenth-century legacy of Earl Guy de Beauchamp of Warwick). It may be that a number of copies had been made in the 1220s as gifts to the old Marshal's children and friends and were eventually scattered all over England.

Those copies might well have been more polished and elaborate than the version we have now. If these are the ones that have been lost, we are in fact lucky, not unlucky, because the one text of the *History* that has survived is the one that was most revealing of the way the author worked. The manuscript of the *History* we have now was acquired either by Sir John Savile (died 1607) or his brother Henry, Provost of Eton (died 1622), late in the reign of Queen Elizabeth I, perhaps ultimately from a monastic library. It lay untouched and unnoticed in his family's collection for centuries until February 1861 when the Savile Library was sold off. It was noted only as a 'Norman–French chronicle on English affairs in verse' in the sale catalogue.

In Sotheby's saleroom, the manuscript of the *History* was picked up and examined by the great historian and linguist Paul Meyer, then a young French scholar working in London. He was intrigued by what he saw, but failed at that point to realise its true significance. The book was sold to the collector Sir Thomas Phillipps, and disappeared into his vast collection at Cheltenham. By the time Meyer realised what he had let slip through his fingers, there was no chance to get it back, as Sir Thomas did not answer letters. In 1881 – long after Sir Thomas's death in

1872 – the Phillipps estate let Meyer have access to the book and copy the text. The book was eventually purchased by the illustrator and cartoonist W. Heath Robinson. After his death, it was bought for the Pierpont Morgan Library in New York, where it now resides as its manuscript M.888. Meyer, meanwhile, published his transcript in three volumes between 1891 and 1901, in an edition he called *L'Histoire de Guillaume le Maréchal, comte de Striguil et de Pembroke*, which is now itself a collector's item. He provided no translation, only a digest of the story in modern French; what he did do, however, was to provide extensive indexes and a commentary on the manuscript, which are still very useful.[2]

A word or two needs to be said about John the poet's sources and methods. He wrote a biography. This is itself a remarkable statement, for there were few works written in the Middle Ages that might be called biographies. Studies written by medieval people about their kings generally tell us not so much about their lives, but their times. They give us little or no insight into their subjects' early years, motives and inner life, as a biography should. Quite a number of bishops, abbots and monks were the subjects of Latin lives (*vitae*), but few are truly biographical. Most are 'hagiographies': that is, studies of the lives of saints. They were written to justify their subjects' saintly status and as devotional texts, not as biographies.

There are exceptions, for instance the *Life of Geoffrey Plantagenet, Archbishop of York*, written by Gerald of Wales around the end of 1193. This is a Latin prose biography (there was nothing remotely saintly about Archbishop Geoffrey), and it and its like may have influenced the young Earl William Marshal when he issued his commission to John the poet. But John wrote in vernacular French, even though there is evidence that he could read Latin. His life of the old Marshal is a true biography, because it follows its subject from cradle to grave, and gives many details and insights into what the Marshal did and why he did it. It is also concerned to give a (highly favourable) verdict on his life, and justify his political decisions and actions.

If it was eccentric of John the poet to write a biography, it was even more eccentric of him to choose to write it in French verse. He probably chose to do so because his patron wanted it sung to music. A good time for such a performance would have been on the day of the old Marshal's 'anniversary'. This was the day when all the abbeys and priories in the Marshal lands – and the Temple church where he lay buried – would have celebrated a full mass of the community on the day the old man had died (24 May), with a repetition of the funeral ceremonies and a feast at the family's expense in their refectories. It is tempting to imagine Earl William Marshal the younger riding back from such a festival at one of the monasteries under his patronage and spending the evening in his hall being entertained by a performance of all or part of the *History* – the author does in fact tell us in the surviving text that his performance of his text was happening on an evening. The French verse form allowed the author to draw for inspiration on the well-established framework of the romance-epic.

---

2 The story is engagingly retold in T. Asbridge, *The Greatest Knight* (London, 2015), pp. xv–xviii.

John was not the first author to use French verse for historical purposes. In the mid-1170s, a clergyman called Jordan Fantosme had told the story of the rebellion against King Henry II in just such a way, although in a poem of only one-tenth the length of the *History*. In the 1190s, another writer had used rhymed French verse couplets to tell the story of the conquest of Ireland by the old Marshal's father-in-law, Earl Richard Strongbow, and his followers (a work once called the *Song of Dermot and the Earl*). This poem was not in any way connected with the Marshals, and seems to have been commissioned by a member of the community of barons of Leinster to celebrate their own accomplishments and independence, at a time before William Marshal had taken control of Leinster. It is, however, conceivable that it might have been a background inspiration for the commissioners of the Marshal *History*: John of Earley, for instance, was seneschal of Osraige and Uí Chennselaig in Leinster for the elder Marshal in 1207 and might well have become acquainted with the *Song*.

John the poet was a remarkable man, even if he was not a particularly distinguished poet. He felt he had to do full justice to the subject of his biography, a man five years dead when he started to work. He had no choice but to undertake a major research programme. Most of those who could have told him about the old man's earlier life were long dead in 1224: the Marshal's last surviving brother, Bishop Henry Marshal of Exeter, had died in 1206. The Marshal's widow had survived him by only 10 months, and in 1224 she lay in her tomb under the choir of Tintern Abbey. There still survived, however, many of the old man's household. At least two of his early squires were ready and willing to share their memories, which in the case of Eustace de Bertrimont took John back before 1183.

For the period before the 1180s, the author had to rely on the stories of his early life the old man had told, and often repeated, to his sons and many friends. But John was not entirely confined to oral sources. Wherever it was in South Wales or Gloucestershire that he worked, he had with him a cache of Marshal documents: probably the family archive of accounts, rolls, charters and correspondence. He was able to deploy these to augment the tales of the Marshal household. He even used one Latin chronicle to help him with the earliest period of Marshal history, when William Marshal's father was active in the 1140s. For the period after the 1180s, John got his informants to commit their own recollections to writing, and pass them on to him. One of his main sources for John's reign was the old man's nephew, John Marshal of Hockering, who was William Marshal's chief political adviser at the time and himself no mean figure in English politics. This sort of miscellaneous research does not necessarily produce good poetry, but it is a testimony to the scrupulosity of the author. The *History* he produced was a work of no little historical merit, for all its inevitable bias towards its subject.[3]

---

3 The text is published with English translation as *History of William Marshal*, ed. A.J. Holden and D. Crouch, trans. S. Gregory (3 vols, Anglo-Norman Text Society, Occasional Publications, 3–5, 2002–2007). Portions of the text in English here are from Dr Gregory's translation. The work will be hereafter cited as *History* with line references.

Old work and new questions

The *History* allows us to present to the modern reader a biography of a man of the High Middle Ages in more detail than any other of his lay contemporaries below the rank of sovereign prince (we know contemporary churchmen far better from their letter collections, autobiographies and biographies). His career was important politically: from 1189, he was a leading actor in the history of England and France. His biography is also an important social document for military and aristocratic life in the High Middle Ages. So it should be no surprise that this book is not the first attempt to tell the Marshal's story; it was in fact the fourth in English when first published.[4] Of its three predecessors, the best (and weightiest) by far is that by the American scholar Sidney Painter. I have no hesitation in acknowledging a great debt to his work, not least in inspiration. It is well written, and based on sterling research, but it was published over 80 years ago. Much work on both aristocratic society and political events of the Marshal's lifetime has built up since 1937, and new questions have since been asked by historians.

What are these new questions? Painter's picture of William Marshal has been taken as the portrait of a typical baron of his age: illiterate and socially clumsy; well disposed in general but still grasping; primitively religious; sophisticated only in the technicalities of war. Yet, paradoxically, Painter also portrays his Marshal as respecting the emerging code of chivalry, loving fair play and worshipping the ideal of woman (though not at ease with the real creature). It is remarkable how this stereotype of the 'bold, bad baron'[5] (to quote a commentary on English liberty by a distinguished early modernist) lingers, even among historians who are supposed to beware of stereotypes. Because the Marshal biography is the only one of its kind, it has to be held to account for this.

The Marshal, in my view, was by no means typical. To begin with, there has been sufficient work done recently to indicate that the Marshal was unusual among his fellow magnates in being a complete illiterate, perhaps not even able to read French, let alone Latin.[6] This single fact may have helped to distort our views of the level of sophistication of the aristocracy of his day, as it is difficult to avoid taking the Marshal as typical. But, on the other side of the coin, it is not often remembered that his biography was the work of a layman. His biographer may not have been technically *litteratus* as the thirteenth century understood it (for most

---

4 The three predecessors were: T.L. Jarman, *William Marshal, First Earl of Pembroke and Regent of England* (Oxford, 1930); S. Painter, *William Marshal* (Baltimore, 1933); J. Crossland, *William the Marshal: The Last Great Feudal Baron* (London, 1962). Since 1990, there have been several further book-length studies (as well as two TV documentaries), most of which tend to give priority to William the soldier: C.A. Armstrong, *William Marshal, Earl of Pembroke* (privately printed, 2007); R. Brooks, *The Knight who Saved England: William Marshal and the French Invasion, 1217* (London, 2014); Asbridge, *The Greatest Knight.*

5 Christopher Hill in the *Guardian*, 15 July 1989.

6 M.T. Clanchy, *From Memory to Written Record* (London, 1979), pp. 175–201.

contemporaries believed that the word should be applied to those educated in Latin), but he could clearly write, if only in the vernacular. The Marshal was also not typical in being so exclusively military in his interests. Most of his fellows among the court aristocracy were administrators first and soldiers second, sometimes a long way second. But the Marshal was a captain and soldier by talent and inclination, and an administrator and judge only when he had to be. There are other question marks over the Marshal as Painter has reconstructed him for us. The degree of chivalry he displayed is one question, another is the level of sophistication of his war-making. Painter would have granted that he was a talented and thoughtful soldier, but a study by Professor John Gillingham has elevated his generalship to a higher plane than that.

Lastly, and for me most importantly, there is the question of the Marshal's basic political conduct, and indeed the nature of the political world in which he operated. For Painter, he was an honest, engaging character; not particularly bright, but straightforward enough. He was a feudal lord who built his power on the ties of homage between him and his men. His success was a matter of being a useful soldier and being lucky in his friends and patrons. To me, this is a regrettable misinterpretation of the sources. Rereading the *History* in the light of the celebrated study by Professor Stephen Jaeger, it seems clear to me that the Marshal was one of the great practitioners of courtliness of his age. His political conduct was studied, sophisticated and devious. Nor was the world in which he rose to the top so uncomplicated as Painter wished it to be. The Marshal's England was long past the stage when feudal knight service was important. For him, power was achieved by attracting independent, influential men into his following and making alliances with his equals at court and in the country. His was a world of shifting political affinities. This was why he was so often able to defy King John; the court was so riddled with his friends that none of the magnates would assist the king against him. Those who held land from the Marshal by knights' service provided him with money, when he could get it out of them, and did not in general give him political and military assistance.

The other significant work on the Marshal is in French, by the eminent medieval scholar and academician, Georges Duby, who died in 1996.[7] His is in many ways a fine book, or at least a well-written one: his passages on the Marshal's deathbed and tournament career are models of how a historian should seek to write, be he French or English. But as a biography, the book has many deficiencies. It is based on a perceptive reading of the *History* and little else. Duby preferred to rely on the historical notes of Paul Meyer, the editor of the text of the *History*, without much heeding even what Painter had to add to Meyer's monumental researches. As a consequence, he made numerous errors of chronology and genealogy that sadly devalue his work. Duby was also less than well instructed on

---

7 *Guillaume le Maréchal, ou le meilleur chevalier du monde* (Paris, 1984), trans R. Howard, *William Marshal, Flower of Chivalry* (London, 1986).

English political and social life. Like Painter, he was not critical of the *History*, except in a literary sense. He too had some axes to grind, he was convinced of the Marshal's limitations, and he saw him as a simple warrior carried far beyond his sphere. Duby's work, if rich in insight, fails to provide any serious rethinking of the man's career, nor does it present any new evidence; indeed, in total, it was downright misleading: he took from the *History* that which confirmed his preconceptions about aristocratic society and ignored the rest. Perhaps no historian is entirely guiltless of this, but Duby's Marshal is a warning of how selective historical writing can distort the evidence in a most unacceptable way.

Apart from the *History*, there is one other source for the Marshal's career. Neither Duby nor Painter employed the other main source for his career, or at least his later one: the Marshal's own charters, of which as many as 90 survive in some form or other in archives scattered across Ireland, Britain and Northern France, and even the United States. These, as I will explain, give a picture of the Marshal's activities that differs from that of the *History*; they show us, among other things, the Marshal as businessman and estate manager, an aspect of his character entirely overlooked by Duby, although not ignored by Painter. Most importantly, they allow us to analyse the nature of his political following. The *History* is a mirror of the emotional bonds between the Marshal and his men; but the texts of the charters form a microscope that enables us to look much deeper into their material nature.

The problems of the sources

One of the main problems about the biography of the Marshal is how far the *History* is to be trusted. This is particularly true of what it has to say about the early period of the Marshal's career. At a later stage, when the Marshal gained in fame and wealth, there is more by other authors with which to compare it. But here, the author had no more to go on than his own hazy conceptions of the events of the reigns of Stephen and Henry II in England and France, some few early written records he had seen (a tally of ransoms from the 1170s and a tournament roll of 1180), and the Marshal's own recollections of his early life as remembered by his family and friends. These autobiographical fragments, curiously, would seem to be for the most part unexceptionable. The Marshal, at times clearly a garrulous old man, had a nice line in self-mockery and obviously told a story well; the fact that, no doubt, he repeated them over and over again may have fixed them in the family mythology. These stories do not always portray the Marshal in a favourable light, and so the element of truth in them may be high. Oral sources can be difficult to assess as historical evidence, but once the anecdotes that lie behind them become stabilised and fossilised by repetition ('pericopic') they pass from teller to hearer with little variation. We can therefore be confident that we are hearing something close to the Marshal's own voice at times.

'When telling a true story nobody does right to lie', said the pious author of the *History* as he reflected on his duty to write an accurate account of the Battle of Lincoln.[8] But he did not avoid the odd half-truth or evasion elsewhere in his work when it suited him. He left gaps in the Marshal's story. He was reticent about his political career from 1170 to 1183, when the Marshal was in the centre of events, but in the disreputable entourage of Henry II's eldest son, Henry. He disguised quite how closely the Marshal worked in the interest of the future King John before his succession to the throne, and how generously John rewarded him. Again, there is a curious ignorance shown by the *History* about the Marshal's immediate family. Although we hear a lot about the Marshal's father (a favourite subject of his stories, apparently), we hear little of the fate of his brothers, Walter and Gilbert (who had died before 1166), and the *History* gives a distorted picture of how the Marshal estate descended through the family. The career of William's brother John Marshal barely features in the *History*, although there is good evidence that John was very important to him in the reign of Richard. There is every reason to believe that William was for a long time estranged from his siblings, which led to his silence on the subject. As a result, the author of the *History* fills in the gap with passages of pure fiction, particularly his treatment of the sad deaths of Walter and Gilbert Marshal.

The element of identifiable fiction in the *History* is a warning that we must treat it carefully. Analysis of its composition revealed that the author was quite capable of inventing likely sounding but quite imaginary royal itineraries to get his action from one point in his story to the next. More difficult to assess is that fact that – aside from the influence on the text of the author's obvious bias towards its subject – the *History* is written in a literary tradition that must have distorted its reconstruction of the past. Although it is unique in its content and aims, the *History* is far from unique in its form. It was written in the tradition of French epics and romances whose known pedigree stretches back to the beginning of the twelfth century in England, with the epic *The Song of Roland*. In one particular instance, the portrayal of tournaments, it has been pointed out by Professor Larry Benson that the *History*'s account of certain of them seems to have been inspired directly by the writings of Chrétien de Troyes, a half-century before. A good example of this romantic influence is the description of William Marshal with which the author provides us. Phrases such as 'He was so noble a man that he might have been taken for the emperor of Rome!' do not in fact tell us much, but even when the poet seems to get more specific he cannot be trusted.

The key to this is, I regret to say, the size of the Marshal's crutch. 'He had a crutch so large, and was so handsomely formed, that no noble could be his peer.'[9] Large crutches (or wide hips, if you prefer a more modest translation), being an obviously desirable feature in a horse-riding society, were regarded as a badge of male aristocratic beauty. We find such a feature praised as early as *The Song of Roland*. In a romance composed in the household of the Earl of Warwick some 10 to 20

8 *History* II, lines 16408–9.
9 *History* I, lines 733–5.

years before the *History*, a popular work called *Gui de Warewic*, one of Guy's great friends, Count Thierry of 'Guaremaise' (that is, Worms in Germany), is described in just such terms as the Marshal: well made, tall in stature with a large crutch.[10] The Marshal was held to have been a handsome man when he was young, so his biographer describes him according to the conventional, contemporary canons of what a young, handsome man should look like (except he was dark-skinned and brown-haired, not a blond, as heroes normally were).

Does the same apply to the author's descriptions of events? This is a disturbing question for a historian, and not an easy one to answer. It is, however, probable that to a degree the poet-biographer did allow his stock of epic verse to intrude into events, particularly the early events of the Marshal's life. This is nowhere more obvious than in the totally fictitious account the *History* gives of the deaths of the Marshal's elder brothers, Walter and Gilbert. It is a good story, but it is contradicted decisively by the historical evidence of the English government's pipe rolls. In other cases, the intrusion of the world of the romance-epic is confined to the details of the story, such as the author's evocation of the flower-strewn pavilion of King Stephen of England.

However, there is a distinct change of gear in the pace of the *History* after the Marshal joins Henry II's household in 1186. Names and events then begin to come thick and fast, digressive anecdotes grow few. The reason for this is given us by the author himself: he was drawing on the written memoirs made for him by (among others) John of Earley, the West Country knight who was the Marshal's ward and body squire from 1187, and household knight after 1194. Of all the *History*, the tournament scenes in the Marshal's bachelorhood are the most suspect. He wins the prize and ransom far too often for my comfort, and indeed the author sheepishly confesses at one point that the younger Marshal's career was not uniformly successful. The hero's winning of the prize in the tournament was a stock romantic episode, such as in Chrétien de Troyes' *Erec and Enide*, a romance of the 1170s, where the eponymous hero overrides all opposition in the tournament to celebrate his marriage and in the end 'everyone on both sides said that by his lance and shield he had become victor in the tournament'.[11] Perhaps the Pembrokes were sneering at the pretensions of the Warwicks, pointing to a real-life hero in their family tree, not a myth. Guy of Warwick is described on occasion as 'the best knight in all the world', and this is the title appropriated by the *History* to William Marshal. If this were so, then the Warwicks had the last laugh, for *Gui*

10 For Thierry, *Gui de Warewic, roman du xiiie siècle*, ed. A. Ewert (2 vols, Classiques français du moyen âge, Paris, 1932–1933) I, lines 4583–4. For other twelfth-century examples of this topos, see the descriptions of William Longsword, Duke of Normandy, in Wace, *Le Roman de Rou*, ed. A.J. Holden (3 vols, Société des anciens textes français, 1970–1973) I, pt 2, lines 1316–17; of Duke Atys, in *Le Roman de Thèbes*, ed. F. Mora-Lebrun (Paris, 1995), lines 6655–6; and of Alexander the Great, in Thomas of Kent, *Le Roman de Toute Chevalerie*, ed. B. Foster (2 vols, Anglo-Norman Text Society, 1976–1977) I, lines 4040–5.

11 Translated by D.D.R. Owen, in *Arthurian Romances* (London, 1987), p. 30.

de Warewic went on to be one of the most popular romances in England for several centuries, while the *History* had no circulation in the Middle Ages.

This book is not therefore just a biography of William Marshal and a survey of his times; it is also an attempt to disentangle at least the historical problems posed by the *History*. One need not be unduly pessimistic about the task. There is much with which to compare it, and although John, the Marshal's biographer, had prejudices, in general they are well advertised: he bitterly loathed King John, for instance, and the king does not appear to any advantage in the work (except when he is said to have died extolling the Marshal's virtues with all but his last breath). The *History* studiously avoids mentioning John's creation of the Marshal as Earl of Pembroke and the remarkable number of grants with which he favoured him. If such prejudices are understood, then the work can be used to some effect, and whatever its faults it is undeniably a brilliant window on to contemporary life and customs. It brings alive the courtly world of the late twelfth and early thirteenth centuries as do few other sources.

1
CHILDHOOD AND SQUIREHOOD

His name was John and he was a Frenchman from the Loire Valley, and that really is about all we know of him, other than that he had a facility in French verse and made his living by it. But at some point early in the year 1224, this young poet was well enough known to receive an invitation from the greatest earl in England, William Marshal the younger, the king's brother-in-law, to cross to Britain and attend his court. The great earl had just been commissioned to take up the rule of English Ireland as the king's justiciar, and curb the power of the rebel Lacy family, lords of Meath and Ulster. To do so meant Earl William had to cross a stormy sea to wage war in a turbulent and dangerous land. So before he went, he intended to put his affairs in order, as any sensible businessman would do.

One of the obligations Young William had on his mind was to his father's memory. His father had died five years before, a man still venerated by many for his military prowess and great loyalty to the House of Anjou, whose throne he had preserved against a French invasion. But not all were convinced the old earl had been quite so selfless and beyond reproach as his admirers and household believed. So the young Marshal was going to put the record straight, with the assistance of his brothers and the old earl's surviving executors and friends. The young earl was a well-educated and sophisticated man, and knew very well the potential of the written word to shape people's opinions; his surviving letters are models of evasiveness and courtly manipulation.

John the poet accepted the earl's commission, and took up residence in the Marshal lands in South Wales. He began his work with enthusiasm that very summer of 1224, interviewing people who knew the old earl, collecting written memoranda of events from witnesses and finding in one of the Marshal castles or abbeys a trove of old documents and letters that much assisted his task. He even made research trips. He seems at one point to have used the library of Gloucester Abbey, and it is clear enough from his work that he travelled north to Lincoln to visit and examine the site of the battle that the hero of his work had won in 1217, and thus decisively defeated the French invasion of England.

In the late summer of 1226, just before the earl, his patron, returned from Ireland, John had completed his work, one copy of which still exists. It is a remarkable book if for nothing else as being the only extended biography of a layman that survives from the Middle Ages. The poem as he finished it ran to over 19,000 lines and tells the story of William Marshal the elder from cradle to grave. John fully lived up to his patron's expectations and we can only hope he was well rewarded for his labours. Eight centuries later, the subject of his biography is now the best known and most admired of medieval knights. Because of the *History of William Marshal*, modern scholars can reconstruct a full medieval life, and explain the society that formed it. This, then, is the story of William Marshal of Hamstead in the county of Berkshire, knight, earl and Regent of England.

John Marshal: father and son

William was born around 1147 into the middle of a war: the civil war between the supporters of Stephen and Matilda that plagued England between 1139 and 1153. In a way, it was in warfare that he was conceived. John Marshal, his father, and Sybil of Salisbury, his mother, were married to seal a pact with Sybil's brother Patrick, Earl of Salisbury, who was John's rival for power in Wiltshire. Even William's name may have been a political stratagem. It recalled his mother's eldest brother, William of Salisbury. He had died three or four years before William Marshal was born.

Civil wars are evil affairs. The war of Stephen's reign was grimmer than most. It came after the reigns of the first three Norman kings, peaceful and prosperous for the most part in England, once the time of conquest and colonisation had ended. People had come to regard peace and strong royal government as the natural order of things, so their disruption was all the worse.

In December 1135, Stephen of Blois seized the crown on the death of his great patron and uncle, King Henry I. He was not the most obvious candidate for the succession: that would have been his first cousin Matilda, the king's daughter and surviving legitimate child, who between 1110 and 1125 had been the wife of Henry V of Germany, and thus empress, but who had returned to England and her father's court to be adopted by him as his nominated heir. But in 1135, Matilda and her second husband, Count Geoffrey of Anjou, were at odds with her father and, as it turned out, when the old king died, hardly any of the barons who had sworn to the king's face to support her had any serious intention of doing so. Most of them did not support Stephen either.

In a series of conferences in Normandy in the week after Henry died, the greatest magnates of the Anglo-Norman realm decided to elect as their duke Stephen's elder brother, the celebrated and pious prince Count Theobald of Blois, who would then automatically have progressed to the throne of England. But by then, Stephen was already sitting on that very throne, having made a dash for London when he heard the news of his uncle's death, and there he found the support of two key bishops, his younger brother Henry of Winchester and the old king's trusted friend and chief minister, Roger of Salisbury, who between them masterminded his acceptance by the city of London and his rapid consecration in Westminster Abbey.

We know a good deal about Stephen of Blois, for the historical record of his reign is quite a rich one. It tells us he was an attractive man, quite unlike his remorseless, devious and formidable predecessor. Stephen's personal charm, loyalty and courage, and in particular his religious devotion, are what commentators who knew him remark upon. The intense loyalty showed by his household officers to him over the years indicates that these character traits had their political uses. He developed also into a successful and stubborn soldier, demonstrating an impressive coolness and bravery on the field. When abandoned by his earls at Lincoln in February 1141, the 45-year-old king stoutly held off the rebels who surrounded him and his household guard with a hand axe until floored by a stone to his helmet and wrestled struggling to the ground.

Stephen's problem was his limited political judgement and vision. He could not manage his nobility. He tried hard to be the sort of king that Henry I had been, but he did not have his uncle's political skill and breadth of intellect. He did not know how to use fear to keep his nobles uneasy, nor favour to entice them into his court. He relied far too much on one particular aristocratic faction, and so destabilised the English political community. Within two years, there was a catastrophic breakdown of the balance at court. The estranged barons took their differences to the country, and those opposed to the king found a ready-made cause in Matilda. With the help of her half-brother, Earl Robert of Gloucester, she landed in England to claim the throne in 1139, and was foolishly allowed by Stephen to secure a foothold in the realm, which expanded by 1140 into control of the south-west of England and the southern March of Wales.

Memories of that evil time were still strong some three generations later, especially on the political fault line between the royalist and rebel areas, the place in fact where John Marshal had his stronghold. The Marshal's biographer preserved the local memories of the time when he wrote that 'no peace, truce or agreement was kept, and the law of the land was disregarded'.[1]

But the civil war was not without compensations for a man of a certain sort. John Marshal was just the type who could take advantage of the peculiar opportunities those troubled times offered. He was cool-headed, whether in battle or bargaining, ruthless in his ambition and a hero to his followers and knights. He knew how to reward and how to punish, when to attack and (less common in such a man) when to retreat. To his son, William, he could not have been more than the memory of a strong man, fearfully scarred on the face by battle, a man he believed to be all-powerful. From his father he expected protection; from his mother he had love and care. William never saw his father after his childhood,

---

1 *History* I, lines 128–30.

and would have not seen too much of him then, as his father toured his estates, discharged his office of marshal at Winchester and Westminster and frequented the courts of greater men. But he remembered stories of his father's prowess that the women, his brothers and the servants would have told him. He would remember the awe that gathered about such a paterfamilias. His cunning was legendary, his military skill in castle building and tactics a marvel to his contemporaries.

So it is that the first part of William's biography, the *History*, is dominated by John Marshal. The biography is honest enough about John's origins. 'Though he was no earl and no baron with fabulous wealth, yet his generosity so increased that all were amazed by it.'[2] He was the hereditary royal master-marshal, son of the marshal Gilbert, who acquired the office in the reign of William Rufus or early in that of Henry I. Gilbert was in turn the son (or son-in-law) of a Gilbert Giffard, who was holding lands in Wiltshire at the time of Domesday Book in 1086.[3] As a royal marshal, John was a dignified enough man, and in King Henry I's reign he lived at a court where he could find some opportunity to further himself, in a modest way. In 1130, we know that he was able to dispose of large sums of money to pay for his succession to his father's office and buy control of the marriage of a Wiltshire heiress. His actual landed endowment was small. He owned houses on the corner of what was later to be called Jewry Street in Winchester, not far from the royal castle and palace, place of his duty. Elsewhere, there were lands held from the king in Somerset, Wiltshire and Berkshire. The family centre in Henry I's days would have been at Hamstead Marshall, in the Kennet Valley in Berkshire, close to the Wiltshire border. Here, there was a hall and other houses within a large enclosure, which John Marshal transformed into an earth-and-timber castle in Stephen's reign.

Apart from these possessions, John and his father were able, like other royal ministers, to pick up pieces of land from powerful barons and churchmen who thought them worthy of attracting into their orbits, rather like a consultant's retaining fees; so John had scattered lands in Herefordshire of the Candos family, in Oxfordshire of the Arsic family, and in Wiltshire of the Salisbury family. There were fees besides from the bishops of Exeter, Winchester and Worcester, and the abbots of Glastonbury and Abingdon. In 1130, his total lands were assessed, for the purpose of a tax exemption, as 35¼ hides, about the amount of land a prosperous minor baron might hold.

John's great days began with the death of King Henry I and the accession of Stephen in 1135. Although the *History* says that John joined Matilda 'without

---

2 *History* I, lines 32–5.
3 For the identity of William Marshal's grandfather, see N.E. Stacy, 'Henry of Blois and the Glastonbury connection', *English Historical Review*, 114 (1999), pp. 32–3 and nn., and see also *Acts and Letters*, pp. 1–2. The surname 'Giffard' is a common Norman soubriquet and means 'moon-face' or 'chubby cheeks'. It is highly unlikely that Gilbert Giffard was related to the Conqueror's leading follower, Walter Giffard, Earl of Buckingham; it is conceivable on the grounds of proximity, however, that he might have had a connection with the unrelated West Country barons, the Giffards of Brimpsfield.

hesitation',[4] we know from other sources that he promptly accepted Stephen once he was crowned, along with almost everybody else who had frequented Henry I's court. Stephen exerted himself to reward prompt allegiance, nowhere more so than in the south-west of England. Here, he feared (groundlessly as it turned out) the opposition of Earl Robert of Gloucester, King Henry's eldest bastard.

Early in the reign, John Marshal received custody of the royal town and castle of Marlborough, along with other lands in north Wiltshire at Wexcombe and Cherhill, which he was still holding at the king's pleasure at the end of the civil war. With Wexcombe, he acquired for his own profit the court of the large hundred of Kinwardstone or Bedwyn, south-east of Marlborough.[5] This windfall transformed him into a castellan of some power. Marlborough, at that date an earth-and-timber castle on a strong site with an impressive motte, commanded the route along the Kennet Valley across the downs from London to Earl Robert's centre of Bristol. John may have been expected to watch the road from the west, but the king's generosity also made him the most formidable man in north-east Wiltshire, with control of the Kennet Valley and the downlands between Swindon and Hungerford. Littered with the ominous and mysterious relics of the Neolithic past, the downs overlook wide stretches of the surrounding country. Even in those days, the hills were bare, cropped by thousands of sheep. From the window of a train from Paddington to the west, they can still look haunted and formidable on a dark afternoon at the year's end. In the 1140s, the menace would have been real. John Marshal's squadrons of mercenary knights issued regularly from the defiles of those grey hills, demanding tribute and obedience from all the lowlanders who had no protector of their own.

When in 1138 Earl Robert was finally driven into revolt by King Stephen's suspicions and slights, John Marshal, along with others in the earl's reach, had a difficult decision to make. For example, Milo, Sheriff of Gloucester, had done well out of the king's attempts to ring in the earl with royalists, but he could not resist crossing into Earl Robert's camp when he arrived in England in person in 1139. John's actions were more ambiguous. He provisioned his castle of Marlborough and another he had acquired or built at Ludgershall, which blocked the road from Marlborough to Salisbury.[6] He must have hesitated a little too long in supporting the king for, when Matilda landed in Sussex in September 1139, we find that the king was engaged in a siege of Marlborough, his patience with his marshal clearly at an end. When war broke out in earnest between the royalists and Angevins (that

---

4 'sanz faille': *History* I, line 47.
5 We know that he had Marlborough in 1138; the likelihood is that he had the lands and hundred too. He first appears with Wexcombe and Cherhill along with Marlborough in the pipe roll of 1156: but lands called *terris datis* (distributed lands) in the early pipe rolls of Henry II were frequently royal concessions of earlier grants of Stephen, *Red Book of the Exchequer*, ed. H. Hall (3 vols, Rolls Series, 1889) II, p. 664.
6 The author of the *Gesta Stephani* mentions John's talent for castle building. There are signs of hasty fortifications at the family home of Hamstead Marshall at this time, later strengthened into a powerful motte and bailey castle.

is, followers of the counts of Anjou, Lat: *Andegavia*) in the autumn of 1139, John may have learned enough caution to give his nominal support to Stephen. In practice, however, he must have sat secure on the downs and done little but recruit and retain knights, and make his presence felt by those among his neighbours whom he could overawe.

Some of his neighbours had to be treated gingerly. The Salisbury family, who were later to be so important in the life of William Marshal, were richer and more powerful than John, holding Salisbury Castle as hereditary castellans and sheriffs. They were at this time loyal to the king, and he had more to fear from them, as the greatest baronial house in Wiltshire, than the Earl of Gloucester. Certainly, early in 1140, the well-informed chronicler John of Worcester believed that John Marshal was still a supporter of the king, and that it was in the king's interest that he had artfully trapped in Marlborough one Robert fitz Hubert, a rogue Flemish mercenary captain of Robert of Gloucester, who had seized Devizes. On the other hand, a royalist prelate who wrote a history of the reign, the *Gesta Stephani* (the Deeds of Stephen), was equally sure that early in 1140, John was an ally of Earl Robert. It was by no means impossible that John was playing a twofold game, nominally the king's man but keeping up friendly relations with dangerous neighbours of the other side – politic duplicity was very much a Marshal family trait, as we will see. Earl Robert's friendship would have protected his Somerset estates. But John needed to stay for a while within the royalist camp while the king and his allies were still dangerous to him. Stephen's reign can provide many examples of such quicksilver loyalties.

By early 1141, however, John had definitely changed sides. It was not just that Earl Robert had captured the king in battle outside Lincoln in the February of that year. King Stephen, who never mastered the intricacies of policy and people, had attempted towards the end of 1140 to impose a Breton governor on Wiltshire. The stranger had been angrily set on and driven out by the united Wiltshire barons. Under such provocation, it would not have been hard then for John and his neighbours, the Salisburys, to go over to Matilda, and both John and the aged Walter of Salisbury were acting as her agents in Wiltshire after the capture of the king.

Marshal family legend told of John's many adventures and enterprises in Matilda's service. How much is legend, and how much truth, is difficult to say. But at least one had substance to it. John was pictured as the hero of the siege of Winchester late in 1141; the *History* tells us that he managed Matilda's escape from the king's army, obliging her to ride astride on the retreat to Ludgershall, so she could spur on her horse, rather than keep her escort back by riding side-saddle, as a noblewoman should. When the royalists closed in, he fought a desperate rearguard action near the nunnery of Wherwell.[7] He took refuge in the abbey

---

7 The *Gesta Stephani* informs us that Wherwell Abbey had been converted by the Angevin forces into a temporary fort to protect their retreat northwards.

church and his pursuers tried to flush him out by setting the church alight. But he would not leave, and threatened to kill the knight who had made it into the church with him when he suggested giving themselves up. He stayed put even when molten lead began to cascade down from the roof of the tower where he was hiding; he was splashed, burned and lost an eye. His pursuers gave him up as a charred corpse, but once they were gone he staggered out and stumbled home to Marlborough on foot, a journey of 25 miles, a whole day's march.

There is some evidence, other than tales of the hall, to suggest that the episode in Wherwell Abbey might well have happened. The burning of a nunnery to flush out a rebel leader was likely to receive more than local attention. The continuation of the Worcester chronicle written at Gloucester Abbey in the 1140s mentions one John, a partisan of the Earl of Gloucester and Matilda, who was chased into Wherwell Abbey church after the rout; who would not come out even when the nunnery was fired around him. The chronicle does not actually make this John the architect of Matilda's escape, or even say he was John Marshal, but the two stories are clearly talking of the same event. The observation may be added to this that the *History*'s account is remarkably close to that of the chronicle in point of detail. It is quite likely that John, author of the biography, had read the Gloucester chronicle or been told of its evidence and used it when writing up his own account.

Another thing that the *History* mentions at this time, which can be borne out from other sources, is a local war that arose between John Marshal and the new head of the rival family of Salisbury, Patrick. For us, this clash has some relevance, for one of its indirect results was William Marshal himself. There is every reason to believe that the Marshals and Salisburys really did come to blows in Stephen's reign, but the exact time and nature of the conflict are impossible to establish. In its account, the *History* places the affair immediately after the siege of Winchester in 1141, and calls Patrick an earl and a follower of Stephen. But Patrick was created Earl of Salisbury by Matilda, not Stephen, and not until after 1144, while, until 1143, Patrick's elder brother, William, was head of the family and was noted as supporting Matilda. Setting aside the unreliable testimony of the *History*, other indications place the Marshal–Salisbury dispute in the mid-1140s.[8] In 1144, the *Gesta Stephani* depicts John Marshal at the height of his power, dominating the region, indifferent to his excommunication, exacting services from churchmen within his reach and compelling their attendance at his court.

8 It is by no means impossible that Patrick changed sides to support Stephen after his recovery in 1141; we have no evidence either way, and family splits are known elsewhere. But it is unlikely that, whatever side he was on, Patrick could have been acting so decisively until after 1143, when his brother William died. Until then, William had been the active leader of the family (Walter, their father, did not die until 1147, but age or illness would seem to have crippled him long before then and he confided the running of his estates to his sons).

The conflict that upset John's hegemony would have happened after 1144, most likely in 1145.[9] It would have been in the middle of the long period of the desultory stalemate between Stephen and Matilda that followed the siege of Winchester. We can dismiss Stephen's part in it altogether. It was purely local power politics, perhaps sparked by a dispute over Ludgershall, a Salisbury family manor commandeered by John as a castle site. There may be some truth in the Marshal source, which talks of aggressive raids by Patrick that John resisted. Patrick's eventual success might explain the willingness of Matilda to grace him with an earldom. Beating down John Marshal would have been the first step to securing Wiltshire for the cause. We find Earl Patrick busy in 1147 campaigning south of Salisbury against another local rival, the Bishop of Winchester: was this another stage in the same campaign?

Despite his reverse, John Marshal escaped utter humiliation. In twelfth-century power politics, as in war, combat was rarely to the death; siege and stratagem were more popular and productive. The final confrontation was avoided wherever possible. John was left with a way out. He must become Patrick's man and marry his sister, Sybil. There was a difficulty with this, for John had been married for many years to another lady, Adelina, by whom he had two sons.[10] But in those days, such an obstacle could be overcome, if the lady's kin and the Church were willing. Both were apparently satisfied. The probable grounds for the separation was the convenient discovery of a relationship between Adelina and John within the degree of kinship prohibited as incestuous. This was beginning to be a popular way of terminating marriages among the aristocracy in the mid-twelfth century. The aristocracy was so closely intermarried by then that it was not always difficult to discover that the wife you wished to set aside was, alas, a cousin anyway up to the seventh degree. Since we know that the two sons of the first marriage did not lose their succession rights by the separation between John and Adelina, this seems to be how the matter was resolved, for such separations left the children of the annulled marriage legitimate.[11]

9 This comment of the *Gesta* is borne out by the chronicle of Abingdon Abbey, Oxon, which names John Marshal as one of its four chief oppressors in Stephen's reign: the abbey had a concentration of lands in Berkshire neighbouring John Marshal's castle of Hamstead. A letter of Gilbert Foliot to the Bishop of Salisbury dated 1144 × 45 reveals that John Marshal (there called 'John of Marlborough') was pillaging Wiltshire outside any control from Earl Patrick at that time, *The Letters and Charters of Gilbert Foliot*, ed. A. Morey and C.N.L. Brooke (Cambridge, 1967), pp. 71–2. (The symbol '×' indicates a date range within which an event took place but which cannot be narrowed down.)

10 Her identity is not fully established. Painter suggested that she was the heiress of the Wiltshire baron, Walter Pipard, for the control of whose marriage John was paying the king in 1130, but that cannot be assumed to be the case automatically, even though one of her sons carried the name of her putative father. For her remarriage, see *Regesta Regum Anglo-Normannorum III 1135–1154*, ed. H.A. Cronne and R.H.C. Davis (Oxford, 1969), no. 339.

11 *Glanvill*, ed. G.D.G. Hall (London, 1965), p. 68.

The first marriage was, whatever the case, set aside. Adelina was honourably remarried to an interesting character, by the name of Stephen Gay, or Gayt. Stephen was a modest landholder of English origins, the Lord of Northbrook Gay in Oxfordshire. He had only one claim to fame: his sister had been the earliest known mistress of Henry, son of William the Conqueror. Many years before he became king, Henry had with her his eldest son, Robert, whom he made Earl of Gloucester around 1121. Stephen Gay was therefore the uncle of the leader of the Angevin party.[12] The fact that Adelina was married to him after her divorce from John Marshal more or less proves that it had been Earl Robert of Gloucester who had been active in settling the Marshal–Salisbury conflict in Wiltshire. Her eldest son by John, Gilbert, was later to have his mother's lands and a share of his father's.

John Marshal settled back into his old life with his new wife after this unwelcome incident: ruling his lordship on the downs, begetting more children and watching the road that led from Windsor and Reading to the west. His marriage did not bring him much in the way of an increase to his lands. Earl Patrick gave John the large manor of Mildenhall with his sister, which may seem generous, but it was a manor over which the earl was in dispute with Glastonbury Abbey.[13] Sybil of Salisbury did, however, help secure her husband's line. She gave him four more sons: John and William before the end of Stephen's reign, then Ansel and Henry, and three daughters besides.

With all going so well, and the ferocity of the civil war dying down, John Marshal became perhaps a little overconfident. At some time in or soon before 1152, he attempted to strengthen his control of the Kennet Valley approaches by advancing eastwards from his castle of Hamstead Marshall and establishing a new outpost at Newbury, where the road from Reading crossed the north–south route from Oxford to Winchester. This brought on him the full attention of King Stephen, who appeared without warning outside Newbury and began a determined siege. The constable of Newbury was low on supplies and men. Although he beat off the attempt of the royalists to storm the castle, he could not hold out long against a blockade. He was granted a day's grace to consult with John Marshal about surrender. John asked for more time, but the king would only grant this if he had in return one of the Marshal's sons as a hostage against trickery. John agreed and sent to the king his youngest son, William.

So it is that the young William Marshal first appears as an actor in these pages. In 1152, he would have been four or five years old. It is impossible to be sure because we do not know precisely when he was born. Earlier writers have favoured a date around 1143 but, from my reconstruction of events, we have his parents marrying *c*.1145, an elder brother appearing *c*.1146 at the earliest, leaving William

12 For Stephen Gay and his royal connections, see D. Crouch, 'Robert Earl of Gloucester's mother and sexual politics in Norman Oxfordshire', *Historical Research*, 72 (1999), pp. 323–33.
13 Stacy, 'Henry of Blois and the Lordship of Glastonbury', pp. 32–3.

to appear no earlier than 1147, a date of birth that is however indicated by other evidence (see below). This would fit in with his own memories of the events he witnessed as the *History* records them. He had by then a certain physical dexterity; he could recall some of the events himself, though did not realise their significance at the time; and, as we shall see, he had the ability to play games happily with someone else.

His father had no intention of keeping his agreement with King Stephen. He reinforced his garrison at Newbury with provisions and determined men, and then refused to surrender it. The king's advisers ('criminal and craven men', as the *History* has it) wanted William hanged in front of the castle. When this was made known to his father, he merely observed to the messenger that he still had the hammers and anvils to make more and better sons. What are we to make of this stunning paternal attitude? Was the slaughter of an infant a matter of such indifference in the twelfth century? Plainly not. Those who advised the king to do it were called by the derisory name *losengiers*, meaning 'deceivers'. The *History* makes much of the unsuspecting innocence of the Young William, and the horror of the doom that was hanging over his head. The writer expects his readers to share with him the enormity of the deed that was being contemplated. What is difficult to understand is the indifference of the father, the 'true and loyal' John Marshal. It may be, as has been suggested, that twelfth-century society would have admired the hard-faced practicality of such a father, even if it did not sympathise with it. For them, the guilt of the killing of the boy would lie then with the king, not indirectly with the father for his indifference. On the other hand, the king obviously expected John to keep to his agreement because he had his son.

Twelfth-century people shared with us the idea that the emotional link between father and son was a potent security. Gerald of Wales, writing later in the century, tells the lurid story of a father who castrated himself at the demand of an enemy who held his son over the edge of a tower, rather than see him dropped to his death. John Marshal had no feelings of that strength (his 'hammers' were not expendable), but that did not make him an unnatural father, by our lights or those of his day. In the imagery of the *History*, he was gambling for high stakes. That he won might indicate how well he knew his opponent. He had had two busy years at the court of King Stephen in England and Normandy between 1136 and 1138. He had been intimate with the king, the sole witness to some of his charters. His gamble with his son's life might not have been so daring if he were convinced that Stephen would never take the forfeit.

So when Young William was escorted to the gallows or placed on a siege catapult, which he took for a swing, no one took any notice in the garrison, whatever the private alarms of the Marshal household back at Marlborough or Hamstead. Even dangling the boy from a wicker shield before the castle gate had no effect on the constable: a great millstone was positioned to be hurled down on the royal troops regardless. Little William, doggedly innocent, called back over his shoulder, wanting to know what sort of funny toy was being hung out of the castle window, which caused the king to smile and have him taken back to safety. After these futile attempts to convince the garrison that the boy was to die, the king gave in. The *History* says Stephen was disgusted by the business of putting a child's life in danger, a strategy that had not in any case been his own idea. Stephen was himself a devoted father who had lost two of his own children in quick succession while they were still infants in 1137 and had been devastated by their loss at the time, suspending a vital military and political campaign in Normandy to go home to his bereaved family. William was too young to serve around the household, but the king kept him by him, the first of many monarchs to be prey to William's confident charm, enjoying his artless and amusing prattle. William later told the story of how the king condescended to play a game of 'knights' with him in his flower-strewn pavilion, a sort of play tournament with soldiers made by medieval boys out of the leaves and heads of the common plantain weed.

It is difficult to know when William was reunited with his family. Newbury Castle eventually fell to the king, who moved on to the more important Angevin stronghold of Wallingford. It was his determined assault on Wallingford that led to the final confrontation between royalist and Angevin in England. Duke Henry of Normandy, Matilda's son, arrived in England at the urgent pleas of his party. One of those who joined his army in the West Country was John Marshal. The barons wanted peace and, after prolonged negotiations, Stephen recognised Henry as his heir in November 1153. Both pledged to return the landed situation to what it had been when Henry I died. It may not have been until then that William returned to his mother, for the *History* talks of a long stay with the king and his release after a general peace was negotiated in the kingdom, in which all grudges were forgotten and men were satisfied with what had always been theirs.

William made another debut in the two years immediately after Stephen died and Henry II succeeded in 1154. This was his first appearance in a charter. In or soon before 1156, his father parted with the Somerset manor of Nettlecombe to Hugh de Ralegh. The price was the service of one knight, a horse, two dogs and 80 marks in cash (£53 6s. 8d.). Hugh had also written into the charter the consent of John's wife and his sons, among them William, now perhaps nine years old. His elder half-brothers, Gilbert and Walter, and his full brother, John, had payments of gold and horses for their consent, William nothing.[14] He was still youngest and least, and we know from what happened later that his father did not plan that he would have a share of the family's lands after he died.

Perhaps in 1156, John's affairs were already taking a downward turn, which is why he was willing to sell off Nettlecombe. Henry II kept him with him in his first tour of his kingdom as king, in 1155 and 1156, but he is not found thereafter at court, and in 1158, when Henry II was preparing to leave for France, John lost Marlborough Castle. He did not lose everything. He kept his exemption from tax, his marshalship, the hundred of Kinwardstone and the royal manors of Cherhill and Wexcombe, but the abrupt resumption of Marlborough shows that the king

---

14 *Acts and Letters*, no. 5. The grant was confirmed by Henry II in 1156 at Bridgnorth.

regarded him, as he regarded many others of the older generation of Angevin supporters, as a man not worth courting, and possibly dangerous. In 1163, a chronicler tells us that John came under a black cloud of the king's anger. He had been dabbling in a current aristocratic craze, attempting to make sense of the fictitious prophecies of Merlin, which were then the subject of much attention. John rashly let it be known that according to Merlin, Henry II would not return again to England after he left for his campaign against Toulouse in 1158; the loss of Marlborough obviously rankled.[15] Henry returned in 1163, and John's speculation looked then very much like treason. John only recovered the king's favour by acting as his inglorious stooge in the persecution of Becket in 1164.[16]

It was in these fading years, as John Marshal grew older and the court hostile, that some provision was made for Young William. The *History* claims that at some time, probably late in the 1150s, John contacted his 'cousin german' William de Tancarville, the Chamberlain of Normandy (often known as 'the Chamberlain of Tancarville'), and arranged that William should cross to Normandy to be schooled in the Tancarville household as a *gentil home* (a man of family).[17] There is no other evidence that John Marshal and the Tancarvilles were related, and it seems that the author of the *History* got it wrong. There *is* evidence that the relationship was in fact between the Salisbury family and the Tancarvilles. So it might well be that William's fostering in Normandy was made possible by his mother's family, even if the suggestion came from his father.[18]

15 Diceto, I, p. 308.
16 For John Marshal's involvement in the Becket affair, see M. Cheney, 'The litigation between John Marshal and Archbishop Thomas Becket in 1164: a pointer to the origin of novel disseisin?' in *Law and Social Change in British History*, ed. J.A. Guy and H.G. Beale (Royal Historical Society, London, 1984), pp. 9–26. The deduction about John's opportunism in the affair is mine, not Mrs Cheney's, and seems to follow from John's problems in 1163.
17 It is worth mentioning that William Marshal was not the only cousin to whom William de Tancarville gave a helping hand. He provided the marriage portion by which his cousin Beatrice could marry a local knight in the Pays de Caux, *Chartes du Prieuré de Longueville*, ed. P. le Cacheux (S.H.N., 1934), p. 50.
18 Lands and houses in Rogerville and Rames (Seine-Maritime, canton St-Romain-de-Colbosc) were held by Edward of Salisbury, Earl Patrick's grandfather, of the honor of Tancarville in the early part of the reign of Henry I, J. le Maho, 'L'apparition des seigneuries châtelaines dans le Grand-Caux à l'époque ducale', *Archéologie Médiévale*, 6 (1977), p. 21. Edward of Salisbury appears in two charters of William (I) de Tancarville, one the foundation charter of the Abbey of St-Georges-de-Boscherville. Edward was a benefactor to the abbey in Normandy. This appearance of a Salisbury–Tancarville link may well bespeak a marriage between the families, perhaps between Edward and a daughter, sister or aunt of William (I) de Tancarville. The Salisbury lands in Normandy would then be the girl's marriage portion. William (I) de Tancarville was very active in England in the reign of Henry I, with lands in Edward's Wiltshire, and also in Gloucestershire and Rutland, with a marcher lordship in Gwent. For these, see *Monasticon*, VI pt. 2, 1066–7; *Llandaff Episcopal Acta, 1140–1287*, ed. D. Crouch (South Wales Record Society, V, 1988) no. 28.

William was already approaching adolescence when he took leave of his weeping mother, sisters and brothers. By then, he was tall enough to ride a horse. Straight-grown, brown-haired and – if the *History* is to be believed – handsome, he rode off to Tancarville attended (as was customary) by another young aspirant (unnamed) who was to be a companion and friend; there was also a serving man to attend to the boy's personal needs. When William returned to England a decade later, his mother would be a widow, and his two older half-brothers would be dead. The Marshal would then be his brother, John, and the elder Marshal would be lying in a tomb in Bradenstoke Priory.

We do not know if William Marshal loved his father; it is rare indeed that the conventional family piety of the Middle Ages can be penetrated. Later, he made pious grants for his parents' souls, but so did others who we know loathed their father, such as the sons of Henry II. The chief purpose of the father in the medieval aristocracy was not to be loved, but to protect and provide, to school and to dominate. John Marshal was a formidable model for his son: astute, physically powerful, an easy companion in the royal chambers and a cool warrior in the field. In his days as castellan of Marlborough, he was no coarse bandit. He was more of a baron than a robber. He played the great game of politics with talent and perception, rising rather than falling among the factions of civil war. Giving ground when defiance would be quixotic, he still ended up on the winning side. So far as his limited resources allowed, he was a generous patron of the Church: a benefactor of abbeys and priories, particularly Bradenstoke Priory, the Salisbury family foundation and mausoleum in Wiltshire, where he was buried himself. He shared the aristocratic fascination of his day with the Knights Templar, to whom he devoted his manor of Rockley in Wiltshire when William was a boy of nine or ten. We may look to him for the beginnings of William's fruitful acquaintance with the crusading orders. John Marshal was the first great exemplar of lordship in his son's life, and even at the distance of centuries we will see, in his strengths and weaknesses, how the son drew himself in some aspects from the pattern of his father, a definitive *preudomme*, or 'man of standing', in his son's eyes.

William de Tancarville: the 'good master'

At the age of 13 or 14, William Marshal came to Normandy and entered a new world, even though Normandy was the land of his fathers (and indeed his father's family may still have held some small Norman properties). But William had known only England, and it may be that for him, as for other Anglo-Norman noblemen, English was the language of his mother's chamber. But William must also have been taught French from his earliest years, or he would never have been able to talk to King Stephen during his time at the king's court. We can only guess at the homesickness and disorientation that he would have experienced: perhaps akin to what the historian Orderic Vitalis, when an old monk and scholar in the 1140s, recorded that he felt when he left his birthplace of Shrewsbury to enter the Norman monastery of St Evroult as a novice in the days of King William Rufus:

'and so, a boy of ten, I crossed the English Channel and came into Normandy as an exile, unknown to all, knowing no one'.[19]

William's biographer has little to tell us of the years spent in the Tancarville household. William must have been uncommunicative on the subject. There was much about his adolescent years that might have given him cause for unhappiness, apart from the usual hormonal upsets: he certainly seems to have been dissatisfied with his treatment from his guardian on more than one occasion. All that the *History*'s author tells us is that he was a docile and well-bred boy, though that may have been no more than his own assumption. But he does include one of those self-deprecatory stories that must stem from the Marshal himself, how he was known at that time for his sleeping and eating, not unusual preoccupations in adolescent boys, it must be said. 'Scoff-food' (*gasteviande*) was his nickname in the Tancarville household, where it was alleged he slept when there was nothing to eat. The Chamberlain was said on one occasion to have predicted great things for him, nonetheless.

One thing we can be sure that he received in those Norman years was a first-class military training. The Chamberlain of Tancarville was known throughout Europe as one of the grander patrons of knighthood, and he was still a young and vigorous warrior when William entered his household. The size of his military retinue was famous, or notorious. To Henry II's clerk, Walter Map, around 1180, the Chamberlain was 'a man of noble race, a remarkable soldier, manly . . . he is the father of knights'; it was his custom to ride everywhere with a great retinue of them.[20]

The Chamberlain was a man of ancient lineage (as Normans went), wide possessions and great generosity. His possessions included substantial estates in England, where he was the absentee lord of the town of Grantham. He held three Norman castles: the powerful and splendid fortress of Tancarville with the square, limestone keep his grandfather had built, rising from a flat-topped hill among the bluffs on the north side of the estuary of the Seine and still impressive in its remains today; Hallebosc, or Albosc, a lesser stronghold some 17 kilometres inland to the north; and Mézidon in Central Normandy, another powerful fortress, above the valley of the Dives. His baronies of Tancarville and Hallebosc made up most of the Pays de Caux between Le Havre and Lillebonne.[21] Even William Marshal's uncle, the Earl of Salisbury, could not command such resources. William's placing in the Chamberlain's household was therefore a great thing, and whichever side of his family placed him there they found for him the best training available both in soldierly skill and courtly graces. The Chamberlain was then in the prime of

---

19 *The Ecclesiastical History*, ed. and trans. M. Chibnall (6 vols, Oxford, 1969–78) v, 554.
20 Walter Map, *De Nugis Curialium*, ed. M.R. James (revised edn, Oxford, 1983), p. 488.
21 For the baronies of the Tancarville family in Normandy, see le Maho, pp. 19–23; for Mézidon, *Complete Peerage* X appendix F 50–1. The Tancarville lands in Normandy answered for 10 knights to the duke in 1172, with 94¾ knights' service at the lord's own disposal, F.M. Powicke, *The Loss of Normandy, 1189–1204* (Manchester, 1913), p. 353.

life, not yet tainted with the rebellion that soured his later career, though his capacity for emotion and ill-judged violence was already evident; as a younger man, he became notorious for the murder of Walter de St Martin, a member of an influential family of western Normandy. To escape a dangerous vendetta, William was forced to pay heavy compensation by the menacing alliance of Geoffrey's kin and friends, including the powerful Count of Eu, who had sworn mortal enmity against him.[22]

The education of William Marshal

We can assume that William would have learned the skills of the hunt in the forest of Tancarville, hawking in the marshes of the Seine estuary, the discipline of arms in the great bailey of the castle, and to sing (once his voice allowed) in the chambers of his lord's wife Isabel, a woman of formidable piety who would one day leave her lord to enter the nunnery of Mostervilliers. These were all things that every young aristocrat must know.[23] One thing we can't be certain that he learnt was his letters. Literacy (that is, the ability to read Latin) began to be seen as a desirable part of a young baron's education before the reign of Henry I. William's father's generation in fact contained many paragons of educated laity: Earl Robert of Gloucester for one. A boy of William's level of society was expected to be schooled, but his biography never says he was literate, even though there was good reason that he should have mentioned it had William acquired his letters.

John Marshal himself had some interests wider than warfare, for he was said to have had some acquaintance with the writings of Geoffrey of Monmouth or one of his imitators. While William was in the Tancarville household, the justiciar of England was Robert, Earl of Leicester, a man who wrote letters on philosophy to learned Cistercian abbots, read treatises on astronomy, and consulted bishops on the problems rich men might encounter entering heaven, which understandably troubled Robert and many of his fellow magnates. He was the first English magnate we know of to own a personal devotional copy of the book of psalms, so he could join in the daily office said by his chapel of clerks. A little later, the seneschal of Normandy was William fitz Ralph, famous for personally examining charters in law cases in his court at Caen. On one occasion, he detected a forgery produced before him, to the horror of the guilty party.

Different virtues were apparently courted at Tancarville. William Marshal's biography betrays no evidence that he ever aspired to anything more than physical and military proficiency as a youth. He was, however, well acquainted already with

---

22 Rouen, Archives départementales de la Seine-Maritime, 17 HP 1; Bibliothèque municipale de Rouen, Y 13, fo. 116v.
23 Hawking, hunting and the discipline of arms were what was taught in Henry II's household late in the 1150s to an Italian youth sent by Pope Adrian IV to England for a knightly education: see *The Letters of Arnulf of Lisieux*, ed. F. Barlow (Camden Society, 3rd ser., LXI, 1939), pp. 18–20.

clerks and chaplains from a very early age: his father employed at least two, his uncle William Giffard, rector of Cheddar, was briefly the chancellor of the Empress Matilda, and his youngest brother Henry was destined for the Church. In fact, William's entire career shows an awareness of the value of literacy and accounting skills, but he employed those who had them, he did not have them himself. He was being fitted out for a career as a professional soldier, and if there was an omission in his upbringing, it is understandable. We will see later that he was quick to take into his service clerks of his own once he had the need for them; before then, he would borrow his master's.

William's accomplishments in Latin were probably no more than the basics required of a layman, as listed by the thirteenth-century moralist and statesman, Philip de Novara: memorising the Lord's Prayer, the Hail Mary and the Creed. Novara says that he ought to have learned these from his mother, father or some other close relative. His religious instruction might well have included at least the importance of the first two commandments, and included moral warning about the dangerous mortal sins that he must avoid and confess to avoid damnation.[24] No doubt he had his memory packed with many biblical stories and tales of saints, particularly warrior saints, from an early age. French (Romance) literature was a rising interest of his generation. At Tancarville, William would have gained acquaintance with, and perhaps memorised, a whole range of fables, gestes and lesser romances: epic tales of Normandy and Britain's past, of Charlemagne, Roland and the Twelve Peers, and the legendary deeds of the Roman emperors. With them, he would have taken in a mass of ideas that were the common cultural currency of his day, which would have allowed him to pass for a tolerably cultured man and an entertaining dinner guest.

One other necessary skill for survival had to be acquired in the Tancarville household: courtliness. This had as much to do with self-preservation as mastering the sword and lance. William lived between the ages of 13 and 20 in a great aristocratic court among a crowd of his peers, boys as likely to be his rivals as his friends. To survive in such an environment, he had to use his wits and every advantage nature had given him. In his day, and in that of his father, society across Western Europe had already developed a code of behaviour that taught how to get on in public life. William would have known it as *courtoisie* (Lat. *curialitas*, Eng. 'courtliness') – the behaviour appropriate to courts and public assemblies. His father had already been his first great tutor in the school of courtliness, for John Marshal was universally recognised as a great practitioner of it. William as a boy would have aspired eventually to graduate into the status of what he and his fellows called a *preudomme*, a man of distinction and a respected actor in public affairs.

Courtliness was taught to up-and-coming youths in the households where they were placed: here, for instance, is the recommendation given to the young people

---

24 For some mid-thirteenth-century advice as to educating a young medieval aristocrat, see *Les Quatre Ages de l'Homme*, ed. M. de Fréville (Société des anciens textes français, Paris, 1888), cc. 12–20, pp. 9–14.

in his own court by the aristocratic poet Garin lo Brun, castellan of Veillac in the Auvergne, a contemporary of John Marshal: 'Courtliness (*cortesia*) makes a man to be held in esteem', he said, and again, 'Courtliness resides in rich display and in being a gracious host; it lies in doing honour to others and in elevated speech.' Garin said it was a complicated business to acquire it, and as hard to define it. Some people had a natural aptitude for it and others found it difficult to acquire. Courtliness was therefore nothing to do with birth: 'there are honest peasants who are reckoned courteous'.[25]

What Garin was talking about was not 'chivalry', which did not fully develop as a self-conscious aristocratic code for males until after William Marshal's death. He was talking about the social skills and amiable self-confidence necessary to get on in the environment of courts and public assemblies, skills that anyone, man or woman, could acquire and display to advantage, even a peasant, as he says. Garin wrote in central France, but the same idea was recognised in contemporary England. From England comes another little tract on the subject for youths, written by a cleric called Robert of Ho probably not long after the time William Marshal emerged into public life:

> My son, I understand this about courtliness (*corteisie*), that a fellow should know knightly skills and how to ride a horse skilfully and gallop his destrier; he should know how to make poetry; he shouldn't take a risk without good reason; he should be a connoisseur of hounds, hawks and hunting; he should speak well and be moderate in his replies, and stick to what he says: the better he understands these matters the more respect he'll have in every land.[26]

William Marshal's career tells us these were exactly the sentiments he picked up at the court of Tancarville, and 'respect in every land' as a *preudomme* was the ambition his Norman mentor placed in his heart. To acquire that, he must project social ease and acquire a facility with words, though not be reckless with them. He must have the skills of the hunting field and the stable, so he could talk intelligently about horses and hounds with his peers, as well as being able to impress and amuse them with his wit. As Garin said, not everyone was born with the abilities to attain this happy state, but young William Marshal most certainly was, and he reaped the benefit of them all his long life.

First, however, William had to survive the many and various trials of adolescence, not all of them hormonal. The Lord of Tancarville was surrounded by a great retinue of knights, squires and servants, greater and lesser. Even a humble squire might find himself the object of envy and plot. The *History* is full of the doings of the Marshal's detractors, who cropped up everywhere he went to

---

25 Garin lo Brun, *Ensenhamen* in, *Testi Didattico-Cortesi di Provenza*, ed. and (Italian) trans. G.E. Sansone (Bari, 1977), pp. 67–8.

26 *Les Enseignements de Robert de Ho: dits Enseignements Trebor*, ed. Mary Vance Young (Paris, 1901), pp. 79–80.

discredit him with his current master. This persecution was no mere literary convention to explain the rough patches in his career. At Tancarville, his kinship with the lord, and the lord's initial satisfaction in the boy's looks, humour and address, brought on him the envy of others who were competing for the rewards of their master's favour. His master also was a mercurial and emotional man, whose moods were equally dangerous reefs in William's voyage into his perilous future.

The biography says that William coped with these rivals in the approved manner of courtly heroes: 'he was of such a docile and well-bred disposition that he would never show signs of noticing any slur spoken against him'. He endured backbiting in silence, behaved with modesty, and confounded envy by great deeds.[27] His line in self-deprecation is a very good example of this form of defence. He was filing down the teeth of persecution by jokes against himself – a ploy that is still to be found alive and well in the playgrounds of the schools of England, as every teacher knows. William de Tancarville did his duty by him. In his overpopulated retinue, William learned, as no doubt his father had intended, all that was necessary for a household knight to know. Not merely the physical skills, but some of the political ones too.

John Marshal died on 22 July 1165, as we learn from his son's expensive foundation of a mass to be said on the anniversary of his father's death at the priory of Longueville in Normandy. Since William did this on the new estates he had acquired in Normandy more than 30 years after his father died, we get a glimpse of a real commitment to his father's memory, which seems a little more than dutiful.[28] When he had the resources, he invested them in an act of piety that betrays a need to connect still with his father, a man long distant from him emotionally, and also – as all would have acknowledged at the time – undoubtedly after his death experiencing the pains of Purgatory, not least because of his ruthless persecution of the Church in the days of warfare in England. We know John's death was not sudden. He had time to draw up a testament, in which he made no known provision for William. His lands were divided between his two surviving eldest sons: Gilbert and John. Gilbert himself was to die only months after his father, leaving all the Marshal inheritance in the hands of the younger John.

Premature mortality afflicted not just this generation of the Marshal family, but that of William's own children. His elder half-brothers Walter and Gilbert barely made it to adulthood, yet they did not die in warfare or on the tournament field. His sons Walter and Ansel would also die within months of each other as young men, and in their case we know that both died after months of debilitating, mortal sickness. There were a number of conditions that could have carried off either group of brothers well before their time, but one that was widespread during

---

27 For the quotation, *History* I, lines 802–3. On the subject of courtliness in aristocratic education, see C.S. Jaeger, *The Origins of Courtliness* (Philadelphia, 1985), pp. 211ff., 257–68.

28 *Acts and Letters*, no. 66, pp. 135–7.

the twelfth century was pulmonary tuberculosis.[29] It tended to run in close-knit families where it became established, and in the case of both sets of these Marshal brothers, we happen to know they were very close to each other emotionally and physically, and so ripe for cross infection. This may have been a more likely source of the curse of premature death that contemporaries believed afflicted the Marshals than the spiteful malediction of the Irish Bishop of Ferns, with whom William Marshal was to have a long-running vendetta.

William did not return to England for the obsequies of his father and half-brother as far as we know. Indeed, the *History* has nothing to say on his father's death. Even more strangely, it places the deaths of both his half-brothers, Gilbert and Walter, in their parents' lifetime, and betrays no knowledge of the family succession arrangements. Such things were obviously not talked about among the later Marshals, and may have been forgotten, so the author of the biography was silent about them. And if there were a reason for this, it must be because these important events in England touched not at all on Young William in Normandy, where his career was not dependent on his brothers, but on his relations with the Chamberlain, his master.

In 1166, when his brother John was taking on the headship of his family and government of their lands, William was fast approaching the end of his squirehood. At some time in that year, perhaps with a batch of companions, he was knighted by William de Tancarville. William's knighting was not the great festival it would have been if he had been a young baron. William de Tancarville's own knighting in Stephen's reign had been a solemn and lavish occasion, with a week of festivities ending in his reception with a great crowd of kinsmen and knights by the abbot of the family monastery of St-Georges-de-Boscherville in solemn procession at the abbey door; he was received as the abbey's protector, and offered his sword on the high altar, which he and his friends redeemed by great gifts.[30]

William had to be satisfied with much less. The ceremony was carried out when he was 20 years old after perhaps as many as six years in the Tancarville household.[31]

29 Rawcliffe, C. *Urban Bodies: Communal Health in Late Medieval English Towns and Cities* (Woodbridge, 2013), pp. 63–5.

30 This information can be reconstructed from a charter in the Archives départementales de la Seine-Maritime, 13 H 15, printed in A. Deville, *Essai historique et descriptif sur . . . l'abbaye de St-Georges-de-Boscherville* (Rouen, 1827), pp. 73–6.

31 The question of the Marshal's age at his knighting is difficult to resolve because of the obscurity of the relevant passage in the *History* (lines 772–3), which Paul Meyer read as *Mès l'om dist que vint anz enters/Fu il ben eskuers*, that is, 'people say that he remained a fine squire for a full twenty years'. If 'esquire' refers to his training at Tancarville, then this is obvious nonsense. Meyer, the first editor of the text, thought *vint* was a misreading for *huit* (eight), but since he placed the knighting incorrectly in 1173 and thought that William had been born in 1143, this contorted the chronology unbearably, and Meyer confessed that he was confused by the text here. If, however, we take it to refer to William's age, applying 'squirehood' to the whole passage of his life before his knighting, then the reference does make at least chronological sense and vindicates Meyer's reading.

It happened when the Chamberlain was on campaign on Normandy's northern border, in garrison at Neufchâtel-en-Bray. The ceremony is simply, perhaps shamefacedly, described by the *History*. In his new cloak, William had a sword girded to his side by his master, and received a ritual blow on his shoulder – the dubbing or, in French, *colée*. There may have been a vigil, a bath, and a subsequent mass and feast, all eventual features of the ritual of becoming a knight, but we hear nothing of them here. So he entered into what was already being described in his time as the 'order' of knighthood with very little fuss, considering how great an ornament to it he was to become.

2

THE HOUSEHOLD KNIGHT

The twelfth century was the first medieval century to know the sorry plight of distressed gentlefolk. Western society had, by then, discovered standards of display that the man of blood had to live up to, or fall in dignity. When William Marshal had become a knight, these standards of style, dress and display were not as elaborate as they were to become in his later days,[1] but they still required that he have: three horses (a sumpter for his baggage, a palfrey for riding about, and a big-boned warhorse for the tournament and battle); the long, rich cloak of a gentleman and the ironmongery of war (a hauberk and hood of mail, mail and plate leggings and a helmet). William Marshal was in the tidal reaches of aristocracy, a younger son with no resources other than his wits. He knew how a man of good family should live, eat, dress and spend, but did not inherit the means to keep up with his more fortunate fellows. In his time, there was a social beach to be swept down by the ebb tide of poverty. He might well have known the sad story of Hugh Poer, whom his father would have met at Stephen's court. He too was the younger son of a baron, but had been raised briefly to the earldom of Bedford, then tumbled to common knight and total obscurity in a few years.

William was a man with a dignity to support, and for such a man his dignity was a great burden. He was one of the Honourable Georges and Honourable Johns of his day. Since his father had not been inclined to reserve him a share of his lands, his options were limited. If he had not gone on to seek his fortune, he had only one other resort: his family home. He would have had to live on in his brother's

---

1 The *History* notices this elaboration of expectations between the 1160s and the 1220s when it describes William leaving his family for France with no more than a friend and a manservant: 'in those days people were not so proud; the son of a king rode out with a cloak rolled up behind him, with but a squire, who did not expect a pack-horse', *History* I, lines 763–8.

hall, to grow old, unmarried, in hopes of something turning up, but at least keeping up appearances in the glow of the nearness to a great relation. On occasion, the sources allow us glimpses of such men. Geoffrey du Neubourg, the fourth son of Earl Henry of Warwick, was, like William Marshal, brought up in Normandy by a relation, this time his adult brother. In Stephen's reign, he returned to England to live off his eldest brother, Earl Roger of Warwick. When Roger died in 1153, Geoffrey 'the earl's uncle' lived on for many years at Warwick in his nephew's household, occupying a place in his charter witness lists. Geoffrey was still there in the 1170s, when William Marshal was making his way in the world, and by then he was in his sixties. He never married nor had land. He must have had some money from the earl, or the family would have been embarrassed by his poverty. It may even be that he had a high old time, like one of P.G. Wodehouse's aristocratic drones, but we do not know. His sort of existence does not sound very attractive. Yet there were enough of these aristocratic supernumeraries around in William Marshal's day to acquire a group name in English law books; they were the 'hearth sons'.

William Marshal did not choose to seek a living from his brother, John, in 1167. Why he did not do so is something of a puzzle. It may be that some personal difference was responsible for this, or at least a determination that he could do better. On the other hand, there is some evidence that his brother could not have done much for him immediately after their father's death, even if he had wanted to. John Marshal was underage when the elder John died, and spent a period of as much as a year in royal wardship, his lands in the custody of an officer notorious for his rapacity, Alan de Neuville.[2] But by 1167, John must have been free and of full age, and William now had some claim on his brother. He must have known that by then, he was the heir to John's lands and office, at least until John produced legitimate children. But this did not persuade him to go home, as others we know of did in his circumstances. There was therefore only one course open to him: his family had given him but one possible profession, arms, and he had to pursue it.

Fighting had been a way of life for a man for many centuries before William's time. What was new in the twelfth century was the nature the calling had assumed. Armed bands had surrounded great men since the Late Empire, but in the mid-twelfth century in Western Europe such bands had been refined into the *mesnie* (the French word comes from the Latin *mansio*, meaning household, but the usual Latin equivalent in the twelfth century was *familia*), the military household. Kings and great barons recruited men of mixed backgrounds into their service, but all were trained and disciplined to the same degree, and as long as the lord was happy with his service and could afford it, the household knight had a permanent income and other benefits, such as bed and board, several mounts and the

---

2 We know of this from the recollection of a Wiltshire jury of 1201, *Curia Regis Rolls* I, p. 424.

full range of knightly equipment. By the early twelfth century, household knights were uniformly equipped in armour and trappings, bearing a lord's device or colours.

The earliest such unit of which we get a close glimpse was the household guard of King Henry I of England. He had the wealth to employ several hundreds of horsemen, formidably skilled and organised. Some were landed men with a penchant for war; others were royal bastards; some were younger sons or heirs in search of profit, glamour and opportunity; others again were men of obscure birth with no other resource than their sword and strong arm.[3] It is certain that Henry I's *mesnie* was not the first such band; it had its predecessors under earlier Norman kings and dukes, but it is unlikely that they would have been as well organised as his. In his day, the *mesnie* was a separate department of the royal household, under its constables and marshals, each soldier receiving pay. Such *mesnies*, whether in the service of the king of England or of France, or of the lesser French princes, were bodies of soldiers unique in Western Europe since the collapse of the Late Imperial army. Indeed, contemporaries compared the English royal *mesnie* favourably with Caesar's legionaries, adopting a certain self-satisfaction when they did.

The *mesnie* had high morale and cultivated specialised military skills, but, above and beyond this, it had its own military rituals and respected a set of military customs that united all knights in a sort of freemasonry, even if they had different employers. As we'll see, this had a lot to do with the fact that the knights of Western Europe had a common meeting place in the international tournament events that had been going on since at least the 1120s, and probably some time before then. This freemasonry was not in William Marshal's day what we call 'chivalry' (a word that literally means 'what the horse soldiers did'). Chivalry appears fully formed as a code of exclusive male aristocratic behaviour in the time of the Marshal's sons, and when it did, it had more to do with defining who was or was not a privileged nobleman than who was a skilful knight.[4] But already by William Marshal's day, embracing courtliness and living like the horse soldiers did was the epitome of what made a layman distinguished among his fellows, a *preudomme*. William Marshal's biography is as a result a key source in examining what was going on in twelfth-century male aspirations and aristocracy.

The device of Tancarville

A settled position in someone's *mesnie* was what William Marshal was looking for in 1166, but such opportunities were limited; a baron or earl might retain no more

---

3 M. Chibnall, 'Mercenaries and the *familia regis* under Henry I', *History*, 62 (1977), pp. 15–23.
4 Such a meaning is evoked by the *History*'s use of the word *chevalerie*, as when the royal garrison at Winchester in 1141 rode out daily 'for to do *chevalerie*' (*History* I, lines 174–8), meaning manly deeds of horsemanship and arms.

than six to twelve of such fortunate creatures. In many ways, he was in the same position as a contemporary graduate after the close of the last examination booklet. He was free, but free to starve as much as prosper, at the mercy of the job market. There were thin pickings for young knights, and what was to be had depended on luck and notice. Failure meant a return to kick his heels in the family home, whether he was welcome or not. At this point in his life, William would have been ticking off in his mind the possible openings his network of kinship offered him. The wider circle of kinship did not play much of an active part in twelfth-century society. Family affections, then as now, embraced little more than the nuclear family we acknowledge today: uncles, aunts, perhaps first cousins, were the remotest relations a man was expected to cherish. However, when a man increased in wealth and needed followers, it seems to have been the general rule to look to kinsfolk, the people horizontally connected with you through a common ancestry, the group William would have called (in French) his 'parage'. As Abbot Samson of Bury St Edmunds discovered, alleged kinsfolk were not shy of waylaying him on his return from his blessing as abbot, seeking places in his household and administration. Samson resisted their pleas at the time, but certainly later took on those of his kin whom he thought had the talent to be of use to him. Kin were not necessarily trustworthy, or even grateful, but medieval society valued blood, and believed it strengthened the link between lord and man, patron and client.[5]

In 1166, William Marshal seems to have had hopes of a postgraduate career in the Tancarville household, but for reasons that are not entirely clear this was to be denied him. Part of the reason at least is clear: William de Tancarville had decided he was not the sort of tyro knight he wanted in his household, whether because there were better candidates or because he was not convinced of the boy's talents, cousin or not. However, to begin with, luck gave Young William a stay of execution on the termination of his career at Tancarville. In the summer of 1166, there was trouble on the northern borders of Normandy. The decisive way that Henry II had with the Norman aristocracy sometimes backfired on him. He had denied his ancestral lands to the nobleman William Talvas, and William was better able than most to make his displeasure known, for as well as being a Norman nobleman he was also Count of Ponthieu on the estuary of the Somme north of Normandy. Talvas made common cause against Henry in 1166 with his neighbours, the counts of Flanders and Boulogne. The result was the invasion of the Norman county of Eu, across the border from Ponthieu.[6]

5 Raymond le Gros, an Anglo-Welsh settler in Ireland, was escorted by a *mesnie* of knights in 1176 whose special feature was that all its members were his kinsfolk, a point that seems to contemporaries to have enhanced its military usefulness.

6 I suggest here that the warfare to which the *History* refers in its account of the Marshal's first expedition is to be located in 1166. It fits the report by Robert de Torigny of a campaign where William Talvas, count of neighbouring Ponthieu, was in conflict with Henry II over the confiscation of his castles in the south of Normandy, Torigny, p. 227. I differ here from Painter, *William Marshal*, pp. 19–20, 20n., who suggests that the conflict

The allied counts of Flanders, Boulogne and Ponthieu camped with a formidable army on the northern border of Normandy, threatening to break across it anywhere along its 50-kilometre length. A Norman force was based at old King Henry's proud fortress of Neufchâtel-en-Bray deep within the frontier to counter any incursion and foil a strike at the capital city of Rouen. The Norman marcher lord, the Count of Eu, along with the Constable of Normandy, William de Mandeville, the dashing and distinguished heir to the earldom of Essex, and the Chamberlain of Tancarville, led the defending army. It was in camp with this force, in the early stages of the campaign, that William Marshal was knighted. It is possible that the nature of the military emergency encouraged his master to knight him early. William's elder brother, John Marshal, was not knighted until he came of age the next year, 1167, but with John the knighting was part of the process by which he obtained his father's lands and shook free of his wardship. William Marshal had no inheritance to which he could look forward, so nothing prevented his premature knighting at the age of 19 or 20.

Neufchâtel was one of an inner line of fortresses along the river Béthune, built to defend the northern approaches to the Norman capital, Rouen. It was some 25 kilometres from the Norman border to north and east. As such, it was a good base to await an expected onset, if its direction was uncertain. The way that the *History* describes the ensuing campaign, it would seem that the thrust when it came still took the Normans off balance. The invaders reached Neufchâtel with almost no warning. The border counties of Eu and Aumale were already lost before the Chamberlain and his colleagues were aware of their danger. The contemporary historian Gervase of Canterbury tells us that the county of Eu was looted and burned by the Flemings. This probably means that the enemy entered Normandy across the river Bresle, between Eu and Blangy, and spread out in several parties to waste and pillage the land, the preferred strategy in medieval armies when their leaders wanted to humiliate and put pressure on an adversary. It would have been the main column, commanded by Count Matthew of Boulogne, that surprised the Normans at Neufchâtel.

The Normans were in total disarray when news reached them of the imminent descent of the Flemings. The Count of Eu wandered about, unarmed, his

---

described by the *History* is the invasion of the county of Eu by Louis VII in association with the Count of Boulogne, referred to by Gervase of Canterbury under the year 1167, *Opera Historica*, ed. W. Stubbs (2 vols, Rolls Series, 1879–1880) I, pp. 203–4. But Stephen de Rouen tells us that in June 1167, Philip, Count of Flanders, was fighting on the side of King Henry, *Draco Normannicus*, in *Chronicles of the Reigns of Stephen, Henry II and Richard*, ed. R. Howlett, II (Rolls Series, 1885), pp. 688–9, whereas in the *History* he is fighting against the king. Moreover, the next incident in the *History*'s supposedly chronological narrative (the tournament between Sainte-Jamme-sur-Sarthe and Valennes) can be firmly dated to a time late in summer 1166. Another indication for setting the incursion described here early in 1166 is that William de Mandeville is referred to in the *History* (lines 863 and 1144) as not yet – but about to be – Earl of Essex, which he became in October 1166.

imagination undoubtedly warning him what was happening to his estates and revenues. We know from other sources that he was impoverished by the pillaging of his county, and later had to raise money to pay the knights and serjeants he enlisted for the campaign by confiscating the treasure of his abbey of Le Tréport.[7] Other Normans rode off in an undisciplined attempt to meet the enemy before they forced a passage into the town. The young William de Mandeville and a few men had the presence of mind to head for the bridge outside what seems to have been the town's west gate. Here, the road ran out over a ditch into a faubourg, or suburb, then called the Chaussée d'Eu (nowadays the area called St Vincent). The Chamberlain of Tancarville was not so headlong in the crisis. He stumped about the castle dragooning together a company of his men, including William. Together, they rode down to the bridge. The excitement of the day carried William away. He forgot himself, and was on the point of passing his master when the Chamberlain halted him with the jovial cry of: 'William, get back! Don't be so hot-headed! Let these knights get through!' He wished he had never been born, the biographer said, for William had thought he was a knight the equal of the others in his master's eyes.

The put-down seems to have been one of the Marshal's favourite stories in later life. But, characteristically, he did not fail to add that despite the rebuke, he let a few of his elders get by, and then spurred on his horse and got near the front again. At the bridge, the Chamberlain's company joined up with William de Mandeville and almost immediately encountered Flemings pouring into the suburbs of Neufchâtel. The leading ranks of each side spurred into a charge in the suburban street of the town outside the gate. William's lance was broken by the shock of the meeting of the hemmed-in ranks, but he laid about with his sword to some good effect. The Normans even managed to drive the Flemings back to the barrier that closed off the suburb. However, despite the Normans' efforts, they were pushed back in turn by the press of the enemy to the town bridge. A general melee developed in the crush before the bridge as Count Matthew committed new forces to break into the town. For a while, the struggle swayed about as the Normans, helped by the townsfolk, rallied in their turn. At some point, William's luck ran out. He had found a stone-walled animal fold just off the road, and was using it to good effect as a temporary fort where he couldn't be surrounded, and from which he could sally out into the street when he was able. But a party of Flemish foot soldiers got hold of an iron hook from the roadside – a fire precaution to pull down burning thatch from the surrounding houses. They used it to catch William on his shoulder and struggled to pull him down and take him. He pulled free despite a torn shoulder, but in the meantime his horse was fatally wounded. Fortunately, the battle had swept by and the Flemish forces were withdrawn as the town militia

---

7 *Cartulaire de l'abbaye de St-Michel du Tréport*, ed. P. Lafleur de Kermaingant (Paris, 1880), pp. 63–4. The count took two rich gospel books, two thuribles, a gilded silver chalice and over two dozen vestments, and pawned them. On his deathbed, a few years later, he regretted his action and compensated for it by an annual rent.

came to William's aid. Count Matthew was perhaps unwilling to prolong the skirmish into a risky general action, once he had lost the advantage of surprise.

As a first taste of the excitement of combat, William's experience that day might have been a lot worse. For what it is worth, the *History* tells us that Normans, captured French and Flemish, and townspeople alike were all agreed that he had distinguished himself. An idea corresponding to our 'man of the match' was known then and was the culmination of every tournament. William might have done better, however, had he remembered what the more experienced knights knew. War in the twelfth century was not fought wholly for honour, or even for salaries. Profit was there to be made – and the men who must make it were precisely those in William Marshal's position: the household knights with no other resource. His failure to convert his valour into more tangible benefits was a sad failing in one in his position. His elders were not slow to remind him of this.

The evening was given over to a celebration of the sort familiar to anyone who has been in the bar of a rugby club after a home win; an evening of drink, loud laughter, reminiscence and practical joking of a peculiarly unsubtle sort. William de Mandeville, the heir to the Earl of Essex and a man already reckoned as one of the great knights of his day, called down to William.

'Marshal! make me a gift, out of friendship and as a reward.'

'Willingly! What will it be?'

'A crupper, or, failing that, an old horse collar.'

The request for a gift of assorted items of saddlery rather puzzled the naive William, for, as he said, he had never owned such things in his life, but used his lord's.

'Marshal, what's that you say? Today you got forty of them before my very eyes, or even sixty, and now you intend to refuse me one!'[8]

There was a general belly laugh around the hall at William's expense. It penetrated the elation and exhaustion of the day, and entered his store of instructive stories with which he regaled the sponsors of his eventual biography, when no doubt they were squires needing instruction. The point of Mandeville's joke was that William had failed to profit by his chances. If his calling was now arms, its fees were the ransoms and equipment of the men he had defeated. He had acted the epic hero, and although his efforts were ungrudgingly respected, his lack of realism – given his circumstances – was not.

The 1166 campaign was fierce, but apparently brief: the Count of Flanders was Henry II's ally by the next year. Peace was a problem for a man in the position of the young William Marshal. It was especially unwelcome in 1166, for the skirmish at Neufchâtel had lost him his expensive warhorse, which left him as much a knight as an admiral would be a flag officer without a fleet. The Chamberlain, on his return home, decided to economise on his retinue. He let it be known that those of his knights who wished to go off in search of fortune would have free licence

---

8 *History* I, lines 1145–57.

from him. This was tantamount to giving notice to such knights as he did not particularly pick out to quit his hall. William Marshal was meant to go too, but his cousinship to the Chamberlain made an outright command to leave difficult, but hints were dropped. No support was given to him to replace his horse. To buy one, he had to sell the new cloak he had for his knighting. With the 22 shillings this raised, William bought a passable mount, a rouncy, a squire's horse, but, with no money for a packhorse, the new warhorse had to double as the transport for his armour and baggage, while he rode his palfrey. While his fortunes were still undecided, his luck resurfaced. News reached Tancarville of a tournament in Maine. The Chamberlain decided to participate, and as a result William's fortunes took a turn for the better. The Chamberlain was now willing to retain him for the occasion, and as a result new equipment was forthcoming and, ironically and belatedly, a warhorse. But the Chamberlain was a whimsical and unpredictable man, and he did not want William Marshal to feel too convinced of his continuing good will. He deliberately left him out when the horses were given out to the other knights. When William reminded him of his promise, a white horse was forthcoming. It was a fine horse, but wild and difficult to control. We are told that William needed all his emerging skill to break in his Bucephalus. If the biographer is not just making it up, William called the horse 'Blancart', a name given to the mounts of several young epic heroes. It may be that in doing so, young William Marshal was flipping a defiant finger at his stingy patron.

This first tournament was a particular success for William. His performance was once again remarked upon; more important, he made three captures, one of them a leading courtier of the King of Scotland. This time, he did not forget his own needs. The ransoms of horses and money he collected helped him break even and gave him the confidence to bid for independence. The Chamberlain was happy to let him go off on his own account to a second tournament a few days' ride away, perhaps hoping his needy young cousin would not come back. Again, William distinguished himself, and it must be that as a result, he embarked on his first extended tour of the tournament circuit, which the *History* hints at. He was learning technique and establishing a reputation. The *History* indicates that he travelled across France at least as far as Hainault, one of the great centres of the sport. But it also had to admit that his first tournaments in these years of 1166 and 1167 were not invariably successful. On one occasion, he fell victim to an older and more experienced Hainaulter knight, Matthew de Walincourt, who humiliated him by claiming his entire harness, despite William's obvious poverty. It is rather significant for our understanding of William's character that he bore a grudge against Matthew for a decade, and saw nothing wrong in humiliating the older man in turn when he had a chance, though Matthew was by then well past his prime and there was little honour in making a fool of him. But what had been done to William he felt was not fair; he resented it and stored the grievance away for future settlement. He would not rest till he paid back the man who had put him down as a youth.

On his eventual return to Normandy in 1168, William went back to Tancarville – for he still wore the colours and device of the Chamberlain. Here, he finally made up his mind and got leave to cross the Channel to return to England, in effect resigning any expectation of a household place with his cousin. The Chamberlain willingly bid him farewell, with an amiable jibe that he should not stay too long there and a vague invitation that he should come back to Normandy some time. England (despite the military tumult of Stephen's reign) had acquired, or perhaps retained, a reputation as a dull place for knights fond of active exercise. Henry II did not allow tournaments there, and those barons and knights who had a taste for the sport had to cross to the Continent. That the English were more fond of drinking and boasting than of fighting was a routine insult thrown by the Norman French at their English cousins. Twelfth-century English writers took great exception to it. Like the well-established contemporary joke that Englishmen secretly had tails hidden about them, it was one of those tedious pleasantries that marked a growing divergence in feeling between the English and Norman components of Henry II's realm. This emotional separation between peoples is a theme that surfaces again and again in the Marshal's biography.

Patrick, Earl of Salisbury

We are told that William went to England to see his family, from whom he had been separated now for five years and more. But it was one particular member of his family that he really wanted to meet, and the *History* does not disguise it. He had cast off from the insecure refuge of Tancarville, hoping to find a safe harbour in England. His uncle, Earl Patrick of Salisbury, as one of his most potent relatives, was the first port of call. He found the earl somewhere in southern England early in 1168. The *History* says the earl was newly returned from the king's side; if so, Patrick had been in France, because that was where the king was during 1168 and 1169. A campaign was being planned to subdue the rebellious Lusignan family in Poitou, one of Henry II's most troublesome provinces, and Earl Patrick was to be one of the leaders of the expedition. With a campaign in the offing, the earl readily found his courtly and confident young nephew a place in his *mesnie*. William was very soon at sea again with his uncle. The *History* fails to tell us whether he found the time to see the rest of his family while he was in England.

So William embarked optimistically on his second campaign under a new banner. Just after Easter 1168, his uncle had been given the task of assisting Queen Eleanor to govern Poitou. It does not seem that he had long to discover the difficulties of his position. Accounts differ as to the precise circumstances of what happened. The Angevin court historian, Roger of Howden, says that the earl was returning from a pilgrimage to Santiago de Compostella in Spain, presumably before assuming his responsibilities. This snippet may be just a device to underline the vileness of the earl's murder: the brutal assassination of a pilgrim. The *History*'s more detailed account has the earl escorting the queen peacefully between castles. Both accounts, however, are clear that a party of Poitevins led by the Lusignan brothers, Geoffrey and Guy, ambushed the earl's party as it was riding unarmed and comfortably on their palfreys through the countryside. When the ambush erupted around them,

Earl Patrick's *mesnie* grappled for their hauberks, helmets and arms. The queen was hustled off to the protection of a nearby castle. The defenceless earl struggled to mount his warhorse and once in the saddle rode defiantly towards the Lusignans. But a passing Poitevin knight (the Lusignans always denied it was at their orders) ran him through with a lance from behind, and he died under his nephew's eyes.

In a rage of anger and horror, the young Marshal, protected only by his hauberk, rode into the Poitevins, hacking at the murderers. He did not last long, for his horse was killed under him and he was surrounded. He set his back to a hedgerow, and stood the Poitevins off 'like a wild boar amongst the dogs', mouthing threats and insults. But soon enough a knight got behind the hedge and struck at him through the foliage with a spear, slashing into and through his thigh. Felled, he was taken as a knight worth ransoming and bundled off, bleeding heavily, placed on an ass, a baggage animal. Meanwhile, his dead uncle was also being carried off by such of his men as survived. The corpse was laid to rest at the great church of St Hilary outside the city of Poitiers, a rather more remote tomb than the Wiltshire priory of Bradenstoke that was the mausoleum of his and the Marshal's families, where no doubt he had intended to lie one day.

William's period of captivity, the only such episode in his life, may not have lasted more than a few months, but it was not made comfortable for him. His captors carried him around with them like an awkward bundle. His wound was not treated: they wanted him to pay up his ransom and go home, though who it was they thought would pay is difficult to say. This was not the age of 'chivalry', as it later came to be. William's Poitevin hosts were desperate and dispossessed men; William was a hostage and a source of profit, not a fellow knight in difficulties. So in his captivity, he had to be his own doctor, staunching the lance wound with the bindings from his legging. The only assistance he had was from a kindly gentlewoman in one of his captors' temporary hideouts, who smuggled clean linen bandages to him concealed in a hollowed-out loaf. Luckily for the young Marshal, his body was resilient and his wound healed, not that he helped the process along himself. Observing a group of young knights and squires competing in throwing a heavy rock, he was pressed by them to join in the game. After a show of modest resistance and an allusion to his wound, he allowed himself to be persuaded. He hurled the rock a good half a metre beyond the previous champion, and in doing so tore open his wound once more. Like most of the Marshal's stories, this one had a point, and it was not just to point out the man's physical excellence and endurance of pain. What he accomplished was a courtly exercise. He did not put himself forward in competition and deprecated his own talents, but when he was brought to the point he performed beyond expectations and earned unbidden praise.

In the end, he was freed by a means that must have surprised even him. He had come to the attention of Queen Eleanor, and, whether it was a whim, or whether she had decided that William was one of the best bargains on offer in the military marketplace, or whether she had admired his reckless attempt to avenge his stricken uncle, she decided to buy him free. Once pledges had been given acceptable to both parties, William was freed into her hands, and he was retained in her own household. So at the age of but 21, he re-entered the golden circle of royalty he had first glimpsed as a small boy, and had never forgotten. Indeed, his biographer says as much, saying from now on he was 'in the gold', meaning in clover. He was well aware of the dramatic jolt this gave William's fortunes. He chooses this point in his narration to break into a paean of anticipated triumph: deeds of prowess, wealth and the respect and confidence of kings and princes.

What was it about William Marshal that won him so much, so easily? He was well connected, so much is true. No one could deny his 'lineage' (vertical descent) was respectable and his 'parage' (his contemporary relations) was distinguished. The Earl of Salisbury had been an uncle, the Chamberlain of Tancarville and the Count of Perche close cousins (see Table 1). His father and grandfather had been in office at the court of England for half a century. But success needed to be founded on more than the web of kinship. He had luck in abundance that would have ensured him a marshal's baton from Napoleon. But it was the man himself that counted. He was no deep thinker, and as far as we can tell his educational level was below the ideal for an aristocrat of his day. What he did have was a practical intelligence, and the assurance to make quick and confident decisions – the prized quality his contemporaries called in French, *sens*. His attempts at sophistry, where the *History* preserves them, are little more than stubborn and shallow attempts to justify his own reputation and self-interest. The mental assurance was complemented by physical coordination and confidence. He was undoubtedly a big, healthy and prepossessing man, a fine athlete and horseman. This mixture of quick wit and hand made him as perfect a warrior as he was to become in time a commander. The crown of his fortune was that he had an open face, a ready humour, an imperturbable temper and an underlying alertness for his own advantage that made him as natural a courtier as he was a soldier. The Queen of England, as good a judge of a male animal as might be found in mid-twelfth-century France, was bound to be impressed. William's face was his fortune.

At the court of the Young King

For the next 15 years of his life, William was dependent on the fees and wages of the various Plantagenet royal households of which he was a member; these and the profits he amassed on his own account on the tournament circuit. For the first six years of this happy period, he was still what he would have called a *bacheler* (or, if he was in a particularly carefree, sword-tossing mood, a *bacheler leger*), a retained knight and professional soldier without responsibilities to dependents of his own. Until June 1170, he remained with the Queen; in that year, he transferred to the household of her eldest surviving son, Henry, and in 1186 he entered the retinue of the old king himself. He would be 43 years old before the royal *mesnie* stopped being the focus of his career. These were the years of his prime, and, what was more, he spent them doing what he deeply loved. Even allowing for the bias of his biography, the bare chronology of his career demonstrates that he was valued and respected and never short of employment by the greatest of his world. After 1168, money was easy and he had no responsibility to anyone but himself, except in his latter days to his own squires and retainers. In old age, he could not let a campaign pass without pushing himself forward, a boy again, even to the extent of becoming a nuisance to a new generation of bachelors. His old age must have been a time of gnawing regret to him: a world-class sportsman grown old and stiff, sentenced forever to the club bar and committee room. Golf and bowls might be the consolation that history now offers such men; for him, it would have been hawks and hounds (although, oddly, no source mentions his enjoyment of the hunt).

It is very curious that we hear little from the *History* of what happened to him in these, the best years of his life. Only two incidents of any political importance are recorded by his biography between 1170 and 1182; we know rather more about his childhood and apprenticeship in arms. There are reasons for this. The men who provided details of his life for his biographer did not really get to know him till the very end of the period. But over and above this is the fact that much of what happened in this period was less than creditable to him considering what his later career was. He participated in plots and scenes that were distinctly unsavoury. A mist was therefore allowed to obscure this period of his career – a golden mist full of the shapes of grand tournaments and festivities, of kings, dukes and counts of great renown. But despite this, it is possible to recover something of what was really happening at this time. The cold evidence of charters and the sombre chronicles of Roger of Howden, the court historian of the early Angevin kings, give a very different picture of the Marshal's world, particularly when he was in the retinue of the king's son between 1170 and 1183.

And so we come to the defining relationship in William Marshal's life. This was William's own assessment. When early in King Richard's reign he made his first great religious foundation, he did so dutifully for the souls of all the kings he had served till that time, but it was the Young King Henry – then nearly a decade dead – his charter deliberately identifies as 'his lord', not Henry II nor Richard, and that can only be because William himself authorised that precise wording.[9] When the Marshal was placed in the household of Young Henry (as he was often called), the boy was 15, newly crowned as his father's associate-king on 14 June 1170. He was an engaging youth, generous, likable and determined to be liked. His epicene teenage beauty at that point was celebrated in a somewhat homoerotic poem 'In Praise of the King's Son' that survives copied on the margins of a manuscript of Roger of Howden's history, though it wasn't written by him. It was written by someone who had apparently seen the boy, and remarks on his striking carriage, his peaches-and-cream complexion, his athletic frame and his shock of bright gold hair: 'gifts which having given left Nature all but a pauper'.[10] His

---

9 *Acts and Letters*, no. 21, p. 77.
10 Howden V: 4–5n. His remarkable good looks are also mentioned in the description of him by his one-time chaplain, Gervase of Tilbury, *Otia Imperialia*, ed. and trans. S.E. Banks and J.W. Binns (Oxford, 2002), pp. 486–7.

TABLE 1 Selective genealogy of the Marshal and Salisbury families

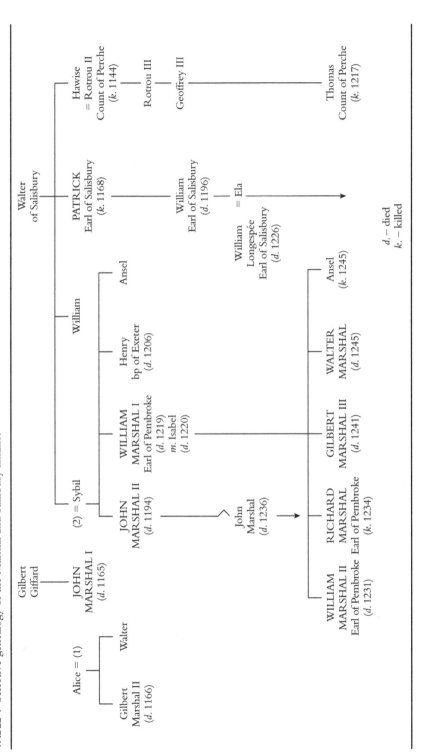

most formidable quality was his charm; it won him friends and a loyal following, both men and women. But charm is a useless commodity in the political marketplace unless stiffened with more solid virtues, and historians have always been divided as to whether there was much in the way of judgement or calculation behind the glamour and physical beauty of the young man he became.

Henry certainly had an uncheckable humour that might better have been checked. People told stories about him as a result. In the thirteenth century, people still recalled a story that when the archbishop congratulated the boy on his coronation in 1170, saying that he had been raised to an equality with his father, Henry is said to have denied it, for, he said, he was the son of a king, and his father only the son of a count. The story is unlikely to be true, as Young Henry would have known and been proud of the fact that his father may have been the son of a count, but he was also the grandson of a king, Fulk of Jerusalem, who had left Anjou for the Holy Land to marry the heir of the Latin Kingdom in 1128. Henry was nevertheless undoubtedly a creature of irrepressible whim, choosing one day in Normandy in 1172 to eject from a packed dinner everyone who was not called William (which being the commonest Norman name left him still with numerous guests, including his *carissimus*, his most intimate intimate, William Marshal).

There is little evidence that Henry developed much in the way of the administrative and juristic talents for which his father is famous, but then since he was never given lands to rule he had no chance to show he possessed them. What he was given was money, and plenty of it, and recently historians have become inclined to think that the way he spent it showed some calculation and investment. Since in his day the tournament circuit of Western Europe was the centre of what it meant to be an aristocrat, he made himself one of the biggest promoters of the sport in Europe. He had great fun doing so, but his tourneying was not just the self-gratification of the playboy he has been characterised as. There was a return for the expense in the shape of celebrity and international fame. Young Henry might have been a king without a kingdom, but he did rule over the international world of martial celebrity and so accumulated prestige and political capital, which in due course might have stood him in good stead had he ever succeeded his father.

We know rather more about his early life than is usual for Young Henry's day and age. He had been educated by a private tutor from his early years and so must have been literate at least. Some attempt was made to give him instruction in business from some of the king's principal justices. We don't know if his interests ran to any branch of the liberal arts, though there is some evidence he studied the art of rhetoric to good effect, which meant that he likewise had an education in grammar and logic, of which rhetoric was a companion study. Nobody ever remarks on his learning, but if he were anything like his brother John, who had a similar education, he would have had a mastery of Latin, both spoken and written, and would have read widely in history and theology. His court was to acquire some celebrated literary names: notably Ralph Niger, a master of the Parisian schools, a prolific commentator on scripture and a historian of his age.

Henry was placed for a few years from the age of seven or eight in the household of Chancellor Thomas Becket, who became Archbishop of Canterbury in 1162, which would have brought Henry into contact with some of the finer minds of his age, though he was there principally to associate with other noble children at the chancellor's court and to acquire the social ease and grace expected of him. Becket was renowned for the ceremony and expense with which he conducted his hall both before and after he became archbishop. Henry could, however, have acquired some early training in arms there, for Becket employed a distinguished knightly household, and indeed is known on more than one occasion (before he became archbishop) to have participated with credit in military actions in France. The boy Henry had been married to Margaret of France in Normandy at the age of only five, though he did not cohabit with his child bride till many years later, probably not till after their joint coronation in 1172. She too would in due course become an important character in William Marshal's life.[11]

Such was the gilded youth to whom William Marshal became as much a companion as a tutor. He would already have known the boy before his coronation if only at a distance, because Young Henry was with Queen Eleanor's household in Normandy in the months leading up to the event. We don't know whether or not William was present at his new master's consecration; his biography says he was, but the historical record indicates otherwise, that the queen remained in Normandy when her son crossed to England. The *History* says William was later summoned by the old king and offered the job of tutor in arms to his son, promising much in return for his labours (with the usual implication that the elder Henry did not live up to his pledges). Literary and charter sources mention just such figures in the education of the greatest among young aristocrats. The Marshal biographer proudly states that he was to be 'lord and master of his lord'.

There is supporting evidence elsewhere for his closeness to the boy king. Young Henry's charters reveal a permanent group of some eight retained knights in his entourage, and of these William is almost invariably placed first, with the only exception of Peter fitz Guy, the Young King's seneschal in the 1170s. This inner retinue, the *mesnie privée* as it was called, contained a majority of Normans, with two Englishmen: William himself and Simon de Marisco. Some of the eight were from minor baronial families; the Normans, Adam d'Yquebeuf and Robert de Tresgoz. They were, like William, in expectation of succession to the family lands. We glimpse besides these men a much larger group of squires surrounding the knights, men such as Henry Norreis, a sycophantic hanger-on of the Marshal, who was the unintentional cause of his downfall at court. But above both these and the knights were a group of glittering young magnates who moved in and out of the Young King's court, men who enhanced the glamour and fashion of his following. Chief among them was Robert, Count of Meulan, a man in his late twenties when

---

11 See on this, M. Strickland, 'The upbringing of Henry, the Young King', in *Henry II: New Interpretations*, ed. C. Harper-Bill and N. Vincent (Woodbridge, 2007), pp. 184–214.

the Young King was crowned. He was the greatest magnate in Normandy, and a cousin of the King of France, but had been excluded from the favour of Henry II, so perhaps fixed on the old king's son in compensation. Others were less substantial men, but still more than common knights: Judhael de Mayenne, Baldwin de Béthune and John des Préaux.

In this rich and glamorous gathering were abundant opportunities for the young Marshal, and he used them. He cultivated useful friends such as Baldwin de Béthune, brother of the great Picard magnate Robert, Advocate of Arras. Baldwin eventually received the county of Aumale, and the close and honest friendship between the two men was a great help to both, particularly as they inhabited a little world where enemies were common and not open. William gained a more than nodding acquaintance besides with dukes, counts and even kings, a celebrity in which the *History* frequently rejoices.

The mid-twelfth century was a great age of the lay courtier. Courtiers were nothing new at this time, but what was new was the amount of thought, and even study, that went into their careers in the households of the great. As we have already seen, courtly qualities were discussed and cultivated: a man must be cheerful, urbane, witty and wise, as well as having the innate qualities of nobility and good looks. The bare facts of his career, setting aside the bias of the *History*, tell us that the Marshal must have been a very icon of courtliness, innately good-humoured, charming and amusing. With tact and a well-bridled tongue, he had no need to be a master of manoeuvre and dissembling. What for others was merely the carefully constructed outer mask was for him his natural disposition. In the words attributed to King Richard of him, he was '*molt corteis*' (most courtly). His ambition rode easily beside his own disposition. His aggression and competitiveness were channelled into the tournament and warfare. After he had put off his armour and sword, he could lapse into the companionship of the household with ease. He rose effortlessly, without needing to plot or subvert the position of others. His only danger was his own success.

The courtly world of the Plantagenets had its dark side. Courts could be ugly places, sinks of treachery and conspiracy. The greater the ruler, the more there was to be gained by intrigue and slander against one's rivals for men of few scruples. Behind the mask of some of these courtiers was deceit and treachery. There did not lack for such men at Henry II's court. It can be no coincidence that his reign produced the first great crop of satirists of the court: men such as his distinguished clerical courtiers, John of Salisbury, Walter Map, Gerald of Wales and, above all, Peter de Blois, who turned to bitter essays on the courtly life to relieve their anger and frustration at the daily pettiness, stress and intrigue of their lives. William Marshal's biography, as well as contemporary courtly romances, contains similar sentiments, although in general his biographer is more stoic in his approach to difficulties at court. The *losengiers* and *paltoners* (deceivers and traitors), who haunt the Marshal from his earliest exposure at court as a boy in Stephen's reign, were for him just one more set of opponents to be overcome, not evils to be bewailed – the Marshal was, after all, a soldier.

What applied to the court of Henry II was true to an even greater degree of that of his son, the Young King. The boy had little power and no responsibilities, just time to kill in the most elegant and expensive ways his day could offer. The inhabitants of his court were young and ambitious men, and he was eager for an independence and influence that he gradually came to realise would not be his until his father died. Time, money and a grievance added to a bright and inexperienced court could only mean trouble. Henry II realised this and in a desultory, abstracted way did something to damp it down. Smothering the problem with money for amusement and display in fact did little to help, for there was never enough for his son, and attempted economies only provided more grievances. What could you do with a prince who retained knights for his tournament team at the astonishing rate of 20 shillings a day? Picking sensible men to fill positions at his son's court was another way. In 1170, William Marshal's apparent steadiness would seem to have secured him his tutorship to the Young King. Yet Henry II could not prevent his son taking on men more to his own liking. The clerks the elder king placed with his son would be truest to his interests. The staff of the Young King's miniature chancery in fact depended on the father for their advancement in the Church hierarchy. This section of his son's household may have been intended to be Henry II's hold on his son's political activities. If this were so, he miscalculated badly.

Royal and baronial households by the twelfth century had two broad departments: the lay household, the *mesnie* and the officers of the hall, and the clerical household (called the chancery in the royal households and those of certain great magnates). In general, there seems every reason to believe that the two sections got on very well together. Clerks and knights were after all usually men of the same class and shared certain interests, and they weren't competing for the same sort of patronage to make them rivals. There are numerous examples of lords displaying great affection for their household clerks and chaplains, lavishing rewards on them and their relations, just as they did on their knights. Even in the Young King's household, William Marshal could enjoy a good working relationship with his master's kitchen clerk, Wigain, who kept for him a running tally of his tournament wins in the 1170s and 1180s.

Literacy was in great demand in the twelfth century, and deeply respected by an aristocracy that itself aspired to learning. It was an age of earnest religion among laymen. But still, there were two distinct departments in the households of the great, and their respective members were sharply distinguished by different dress, education, skills and ideals. There was at least the potential for anticlericalism, and in the Young King's household there was every necessary ground for an unhappy schism. There is good evidence from the writings of John of Salisbury of a feeling of clerical contempt for the knight in Henry II's efficient household. Henry's son, a lord devoted entirely to military pleasures, held the ring between, on the one hand, an arrogant young *mesnie* and, on the other hand, senior clerks with loyalties elsewhere, and no useful work to do.[12] It was hardly to be wondered at that his

12 See G. Duby, *The Three Orders*, trans. A. Goldhammer (Chicago, 1980), pp. 263–8.

knights and clerks must come into conflict, and the Young King would fail to keep them apart.

In 1173, the Young King's irritation with his father's restraints on his power and purse led him to rebel and ally himself with the King of France. All of the knights who can be identified as his intimates from his charters joined him. They appear in a list of rebels drawn up by Henry II's government and preserved in Roger of Howden's chronicle. William Marshal appears along with them, his first appearance in a surviving contemporary history. But it is notable that the boy's then chancellor, Richard Barre, and Walter, the royal chaplain, as well as the Young King's chamberlain and usher, his father's appointees, promptly defected to Henry II. Richard was of a Buckinghamshire knightly family, had received promotions to archdeaconries from Henry II, and had been one of his ambassadors to the Pope on the dangerous mission to Rome after the murder of Becket in 1170. It was inconceivable that such a man could have much sympathy with his nominal master's cause, and would return in such a crisis to his true lord.[13]

Later, in 1176, after the failure of the rebellion and the Young King's reinstatement, Howden tells us of his vice chancellor, Adam (the then chancellor, Geoffrey, Henry II's eldest bastard, did not reside with the household, perhaps wisely). Adam did not like what he saw going on at Young Henry's court, and 'as he owed everything to the lord king (i.e. Henry II) who had found him a place with his son', he attempted to inform on him by letter, in secret. Unfortunately for him, his intrigue was discovered. The Young King and his intimates tried Adam for his life, and the death sentence was being pondered when a friendly bishop stepped in and saved the hapless clerk. Nonetheless, Adam was whipped naked through the streets of the Norman town of Argentan and incarcerated, until Henry II intervened and had him transferred to the friendlier custody of Hyde Abbey in Winchester.

No wonder, perhaps, that William Marshal did not speak overmuch of his long residence in such a menagerie, except of his glorious tours of the tournament fields. Who knows but that the tournament may have seemed for him a place of freedom; above him the empty sky rather than the roof timbers of the packed hall, around him the hoarse bellows of combat rather than the whispers of conspiracy behind stone arcades. No need for the courtier's mask of mannered indifference under a helmet: he could let his animal spirits and aggression rip. The *History* records the position he was in when he was off the sports field. Speaking of his appointment by Henry II to be his son's companion and tutor, it says:

> There were many in the father's entourage who said: 'My lord! It is this person and that who is doing this to him, I mean those whom you have assigned to him as tutors; it is they who determine his behaviour. The day

---

13 For the career of Richard Barre, see R.V. Turner, 'Richard Barre and Michael Belet', *Medieval Prosopography*, 6 (1985), pp. 12–34.

before yesterday he had five hundred pounds, and now already he has been quickly relieved of them, and once, I cannot remember when, he had a thousand. If he carries on like this, he will ruin you and take from you all you have got!'[14]

As William grew in intimacy with the Young King, it became clear that he had no friend in Henry II, and his entire livelihood depended on an untried youth, in a court riven with faction and laced with informers.

Rebellion and disfavour

For a long time, the Marshal trod the tightrope of favour with confidence and success. It probably helped that he was unaware that there was a chasm below his feet. In 1173, however, he collided hard with political reality when the Young King put himself at the head of a powerful dissident Anglo-Norman aristocratic faction that had tired of the rule of his father. Henry II had begun his reign with a deliberate show of consultation with his magnates and bishops, united together in regular great councils. What had been till his succession a disunited and war-torn realm was now to be shown to be under Henry a land of peace and harmony. Within a decade, however, it became clear that the king's natural tendency in the way he governed was not consensus. He was by nature impatient and decisive, particularly with magnates he regarded as useless to him or possibly dangerous. He had no time for certain very powerful earls and counts, and they were excluded from his inner counsels. By 1170, the three most powerful earls in England (Chester, Leicester and Gloucester) had been either cut down to size by reneging on promised favours, or simply sidelined. The same happened in Normandy, where the great counts of Meulan and Eu were ignored by the king, and it seems that William's old master, the Chamberlain of Tancarville, felt badly treated. He too allied with the dissidents in the duchy.

The king, always on the road in his great continental dominions, preferred to rely on an inner group of bureaucrats and churchmen who toured with him. Some earls were valued for their military skills, as were Earl Patrick of Salisbury and Earl William of Arundel, and deployed to danger points, such as Poitou and the Welsh March. Others were valued in diplomatic missions. But a rather large group of them were almost invisible in Henry's entourage. The only earl ever rehabilitated in Henry II's mind was Richard fitz Gilbert (known to history as Strongbow), who was to be William Marshal's posthumous father-in-law. The king belittled Earl Richard right from the beginning of his reign when he denied him his father's lordship of Pembroke. It took Earl Richard's dramatic and sensational conquest of Leinster and Dublin to change the king's mind, and even then he laid harsh conditions on Earl Richard's rule over Ireland as the king's lieutenant. This weakness

14 *History* I, lines 1975–84.

in Henry's government widened into a fissure in the years after Thomas Becket's assassination, which was carried out by a group of those very bureaucrat-barons close to the king. In the light of this, the collapse of Henry II's great realm into civil war in 1173 is not so surprising. But the detonation that blew it apart was set off by the Young King.

The immediate cause of the explosion was Young King Henry's dissatisfaction with his lack of any sort of authority within the Angevin realm. His father did not consult him when he planned to alienate castles for his little brother John's marriage settlement, though it would come out of Henry's future realm. His father seems to have allowed him little authority over any part of his future realm, not even his wife's dower lands in the Vexin. In the year before his rebellion, his only recorded governmental action was a punitive one against a dissident Norman baron, and his arbitrary if successful actions in raising money in carrying it out gained him criticism.[15] In the meantime, his brother Richard (still only 15) had already been invested as the ruler of their mother's own realm of Aquitaine and his next youngest brother Geoffrey was promised the heir of Brittany. It is unlikely that Young Henry kept quiet about his resentments, and there is some evidence that he found his father-in-law, the King of France, all too sympathetic to his grievances. This is the context for a bitter dispute that flared up between father and son at the elder Henry's court early in March 1173 at Chinon in Anjou.

Robert de Torigny, the well-informed abbot of Mont-St-Michel, identified the flashpoint as Henry II's abrupt dismissal of a particular baron from Young Henry's entourage whom he found objectionable, Hasculf de St-Hilaire, as well as lesser knights in his retinue. William Marshal was not among this group apparently. The father's action was unpardonable, and was a direct insult to his son both as a king and as lord of his own household. It must have underlined for Young Henry the impossibility of the situation he was in. There seems to have been an angry face-to-face confrontation between father and son, followed by Young Henry's withdrawal from his father's court to Argentan in Normandy. Then – carefully concealing his plans from his father's agents and appointees in his household – Henry slipped across the Norman frontier into the county of Perche. The Count of Meulan and Earl of Chester, as well as his brothers Richard and Geoffrey, joined Henry at the court of his natural ally, his father-in-law, Louis VII of France, at Chartres, with whom he had made a long and apparently happy visit at Paris the previous year. They were soon joined also by William's old master, the Chamberlain, who came hotfoot to Young Henry from England, which is perhaps good evidence that though an outbreak of revolt may well have been looming, the flashpoint

---

15 He was involved in a successful action before his rebellion against the baron Hugh de Gournay in the Norman Vexin, though the historian who records it says disapprovingly he won more by a trick than force of arms. Henry laid a heavy ransom on the town of Gournay to avoid it being burned down, Diceto I, 369. This episode has been placed in the period of the 1173–1174 rebellion, though it precedes the account of it in Diceto's work.

took everyone by surprise and was unplanned. In this period of confusion, which lasted several weeks, the old king was able to seize the castles of many of the Norman rebels before they could be put in defence.

The rebellion continued to be a fiasco, despite it being joined by many of the great earls, counts and barons of England and Normandy, not to mention others from Poitou and Anjou. The rebellion also had the support of the foreign powers of Flanders and Scotland, who invaded Henry II's lands in support of the rebels. But even with that support and the backing of Louis VII, the rebellion still ultimately collapsed. Henry II's decisiveness, the support of his justiciar and loyal bureaucrats in England, heavy recruitment of mercenaries, the incompetence of the rebel leadership and sheer luck defeated the most serious challenge he experienced in all his long reign.

The Angevin government kept on file meticulous lists of the rebels of 1173, which we know of because they were copied into the historical works of Roger of Howden, one of Henry II's loyal clerical followers. One particular list tells us it was copied from the letter of defiance addressed to Henry II by the group of rebels gathered around the Young King at the Capetian court. It was the usual formal act of any punctilious rebel at the time. The letter withdrew allegiance to the old king and cancelled the homage that had been done to him. By sending it, the rebel could defend himself from the charge of being treasonous. One of those 'who returned the faith they swore to the king' was William Marshal, who must have put his seal to the joint letter.[16]

Not surprisingly, the *History* has very little indeed to say of William Marshal's part in these tumultuous but disreputable events; it does not even tell us explicitly whether he was one of those in his young master's council who argued for rebellion. But since his biography would have told us had he argued against it, the likelihood is that he had supported his lord's decision. Its author's intention was to prove William to be the most loyal of men, and a walk-on part in a great rebellion did not help cultivate that image, so he was evasive. In fact, he reports only one incident in the 1173–1174 rising that concerned William. While the Young King's *mesnie* was awaiting an onset by his father's forces in the very first days of the rising, the *History* claims that it was to William that the Young King turned to knight him. This William supposedly did, and gladly, though it would not have gained him the friendship of Henry II, who, we are told, had reserved that honour for Louis VII of France as a matter of policy.

The biographer's claim is extravagant and unreliable, though maybe not without some basis in fact. We know that Young Henry had in fact received arms from his father immediately before his coronation in 1170, the ceremony called *adoubement* (equipping), which was the central act of what we call 'knighting'. But even though William Marshal could not have been the man who made his master a knight, he might well have presided at a camp ceremony of acceptance into the

---

16 Howden, *Gesta* I, pp. 45–6.

order of knighthood before the Young King's first battle.[17] If so, it underlines how much favour the Young King offered William. The root of their deep friendship was their joint addiction to the tournament, and that addiction guaranteed favour to William, so long as he did not become the object of factional hatred. In that respect, the tournament was both the making and unmaking of William as a courtier.

On the tournament circuit

The rebellion lasted well over a year, though by August 1174 it was clear to everyone that it had failed. Young Henry and his brothers were received back into their father's peace without penalty, along with their households. One of the witnesses to the peace settlement between the king and his sons was no less than William Marshal, making his second appearance in the record of his times. His former lady, Queen Eleanor, apprehended by the king's agents trying to join them, was not so lucky as her sons. She began a long period of house arrest in England. As part of the settlement, Young Henry was conceded two Norman castles for his very own and given annually 10,000 pounds in the currency of Anjou, which still amounted to the substantial sum of £2,500 in sterling. None of this resolved the tensions that had inspired the Young King to rebel, and Henry II himself had no solution, other than to keep his eldest son close by his side and constantly under watch.

By the beginning of 1176, all Young Henry wanted was to escape supervision. His first tactic was to argue his father into letting him go on a grand state pilgrimage to the great shrine of St James at Compostella in Galicia, but this was forbidden. The king didn't think it likely that the plan came from any deep-seated religious devotion on his son's part, so refused him. He instead suggested that they go together on a joint campaign against a faction of the nobility of Poitou that had rebelled against Richard, his brother.[18]

After a successful campaign, which ended in yet another dispute between the old king and the younger one, this time about his freedom to employ knights of his choice, Henry II proved willing to entertain a second suggestion by which his son might escape his supervision. The Young King had already been trained by William Marshal in the techniques of the tourneyer, and the *History* tells us he had

17 *History* I, lines 2072–95. The *History*'s claim is inaccurate, for the Young King had delivery of arms from his father in 1170 at the age of 15 immediately before his coronation, according to one of Thomas Becket's correspondents, *Materials for the History of Thomas Becket Archbishop of Canterbury*, ed. J.C. Robertson (7 vols, Rolls Series, 1875–1885) VII, *Epistolae*, no. 476 (p. 316): *rex apud Londonias filium suum cingulo militiae donavit* . . . and there is no reason to doubt this source, a well-informed cleric and courtier. A defence of the *History* is possible if we suggest that the Young King's cronies argued that their young master was not of proper age for knighting when girded by his father, and he was now well over 18 (while his younger brother Richard had been knighted at 16). For a distinction between knighting and delivery of arms, see J. Flori, *L'Essor de la Chevalerie, xiᵉ–xiiᵉ siècles* (Geneva, 1986), pp. 113–15.

18 Howden, *Gesta* I, pp. 114–16.

frequented tournament fields in the years between his coronation and rebellion, but now he had something bigger and quite unique planned. It may even be that it was William Marshal who suggested as a solution to his master's difficulties that he should make an extended tour of the great tournament events of France and the Rhineland over the next several years, and for whatever reason this request was agreed to. More than one writer says that the old king took great pleasure subsequently in hearing how his son carried all before him on the tournament fields of Europe, though the expense of it all caused him to grit his teeth. His calculation may have been that such success enhanced the prestige of his dynasty and could be turned eventually to political and diplomatic capital. The *History* comments on the king's willingness to let the tour commence, and mentions that as they left, the old king specifically charged William to take care of his son 'for he trusted no man as much as him'.[19]

So began one of the grandest and most expensive tourneying tours of the age. A generation later, it was acknowledged as having been the high point of the sport. It was so grand that one of the heralds or clerks resident at the Young King's court undertook to create a chronicle of the tour, recording the dates of meetings and the feats of the king and his household in each event. The reason we know of this 'Tournament List' was because the Marshal's biographer encountered a copy of it over 40 years later in the family archive of letters and papers where he found much of his source material for the Marshal's early life. It provided him with the framework of his narrative between 1176 and 1182, and his extracts from it constitute now one of the principal sources for tournament practice in the twelfth century.[20] Why was it in the Marshal archive? Copies of it may well have been circulated in the king's household as souvenirs, and one can imagine why the Marshal would have kept it as a memento of the heyday of his career, even if he found reading it difficult.

It was in these years that William came fully into his own. The tournament – or to be precise the *mêlée* tournament – had been popular for generations among men of his class. It's perfectly possible that his father John would have ridden in such events, as we know they were staged in England in the reigns of Henry I and Stephen. As we've seen, they were already in John's day an obsession among greater barons, such as his son's own master, William de Tancarville, who lavished money on tourneying retinues of practised knights so they could excel in the field and bring him martial honour. The practice of the tournaments in William Marshal's day will be gone into in detail later in this book (see Chapter 8), but it can be described briefly here.

The tournament in its twelfth-century heyday was usually a three-day event, and it was best experienced in the heartland of the sport in Picardy, Flanders and the Western Empire, where the greatest of them were staged. Tournaments by

19 *History* I, lines 2421–32.
20 *History* III, pp. 25–7.

the Marshal's day were in fact staged all over Europe, from Iberia to Poland, though not in England, where King Henry II had banned them. But the biggest international gatherings were held in the lands ruled by the counts of Flanders and Hainaut and the Duke of Brabant. These lords, and any other lord or lady willing to earn celebrity by paying for them, provided funds for the publicising of the event, the erection of stands for the many spectators, the organisation of the events, the lavish entertainment and the prizes. Two neighbouring towns were designated as bases and lodgings for two teams and the landscape between them was designated as the tournament field. Thousands of knights, their lady companions and attendants would turn up to watch the spectacle as much as to participate. They were staged the whole year long, apart from the penitential season of Lent, the 40 days preceding Easter. January was as popular a tournament month as June, winter cold notwithstanding.

The most spectacular event associated with the tournament was the grand charge, which took place on its second or third day after a grand review and parade, when the mounted teams lined up opposite each other in full armour and rode across the field in front of the main team base, lances down, to smash into each other and then skirmish, as knights sought to take prisoners and secure their ransoms. This was where William Marshal came into his own. He was responsible for the training and conduct of his lord's *mesnie* in the field, which was no small job. When on tour, the Young King expanded his retinue by short-term contracts and by attracting into it noblemen who wanted the distinction of being in its ranks. On one occasion, his retinue was expanded to over 200 knights, of whom 15 were magnate-knights, or bannerets, with *mesnies* of their own. William marshalled them – it may even be he occupied the formal office of marshal of the Young King's household as his brother was of the old king's – and suggested the day's strategy.

Once the great charge began, William's job was more physical and simple. His lord was conspicuous on the field: his full heraldic device was painted on his shield and displayed on his robe, his banner and – if that were not enough – draped on great cloths over his horse (see Figure 4 for an illustration of this). The Young King was very visible on the tournament field, and had to be if his *mesnie* was to protect him from capture, because as soon as the main event began he would be the target of every ambitious and needy knight on the field. A king's ransom was always welcome, and Young King Henry was one of the few kings who ever ventured himself on a tournament field. Once the great charge began, William Marshal became the king's bodyguard, he and the inner retinue clearing Young Henry's way and fending off would-be captors.

The Anglo-Norman retinue managed to avoid the disgrace of losing their lord to hungry tournament predators, though the biographer implies that the ill luck that had dogged Young Henry in war followed him on to the tournament field in 1176. But slowly his retinue learned the discipline necessary to survive in the great charge of the tournament, by holding together in a wedge around their master and, when the other retinues were disorganised, turn on them and pick them off, sweeping up ransoms across the disorganised field once the immediate danger to their lord dissipated. The Marshal was not above employing dubious stratagems at times. He acquired one from the celebrated tourneyer the Count of Flanders, the king's first cousin and great rival on the circuit. The Flemish team would give out that they had decided not to join the grand charge, but just joined the review parade that preceded it then stationed themselves at the lists without arms and unhelmeted. Yet once the grand charge had occurred, they would suddenly equip themselves and launch at the disorganised throng on the field with little resistance, sweeping all before them. The Young King had the satisfaction of successfully employing the same trick on the Count of Flanders: 'trickery' and 'deception' were all part of the sport.

The pages of his biography still glow with the pride William Marshal took in these, the great days of his career, when he rose to martial celebrity and became the friend and associate of the princes and peers of Western Europe at the side of his beloved lord, the Young King. He was full of tales about those days in his later years, and his sons and squires had the benefit of hearing them, probably several times. And so in due course, they were transmitted to his biographer, who fitted them carefully into what the written record told him, and produced quite an effective reconstruction of the heyday of Marshal's tourneying career. We occasionally catch glimpses of how exalted and hilarious a time he and the king, his lord, were having. Very striking is the story of what happened at Anet on the Norman border in the spring of 1178. The Anglo-Norman team had carried all before them and driven the defending French team back through the lists, seeking safety in the neutral ground. Henry and William were not going to let that stop their fun. They rode down the spears of the infantry posted to protect the lists: none of the soldiers willing perhaps to oppose the lord of Normandy who was suddenly upon them. As they went through the lists and down into the town, Marshal grabbed the bridle of a French baron who had incited the soldiers to stop them, and the pair, laughing hilariously, rode back up the main street of Anet with the man flailing in his saddle behind them. But when he got to lists and encountered a squire to whom he could hand the man over, William turned to find the saddle empty. The man had grabbed a low-hanging gutter as he was dragged past and clung on to it. The king had seen all this and was speechless with laughter. The story of William's mishap ran the round of the circuit, and it seems that he enjoyed telling it against himself too for many years.

The events of 1179–1180, while the grand tour was still going on, are the key to William's eventual fall from his happy state of grace. In November 1179, the Young King had represented his father at Reims when Louis VII's son and heir, Philip, was crowned as Associate-King of France. Henry had borne the crown of France ahead of Philip in the procession, and had shouted '*Vive le roi!*' along with the rest of the nobles present. The Young King attended the subsequent tournament at Lagny, some 17 kilometres east of Paris, held to advertise the munificence of the new French king. William Marshal's name featured high among those who participated at Lagny, in a list that the *History* preserves embedded in its text, for its author found for his source a celebratory 'tournament roll' of the great

Lagny meeting among the souvenirs in the Marshal archive, which listed all the participants.

Here, for the first time, William Marshal appeared as a superior knight *portant banière*, that is, he had gained sufficient wealth and prestige to raise his own banner as leader of a company of knights who wore his colours, not his lord's. This must have been the occasion when he first displayed his own bearings. Individual devices, the prototypes of heraldic arms, were at that date reserved for counts, barons and a few more famous knights. We know from the thirteenth-century artist-historian Matthew Paris that William Marshal adopted a banner divided vertically half-green and half-yellow, featuring a red lion rampant.[21] Ever the courtier, the Marshal, like other prominent royal followers, chose to incorporate in his design the lion device that had been associated with the English kings since the reign of Henry I.

Losengiers and *lèse majesté*

William had now left his former colleagues in the *mesnie* far behind, and they resented it. Perhaps they had resented it since 1173 if the Marshal had indeed knighted the 18-year-old king. Now he was so obviously set socially above them, they chose to move. A cabal was formed of, appropriately, five members. The *History* chooses to be coy about who they all were, but it does at least name the two leaders, Adam d'Yquebeuf and Thomas de Coulonces. Adam had much in common with William Marshal in origins and expectations; he even shared a connection with the Tancarville household. He had served the Young King as long as had the Marshal, and had attained a high position in the *mesnie*, but nowhere near that of the Marshal. It may well be, therefore, that we should look to envy as the root cause of the plot against William, as the *History* suggests. Sayings written down in this very decade do indeed tell us that envy was the courtier's bane: 'Don't be envious of a colleague promoted to a position of authority', says a popular schoolbook intended for adolescents, 'you shouldn't direct poison darts at such men behind their backs'. A common proverb had it that, 'No one lives so good a life that Envy does not wish to harm him.'[22]

The *History* also mentions another cause for concern about William Marshal when it pictures the cabal attempting to entice other reluctant members of the *mesnie* into their web. It was inappropriate, they said, that the Marshal should be set above the rest of them, equal with dukes and counts, when they were Normans and he was English. We will see in a later chapter from what source the *History* acquired that particular prejudice, but for now it might be observed that the use of such an argument, however ineffectual it was, did not promise well for the future unity of Henry II's realm.

---

21 In heraldic parlance: 'party per pale or and vert, a lion rampant gules'.
22 *Urbanus Magnus Danielis Becclesiensis*, ed. J.G. Smyly (Dublin, 1939), p. 40 (a work of around 1180); Walter of Arras, *Eracle*, ed. G. Raynaud de Lage (Classiques français du moyen âge, 1976), lines 1252–3 (a work dated 1176 × 84).

According to the *History*, the plotters adopted two lines of attack. The Marshal, they said, was haughty and arrogant to the point of *lèse majesté*. When the Young King went into action alongside the Marshal in tournaments, the Marshal's own followers had raised the cry 'God for the Marshal!' (*Dex aïe li Mareschal*), and scooped up prisoners and ransoms for their master, and not the king. The Marshal's enemies said he employed a servant (we might call him a 'herald') called Henry Norreis whose job was to go around promoting the Marshal's celebrity, and to draw attention to his exploits whether or not the Young King was in the field.

The *History* is very sensitive about this particular charge. On several occasions, it portrays its hero giving up chances to make captures so as to safeguard his royal master; indeed, he is depicted as ever at the king's shoulder, fending off those who desired to seize him and earn the proverbial king's ransom. This sensitivity tells us that there was a charge to answer, and indeed the author confronts it head-on. In his account of a tournament in Picardy early in the tour, he says William abandoned his lord's side to take on another ineptly managed retinue only to find the king besieged and on the point of capture when he returned. He was sternly scolded: 'Any man who leaves his lord in such a situation behaves very badly!' The Marshal, ever courtly, accepted the rebuke but turned it with the flattering comment that he had thought his lord was happy to take the risk, so as to excel his forebears in prowess.[23] Thereafter, William confined his profiteering to events he was attending on his own account, on leave of absence from the king, putting aside the livery of England.

Besides a tendency to be selfish in the matter of ransoms, the Marshal and his men were foolish in the way they went about promoting themselves. The most tactless of the Marshal's decisions was his choice of '*Dex aïe li Mareschal*' for his war cry or *enseigne*. This was tactless because the ancient war cry and password of the Duke of Normandy and later the King of England, as attested by Wace of Bayeux in the 1150s, was '*Dex aïe*' ('God my help!'). What the Marshal had done was to make free with a treasured shibboleth of the Norman dukes: and if that was not *lèse majesté*, it is difficult to see what would be.[24]

More subtle, difficult and insidious was the plotters' supposed allegation that William had a sexual affair with the Young King's wife, Margaret, daughter of Louis VII. We may be sure that the insinuation was actually made, otherwise the *History* would not have leapt to its hero's defence. Such a titillating rumour must spread uncontrollably in the crowded life of the royal household. It was soon known to William's friends, and then to the Marshal himself. But there was not much he could do to stem its spread, and so he chose to keep a dignified silence.

---

23 *History* I, lines 2541–62.
24 The war cry of the Marshal and his men is attested in *History* I, lines 5226, 5862, 6226. It continued to be used in the 1230s by his son, Earl Richard Marshal, whose household knights shouted (presumably in the vernacular) '*Deus adiuuet Marescallum*' as they escorted Hubert de Burgh out of Devizes church, in which he had been cornered in 1233, M.L. Colker, 'The "Margam Chronicle" in a Dublin manuscript', *Haskins Society Journal*, 4 (1992), p. 137.

The allegation of adultery with a queen that the *History* presents us with as the chief cause of its hero's fall from grace creates some difficulties for us. Not the least of these is the fact that it is an allegation that a number of fictional epic heroes had to contend with in works written well before the *History*. Tristan's encounter with King Mark of Cornwall's wife led to his overthrow at court. In the English romance *Gui de Warewic*, written in the Marshal's lifetime, the hero is accused by the evil seneschal of the Emperor of Constantinople of just such an unfounded crime, and temporarily withdrew from court, but, unlike the Young King, the emperor did not give the charge any countenance.

Another problem is that, unfounded or not, the allegation did tend to enhance the Marshal's status in a seedy sort of way. He had been thought worthy to knight a king, and now was thought capable of having seduced a queen, or at least of having been thought worthy by her of seduction. The fictional precedent of Lancelot comes to mind: hero and adulterer. On the other hand, it cannot be denied that adultery among the great and famous was a salacious twelfth-century fascination. In 1182, memories would still have been fresh in England of the sensational events reported to have happened at the court of Flanders seven years earlier when Count Philip had supposedly discovered one of his *mesnie* in a secret liaison with his wife. It was said that the culprit had been denied a hearing and ignominiously executed: beaten by the household butchers and hung head down in a sewer until he suffocated.

It was accepted in the Marshal's time that dangerous liaisons with female royalty could have disastrous consequences. In the popular mystical romance *Ami et Amile*, written around 1200, the position of Count Amile at Charlemagne's court is subverted when it was revealed that he had (innocently) slept with the emperor's daughter. The penalty with which Amile was threatened was decapitation.[25] Perhaps the Marshal's enemies had hopes of just that fate befalling him.

We cannot tell for sure whether the allegation of adultery against the Marshal was ever taken seriously or even got as far as the king's ears. The next year, the Marshal visited the French court where Queen Margaret was in residence and was received in a friendly way by her brother King Philip. It would have been a dangerous thing to do if anyone in Paris countenanced the charge. For me, the most telling evidence against its importance is that, if it was made, the Marshal survived it suspiciously easily. One would expect that a sexual encounter with his lord's wife would have raised some genuine Plantagenet passion in the allegedly cuckolded Young King when he got to hear of it.

All we find in the *History* is a description of a period of royal coldness to William, which William found deeply wounding, but which did not get in the way of the

25 Howden, *Chronica*, II, pp. 82–3; *Ami et Amile*, ed. P.F. Dembowski (Classiques français du moyen âge, 1987), lines 713ff. The difficulties in accepting Howden's story as little more than gossip are dealt with in R.E. Harvey, 'Cross-Channel gossip in the twelfth century', in *England and the Continent in the Middle Ages: Studies in Memory of Andrew Martindale*, ed. J. Mitchell (Harlaxton Medieval Studies, VIII, Stamford, 2000), pp. 48–59.

Young King continuing to employ him as team manager on the tournament field. No other source mentions the affair at all, which is a little odd in such a well-documented age that had a taste for salacious gossip. Only Roger of Howden provides what might be a speck of confirmation, when he reports that early in 1183, the Young King sent his wife to her brother, King Philip, and does not explain why. But an innocent explanation might be found in the other events of that time. The Young King was preparing war against his brother, Richard. He might well have been sending his wife out of the way of a coming conflict. In the face of such ambiguous evidence, I would put down the allegations of adultery with Queen Margaret as a stratagem of the author of the *History* derived from contemporary romances and erroneous gossip, not taken seriously at the time but a welcome distraction from the more difficult accusation of *lèse majesté*.

William distanced himself from the king, whatever the cause of his disgrace. First, he stayed with friends, but was soon recalled for the purpose of a tournament at Epernon in the Île-de-France. At the dinner afterwards, says the *History*, the Count of Flanders publicly lectured the Young King on the stupidity of quarrelling with the Marshal, to no good effect.

In the meantime, Henry II had got to hear of the rumours of the estrangement. He was rather more pleased than otherwise; the *History* has the honesty to admit that William was by then seen by the elder king as one of the least desirable of his son's companions. When a little later William attempted to appeal to Henry II at Caen at his magnificent Christmas court of 1182, his suggestion of a battle to prove his innocence was brushed off. This was not the only time in his career that the Marshal challenged his detractors to prove their accusations in battle with him. He was to do it again before John in 1205 and 1210, when charges of treason hung over his head. It was as if the very threat of a physical encounter would absolve him of suspicion, a clean act of the body to override the dark and dirty insinuations of wicked and envious minds. The *History* puts a grand speech into the Marshal's mouth by way of reply, which we may well doubt was ever spoken. He had been denied justice. He must leave the Plantagenet lands and find a more welcoming place to live. A false accusation had been made, and his accusers did not dare to lift their heads, yet still he suffered wrong. So a safe conduct to the frontier was given him, and he and his men departed south to the county of Perche, leaving behind him his relieved and exulting enemies. He was an exile from his lord and his land.

3

THE MAKING OF A MAGNATE, 1183–1190

As he left Normandy in January 1183 and took the road to Paris, William Marshal no doubt at this point thought, or at least feared, that his prestigious connection with the English royal house had come to an end. At any rate, he must have worked up a plan if the worst had in fact happened. He was now 35 years of age. He was still in his prime, and a man so practised and active would not have lost any of his prowess. But 35 is a time to look both back and forwards. Balanced on the midpoint of man's allotted span, it is a time to begin to think of a colder future. 'He that ever hopes to thrive, must begin by thirty-five.' The Marshal would have taken the moral in Johnson's verse. Neither he nor his contemporaries would have considered him to be on the shelf at 35. When Wace depicts the Roman Emperor Lucius in battle with Arthur, it is as: 'Still in youthful condition, less than forty and more than thirty, a tough and brave man.'[1] In the event, he reverted to the strategy of his younger days. He sought the tournament field, advertising his availability. But at the same time, he kept in touch with subsequent doings at the Young King's court. His great friend Baldwin de Béthune undertook a correspondence with him, although William needed a clerk to read to him the letters Baldwin sent.

William passed into the tournament heartland and found an event in mid-January 1183 some kilometres east of Paris. If finding employment was his plan, he could not have done better. The *History* talks of dukes and counts outbidding each other for his service and there is some confirmation that this really happened, for although the *History* says he regretfully declined the offers, there is other evidence that he accepted a particularly tempting one. Unlike the author of his biography,

---

1 *Roman de Brut*, ed. I. Arnold (2 vols, Société des anciens textes français, 1938–1940) II, lines 12453–5.

the Marshal did not know that he would be recalled to the Young King in a couple
of months. He was at a loose end, unemployed and still landless; his brother might
yet produce an heir to the Marshal estate. When so great a patron as Count Philip
of Flanders offered him a substantial fee to retain his service, he took it gratefully.
He was too pragmatic a man to risk turning it down. The count's offer was indeed
generous. It was a quarter of the rents of the great Flemish city of St-Omer, one
of the count's personal estates.[2]

There is some evidence that William was more disconsolate than his pragmatic
and down-to-earth search for a substitute income might indicate. He joined one
of his greatest friends from the circuit, James d'Avesnes, Lord of Guise, in a
pilgrimage to the Rhineland, to visit the shrine of the Three Kings at Cologne
bearing, as was appropriate, rich gifts. He can only have wanted the intercession
of those mystical, royal saints at the throne of the King of the Universe to mend
his breach with the terrestrial king who had cast him off. And it seems they were
listening.

As the Marshal was sizing up possible futures, a counter-conspiracy was under
way at the court of his former master. Circumstances favoured a reconciliation. In
January 1183, not long after William took himself off into exile, the sons of Henry
II fell out among themselves, Henry and Geoffrey taking on Richard. The issue
as ever was the veil of uncertainty the elder Henry could not help himself casting
over his sons' future. But the old king seems finally to have come to realise that
the security of his realm demanded that the succession question must be settled.
So not long after the showdown at Caen, he proposed that Young Henry's primacy
over his brothers should be acknowledged. They must do homage to him, Richard
for Aquitaine and Geoffrey for Brittany. But as this arrangement was being ironed
out, the Young King caught his father on the back foot by announcing that he
had entered into a pact with the barons of Aquitaine against their now feared and
hated lord, Richard, and that he intended to prosecute a war in the south against
his brother. The Young King's motives are not easy to make sense of, but, in the
opinion of Ralph de Diceto, a contemporary, Henry may simply have identified

---

2 That the Marshal possessed a fee in Flanders was known to Painter (*William Marshal*, p.
   49 and n.), and he made the logical connection that this fee must have been acquired in
   1182–1183, when the Marshal was free and his friend Philip was still count. The location
   of the fee in St-Omer is mentioned in an inquest long after William's death, along with
   the information that he exchanged it with the Count of Guines (a potentate of the area
   around St-Omer) before 1204 for the count's English estate of Trumpington, Cambs,
   see TNA: PRO, KB26/146 m. 9. For the status of St-Omer as comital demesne, see a
   charter in *Les chartes de St-Bertin*, ed. D. Haigneré (4 vols, St-Omer, 1886–1890) I, p.
   188. There is the alternative suggestion that the Marshal had the fee in St-Omer in 1197
   when he was on an embassy to Count Baldwin. He is said to have done the count good
   service in battle when he was in Flanders, and it is possible that the St-Omer fee was a
   reward for that. But, on the other hand, his stay there was brief, and service in battle
   was rewarded usually by gifts of ransoms or money, not rents.

Richard as the chief danger to his future overlordship and had decided on a pre-emptive strike to reduce his warrior brother in both status and lands.

In February 1183, Young Henry put his household on a war footing. At this point, he was vulnerable to the blandishments of William's friends at court. Everyone seemed to interest themselves in his recall, even Geoffrey de Lusignan, whom the Marshal still blamed for his uncle's death 14 years before. Obligingly, the triumphant Yquebeuf faction discredited itself by arguing against war as soon as it became apparent in March 1183 that Henry II was likely to move to support Richard against his brothers. William was therefore recalled from Paris to resume his position at the head of the Young King's *mesnie*. The messenger sent galloping into the Île-de-France was carefully chosen. It was an Englishman, Ralph son of Godfrey, a close friend of the Marshal and the king's chamberlain. He would later support Ralph financially when he took the cross with King Richard.

Death in Limoges

So William returned to his young master, preceded by letters of safe conduct and recommendation from King Philip and others at the French court to Henry II, all taking the Marshal's part in the late differences. These apparently stood him in good stead with the elder king, who signalled his willingness that the Marshal should resume his old position in his son's household, despite being now at war with him. Along with Baldwin de Béthune, William rejoined Young Henry late in the season of Lent, probably in April or May 1183. William and Baldwin were received honourably, and perhaps with relief, for the campaign had been hard going.

Young Henry, his brother Geoffrey and a party of rebel Poitevins were based on the city of Limoges, threatened by Henry II and Richard. They had successfully weathered a siege of the city, and their father and brother had been compelled to withdraw, so the campaign had reached a critical point. The main problem for them was finding money to maintain the mercenaries who made up the Young King's army. To find it, Henry had ordered the forced seizure of the treasures of surrounding monasteries. It was on a gathering tour, late in May 1183, that Young Henry contracted dysentery; out of sheer pique with his father, according to the implacable court historian, Howden. Henry grimly carried on the work but he was weakening rapidly. In the first days of June, he was carried by his household back to his base at the castle of Martel, near Limoges. The old king was informed but would not come, sending only a ring in token of forgiveness. He had been shot at by his sons' crossbowmen earlier in the campaign (by mistake, they said).

By 7 June, it was apparent that the Young King was dying, and so the solemn medieval pomp of death was begun. We have very good sources for what happened in Young Henry's last days. On that day, he was confessed privately in his chamber by the Bishop of Cahors and an abbot, prostrating himself naked on the floor before the bishop's crucifix, despite his obvious agony. He renounced his recent actions and received the sacrament. Four days later, in front of his retinue, the Marshal among them, feverish and weak but still coherent, Henry made a public confession and received the last rites. As frequently happened in those days, he made his written testament as one of his last conscious acts when it was evident that everything was nearly played out and there would be no recovery.

By the bedside at that point on 11 June was Count Raymond of Toulouse. Remarkably, a letter he later wrote to Pope Lucius on what he had heard and witnessed in the death chamber still survives.[3] Raymond tells us the room was crammed with Henry's advisers and knights, attentively listening to their lord's wishes as his testament was drawn up. Solemn occasion or not, his men robustly disputed Henry's desire to be buried in the choir of the Cathedral of Rouen, near to his late uncle William, his father's younger brother. No, they pressed him to seek burial in the fashionable monastery of Grandmont, only some 20 kilometres north of Limoges, one of his father's favourite houses, which Henry II had selected himself in 1170 for his own burial site when seriously ill and in fear of death. The old king's advisers on that occasion had been loud in their objections to his choice. But in June 1183, a royal burial at Grandmont would be some compensation to the abbey for the damage the Young King had recently done to its estates. However, the dying king was adamant. He would rest in the capital of the duchy he would not now rule.

There was another pressing spiritual concern at the deathbed. Henry had at some time had his servants stitch on to his cloak the white cross a crusader sported on his clothing as a sign of his vow. He was evidently now troubled by the lightness with which he had made the promise. Not only the *History*, but two historians independently record that, at the last, he committed the cloak to William Marshal, 'his most intimate friend', to take to the Holy Sepulchre in Jerusalem as fulfilment of the vow, and according to the biographer, the legacy of the cloak and the obligation that went with it was written into the king's will. As an extravagant display of repentance, in the way of a dying monk, Henry then had himself taken from his bed and laid on one of ashes, with a stone pillow, a hair shirt on his back and the noose of a condemned criminal about his neck. Clasping or kissing the ring that his father had sent him as a token of peace, he lapsed into unconsciousness and died soon after.[4]

Whatever the grief and hopelessness of the occasion, the Marshal had received his first lesson in how a great man must die. For him, it would be some 36 years before he would need to put it into practice. Unfortunately, he also got a first taste of the chaos that follows the death of a king. The Young King had died penniless, and had left some pressing debts. The Marshal was promptly seized by a company of Basque or Spanish mercenaries demanding their arrears of pay. It took all his

---

3 Rouen, Archives départementales de la Seine-Maritime, G 3569 (3).
4 For the death scene, see particularly Geoffrey, prior of Vigeois, *Chronicon Lemovicense*, in *Recueil des historiens France* XVIII, pp. 216–20. It is Geoffrey who favours us with the description of William Marshal as the king's *carissimus*.

personal authority for them to take his pledge that the debt would be paid. In the meantime, the corpse was prepared for the long journey to Rouen, where the Young King had requested burial. Its bowels, brain and eyes were removed as part of the embalming process, and it was in burying these parts of his body that Grandmont Abbey had to be satisfied.

The rest of the Young King's body was packed with salt and stitched into bull's hide. A lead coffin and pall were found and the cortège moved off in procession in fine weather. At the monastery of Vigeois, its prior recorded that the late king's entourage was so impoverished that a collection at a requiem on an overnight stop there raised but 12 pence (which the Young King's chaplain filched). A friendly abbot had to provide the candles about the bier, and the knights had to be fed by the priory's charity.

Heading north, the cortège crossed Poitou and Anjou. But now they were faced with more difficulties. It is not often that we encounter 'public opinion' in the Middle Ages, but in a rudimentary way it existed and expressed itself, frequently through popular religious movements. The common people of that region of France were already in a state of excitement. The depredations of the bands of mercenaries employed by the late Henry among others had sparked off a resistance movement. For a month or two before Henry died, men had been banding together under the inspiration of a carpenter called Durand, who was said to have been inspired by a vision of the Virgin. Under his leadership, companies of 'peace men' clothed in white cloaks, and supported by local knights and the Church, took on and routed the Brabançons and Navarrese who were terrorising their land in the pay of the elder and younger king of England.

Odd though it may seem, the Young King's death must have tapped this same vein of popular emotion. However feckless he had been, he was not his father, and hopes had grown about his succession, which would lift the harsh gloom of the present. Now this longed-for event would not happen and a regret infected all levels of society. In those days, such a regret would be expressed by claims for the sanctity of the lamented deceased, and acclamations of miracles at his bier, or tomb. Over a decade later, such claims would be made in London after the execution of William Longbeard, a city magnate who had been credited with a desire to improve the lot of the poorer citizens.[5] The same claims to sainthood were made in the French countryside for Young Henry, and for the same reasons: an expression of the grief of the inarticulate for lost and buried hopes.

Cures were claimed at overnight stops, lepers were cleansed by touching the Young King's bier, a column of light appeared above the coffin at night. The historian William of Newburgh accused 'certain people' of fostering this nascent cult either to justify the son's campaign against his father or to claim that God had

5 C.N.L. Brooke and G. Keir, *London, 800–1219* (London, 1975), pp. 48–9.

accepted his final penitence. At Le Mans, the countryside was so feverish that the bishop halted the cortège, and the Young King was buried at the cathedral along with one of his household squires who had sickened and died on the way. The Dean of Rouen had later to claim the body with a royal warrant to get it to the dead king's chosen resting place in his cathedral. It was buried there well over a month after his death. Le Mans did not give up easily, and an enquiry into the incident went as far as the Pope.[6]

William Marshal undoubtedly played a part in these tumultuous scenes, for the *History* tells us that he escorted the corpse to its grave. It is, however, unclear whether he was one of those who were promoting the excitement. Probably he was not, because the *History* begins to signal a *rapprochement* with King Henry the father even before the Young King's death. After the burial of his young master, he sought out Henry II, characteristically taking in a money-raising expedition to a tournament on the way to court. The Marshal found the king softened towards him.

There is no doubt that Henry had been as much shaken by his eldest son's death as had the rest of the knightly world. The poet-castellan Bertran de Born, one of the Young King's supporters in the Limousin, published a rather affecting lament for the dead king, taking advantage of the public mood and the sense of loss affecting tourneyers in particular: 'even the Germans weep!' he comments. Another Limousin lament also survives from this time, which put the effects of the king's death starkly and, as it turned out, accurately. Knights and troubadors would go now without their greatest patron, he said; 'the bravest and best' knight would no longer charm the ladies. It was a new and joyless world that opened up before the knightly world. And the poet was right. His verdict was echoed by the Marshal biography 40 years later. The tourneying craze ebbed without the patronage of the Young King of the English, and its great days were done.[7] William Marshal, too, may have sensed this, for his actions show he was ready to move on and seek other rewards than those of the tourneying circuit.

6 For the cult of Young Henry, the most judicious source is Newburgh, I, p. 234; and the most revealing a sermon by Thomas of Earley, or de Agnellis, Archdeacon of Wells, 'On the death and burial of Young King Henry', in *Radulphi de Coggeshall Chronicon Angicanum*, ed. J. Stevenson (Rolls Series, 1875), pp. 263–73. Thomas fulsomely advocated the sanctity of the Young King, and made no secret of his connection with Henry's mother, who had been imprisoned in England for many years by her husband when her son died. It is likely enough that she and the Young King's friends were the 'certain people' supporting the cult referred to by William of Newburgh, rather than the Capuciati of Berry and the Limousin. For this movement, see Duby, *The Three Orders*, pp. 327–36.

7 For Bertran's lament, *Mon chan fenis*, see *The Poems of the Troubadour Bertran de Born*, ed. W. Paden and others (Berkeley, 1986), pp. 215–23. The second lament, attributed by some to Bertran, can be found in R. du Boysson, *Etudes sur Bertrand de Born* (repr. Geneva, 1973), pp. 158–9.

In the East

Henry II knew the nature of his son's last command to William. When William appeared before him to request formal permission to leave his lands, the king undertook to retain the Marshal in his household when he returned. To demonstrate he was in earnest, he took two of the Marshal's horses as a guarantee of his return to him. He then conferred a purse of 100 Angevin pounds on the Marshal for his expenses. It was not in fact a very generous gesture, as the sum amounted to only £25 sterling. The *History* dryly notes that a single one of the horses the king kept was worth that much, but doubtless the Marshal would have seen the advantages of the bargain. After a visit to his family in England, which in its way formed part of the settlement of his worldly affairs, the Marshal took ship for the Holy Lands, perhaps not until the change of weather opened the Mediterranean in early 1184, the point at which most pilgrims departed. There he stayed for over two years, two of the final few years of the Latin Kingdom of Jerusalem.

The *History* is strangely silent as to what William did in the Kingdom of Jerusalem, save commenting that he accomplished his mission and did as much in two years as others did in seven. A cynic might conclude from this turn of phrase and then silence that the Marshal, in that case, had done very little. This would be unjust. Before he left, William had been the witness of the last gloomy weeks of a wasted young life. We do not need the assurances of the *History* to know that he was deeply moved. For all his undoubted ambition and worldliness, William took the cross and the road eastwards from which so many did not come back. By no stretch of the imagination could this be interpreted as a career move or a manoeuvre. He went to discharge his duty to his dead lord and to God.

In his last days, he was to reveal to his knights that he had been smitten in the East with thoughts of his own mortality, thoughts gloomy enough to cause him to buy a cloth to lay on his own bier, and to make an informal commitment to end his days among the Templars and be buried in a Templar house. The Marshal had a spiritual life (although the *History* does not rhapsodise about it). We might believe that what he saw and did in Palestine satisfied a longing deeper than the thirst for wealth and fame that had pushed him so far. He did not need to talk about it. The twitterings of his vague successes in the East are his biographer's vanity, not his own.

Though we have little evidence from his biography and none from any other source as to what William did in the East, the two years he spent in the Kingdom of Jerusalem were tumultuous and difficult ones. His biographer believed that he had accomplished deeds of arms there, though he was not specific about them, which may be because for most of William's time there, the crusading kingdom was in a state of truce with Saladin, the King of Egypt and Damascus. From the perspective of the decade in which the biographer wrote, the Kingdom of Jerusalem was a tragically failed project. It has been suggested that the entire crusading enterprise was regarded with disillusion in the West by the 1220s, so the author felt inclined to pass over the whole episode of its decline, the way he glossed over the failed revolt of 1173–1174. But since he was willing enough to recall events creditable to William even in that war, that may not be enough to explain the silence. But he does mention one curious fact, and that is that William encountered Guy de Lusignan in the East, and not at the point of his sword.[8]

Guy and his brother Amaury had migrated to the Holy Land some time early in the 1180s, largely because their activities in Poitou had left them with few options. Guy did well in the Kingdom of Jerusalem, and in 1184 held a military command under the young leper-king Baldwin IV, whose sister he married. This could have been inconvenient, because William Marshal and the Lusignans were in a state of mortal enmity, a condition of personal hostility that the society of the time recognised. It did not mean that they were pledged to kill each other if they got the chance, but it meant that they and their supporters were enemies till death. They would not be expected to associate publicly and would use every opportunity to frustrate the designs of the other.

Yet when he left Jerusalem in 1186, William is depicted as taking a peacable leave of Guy, one of his uncle's murderers. Since the biographer had earlier numbered Guy's brother Geoffrey as one of the advocates for the recall of William to the Young King's side, it seems that the mortal enmity between the Lusignans and the kin of Earl Patrick had been ended, at least as far as William Marshal was concerned. Yet it was not his decision to make: in 1184, that rested with Earl William fitz Patrick of Salisbury and his brothers, and it could only have happened after a major act of atonement by the Lusignans, which, as far we know, they did not make. Could it be that William, in his desire to get on in the world, trespassed against the norms of his social class in the East and that the family storm that he kicked up on his return rather spoiled his recollection of his time there?

Captain of the Guard

William returned from the East to pick up the threads of his career in the spring of 1186. He found the king in Normandy, in his hunting lodge of Lyons-la-Forêt.[9]

---

8 I draw here on two recent thoughtful reflections on this episode, N. Paul, 'In search of the Marshal's lost crusade', *Journal of Medieval History*, 40 (2014), pp. 292–310; Asbridge, *Greatest Knight*, pp. 160–8.

9 Following Meyer, Painter believed William returned to the Angevin court in 1187, because 'a little after he returned' the True Cross was lost to the Saracens. The *History* also says that William took leave of King Guy before he left, and Guy took the throne in late summer 1186. If the Marshal took leave of King Guy, then he could not have returned to France before the end of 1186. But there are several reasons why such a late date is impossible. The Marshal was in the Holy Land by early 1184, and if he then stayed two years, as the *History* says (line 7276), he would have left long before King Guy's succession. In fact, one terminal date for the Marshal's return can be established by King Henry's grant to him of the estate of Cartmel in the honor of Lancaster, which is dated by the pipe rolls to Christmas 1186, *Pipe Roll of 34 Henry II*, p. 50. The king's grant no doubt was preceded by some time in his service, and if the *History* is right, and the Marshal encountered Henry II at Lyons-la-Forêt, then the Marshal must have met the king before

He was welcomed and found the king as good as his word; he was retained to serve in the military household of Henry II, still then the most potent ruler in Christendom. He found several familiar faces in the royal retinue: Peter fitz Guy, Gerard Talbot and Robert de Tresgoz, also sometime members of the Young King's household. The king was now 63 years of age, with two legitimate sons left to him. Richard, the Count of Poitou and his presumed heir, was approaching 30; John, the youngest, was nearly 20: recently, he had been made Lord of Ireland, but his father's attempt to give the title reality had come to grief ominously on the young man's incompetence.

The next few years were busy ones. William was constantly engaged on active military service. The tournament makes no further appearance in his life (except when, as regent, he banned one in 1217). War, counsel and command were now his daily business, and the *History* gives us accounts of his campaigns rich in detail. Indeed, the *History* is now an altered creature. It abandons its anecdotal, patchy approach and we begin to get a more methodical, less embroidered picture of its subject's life and times. This is largely because the *History*'s informants, particularly John of Earley, the Marshal's squire and ward, were taken into the Marshal's own small household during this time. But also it is describing events less far removed from the days when it was composed. The author's own memories and those of his contemporaries could be tapped.

However, this does not mean that the *History* is to be wholly trusted in its account after 1186. The Marshal is its central character, and by magnifying him (as in a Romanesque sculpture) all the other characters about him are dwarfed. The picture of indispensable royal aide and commandant that the *History* contrives to project has its element of truth. A loyal servant by temperament and family tradition, William was probably the king's most reliable and accomplished captain, and his importance grew towards the end as the fabric of Henry II's continental government loosened and slid into ruin in the face of the king's growing illness, internal rebellion and the aggression of Philip II of France. But the king's business was not principally war. Within the world of the court, William Marshal was but a small creature as yet. He did not have the sources of external power, the lands and followings that made bishops, earls and barons men of note. He was not of the king's own generation, and all his skills as a courtier could not make up for the lack of a common experience that gave the older men at the court of an ageing king such an advantage. He could not talk of old triumphs and failures, or reminisce about the old battles and conspiracies. Indeed, in some of the more recent ones, he had been on the wrong side. His face was a new one; it fitted, but that was all.

he left for England in April 1186. In March 1186, the king is known to have been at Gisors on the frontier of Normandy, from which Lyons is not too far, R.W. Eyton, *Court, Household and Itinerary of Henry II* (London, 1878), pp. 267–8. Professor Nicholas Vincent lists royal acts to which the Marshal was witness in England during 1186, 'William Marshal, King Henry II and the Honour of Châteauroux', *Archives*, 25 (2000), pp. 6–7, 7n.

Sources outside the *History* give a truer picture. The Marshal appears in the royal acts of the last years of the reign infrequently and in a junior position, on occasion alongside another promising newcomer, the young administrator and justice, Geoffrey fitz Peter, whose career paralleled his own in many ways.[10] The two were to become allies at court, and there is some evidence of friendship. Rewards began to come the Marshal's way, as they did Geoffrey's. One of the most economical means of royal patronage was the granting of wardships: the keeping of the lands and persons of underage boys or female heirs, whose custody belonged to the king if their fathers held their lands directly from the Crown. One of the first grants that William had was the keeping of the 15- or 16-year-old John of Earley (but not his lands), son of William of Earley, a minor baron of Somerset and Berkshire and a royal chamberlain.[11] He took John into his household as his squire; it is probable that he was given also the right to marry him off to whomever he pleased.

There is a pattern to some of the other early grants that came William's way. In 1186, and perhaps as early as Christmas 1185, he had the grant in England of the large royal estate of Cartmel in Lancashire, between Lake Windermere and Morecambe Bay. At about the same time, William was given the keeping of one of the king's female wards, Heloise of Lancaster, the heiress since 1184 of the Barony of Kendal in Westmoreland, which neighboured Cartmel to the east. The plan was, it seems, to raise William to the standing of a minor baron in the north of England. He could, if he so wished, have married the Lady of Kendal, and then her lands would have been his and the heirs he had from her. It would have brought him to a level with his elder brother, John Marshal, and have been a handsome reward enough. The barony of Kendal spread across Westmoreland, Lancashire and the West Riding of Yorkshire, and as Lord of Kendal he would have had castles, the priory of Cockerham and great tracts of forest.

The Marshal made at least one tour of Kendal and Cartmel, issuing a confirmation charter for an estate at Sizergh in Westmoreland to one of Heloise's dependants. In that charter, it is clear that he was still keeping open the possibility of a marriage with the girl, for he refers to the possibility that he and Heloise might in future have heirs between them.[12] So it seems that for a couple of years, the Marshal was reconciling himself to a future in the north of England, distant though it was from the scenes and triumphs of his youth.

---

10 See R.V. Turner, *Men Raised from the Dust* (Philadelphia, 1988), pp. 35–70.

11 For William and John of Earley, see p. 212. Coincidentally, John of Earley was the great-nephew of Thomas of Earley (or de Agnellis), Archdeacon of Wells (died *c*.1195), the cleric who attempted to promote the cult of the Young King Henry after 1183.

12 For the extent of the royal lordship of Cartmel (an area of 28,747 acres) and the barony of Kendal, see *Victoria County History of Lancashire* VIII, p. 254; W. Farrer, *Lancashire Pipe Rolls and Early Charters* (Liverpool, 1902), pp. 389–90. For the Sizergh charter, *Acts and Letters*, no. 9, pp. 63–4.

The last days of Henry II

Circumstances did not in the end favour the marriage alliance of Heloise of Lancaster and William Marshal. He and the lady remained 'just good friends', as the *History* puts it with a certain anachronistic tact. Events began to gather a speed in 1188 that would have left neither the king nor William with time to plan marriage alliances, and William Marshal found himself in the thick of international action. The centre of the storm was the castle and lordship of Châteauroux in the central French region of Berry, an area nominally under the overlordship of Henry II in his role as Duke of Aquitaine, and adjacent to his regional centre of Tours. But Châteauroux was also in the front line created by the ambition of the Capetian monarchy, moving its power southwards from its rival centre of Orléans and taking control of Bourges, an archbishopric and the provincial capital of Berry. In 1176, Henry II had acquired custody of Châteauroux when its lord died, leaving as its heir an infant daughter, Denise. Although they were unable to do much about this extension of Plantagenet power, both Louis VII and Philip II had ambitions to curtail it. In May 1187, King Philip led an army into Berry and attempted to seize Châteauroux, but was beaten off; yet despite this failure, the attack led to a major crisis in the Angevin monarchy.

As with so many crises in the English monarchy, the problem was created by doubts over the succession. The king's relations with Count Richard, his heir since 1183, were no more successful than they had been with the Young Henry, and for the same reason: the king would not resign into Richard's hands any more power than he could get away with. Richard could count on the support of Philip II of France in any confrontation with his father, the same way as the Young King had counted on Louis VII, and Philip was assiduous in raising doubt in Richard's mind about Henry's ultimate intentions. He found an opportunity when he and King Henry came together on the Norman frontier in January 1188. Jerusalem had been lost the previous year to the Saracens, and the Archbishop of Tyre was present to preach the renewal of the crusade. The two kings and several other princes responded and took the cross. But if Henry went, what of the succession? The time had clearly come for a firm statement as to his intentions, but almost by reflex Henry avoided the issue.

A rumour arose that Henry intended to cut Richard out of the succession and make John his heir, and most likely it started in Paris. It began to circulate at a critical time. Henry II had been subject to recurrent and serious illness since 1182, and the organisation of the crusade further aggravated the uncertain situation. In June 1188, Philip added further ingredients to the volatile brew. He and Count Richard had come to blows over Toulouse, and, in retaliation for his losses, Philip launched a second, and this time successful, assault on Châteauroux. Instead of a time of pious preparation, the summer of 1188 became a period of renewed Anglo-French warfare. Ill though he was, King Henry applied himself to the preparation of a mighty army that would humiliate Philip. Thousands of Welsh mercenaries were assembled and marched to the Channel ports, and military summonses went out to the king's principal captains. We know this because Nicholas Vincent in 1996 discovered a fragmentary text of the summons sent to no less than William Marshal, which tells us quite how close he was now to the centre of the Plantagenet world, as well as adding some details about his character. It runs as follows (in my translation):

> Henry, by the grace of God, King of England greets William Marshal. I request that you come to me fully equipped as soon as may be, with as many knights as you can get, to support me in my war, and [that you let me know] how many and of what sort of troops will be in your company. You have ever so often moaned to me that I have bestowed on you a small fee. Know for sure that if you serve me faithfully, I will give you in addition Châteauroux with all its lordship and whatever belongs to it [as soon as] we may be able.[13]

The king had decided that his long-suffering (but hardly uncomplaining) servant, William Marshal – lord of what he at least considered the small fee of Cartmel – should be offered the chance of consolidating the Angevin hold on Berry, if the campaign was successful. Heloise of Lancaster was to be superseded by the superior enticements of Denise of Châteauroux.

King Henry landed in Normandy on 11 July 1188, and a period of intense warfare followed along the Norman frontier in which the Marshal took a prominent part. But a storm over the succession blew up as peace seemed on the point of being made in November when his allies, the counts of Flanders and Blois, abandoned Philip. Philip then artfully proposed at a meeting on the Norman frontier that he would relinquish the lands in dispute between Henry and himself to Richard, providing Richard married his sister, Alice, as had long been proposed, and that Richard be recognised as his father's heir. In proposing this recognition, Philip stabbed to the heart of the troubled relationship between Henry and his son and drew blood. Henry would not answer the proposal and so Richard's active and suspicious mind drew the fatal conclusion that his disinheritance was indeed being considered. He drew off to Poitou in haste, summoning all his forces as he went.

William Marshal was one of the king's messengers who pursued Richard into Poitou, demanding that he return and talk again to his father. The *History* claims that this mission of reconciliation was William's idea, but, whether it was or not, it was abruptly abandoned when the envoys reached Amboise hot on the count's heels, and found that the night before Richard's clerks had written and sealed over 200 letters summoning men to their master's side. A desultory border war followed through that winter and spring, with Richard actively assisting Philip. Henry II fell ill again in the new year, and a proposed peace conference was continually postponed. From Christmas 1188 until his death in July 1189, the sick king languished

---

13 Latin text in Vincent, 'The Honour of Châteauroux', p. 15. The square brackets indicate hypothetical additions where the text is incomplete.

in Maine and Anjou, the heart and centre of his family's ancestral domain: it was a place convenient to monitor events both in Berry and Normandy.

The knights and barons of his household at his side may well have come to seem more important to him at this time, which must often have found him weak and fearful, for he moved to secure their allegiance more firmly. The young Gilbert fitz Reinfrid, son of a royal justice and nephew of Walter de Coutances, Archbishop of Rouen, and recently appointed the steward of the royal household, was one of those favoured.[14] At some time in Lent 1189, William Marshal was asked to give up the wardship of Kendal and its lady, and it was eventually transferred to Gilbert by a charter that William himself witnessed.[15] In this way, the king would not just have rewarded young Gilbert, but gratified the powerful official dynasty to which he belonged, and of which he was the chief heir.

No slight to the Marshal was intended, however. As we now know, he had been given hopes of something greater in the offing. Châteauroux may have been out of reach for the moment but he had instead a promise from the ailing king of one of the greatest heiresses then in England, Isabel, the daughter and heir of Earl Richard fitz Gilbert of Striguil, with estates and claims that dwarfed Kendal and Châteauroux. A number of others of Henry II's household had promises of great reward at this time, including the Marshal's friend, Baldwin de Béthune, to whom the promise of the heiress of Châteauroux was now transferred.

Eventually, in the late spring and early summer of 1189, when Henry was feeling better, the parties came together for a protracted series of conferences in Maine and the county of Perche, but no good resulted. Henry's continued prevarication simply served to confirm for Richard the danger he was in of disinheritance. Henry, for his part, did not realise his own danger. Richard has been criticised for lacking subtlety, but he was a determined, perhaps brilliant, general, and he did not mitigate that quality just because he was dealing with his father. After leaving this last conference, he and Philip launched a vigorous assault on Henry as he was retreating back into Maine. Castles fell with a rapidity that can only suggest that their keepers were aware that the old king was labouring in his last illness, and that their new

14 For the genealogy and origins of the family of fitz Reinfrid, which derived from relatively humble origins in Cornwall, and was represented at Henry II's court by the brothers Walter de Coutances (died 1207) and Roger fitz Reinfrid (died 1196), as well as Roger's son Gilbert and a host of siblings in canonries and archdeaconries in England and Normandy, see the Rouen obits printed in *Recueil des historiens de la France* XXIII, pp. 359, 362, and *Oxford Dictionary of National Biography*, s.n., 'Walter de Coutances'. Archbishop Walter had been a member of the Young King's household at some point, alongside William Marshal.

15 *Lancashire Pipe Rolls*, p. 395. The charter is undated, but it calls Gilbert a royal steward, which he had become only recently in 1189; the witness list parallels a similar grant to the royal usher, Walter, datable to 1188 × 89; also it is addressed to Count Richard, something that a prudent beneficiary might well have asked for if the king was ailing and Richard the next heir. Because of this, Professor Vincent suggests it may have been issued as late as July 1189 in the few days between the settlement with Richard and the king's death, 'The Honour of Châteauroux', p. 11.

master was at their gates. Richard caught up with his father at Le Mans (where Henry had been born) on 12 June. Henry was accompanied by his servants and household guards, but no army. The barons of Normandy had been summoned to join Henry, but had halted at Alençon, troubled by the combination of King Philip and Count Richard, and reluctant to proceed into the war zone of northern Maine.

King Henry was now in a very difficult position. He gloomily took up quarters in the palace of Le Mans in the evening of 11 June, and awaited the arrival of his enemies. The Marshal was sent out to try to make contact with the king's pursuers as soon as the sun came up. He and his small party of royal officers rode southwards out of the postern gate of the palace of Le Mans in the misty first light of morning, south along the built-up suburban road that led to a bridge over the river Huisne by which one would reach Tours. Just across the bridge, they spotted some unsuspecting French scouts trotting along the riverbank looking for a crossing by which their army could force an entry into the city. Rather than disperse the tempting target of unarmoured horsemen, the Marshal and his colleagues galloped back promptly to tell their master that the city would soon be under attack. The king had his men break down the bridge over the wide stream of the Huisne, and place stakes on the banks to block any attempt to swim horses across the shallower part of the river. This was done just in time, as the King of France and Count Richard's main army arrived in force. Frustrated, the French made camp.

The next morning, after a dawn mass, the king rode south to the broken bridge with his officers to try to see what Philip and Richard were planning. He was unarmed, and seemed to believe that no action would happen that day. The Marshal was less sure, and rode fully equipped despite the king's querulous annoyance with his precaution, which implicitly questioned the royal judgement. At the bridge, they were all taken aback to find that the French had been able to find a crossing point and scattered French knights were feeling their way over the river Huisne using their lances to test the water's depth. The detachment of royal guards at the bridge tried to hold them up, but could not prevent a company of the enemy mustering in the suburban street by the hospital of La Maison-Dieu de Coëffort.

The Marshal rallied a company of the king's knights and drove the French and Poitevins back down the road to the bridge, but in the end found himself retreating back to the city wall as the number of their assailants grew. Nonetheless, he skilfully seized several knights in the street fight, who only escaped by cutting free their bridles and fleeing with only spurs to guide their horses. John of Earley was later to tell all this to the biographer. He witnessed the fight for Le Mans as his master's young squire, and he deftly caught the bridles as the Marshal caracoled his horse before the city gate and threw them back through the arch. The Marshal escaped unscathed from this intense skirmish, with only a wound to his horse's leg to show for it.

However, the day was not to end in victory, despite the Marshal's heroics. The king or the city's governor ordered the suburb between the river Huisne and the city gate to be set alight, to discourage the French assault. As a tactic, it was less than successful, for the French army had by now pushed detachments south around the city bypassing the crossing of the Huisne. They managed to cross the river Sarthe below its junction with the Huisne, and were able to swing around and approach the city from the west, where defence was light. At least one bridge over the river Sarthe into Le Mans was forced and the French poured in. A trap was now closing around King Henry. His last chance was to break out of the city with his knights and head along the road towards Fresnay-sur-Sarthe (35 kilometres to the north-west), the only route now left open.

The king departed Le Mans in haste with his guards, leaving the city in flames, and its castle eventually to fall to the French. The pursuit was hot behind him. William Marshal and a few others were left to delay the pursuers. It seems that the Marshal had in mind his father's tactics against a raid by King Stephen on Ludgershall in the 1140s. Count Richard, unarmed except for an iron cap so as to ride all the faster, was leading the party of pursuers. He plainly thought that his father's men were routed. The Marshal waylaid him with a party of the royal *mesnie*. The ambush was unexpected, and could have been fatal for the count. The Marshal himself, fully armed, rode him down. Richard, finally realising his position and recognising his assailant, shouted out that he was unarmed and that it would be an evil deed so to kill him. The Marshal cursed him, lowered his lance point, and killed the count's horse, calling on the devil to despatch Richard himself.

This reverse halted the pursuit and the king proceeded at a more leisurely pace to Fresnay. There, the king despatched his officers in different directions to rally resistance. The Marshal was sent north with the Earl of Essex and his colleague, William fitz Ralph, to Alençon to take responsibility for the defence of southern Normandy. The disconsolate and sick king rode on by a circuitous route to Angers and Chinon, to be followed by the dreadful news of the fall of Tours, the great Angevin bastion on the Loire, against the Capetians.

Even before he reached Chinon, it was evident that Henry had made his last rally. His spirits sank, he failed to assemble such forces as he had available, and consented to a last bitter interview with Philip and Richard. He rose with great pain from his bed for a conference near Tours and accepted the terms that were dictated to him by Philip (to his credit, embarrassed to find how feeble and wretched his adversary had become). Henry then returned to Chinon and what was to be his deathbed, although to the end he hoped to recover and revenge himself. The end was not long in coming. He fell into a stupor and delirium on hearing that his beloved son John – who had been with him at Le Mans – had joined Philip and Richard against him.

After three days of fitful semi-consciousness, Henry died on 6 July attended by none but his menial servants. His chamber was rifled before the knights of his *mesnie* learned of his death, and the corpse tipped out of its bedclothes, exposed and naked (the king's body would not have been stripped by the looters, for the sick were customarily left unclothed in bed). The household knights found Henry's body abandoned, cold and stiffening in an empty room, black blood staining the nostrils and mouth from a final paroxysm. For decency's sake, one of his knights (or a faithful servant, according to another account) cast his cloak over the dead king.

The Marshal was a witness to all of this. He had been recalled from Alençon in the last week of June to the king's side at Chinon. In the aftermath of the settlement with Richard, in the old king's last few days of life, William had helped in the arrangements to transfer his claims on Kendal to his younger colleague, Gilbert fitz Reinfrid. He and the rest of the *mesnie* did what they could for their late master and had the body prepared and dressed in its royal robes. William Marshal attempted to get the seneschal of Anjou to open the treasury of Chinon to scatter the customary alms to the poor, but the seneschal stubbornly refused. This must have all seemed depressingly similar to William to the shabby aftermath of Young Henry's death. The day after the king's death, his bier was escorted by the *mesnie* and the barons of Anjou and Touraine downriver to the Loire valley and the abbey of Fontevrault, a house of nuns particularly favoured by Henry II. There, the body was received and lay in state till the arrival of Count Richard.

William did his last duty to his master, and followed the body to Fontevrault. There, with the rest of the *mesnie* and household, he awaited the arrival of the count. His situation was not a happy one. He and everyone else knew how he had covered Henry's retreat from Le Mans, and the expectations of the men standing around waiting with him at the abbey were that his career in royal service had ended. Several, we are told, rather generously offered to settle a modest competence on him to tide him over. William had now only his rents in St-Omer and the land of Cartmel, if the new king let him keep even that. He had let both Kendal and Châteauroux go earlier in the year, and had not had time to take possession of the heiress of Striguil.

Lord of Striguil

If those at Fontevrault could have known what plans were forming in Count Richard's head as he rode to join them, they would not have needed to commit themselves so hastily to William's future upkeep. The count, soon to be king, was already turning in his mind the execution of the grand plan that was to become the third crusade. To quit his new kingdom for several years and yet ensure its safety in his absence was already his great concern. Before he even reached Fontevrault, he must have decided that William Marshal was to be part of that plan. Richard meant to secure England by raising such men as he knew were tested, capable and, above all, loyal to great power in the kingdom and leave them to guard it for him. William Marshal, whose loyalty to his current lord was his most famous quality, was to be one of them: there was to be no small-mindedness about the ambush on the road from Le Mans to Fresnay.[16]

---

16 Roger of Howden remarks how the count retained all the servants of his father whom he knew to be true men (*fideles*) and these he rewarded each according to their desserts; he treated with contempt those who had abandoned his father, *Gesta* II, pp. 72–3. The *History* lists some of these deserving men as Baldwin de Béthune, Reginald fitz Herbert and Reginald de Dammartin.

TABLE 2 The children and grandchildren of Henry II and Eleanor of Aquitaine

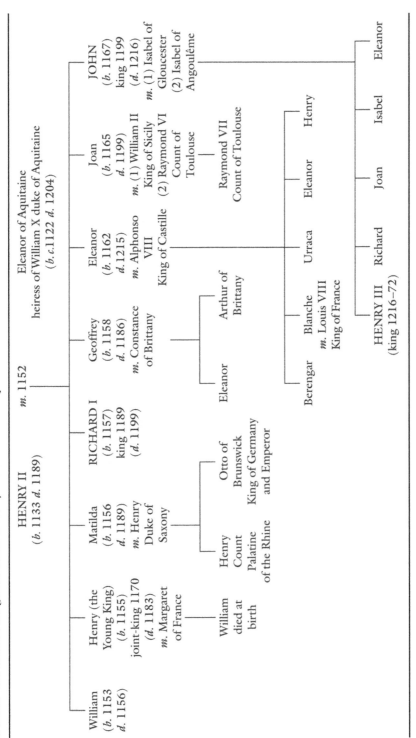

The count arrived at the abbey. The author of the *History*, in one of his most telling asides, recalls either his or one of his source's impressions of Richard on the point of becoming the most powerful king in Christendom (John of Earley and others of the Marshal's knights would have been there to see him). 'I can tell you that, on his arrival, he showed neither joy nor sorrow on his face, and nobody could say if he felt in his heart joy or sadness, sorrow and grief or gladness.'[17] Here was the pattern courtly king, standing impassive beside the corpse of his father whom he could with justice have been said to have harried to his grave, if not driven to his death. But there was no emotion in his face. Whatever his eyes saw was not allowed to speak to his heart. By such acts of self-control were great kings set apart from common humanity.[18]

Richard left the church and summoned William Marshal to him, along with the Manceaux magnate Maurice de Craon, presumably as a witness. According to the *History*, the count first teased the Marshal with attempting to kill him on the road from Le Mans, and claimed that he had deflected the Marshal's spear thrust with his arm. When the Marshal indignantly protested that if he had been aiming at Richard, he would have struck him, not his horse, and that he did not consider it a crime, Richard let be and pardoned him.

William and a colleague were to be sent immediately to England on a mission, the nature of which the *History* does not reveal. At this point, members of the dead king's household, apparently standing around within earshot and perhaps rather gratified at the turn events were taking, protested to the count that his father had given William the heiress of Striguil. The count corrected them. His father had only promised the girl to William: *he* was giving her to him. Others still in expectation of reward were also relieved of their anxieties; the *History* provides an instructive list of them. But this could not have been all that Richard bestowed on William at Fontevrault, for on his subsequent journey to England William paused in the Pays de Caux to take possession of certain unnamed estates, which can only have been the portion of the lands of the Giffard family to which his wife-to-be was also heir. The Marshal must have left Fontevrault armed with a sheaf of Richard's writs directing various bailiffs and officers to surrender their charges to the Marshal.

There remained little more to be said. Following the funeral, William took to his horse and rode north to Normandy and the Channel coast. He seized the

---

17 *History* I, lines 9294–8.
18 Henry of Huntingdon writes in a similar vein about Henry I of England nearly a century before this, 'he was a deep dissimulator and his mind was unreadable', see 'Epistola de contemptu mundi', in *Historia Anglorum*, ed. T. Arnold (Rolls Series, 1879), p. 300. Chrétien de Troyes, the apostle of courtliness, writing in the 1170s, pictures the courtly king, Erec of Brittany, on hearing of his father's death thus: 'Erec's sorrow was far greater than he showed to the people; but grief is not becoming in a king, and it is not seemly for a king to show sorrow', *Erec et Enide*, ed. M. Roquez (Classiques français du moyen age, 1952), lines 6466–9.

opportunity of taking charge of the Giffard lordship of Longueville en route to Dieppe and awaited his servants' news that they had found him a boat at the port at St-Vaast-d'Equiqueville, a Giffard manor east of the town.[19] This would have been the first time the Marshal had spent a night under a roof that he could have called his own.

Before the end of July, William was in England. He sought out first his patron of long ago, Queen Eleanor, still under supervision at Winchester. He delivered to her whatever message Count Richard had entrusted him with and then took to the road again, heading for London and the girl, Isabel of Striguil. Another writ eventually delivered her from the tower into his hands (despite some cavilling by the justiciar, Ranulf de Glanville) and they were married with no delay in the city.

Noble marriages were occasions of great festivity in the twelfth century. When Isabel's great-aunt had married a local baron at Chepstow priory some 40 years before, all the barons and prelates of the country round about had been there. Ten days of festivities had ended in a great cavalcade up the Wye Valley to her new home at Monmouth.[20] The Marshal arrived in London dusty and without the sort of money to hand to afford such a display. However, he did at least find it easy to raise credit. The prominent city magnate and financier Richard fitz Reiner offered him hospitality at his great mansion at the western end of Cheapside in the shadow of St Paul's. Fitz Reiner was willing and eager to ingratiate himself with the new regime and lend sufficient sums to allow the marriage to take place in appropriate state; perhaps it was celebrated in the nearby cathedral.

William's credit rating had improved rapidly since he was last in England. Indeed, there is some evidence that in 1189 he was not in fact short of money. He had his substantial annual rents from St-Omer, and the profits of his wardships. Then there was the accumulation of prizes from the tournament circuit over the years, which we know he had carefully husbanded. Somewhere he had stored up his treasure in a safe deposit, which in those days tended to be within the walls of a monastery. The Templar house on the Strand in London was particularly popular with people of William's background as a secure place to store their treasure. Since in 1189, he embarked on an expensive building campaign at the castle of Chepstow (chief place of the honor of Striguil), William must have had funds stored somewhere on which to draw. The marriage done, William retired to Surrey, where he had borrowed the house of a friend, Enguerrand d'Abenon, at Stoke

---

19 St-Vaast-d'Equiqueville appears in a later grant by William Marshal to Longueville priory as (at least in part) his demesne manor, *Chartes de Longueville*, p. 105 and n. It might be suggested that Marshal had to stay at the lesser manor house of Equiqueville (which is not on the direct road to Dieppe) because the Giffard castles of Meullers and Longueville were not willing to surrender to him, which is why the place stuck in the memories of the biographer's informants.

20 The marriage of Rohese de Clare can be reconstructed from charters granted to Monmouth priory to celebrate the event, printed in T. Madox, *Formulare Anglicanum* (London, 1702), no. 400.

Daubernon, and there he commenced life as a married man, awaiting the arrival of Richard in England.

We have some knowledge of the nature of that life. We know his wife was still very young when they married (she could not have been older than 20, and was probably a few years younger), and that he was uxorious (they produced 10 children in all, and she was pregnant before 1189 was out). William's sexuality is not an unapproachable subject even at the distance of centuries. There is evidence that William had not ignored the possibilities for casual sex on the tournament circuit or in society generally. We know his elder brother John did as much, and entered into an extramarital relationship with a Sussex lady, Alice de Colleville, who was in fact married to another man. The fruit of that liaison was an illegitimate son, whom John acknowledged and who eventually entered his uncle William's household as a squire and then knight. Evidence has recently been found that William Marshal, too, entered into a similar relationship, which produced before his marriage a son called Gilbert Marshal, whom his father endowed in the 1190s with lands in the Marshal manors of South Mundham and Sundon, and whom he married off to the widow of one of his seneschals.[21]

All we know of William's earliest lover is that she was later married off to a respectable landowner and produced another son, the royal justice Roger of Essex, Gilbert's half-brother. Was she an ambitious prostitute who had singled out William as a great opportunity? According to Peter of Blois, the sophisticated courtesans who followed the Angevin court were effective political operators in their own right. The new king's brother, John, for instance, was associated around this time with an apparently well-known high-level prostitute who went by the name of '*la reine Clémence*' (Queen Clemencia), by whom he had his first child, a daughter.[22] The children of such liaisons, if acknowledged, might very well expect to be taken care of, and John and William Marshal and John of England were willing to make provision for their low-born children with a degree of generosity. Count John's illegitimate daughter Joan was to become Princess of Gwynedd and Lady of Snowden.

In 1189, William Marshal became, by right of his wife, Lord of Striguil. It is often wrongly said that he also became Earl of Pembroke. In 1189, and for over a decade afterwards, Pembroke was in the hands of the king, for Henry II had confiscated it from Isabel's father, Earl Richard, in 1153 or 1154 and never let it go. The earldom of Pembroke had been created for Isabel's grandfather in 1138 as a reward by King Stephen. When Earl Richard succeeded in 1148, he was only a child and it was easy for Henry II to reclaim Pembroke from him, almost certainly on the grounds that it had been a royal estate alienated by Stephen that was rightfully

21 *Acts and Letters*, p. 15, nos. 25, 247.
22 A fact known to the monks of Tewkesbury Abbey, see *Annales de Theokesburia*, in *Annales Monastici*, ed. H.R. Luard (5 vols, Rolls Series, 1864–1869) I, p. 101.

his under the peace settlement of 1153.[23] Earl Richard had then to settle for his father's remaining honor of Striguil, which had been given to his family in the days of Henry I and therefore could not lawfully be touched. Earl Gilbert of Pembroke had also enjoyed the possession of the castles of Orbec and Meullers in Normandy, and we find the Marshal later holding them, so his wife brought him them too.

'Striguil' was a contortion of an earlier Welsh name for what we now call Chepstow Castle. This formidable clifftop fortress still dominates the lowest bridging point on the river Wye before it meets the Severn. The name Striguil was applied to the castle and to the honor, the great estate, that depended on it. In 1189, this was a scattering of 65½ knights' fees in several English counties, and several large manors kept in the lord's hand (in 'demesne', as it is called). But the core of the lordship was in south-east Wales, in Lower Gwent or Netherwent. Here, the lord of Striguil controlled most of the lowlands along the Severn estuary between the Usk and Wye, as well as the forest of Wentwood that overlooked the flats. Earl Richard had added to this rump of his father's lordship by a successful campaign against his Welsh neighbour, Iorwerth, Lord of Caerleon. He had taken from Iorwerth the castle and lordship of Usk at some time before 1170. Gwent therefore was the seat of Richard's earldom, not Pembroke, and around 1173 he recognised this by dropping the title 'Earl of Pembroke', which he had kept up to remind the world of his claims; afterwards, he was 'Earl of Striguil'.

Earl Richard had conquered Leinster in Ireland in 1170–1171, but this too was not immediately given to the Marshal in 1189; it was still being held by Count John, the new king's brother, whom their father had made 'Lord of Ireland'. He was not going to give it up without a fight. Leinster amounted to the entire south-eastern quadrant of Ireland, and in the two decades since it had been acquired by the English it had been rapidly transformed into a land of castle-lordships and new towns. The native lords within Leinster found themselves increasingly dispossessed and powerless. The death of Earl Richard should have left the lordship to his widow Aífe (or Eve), the daughter of Leinster's last king. Earl Richard had claimed Leinster by his marriage to her, but her rights were more or less ignored when he died, even though we know she claimed them. Aífe was still alive when William Marshal married her daughter, Isabel, and probably in retirement on an Essex estate she owned, where she was known as 'the countess of Ireland'. At some point not long after her daughter's marriage, she asserted her rights as 'the heir of King Diarmait' when the Archbishop of Dublin, disturbed by the changes in Leinster, asked her

---

23 For the royal hold on Pembroke and other points, see M,T. Flanagan, 'Strongbow, Henry II and the Anglo-Norman intervention in Ireland', in *War and Government in the Middle Ages: Essays in Honour of J.O. Prestwich*, ed. J. Gillingham and J.C. Holt (Woodbridge, 1984), pp. 63–70, and comments in D. Crouch, 'Strategies of lordship in Angevin England and the career of William Marshal', in *The Ideals and Practice of Medieval Knighthood* II, ed. C. Harper-Bill and R. Harvey (Woodbridge, 1988), pp. 16–18.

to confirm the possessions 'which Count John and the other good folk of Leinster' had given his cathedral.[24]

But in reality, Countess Aífe had been sidelined, as her confirmation more or less says, for Count John had in fact been disposing of her lands in Leinster. Between 1176 and 1189, Leinster had been ruled by the king's officers in Dublin, who after 1185 answered to Count John. Even before Richard's coronation, the Marshal was earnestly soliciting the king for his intervention in getting John to release it, according to his biographer. John was reluctant to do this, for in the years of his wardship of Leinster he had, as was not uncommonly done, used it to endow many of his own men. Not unreasonably, he doubted that the Marshal would leave them be if he ever got control of the lordship. So John stalled in the face of the king's wishes. Eventually, he withdrew his opposition to the Marshal's assertion of lordship over Leinster, most probably when he found Marshal obliging to him during the troubles after King Richard left. The cost to Marshal was most probably confirming John's butler, Theobald, in the lands John had given him in Leinster.[25]

Then the Marshal had the problem of how to administer Leinster. He would not go there himself for a decade – it was too far from the warm centre of things where the king was – and any emissary of his would be ineffective. A representative was sent, we are told, the otherwise unknown Reginald de Quetteville, to stake the Marshal's claim: 'God help him!' says the *History*. He was utterly ineffectual, as might reasonably have been expected.[26] There must have been a more resolute attempt to gain control of Leinster later. One reason we know that is because a prominent Leinster knight, Philip of Prendergast, had been taken into William's *mesnie* within a year or two of his acquisition of his Irish lands. Philip had in fact married a niece of Countess Isabel, so he could have been influenced by family links. But apart from that link, evidence as to how William Marshal secured Leinster, his wife's greatest possession, is sadly lacking.

So, in 1189, William Marshal became a magnate, but by no means as great a magnate as Sidney Painter believed. He was ruler of one of the flatter, and therefore richer, marcher lordships. Here, he was lord of two powerful stone fortresses (Chepstow and Usk) and overlord of other lesser castles; he was patron of an abbey (Tintern) and two priories (again, Chepstow and Usk), but in England he held precious little other than the potential to make money that the services of 65½ knights' fees gave him. The fat demesne manors of Weston in Hertfordshire and Parndon and Chesterford in Essex that were the richest part of his honor in England were, until she died at some unknown date in Richard's reign, in the hands of his mother-in-law, Aífe. From this, we can see why King Richard was prepared to

---

24 *Crede Mihi*, ed. John T. Gilbert (Dublin, 1897), p. 50.
25 *Acts and Letters*, no. 94, pp. 173–5.
26 Reginald's existence has been doubted, but it is worth noting that a 'Willelmus de Kettovilla' witnessed one of the Marshal's earliest charters, whose issue has been dated between the years 1186 and 1188, *Acts and Letters*, no. 9. This William might either be a close relative of Reginald de Quetteville, or the man actually sent by the Marshal to Leinster, whose name the biographer got wrong.

add to Striguil half of the great Giffard lordship in Normandy and England, an arrangement confirmed by charter in November 1189.[27] Otherwise, the Marshal could have complained with justice that he had not exchanged much of immediate value for Kendal.

Richard was willing to consolidate William's power in the southern Marches even further. Happy to add to the funds he needed to go on crusade, the king allowed William to buy control over the office of sheriff of Gloucester, and with it Gloucester Castle and the Forest of Dean. This bodily extended the Marshal's influence as a magnate eastwards across the Wye up the Severn Valley. It constructed a bloc of power that the region had not seen since the disgrace of Earl Roger of Hereford in 1155. It may be that Sidney Painter was right to suggest that the king so raised the Marshal in order to use him to counter the power of his brother, Count John, to whom Richard had given the heiress and estates of the earldom of Gloucester, with control of Bristol and the marcher lordships of Glamorgan and Newport. On the other hand, the Marshal's actions were so ambiguous towards John in the king's absence that we might suggest just as plausibly that as things turned out, the Marshal and his brother became, in effect, part of Count John's affinity in the area.

William had married the daughter and heir of an earl, but that did not necessarily make him an earl himself. It had long been accepted in England, before the Conquest indeed, that the king alone might create an earl. The earldoms that were created in England and Wales after the Conquest were hereditary and their creations were acts of royal patronage. But royal control had gone further than that and, strictly speaking, a man might not call himself 'earl', even if his father had been one before him, until he had been invested with his earldom by the king. What this involved by William's day was the belting by the king of a sword around the new earl's waist, and the delivery of a charter granting, or confirming, the earldom. Richard never honoured him with such a ceremony, so he never became earl in his reign according to the royal view of things, and was careful to describe himself simply as 'William Marshal' in his own charters before 1199. He was a courtier and knew when not to press claims too far.

However, whatever was claimed for the king, society's thinking was less clear-cut, and there is plenty of evidence that it was thought generally that a man might automatically succeed to the dignity of earl on his father's death, whether the king belted him or not. There are a number of examples of sons of earls taking up the title on their own initiative. William seems to have thought about this too, and decided that even if he was not an earl, his wife, nonetheless, had the right to be

---

27 The Earl of Hertford brought forward a claim to the Giffard lands when Richard arrived in England. The matter was settled amicably by dividing them, and a copy of the king's grant of his half to Earl Richard of Hertford survives, *Acts and Letters*, pp. 465–6. Earl Richard was given the chief Giffard seat in England, and William the corresponding chief seat in Normandy: Longueville and its honor south of Dieppe. In England, William's chief Giffard possessions were his manors of Caversham, Oxon and Long Crendon, Bucks, which otherwise compensated for his lack of demesne in England.

considered a countess. In one of his charters between 1189 and 1199, he had her carefully described as such, though he did not claim in it to be earl.[28] That did not stop other people calling him one. Seeing that he was enjoying the lands and daughter of Earl Richard of Striguil, a royal clerk in October 1189 unthinkingly described him as 'William Marshal, Earl of Striguil'.[29] Roger of Howden, another royal clerk, usually punctilious in his use of titles, was equally loose in this case, and William is 'Earl of Striguil' in his writings too.[30]

The crowning act of this fortunate year was for William to found a religious house to commemorate, among other things, God's grace to him in raising him to such a height. There were other reasons. The patronage of a house of regular clergy who looked to a magnate as its founder and protector had been since the early eleventh century a mark of the prestige of the greater aristocrats. By the mid-twelfth century, many men with pretensions to weight in society had an abbey or priory as a mausoleum and as a means of intercession between himself and a God who men were well aware was not impressed with great wealth. The Marshal's father had adopted the Salisbury family's house of Bradenstoke in which to be buried, and had patronised it as far as his limited resources allowed. However, by 1190, it was beginning to be *nouveau riche* to advertise power by setting up a monastery; there was a surplus of religious houses, and men of quite low station, mere county knights, were scraping together resources to found tiny and often short-lived priories on corners of their estates. But for a parvenu, such as William Marshal, the gesture still had meaning. So he devoted his estate of Cartmel in Lancashire to the foundation of a house of Augustinian canons.

Two more things are significant about this gesture. He drew the initial colony of canons from the Augustinian house in which his father had been buried, Bradenstoke: a sign, perhaps, of local and filial feeling. Despite the distances he had travelled and the sights he had seen, Wiliam Marshal remained a man of the Kennett Valley: the two knights we know he had retained before 1188, William Waleran and Geoffrey fitz Robert, were also from Wiltshire. The other significant detail in the foundation of Cartmel was the commemoration in the foundation charter of the two late kings he had served: Henry II and the Young Henry whom he named as 'my lord'. This last gesture is not without its poignancy: he was willing to repay some of his first great patron's generosity to him by expending his own resources on masses for his soul. We can like the Marshal for that.[31]

---

28 *Acts and Letters*, no. 14, pp. 69–70.
29 *Calendar of Charter Rolls* II, p. 164: '*Willelmo Marescallo comite de Strugull*'. This was not an isolated instance. When William appeared as witness to a charter of the king's brother, Count John, in London at some time between 1189 and 1193, he appeared as '*comite Willelmo Marescallo*', British Library, ms Egerton 3047, fo. 4r.
30 On the titles of earl and count in general, see D. Crouch, *The Image of Aristocracy in Britain, 1000–1300* (London, 1992), pp. 41–75.
31 *Acts and Letters*, no. 21, pp. 76–8. It mentions William's wife so it has to have been made after the marriage, and the presence in it of John Marshal indicates a time when the two brothers were closest, before July 1190.

4

THE RISE OF THE MARSHALS

In July 1189, Richard had the ducal sword of Normandy belted to him in Rouen Cathedral, and in August he arrived in England, where William was one of the first to greet him. William stayed at the king's side for the next three months. These were great days for him. He had a leading part to play in the coronation at Westminster on 13 September, where he bore the royal sceptre before the king. This was not a hereditary office in the coronation and was customarily awarded to men as a royal recognition of their particular fame, and it is some confirmation that contemporaries shared the *History*'s opinion of the Marshal's warrior prowess.

Also at the coronation was a member of his family of whom William had seen little for many years, his elder brother John. John too had his part to play in the ceremony, carrying before the king a massive pair of golden spurs. Carrying spurs was a rather suitable coronation office for a marshal, and since we know the 1189 coronation followed the ritual used for King Stephen's recrowning in 1142, it must be that this was a customary privilege for the royal marshal at the coronation. In 1142, however, John and William's father would not have been the one carrying the spurs, as he was with the other side in the civil war. For William to have a coronation office allotted to him too in 1189 meant that King Richard was deliberately increasing the Marshal family's dignity.

John Marshal had got nowhere at court in the reign of Henry II, but we do at least know that he was a man eager for court advancement. Failing the king, he had become an intimate of the young Count John before 1189, following him on one occasion as far as Maine in France. As proof of the count's attachment and trust, he was made his seneschal.[1] So when John Marshal appeared at the court of

---

1 In 1185 at Wexford, John's seneschal was Bertram de Verdun, and his household seneschal was William de Wenneval, see Kent Record Office, U1475 (Delisle Deeds), T321/1;

Richard, it was not as a forgotten backwoodsman, blinking in the light of the royal majesty. Like his younger brother, John Marshal wanted to be a creature of the court and reap all the rewards that might bring him. Nonetheless, there was a certain irony that he owed his breakthrough to William. He had had so few contacts with him until Richard was king that there must be some justice in suggesting a long estrangement, or at least indifference between the brothers. John had allotted his brother and heir no lands from the paternal estate (as elder brothers often did), and the *History* records no unequivocal contacts between the two. The *History* does not reserve for John any of the adjectives it bestows liberally on people of whom its author approved: 'the brave', 'prudent', 'hardy' or 'loyal'.

William's family was much honoured in these last months of 1189. The king seemed to be willing to go quite out of his way to build them up at court and in the country. In September, John Marshal was appointed the king's chief escheator in England; that is, the man who supervised the taking into royal hands of the lands of men who died without heirs, or at least without adult ones. Although he was later removed from the office, he had in compensation the office of sheriff of Yorkshire, a county available since the disgrace of the previous sheriff and royal justiciar, Ranulf de Glanville. In November, John had perpetual grants of the private hundreds of Bedwyn in Wiltshire and Bosham in Sussex, which his father and he had held only from year to year until then. William's younger brother, Henry, was elevated in September to the rich deanery of York.[2] John and William Marshal appear together side by side in court from September to December in 1189. In a rather nice touch, when they appear together in royal acts, it is John who usually appears first as the elder, although William had by now outstripped him in influence and lands. When William and many other English magnates were summoned to meet the king in Normandy in March 1190, John Marshal went too, and both stayed with the king until at least June. William went on with Richard to the assembly of the crusaders at the great hilltop town of Vézelay in Burgundy in July, and must have taken leave of him as the army began the slow trip south to Marseilles and the fleet.[3]

Calendar of the Ormond Deeds I, *1172–1350 AD*, ed. E. Curtis (Dublin, 1932), pp. 3–4. So it is likely that when John Marshal appeared as Count John's seneschal in a charter dated at Le Mans, it was at some time after that, but before 1189, see *The Irish Cartularies of Llanthony Prima and Secunda*, ed. E. St John Brooks (Dublin, 1953), pp. 79–80. John appears in at least five acts of Count John datable to 1185 × 1189, and in another after 1189 at Cranborne.

2 Howden, *Gesta* II, pp. 85, 91. On 11 November 1189, King Richard I granted Wexcombe and Bedwyn in heredity *cum hundredo* to John Marshal (II) at a fee farm or perpetual rent of £30 p.a. There was a separate grant of Bosham with lestage (a port due) and its hundred for a fee farm of £42 p.a. the same day, *Acts and Letters*, pp. 466–9.

3 For William's and John's appearances at court in the reign of Richard, see L. Landon, *The Itinerary of Richard I* (Pipe Roll Society, 1935). I have added to this certain references generously made available to me by the Angevin Acta project.

In the meantime, the world had changed for the Marshal. His young wife was pregnant before they left for Normandy and presented him with his eldest son and heir, whom he named William, in Normandy in 1190, perhaps as early as April. The Marshal had, with his accustomed ease, achieved the feat that eluded his brother and so many others of his contemporaries: a lawful son to carry on his surname. A second son called Richard, to recall Isabel's legendary father, appeared the next year to consolidate his lineage. A first daughter, Matilda, appeared in 1192 or 1193, and the other four daughters were likely born over the next decade. Regularly, year by year, Isabel would add to their family until they had a total of five sons and five daughters who grew to adulthood. We can date the birth of the other boys: Gilbert was the child with whom his mother was pregnant in April 1207, his brother Walter was born in Ireland in 1209 and the youngest boy Ansel must have been born a couple of years later, but before the family returned to England.

To return from domestic to political success. It is not easy to work out whether King Richard was smiling on the Marshal family in 1189–1190 entirely for William's sake, or in an attempt to encourage the growth of a Marshal party at court, or even both. That there was such a party, however, can be seen in the reaction of other powerful men to the Marshals at this time. Geoffrey, the archbishop-elect of York, resisted vigorously the installation of Henry Marshal as dean of his chief cathedral until December 1189, although the king favoured the Marshal side. A more dangerous enemy for the Marshals was Richard's chancellor, William de Longchamp. He was one of the more fascinating characters of his age. His background was similar to the Marshal's own, a member of a family of minor royal servants, in his case – like Geoffrey fitz Peter and William Briwerre – a family of foresters. He had served Henry II as a clerk, and was later Count Richard's devoted chancellor. It was that devotion and his fierce energy that persuaded the new king to entrust him with the diocese of Ely, the custody of the Tower of London, the justiciarship and the royal seal in his absence. But William was also an eccentric character. He was a man of considerable learning, an author and a patron of other authors. He was also, according to some indications, a kindly and humorous man. Nonetheless, he had a remarkable ability to infuriate many of his political contemporaries. The reason seems to be that he despised courtiers, their flattery, their posturing and their ambition. He plainly loathed William Marshal. If so, it was because he regarded himself as a more honest and forthright sort of person, who would not play the courtly game, but would do his duty and serve his lord, not himself. A long tract dedicated to him survives, whose subject is, significantly, criticism of the court and courtiers.

His contempt is evident for both William and John Marshal (who plainly was not the most competent of men). It was he who removed John Marshal from office as sheriff of Yorkshire in the spring of 1190 after a serious and murderous anti-Semitic riot in the city of York, which left John's reputation in tatters. The king had left for France, giving Longchamp a free hand. He used it to swat those he saw as the king's enemies. There is some remarkable evidence that he attempted in person to seize Gloucester Castle, the base of William Marshal's under-sheriff and retainer, Nicholas Avenel, at about the same time, while the Marshal was with the king in France.[4] There might have been some justification for this outrage if, as I have already suggested, the Marshals were perceived as auxiliaries of Count John at this time. But Longchamp failed in his attempt, and an oblique answer by the king to his peremptory actions in England was to include William Marshal among the four 'co-justiciars' who were to monitor Longchamp's rule in England.

Count John of Mortain

It was in the year 1190 that John, King Henry II's youngest son, becomes an important character in the story of William Marshal, so now is the time to introduce him properly, for the rest of William's life would be the story of how he struggled to deal with John and, in due course, the fallout from his death. John was born the year after William was knighted, at the end of December 1167. His name was unknown in previous generations of his family, and a French source suggests it was given him because he was born around the feast of John the Evangelist (27 December).[5] He was born in England, at the royal hall of Gillingham in Dorset, and he was brought up in the foster family of the keepers of the hall until maybe he was three, before being transferred to the Abbey of Fontevrault in Anjou to be brought up with his sister Joan by the noble nuns of the wealthy convent.[6] He was in his father's itinerant court with the king's wards probably from 1174 to 1182, when he was transferred for three years into the household of the justiciar, Ranulf de Glanville. During that time, he picked up rather good Latin, a deep interest in the business of government and some quite advanced literary

4 Richard of Devizes, *Chronicle of the Time of Richard I*, ed. J.T. Appleby (London, 1963), pp. 12–13.
5 For the name John, *Recueil des historiens de la France* XIII, p. 679. John's birth year is a vexed question, because two contemporary chroniclers give different ones: Diceto (1166) and Torigny (1167). But what settles the question is that Gerald of Wales, who knew him well, says that John was 17 when he arrived in Ireland in 1185, *Expugnatio Hibernica*, ed. A.B. Scott and F.X. Martin (Dublin, 1978), p. 227. That would make *c.*27 December 1167 the most likely date for his birth, and we know his mother was resident at Winchester at some time in the months preceding. It is likely John was delivered at Gillingham, some 130 kilometres west of Winchester, because a suitable wet nurse was available there. John later took his foster-brother into his household on leaving for Ireland in 1185, where the boy unfortunately died on campaign, *Annals of Loch Cé*, ed. W.M. Hennessy (2 vols, Rolls Series, 1871) I, *s.a.* 1185.
6 John's birthplace at Gillingham is revealed by the fact that in 1212, his foster-father William Baillebien still enjoyed the land given him as a reward for his labours by King Henry II near Gillingham, where the Baillebiens had been keepers of the royal hall throughout his reign, a point I owe to Richard Sharpe, *Book of Fees* I, p. 91. John likely spent his early years in a family where English and French were spoken. For John's childhood stay at Fontevrault, A.W. Lewis, 'The birth and childhood of King John: some revisions', in *Eleanor of Aquitaine, Lord and Lady*, ed. B. Wheeler and J.C. Parsons (Basingstoke, 2002), pp. 159–75, Lewis was unaware of the evidence of Gerald of Wales, however, and opted for 1166 the year of John's birth. His error is repeated in recent biographies of John.

tastes. As we've seen, he produced at least one daughter in his teens from a lady of the court, and also a son from an adolescent encounter with his cousin, one of the daughters of his uncle Earl Hamelin of Surrey. He called the boy Richard, apparently after his brother, who may have consented to be the child's godfather. The character of John is a baffling one, and we can't blame lack of sources for that. Many contemporaries commented on the man he became, and some of them knew him personally. To begin with, the positive features, for there were some. John was extraordinarily loyal and affectionate to those he grew up with: notably, his foster-brother and the other children he encountered at court or in the Glanville household. As soon as he had one, his household was populated by his childhood friends. He furthered them with land grants and favours and rarely shook them off, however problematical they became. So he stood by Fulk fitz Warin, even though he became a notorious murderer, and Theobald Walter, even though he was a singularly corrupt sheriff of Lancashire. John also showed affection and loyalty to his father's mistresses and their offspring, most notably the Welsh lady, Nest of Caerleon and her son and his half-brother, Morgan, to whom he granted rich church patronage, though he failed in his bid to make him Bishop of Durham. John's open-handed generosity was in fact acknowledged by his enemies, even as they deplored the greed that took the virtue out of it.

John's character has been tainted by two deaths, which have been characterised as political murders at his orders. The first was his nephew and rival, Arthur of Brittany, who came into his custody in 1202 and was dead within a year. The second was Matilda, the much-admired wife of William de Briouze, and their son, who both died in the prison John placed them in at the end of 1210. That these political prisoners died in his custody is certainly his responsibility, but that he ordered them done away with is highly unlikely and depends on the imaginative speculation of chroniclers who knew nothing of the circumstances; sources that modern historians have perhaps been too anxious to credit because they make for a spicier narrative.[7] Arthur's body does seem to have been found floating in the river Seine, and a credible and less sinister explanation of his death is that he drowned in an attempted gaol break from the riverside castle of Rouen, where he was confined. We can't really know, but it's more likely than that his uncle mutilated and murdered him, an act that he was singularly careless about covering up, if we believe the chroniclers. Likewise, Matilda and her son kept close in insanitary cells were prey to all sorts of possible mortal dangers, not least typhoid or gaol fever

---

7 See, for instance, the tortuous authority assigned by Lewis Warren (following Sir Maurice Powicke) to the circumstantial account of Arthur's murder in the Margam Annals (a source not compiled till the 1240s). This argument has it that since Margam was a house under the patronage of William de Briouze, who was Arthur's gaoler at one point, the annalist had privileged sources for what happened at Rouen in 1203. But this was wishful thinking: Briouze was not in fact a patron of Margam Abbey, which was a monastery of the Lord of Glamorgan, Earl Amaury of Gloucester, in John's reign; see for the suggestion *King John* (2nd edn, London, 1978), pp. 82–3.

and the ever-present dysentery. Death by disease was the fate of others of John's prisoners, not least William Marshal's knight, close friend and seneschal, Geoffrey fitz Robert. John's guilt was in not taking sufficient care of sensitive and dangerous state prisoners.

People were all too willing to think the worst of John, however, and that is something that needs to be accounted for. William Marshal's biography can be very helpful here. The author portrays the interaction between William and John on occasion, and his sources were the very people who themselves witnessed the tense scenes. He always contrasts the self-control exhibited by his hero, the courtly Marshal, and the lack of control and nervous irritability of John. John was unpredictable, a bad quality in a lord of men. He tended to be at best facile, and at worst deceitful, in conversation. Courtiers never knew what to expect of him and so he generated stress around him. His nature was to be distrustful of those outside his childhood gang of early intimates.

Lack of any courtly sensibility, frankness or ease, unreasonable suspicion and distrust of his true intentions made it all too easy for his courtiers to dislike John. He broke all the cardinal rules for the conduct of a lord of his day, unlike his father and elder brothers. These rules are what the well-travelled and famous courtly poet of John's day, Raimon Vidal, describe in his essay on the very subject of a courtly lord:

> Whether among fools and villains or among worthy and accomplished men [*see*] that your words are [*well-chosen*] and what you do is full of sense, and, above all, pleasant, well-bred and guided by good judgement. Wicked, stupid, petty and foolish people have never been good for anything. Affable conduct provides a man of affairs with an immediate welcome in all his enterprises and allows him to employ his skills freely. It often happens that a polite fool gets more consideration than one who is disagreeable![8]

Raimon had no time for John, but deeply admired his three elder brothers, whom he claims to have met when he visited their courts and took as models of courtly princes.

England without Richard

There was never any question that William Marshal would return to the Holy Land with his new lord, the king. He had already made his pilgrimage and done what the crusaders of 1190 hoped to do, worship at a liberated Holy Sepulchre, walk the Temple Mount and visit the sites associated with Christ's life. His biographer makes a point of telling us this. There are some indications that William

---

8 Raimon Vidal, *Abril issi' e Mays intrava*, in *Nouvelles occitanes du moyen age*, ed. J.-C. Huchet (Paris, 1992), p. 102.

supported others who wanted to join the enterprise, however. In the months before the crusaders left, William assisted at least one of his old friends to make the pilgrimage. In 1190, he acted as surety for the sum of 60 marks Ralph son of Godfrey, his old colleague from the Young King's household, had taken as a loan from Henry of Cornhill, a city financier. William probably took the management of Ralph's lands as a way of reclaiming the sum. Ralph was one of the crusaders who did not return, dying in Tripoli the next year.[9]

So it was, in July 1190, when King Richard departed with Philip of France for the Holy Land, that William commenced the role that the king had begun to fit him for as early as the meeting at Fontevrault, before King Henry's funeral. William became one of four 'co-justiciars', nominal assistants to William de Longchamp. It was for this reason that the king had elevated William and his family as far as he had done. William had to have enough land to give him dignity before the other magnates, whom it was his duty now to help to control. Richard has been criticised for the arrangements he left behind him for governing his lands: for leaving William de Longchamp, an arrogant and tactless man, as chief justiciar; for attempting to buy his brother John's complacency with huge grants of lands and revenues in England, and then expecting to get him to stay on the Continent and not take advantage of the opportunities he had been left with.

This is more than a little unjust. He was sufficiently aware of the problems to construct carefully a team of four experienced courtiers and magnates to supervise Longchamp: William Marshal himself, the talented administrator Geoffrey fitz Peter (who now had the lands of the earldom of Essex), Hugh Bardolf and William Briwerre. William Marshal was very much one with fitz Peter and Briwerre; all three were from families who had spent more than one generation in royal service (the other two came from families of royal foresters); all three men were also from the south-west of England. In the event, when things began to go wrong, Richard's precautions were to have some success. Over and above them, it is difficult to see what more he could have done, unless he had taken a reluctant John along with him, and risked his only viable adult heir alongside himself. The fact was that although Richard's arrangements were imperfect, he did at least find his kingdom intact when he returned after a much longer absence than he had anticipated.[10]

William Marshal's elevation to the higher circles of power in England carried its own problems. Chief of them would have been relations with William de Longchamp, with whom he had already clashed before the king's departure. Almost as difficult was the problem of John, the king's brother, who was in England within months of Richard's departure. Both were impossible men to manage and were plainly going to tussle for control of England as soon as Richard was gone. With John, there was a longer-term problem in that, for years, he would be the

9 *Acts and Letters*, no. 27, pp. 83–4.
10 These arguments are considered by J. Gillingham, *Richard I* (London and New Haven, 1999), pp. 119–22.

most obvious successor to Richard (despite the claims of Richard's nephew, the child Arthur of Brittany) and then there was the fact that John and William had rival interests in Ireland. Their rivalry had already led to a dispute between King Richard and Count John just after the coronation, which was only resolved by William's surrender of a substantial amount of land to one of John's followers.

Now the Marshal was a great magnate he could not afford to thwart John too openly; his interests demanded that he tread a careful line between his present and future lords. William may have had hopes that his own brother, still Count John's intimate friend, might ease him over this difficult patch. Both John and William Marshal in fact appear together in the witness list of an act of the count's before June 1190, which tells us of at least one tête-à-tête the brothers had with him before Richard departed.[11] William had already by 1190 obtained Count John's confirmation of his foundation of Cartmel Priory, which lay within another of John's many lordships, the franchise of Lancaster.

In the event, it was Longchamp who was the easier to deal with. His uncourtly arrogance so alienated the barons that he had no party to support him in England. His actions were peremptory and erratic. Unwilling to work as justiciar with the elderly and respected Bishop of Durham, Hugh du Puiset, Longchamp placed him under arrest. He was determined to have no rival to his authority and the Pope helped him along by commissioning him as papal legate for England. When the archbishopric of Canterbury fell vacant, he made a determined effort to secure election to the most senior church post in the kingdom without first seeking the absent king's consent, which was an act verging on *lèse majesté*. Something had to be done about his rogue justiciar, and a mission was sent to King Richard early in 1191, when he was wintering in Sicily.

William Marshal was deeply implicated in this move, and according to the historian Roger of Howden, he made his way to Sicily in person to inform the king of how his English arrangements were falling apart. Since Howden had himself joined the crusade, his comment that William was in Sicily in February 1191 must be taken seriously, though the biography fails to mention the voyage, and indeed has nothing to say as to how Longchamp came to be removed from power, other than saying William was the moving force. It mentions a letter sent by William and his three colleagues to King Richard, but not that he took it himself. It is therefore possible that the Marshal sailed secretly from England at the end of January 1191 and made his way to Messina to inform the king in person how seriously things had gone wrong back home.[12]

11 *Historical and Municipal Documents of Ireland, AD 1172–1320*, ed. J.T. Gilbert (Rolls Series, 1870), pp. 50–1; another leading witness of this act was Bertram de Verdun, who left with Richard on crusade and died in the Holy Land.

12 Not only did Roger join the crusade, a journal survives describing the voyage he made from the landing of Howden Dyke on the river Ouse, down the Humber estuary and onwards to the Mediterranean, by which we find Roger did not join the king in Sicily, but sailed direct to Acre, so could not have seen William Marshal at Messina, though

The result was several royal mandates authorising the four co-justiciars to remove Longchamp when the time was right, and indeed giving the timing of the decision to William himself. They were to replace him with the Archbishop of Rouen, Walter de Coutances, a man who had grown old and wealthy in the household of Henry II, a man indeed very much like the co-justiciars themselves. Walter was with the crusading army in Sicily, but Richard – anticipating the result – ordered him home, and the probability is he sailed back with William, who is known to have had recent and friendly dealings with him over the lordship of Kendal, which he had courteously conceded to the archbishop's nephew.

A protracted political duel between Count John and Longchamp over control of England was ended in October 1191, when, with John besieging Longchamp in the Tower of London, the co-justiciars produced the royal mandate and replaced Longchamp with Archbishop Walter. Longchamp was bundled out of the country into exile in Flanders. The *History* regards this move with satisfaction. Its author sees the Marshal as a moving spirit in the business, and there are other indications to support his view of William's antagonism to Longchamp. But the *History* is less to be believed on how the *coup d'état* left the Marshal's relations with Count John. It gleefully describes the put-down given John's hopes of power by Archbishop Walter, who is said to have brushed him aside 'seeing to what end he would come'. In fact, John's position after Longchamp's departure remained a powerful one. He had, after all, been recognised by the magnates of England as Richard's heir in 1191 at the time of Longchamp's removal, and John was not obliged to retract this claim.

Over the next year, we find Count John in a position powerful enough to be consulted over the election of a new Archbishop of Canterbury; leading a campaign against the Welsh; and attempting to mediate between the committee of justiciars and Longchamp (for a bribe, we are told by Howden). It would be good to know precisely what the Marshal's relations with the count were in 1191 and 1192, but hindsight persuades the *History*'s author that they were already at daggers drawn. The one real indication is a reference that we have to William's later part in mediating between John and Longchamp over possession of the Castle of Nottingham, which is perhaps ambiguous.[13] But overall, one cannot resist the impression that the Marshal must have found John by far the lesser of two evils, and a settlement that removed Longchamp and benefited John was not one that would have harmed or upset him.

---

that does not mean he was wrong in his assertion about the Marshal in Sicily, see P.G. Dalché, *Du Yorkshire à l'Inde: une géographie urbaine et maritime de la fin du xiie siècle* (Hautes études médiévales et modernes, 89, Geneva, 2005). One of the sheaf of letters the king sent back to England singled out for pre-eminence 'my beloved and loyal' William Marshal among the co-justiciars, which might well indeed reflect the fact that William had personally briefed the king, see Diceto II, p. 91n.

13 Barnwell, I, p. 462; an episode wrongly dated by the *History* to 1193.

Richard of Devizes, no friend of the Archbishop of Rouen, reported Archbishop Walter's careful temporising with Count John at this time, but chose to see it as stabbing Longchamp in the back rather than searching for peace and future security. The Marshal may well have adopted a similar ambivalence. It is significant in this respect that in 1194, after Richard's return, the Marshal refused to do homage to Richard directly for his Irish lands, but reserved his homage for John. The *History* had to record this business, it seems, for it was too notorious an incident in the Marshal's career to gloss over. Longchamp, now back from exile, remarked at the Marshal's refusal: 'Planting vines, Marshal?' That is, he accused him of insinuating himself into the good graces of the future king, sowing the seeds of favour. The *History* puts a huffy and legalistic reply in the Marshal's mouth, but even as the biographer records the exchange it sounds like Longchamp had the best of it.

News of Richard's capture and imprisonment in Germany on his return home, which reached England in December 1192, ruined what seems to have been a very satisfactory year for Count John and the justiciars. John was drawn into a conspiracy with Philip II of France. After a trip to Paris in which he entered into a deeply compromising treaty of alliance with Philip, John returned to England in March 1193 with a company of mercenaries and ambitions to confront the justiciars with his claims to the crown. In the event, he did not secure much support and was besieged at Windsor by the reluctant justiciars aided by Queen Eleanor, whose loyalty was to Richard. The four seem to have been less than happy with developments. One of them, Hugh Bardolf, refused to fight John, saying that he was the count's sworn man and could not fight his lord. William Marshal might have used the same excuse, for he too was John's man for his Irish lands. He must have been heartily relieved when John agreed to a truce till November on hearing news of the ransom terms for Richard's release.

Peace was once more re-established. With John discredited and Richard's return assured (once the money was forthcoming), the justiciars returned to their duties and John disappeared to France. Only in February 1194, with Richard's return imminent, did the Marshal and his colleagues finally take the plunge and move troops against John's supporters and the castles they still held. William Marshal played his part, seizing John's main English stronghold of Bristol and other properties of the count in the south-west – the area, as we will see, in which his political power base lay. But this campaign was to have fatal consequences William did not anticipate.

Richard's captain and courtier, 1194–1199

One of the most revealing episodes in the history of the Marshal's political development occurred in March 1194, when Richard returned to England. It was not Richard's return I refer to, so much as an event that took place at the same time, John Marshal's death. John Marshal had mixed fortunes during the years of King Richard's absence. Although he lost the shrievalty of Yorkshire in 1190, he was compensated after Longchamp's fall with the post of sheriff of Sussex, where he had lands at Bosham, and he retained Sussex till he died. He had married Aline du Port, the daughter of a Hampshire baron, but no children had come from the marriage. This sterile union seems to sum up a career destined to have no continuing success. For his brother Henry Marshal, Dean of York, things were different. Early in 1194, Richard, in Germany, nominated him for the vacant bishopric of Exeter, apparently as a token of his appreciation of William Marshal's services.

John Marshal's death occurred early in March 1194, just after his younger brother Henry's election, and just before Richard landed in England. William Marshal was at Chepstow when the king arrived, and from the account of the *History* seems to have heard the news of the landing at the same time as the news of his elder brother's death. As the *History* portrays it, the Marshal's choice was a pretty quandary for a professional courtier. What should he do? Go first to the king, his lord, or attend the head of his own family to his grave? The *History* carefully weighs up his predicament:

> He was so sad at this news of his brother, when he heard it, that he almost died of grief, and it would have been a very cruel blow to him had there not been another piece of news, thank God, which he found most pleasing. For an eloquent, courtly and wise messenger appeared before him and informed him that the King of England had arrived in his own land in good health and cheer, and completely free. Even if he had been given ten thousand marks he would not have been so relieved of the sorrow that weighed on his heart. 'So help me God!' he said, 'Never before did I feel such great sorrow as I did for my dead brother, but I have received such comfort from the arrival of my lord that I could not have greater. I give thanks to God for the misfortune and equally for the good fortune that I have had in so short a time, for I am so glad at his arrival that I cannot but fight off the pain which I thought never to be free of.[14]

The Marshal's position was in fact more complicated than just a choice between a funeral and a fiesta, although the *History* is tongue-tied as to how to explain his actions without further compromising him. It tells us that his brother had died at Marlborough. But the chronicles of the time tell us that Marlborough was one of those castles that had declared for Count John, whose seneschal John Marshal was, or had once been. Marlborough had been a Marshal possession in Stephen's reign, and what it is likely we are seeing in March 1194 is the consequences of John Marshal's unlucky attempt to use the count, his lord, to recover possession of the castle. No doubt he had resisted the co-justiciars when they ordered Marlborough's surrender in February, and no doubt also he had been mortally wounded resisting

14 *History* II, lines 10023–48.

their troops during the fierce siege that had followed, which had been commanded by the Archbishop of Canterbury.[15]

The Marshal therefore did not go to the funeral of his traitor-brother, but he sent knights from his retinue to escort the body to Cirencester. There, the Marshal met the corpse on his way to the king and viewed it, comforting his brother's widow. A mass was heard at Cirencester Abbey but, we are told, messengers reached him at this point urging him on to meet the king. What could a courtier and magnate do, especially when he dared not slight the king whom his brother had betrayed? William sent his brother's corpse and widow on to Bradenstoke Priory and the interment under his knights' escort, keeping three by him on the road to meet the king at Huntingdon, on the way to reduce the rebel garrison of Nottingham.

This episode tells us more perhaps than anything else about the sort of man William Marshal had become. We may discount the messengers who came to Cirencester urging on the Marshal to the king's side. They are a touch too opportune in their appearance to be credible. Their introduction is, however, significant. They are there to excuse the Marshal, because an excuse is necessary. No king could have cavilled at a day or two's delay in appearing if a courtier had to bury his brother, but William Marshal had chosen not to delay. He came direct to the king after the minimum of a ceremonial adieu to the disgraced head of his family. He could have been criticised in his own day for such self-serving, and the tone of the *History*'s apologetic leads one to suspect that he was. The Marshal was such a courtier that he was as happy in the royal presence as nowhere else, unless it were behind the king's banner in the field. John Marshal was not such a brother to him that his death could have distracted William too long from his natural habitat. Let us believe that William felt grief for his brother, but there are degrees of grief. That which William felt for John Marshal might rate as something a little beyond regret, with some guilt mingled in perhaps; a twist in the soul sapped by years of mutual diffidence and earlier tension. Not enough to keep William from the man who wore the crown, the true object of his affection, the man who could give him what his family had not.

For the rest of Richard's reign, William Marshal was deeply engaged in the business of the court, and for the most part he spent the five years in France. The witness lists to Richard's charters seem to show a pattern to William's attendance between 1195 and 1198. He was with the king from spring to autumn, but was absent in winter. It is tempting to see him wintering in domestic content in his Norman castles, busy on his own affairs and begetting daughters in the least congenial season for campaigning. There is some evidence during this period that he paid attention to his English estates and interests, which he would have had managed for him by his stewards and bailiffs. William's position in Ireland, too, had improved. Count John temporarily lost his lordship of Ireland in 1194, and when he recovered it after a year's dispossession found that King Richard would no longer

15 See for Marlborough, Howden, *Chronica*, III, pp. 237, 238; Newburgh, I, p. 406.

be fobbed off as John's British overlord and that he was now unable do what he liked beyond the Irish Sea.

William was in England briefly in the spring of 1196 and in the autumn of 1198, when he appears on the bench of the royal justices in Westminster Hall.[16] He might have used these opportunities to attend to his own interests and discuss his officers' actions. There is some evidence that these men were busy in his absence. In spring 1198, when William was in fact in Normandy, he recovered a property in Southampton from his brother's inheritance.[17] Although (like the other co-justiciars) he lost his shrievalty in 1194, he was allowed to keep charge of the royal forest of Dean, across the river Wye from his lordship of Netherwent, and his English interests were extended elsewhere by his inheritance of his brother's lands in Berkshire, Wiltshire and in several other counties. He inherited also his brother's shrievalty of Sussex. But as far as England and Wales were concerned, the rival attractions of the royal court drew him away from them, to France where he had spent most of his adult life.

There is a certain evenness about these years that makes me think that the Marshal was happy enough during them. He was in high favour with the king, who was scoring continuing victories over Philip of France; he had a congenial life and growing family in Normandy; his military prowess continued. Such was his influence with Richard that he was able to exert himself on occasions to mitigate the effects of the king's touchy temper. The *History* gives us the example of William's ability to soften the fit of royal choler against the papal legate, Peter of Capua, when no one else dared approach him. But another source confirms this; the Life of St Hugh of Lincoln tells of an incident where William Marshal and his friend, Baldwin de Béthune, saved the bishop from the king's anger over money he was owed.[18]

The campaign of 1197 was a particularly happy time for William. In May, he was part of an expedition to punish Philip, the warlike Bishop of Beauvais, whom King Philip had delegated to keep up pressure on the Norman frontier. The command of the expedition was entrusted by King Richard to his brother, Count John (a point the *History* conveniently disregards by pretending that the king himself led it). The campaign was a brilliant success, and culminated in a successful surprise assault on the French castle of Milly-sur-Thérain, nine kilometres to the north-west of the city of Beauvais. Although the Marshal was now approaching 50, he was irrepressible. Standing on the edge of the castle ditch and urging on the attack,

16 *Pedes Finium, 1195–1214* (2 vols, Record Commission, 1835) I, p. 176; *Feet of Fines, 1182–1196* (Pipe Roll Society, XVII, 1894), p. 110.
17 *Curia Regis Rolls* I, p. 50. The property would seem to have been the large tenement on Westgate Street, near the quayside that was later called 'Ronceval', from being given by the Marshal's son to Roncesvalles Priory in France, C. Platt, *Medieval Southampton* (London, 1973), p. 269.
18 *Magna Vita sancti Hugonis*, ed. D.L. Douie and H. Farmer (2 vols, London, 1961–1962) II, pp. 107–9.

he saw a Flemish knight in difficulties, clinging desperately to the battlements while the garrison tried to push him outwards to his death. The Marshal jumped down into the ditch and clambered up the ladder and drove off the knight's assailants, while climbing past him on to the wall. He then defended a section of it till assistance came, amusing himself by flattening the constable of the castle with a blow to the helmet while he was waiting. The genuine Marshal shines through in this little anecdote. Feeling a little weary after his exertions, he sat on the body of the unconscious constable while his men swept on past him and the castle was taken. After his return to Rouen, Richard chastised the Marshal mildly for pushing himself forward in such a way at his age, but we can well imagine the smugness with which the Marshal must have regarded the incident at Milly, and the pleasure of his numerous followers at their ageing lord's exploit.[19]

Following Sidney Painter's chronology, Milly was followed for the Marshal by a prestigious and expensive embassy along with the Norman baron Peter des Préaux, late in the year, to Count Baldwin of Flanders and Count Reginald of Boulogne, to persuade them to ally with Richard against Philip of France. This was perhaps his first experience of international diplomacy, but the king's choice of the Marshal as a joint ambassador was a logical one. St-Omer was the key to it. The Marshal had once held a large part of this Flemish town, but in 1192 King Philip had deprived the Count of Flanders of it, which might have disrupted the payment of the Marshal's revenues. The new count, Baldwin IX, needed to be motivated to recover his lost towns, and the Marshal was a fitting emissary, since he shared the count's grievance.[20]

The *History*'s account of his great embassy is confused, but what seems to have happened was that the Marshal undertook the preliminary negotiations with Flanders in early summer 1197. He then accompanied Count Baldwin to the formal treaty at Rouen in July, he fought in Berry with King Richard, and went back with the count to Flanders in August. Here, he fought with Baldwin against King Philip at Arras, and the strategy he is said to have advised there was thought by his biographer to have contributed to Philip's spectacular and humiliating surrender to the Flemings, one of the most remarkable military coups of the twelfth century. Following King Philip's capture, the Marshal returned with the count and the king to Normandy for a peace conference in September.[21]

19 *History* II, lines 11169–264. The author of the *History* is alone in stating that King Richard took part in this campaign: Diceto and Newburgh imply that the king was awaiting news of its progress in Rouen, for the captured Bishop of Beauvais was sent there by Count John to him, see Diceto, II, p. 152.

20 The *History*'s account of this is confirmed by a payment of 1,730 marks (£1,153 6s. 8d.) made to William and his colleagues for their expenses by the Exchequer, *Pipe Roll of 10 Richard*, p. 172.

21 Howden, *Chronica*, pp. 20–1. The Marshal and his colleagues, Alan Basset and Peter des Préaux, can be found back with the king in September–October 1197 in Normandy, L. Landon, *Itinerary of King Richard I* (Pipe Roll Society, new ser., XIII, 1935), pp. 122–3.

This happy state of affairs came to an abrupt and unexpected end in April 1199. Early in March, King Richard had marched south from Anjou on a minor campaign into the Limousin. William Marshal took his leave of him and returned to Normandy on royal business. On 26 March, the king, lightly armed as he always was at sieges, received a crossbow bolt in his shoulder while reconnoitring the defences of a small castle he was besieging. Eleven days later, on 6 April, he died. There were two potential heirs: Count John, now aged 31, who had led a blameless and useful life since the troubles of 1194, and Arthur of Brittany, son of Geoffrey, John's elder brother, a young man still underage. Richard, on his deathbed, left the kingdom to John, overriding whatever rights might have been thought to have come to Arthur through his father. There were two schools of thought on this question at the time: whether a younger brother could exclude a dead elder brother's son from the succession. William Marshal had, however, long committed himself to John's side of the question, which seems indeed to have been the traditional view of succession among the Norman aristocracy. The day of strict primogeniture had yet to come.[22]

The day after Richard's death, a courier carrying news of his illness reached the ducal castle of Vaudreuil, where William and others were sitting as justices. It was not until three days later that news of Richard's death finally came to Normandy. When the news eventually reached Rouen, to which William and the Archbishop of Canterbury had moved to secure the city, it was late at night after the Marshal had gone to bed. The *History* tells us of a nocturnal debate between the hastily dressed Marshal and the Archbishop of Canterbury over the suitability of John to succeed. William stood out unequivocally for John, which simply confirms what his actions during the earlier part of the reign hint at. The *History* mitigates what it obviously sees as a rare error of judgement by William in depicting him as gloomily listening to the archbishop's all too accurate warning that he would be sorry for his decision. But in fact, whatever the *History* says, the Marshal must have calculated on John's initial weakness as a time when a discreet, ambitious and circumspect man could easily pick up gains and increase his power. Was that not the lesson he had learned in 1189? Did not every royal succession since the Normans first came to England prove it?

22 For a comprehensive treatment of the debate over the rights of adult younger brothers to succeed despite the existence of children of elder brothers at this time, see J.C. Holt, 'The *Casus Regis*: the law and politics of succession in the Plantagenet dominions, 1185–1247', in *Law in Medieval Life and Thought*, ed. E.B. King and S. Ridyard (University of the South, Sewanee, 1991), pp. 21–42. See also R.V. Turner, *King John* (London, 1994), p. 50.

5

EARL OF PEMBROKE AND LORD OF LEINSTER

William and Archbishop Hubert were very soon dispatched into England by John, and there they received an oath of loyalty to John from the barons and prelates, many of whom attempted to make their oath conditional on the king's respect for their claims. They grumbled, but accepted assurances that the new king would give them a hearing. With England passive, William returned to John in Normandy and escorted him back across the Channel to England.

One wonders if William did not bend the king's ear about what he considered his own claims on the return trip. Whether he did or not, if royal grants were what the Marshal was expecting in 1199, he was not to be disappointed. The author of the *History* declares in a rather unhappy way that he had heard grants were made at this point, but he knew nothing of them, not being in England at the time. He seems to have been reluctant to credit John with any generosity to his lord, and it is very odd indeed that he refused to describe the grants, which other sources tell us were great indeed. One wonders what sort of accusations he was trying to gloss over.

The first, and perhaps the most gratifying grant, was the formal investiture with the title of earl, which William received just before John's coronation in London on 27 May 1199. Howden records that William was invested earl under the name of Striguil, but he was wrong. As early as June 1199, William Marshal appears in royal documents as 'Earl of Pembroke', a title he uses consistently for the rest of his life and the title by which he was generally known by others.[1] There has to be some significance in the revival of this title, and an abundance of other evidence

---

1 William is *comes Penbroc* in a charter of King John dated 20 June 1199, *Rot. Chartarum*, p. 79. His own charters have him either by that title, or *comes de Penbroc*, or some other spelling. The exception is in a charter of his to Bradenstoke Priory, of which the original survives, *Acts and Letters*, no. 36 p. 97, where he is *comes Penbrocsir[e]*, namely 'Earl of Pembrokeshire'.

soon confirms that William had indeed received from John at least the promise of the marcher lordship of Pembroke.

William did not receive Pembroke immediately, for John was at this time engaged in hostilities with Maelgwyn and Gruffudd, sons of the late Prince of Deheubarth (west Wales), the great Rhys ap Gruffudd. During 1199 and 1200, Richard's sheriff of Cornwall, John of Torrington, was transferred to keep what were still the royal castles of Carmarthen and Pembroke, and it is clearly stated that 'Pembrokeshire' too was in his wardship. John was still issuing orders to the sheriff of Pembroke and to 'his' barons and knights of Rhos and Pembroke in October 1200.[2] But in April 1200, John had released some lands in west Wales to Earl William, the territories of Efelffre and Ystlwyf east of the lordship of Pembroke itself, until he should deliver to William his land of Emlyn (then occupied by Maelgwyn ap Rhys, along with its castle of Cilgerran, originally built by the earlier earls of Pembroke). It seems likely that Pembroke came into the hands of its new earl when he arrived there in person en route to Leinster early in autumn 1200. In May 1201, William Marshal appears as the patron of the burgesses of Pembroke, securing trading privileges in London for them from the king.[3]

In reclaiming Pembroke, the lost possession of his wife's family, William Marshal had achieved what her father Earl Richard fitz Gilbert, never a favourite at the Angevin court, had failed in. Pembroke brought him considerable prestige. In terms of land, the area under the earl's jurisdiction was about twice that of his other marcher lordship of Striguil, with much good arable land. This was 'Pembrokeshire', the area of jurisdiction of the earl's own sheriff, who presided over its central county court where criminal and civil justice was administered in the earl's name and by the county's own customary law. Beyond this lordship, the earl had claims on the allegiance of the lord of Cemaes to the north-east, and it was obviously still remembered that the Marshal's wife's grandfather, Earl Gilbert, had included the castles of Cardigan and Cilgerran within his earldom.

Pembroke was one of the most powerful marcher lordships, thoroughly organised for war, which had been its natural state for a good part of the last century. It was a land of powerful castellans: at Roch, Wiston, Carew, Manorbier and Haverford. Perhaps most significant of all, it was the staging post for Ireland. The Marshal's new vassals at Roch, Carew and Manorbier were also some of the greatest men of Leinster. Possession of Pembroke was for him the first step to gaining undisputed control over his Irish lands. It is not surprising that he showed an immediate interest in its potential.

Crossing to Ireland

Although the *History* has nothing to say about it, there is no doubt that the Marshal visited both Pembroke and Ireland during the autumn of 1200. The evidence is

2 *Pipe Roll of 1 John*, p. 182; *Pipe Roll of 2 John*, pp. 226, 230; *Rotuli Chartarum*, p. 98.
3 *Ibid.*, pp. 47, 95.

in a remarkable lost writ of King John that was issued on 3 December 1200 at Hamstead Marshall, during a royal progress through Wiltshire and Berkshire, while the king was a guest of William Marshal, then freshly returned from Leinster. The writ tells us the king had found William a shaken man. He had made his will, and was asking the king to confirm its terms, particularly his promise to found a Cistercian abbey in Ireland. The reason for his troubled state of mind is not hard to find. There is a reference in the Annals of Ireland, apparently quoting a foundation chronicle of Tintern Parva Abbey, to the Marshal founding that same house in Leinster in 1200 in fulfilment of a vow he made when caught 'for a day and a night' in a storm at sea, before safely making Wexford Harbour.[4]

William is last found at court with the king in September 1200, and so in the early autumn he must have travelled westward into South Wales to take formal possession of Pembroke, before taking ship with his retinue for Ireland. Once embarked, the seasonal gales from the Atlantic nearly brought his career to a premature end, probably driving his little fleet off course and back towards Wales before relenting and allowing the ships to limp past Rosslare Point into the safety of Wexford Habour. What made the situation all the more desperate was that William had sailed for Ireland with his wife and probably also his several children.

It was not unprecedented for a stormbound nobleman in such desperate circumstances to attempt a fervent bargain with God as his ship veered and plunged in dark seas. If God would spare him, he would raise a monastery. If God chose not to, then no monastery would be built. Count Waleran of Meulan, caught in a spring storm in the Mediterranean in 1148, did exactly the same. The Cistercian abbey he subsequently raised in Normandy was called 'the Abbey of the Vow' (*de Voto*), and so too was the abbey that William Marshal proceeded to authorise and endow, though it is also called Tintern Parva ('Little Tintern'), for the monks to set it up were drawn from the original Tintern in South Wales, founded by his wife's uncle in the lordship of Netherwent in 1131.[5]

William and Countess Isabel made a great progress across Leinster, holding courts and issuing solemn charters to the tenants who appeared before them. One that has survived is his confirmation of his lands to the veteran colonist Adam of Hereford, authorised perhaps in an assembly at the Castle of Kildare, the lordship where Adam's lands were concentrated. Adam had probably arrived in Leinster with the countess's father in 1170 and by now would have been elderly, possibly some years older even than the earl who had arrived from England to take his

4 *Acts and Letters*, pp. 474–5. The text of this key document was once copied into the historical collections of the Irish antiquary, Sir James Ware. Fortunately, it came to the notice of Sir William Dugdale in the mid-seventeenth century, who copied it into his notebooks and subsequently published it.

5 *Chartularies of St Mary's Abbey, Dublin*, ed. J.T. Gilbert (2 vols, Rolls Series, 1884) II, pp. 307–8.

homage. The issue of the charter would have occurred on Adam's public act of submission to the new lord of Leinster.[6]

The failure of the *History* to mention the Marshal's first visit to Leinster is more than a little odd. It states boldly, on the occasion of the Marshal's crossing to Ireland in 1207, that its hero had never been there before; but this is not true. Not only did he undertake to found the Abbey of the Vow in 1200, William can be proved to have founded another Cistercian abbey on that same autumn tour of Leinster, at Duiske on the boundary of his lordships of Carlow and Kilkenny, which was to be a daughter house of the Wiltshire Abbey of Stanley. While in Leinster, William befriended Hugh le Rous, in 1202 made Bishop of Ossory, the chief religious authority in the south-west of Leinster, who helped move his projects forward and who we know made a return visit to William at Hamstead, at some time in the winter of 1203–1204 after the Marshal's return from Normandy.[7]

William and his council cannot have been entirely happy with what they had found in Ireland. Previous attempts to bring his huge and ramshackle lordship under control had been ineffective, so they agreed a dramatic strategy before he left. Countess Isabel would remain behind and take responsibility for a reform and reorganisation of Leinster, her father's great conquest. At her side would be her husband's leading follower, Geoffrey fitz Robert, a Wiltshire knight whom the biography commends as the earl's good and loyal servant. Geoffrey had been taken into the Marshal *mesnie* some years before William's marriage, in the days when William was still contemplating settling for the lordship of Kendal. Now Geoffrey was appointed seneschal of Leinster to assist the countess. We know this from King John's writ issued after William's return, which notes these arrangements.

After a stay in Ireland of perhaps as long as two months, William Marshal took ship (probably a little nervously) and sailed back to England, leaving his wife and their children behind. It does not seem likely that they were reunited until the close of the Norman campaign in 1203. In the meantime, they communicated by letter. As it happens, one of these actually survives. It is William's response to Isabel's dutiful request to use the wealthy church of Kilcullen in modern County Kildare for the purpose of endowing a mass for her father's soul. William obligingly endorsed whatever she might choose to do with it.[8] Isabel must have had her two sons and several daughters with her in Ireland during this period; her eldest boy was only 10 in 1200. Nothing would be done about the younger William's future till 1203, when the family was once more reunited.

When the *History* can be detected to have kept quiet about an incident, there is a reason for it; it is seeking to protect its hero. There must be more to this reticence than just the memory of the nausea of the rough and dangerous sea crossing. Looking ahead to the problems he was to have in Ireland in 1207–1208, it might be suggested

---

6 *Acts and Letters*, no. 48, pp. 112–14.
7 *Acts and Letters*, no. 53, p. 121.
8 *Acts and Letters*, no. 54, pp. 122–3.

that the Leinster expedition of 1200 did not go smoothly. As we will see, Leinster was a coherent political community, its greatest men closely related and frontier warriors all, with a strong sense of place and identity. They had proved in the past hostile to effeminate courtiers, as they seemed to regard them, from across the Irish Sea (they had handled roughly Henry II's steward, William fitz Adelin, in 1176, and had been less than impressed by John, the king's son, in 1185).

Into this exclusive and hostile community sailed the Marshal. It may well be that they found cause to resent him. A hint of how he might have offended is to be found in his known doings on that expedition. His new monasteries were pious intrusions, acts of patronage directed back across the Irish Sea, colonies of his Abbey of Tintern in Gwent and the Wiltshire Abbey of Stanley. The old colonials of Leinster might have had their hackles raised by this, especially if it was combined with grants to the knights who came to Ireland in the Marshal's entourage: Geoffrey fitz Robert was, we know, given a new lordship for his own based on Kells, south of Kilkenny. Perhaps as a diplomatic gesture to promote solidarity with the colonists, Geoffrey was given as his wife Basilia, the widowed sister of the great Strongbow.

Back once more at the royal court, the Marshal had further grants from John. The shrievalty of Gloucestershire was restored to him and to it was added now the keeping of Gloucester and Bristol castles. By 1201, he had the wardship of the lands and heir of the baronial family of Giffard of Brimpsfield, powerful in the south-west. As in 1189, William's relatives were not forgotten in his surge of good fortune. His nephew and household knight, the bastard John Marshal, was awarded by the king the heiress of the Ryes family, who brought him the Norfolk barony of Hockering and the small honor of Ryes in Normandy. In this way, the illegitimate son of John Marshal found more than enough compensation for the diversion of his father's lands to his uncle.[9]

9 The question of the parentage of this John Marshal was for a long time unnecessarily clouded. Meyer, followed by Painter and Duby, concluded that John could not have been the son of John Marshal (II) because William Marshal was in fact his brother's heir. William's nephew John, they said, must therefore have been the son of a younger brother, perhaps that Ansel who briefly appears in the *History*. The *Complete Peerage*, the bible of English aristocracy, dismisses this, saying that William's nephew John could very easily have been John Marshal's bastard. In fact, there is conclusive proof that he was just that, first in a charter of William Marshal's dating to the 1190s, in which John is called 'the younger John Marshal', and in another charter dating to a time after 1199, in which William confirms his deceased brother's grants to Bradenstoke Priory, his nephew John appears in the witness list, where he is called, significantly and forlornly, 'John Marshal, *the son of John*', see *Acts and Letters*, no. 45, pp. 107–8. Furthermore, a charter of *Johannes Marascallus filius Johannis Marascalli* (that is, William's brother) concerning Nettlecombe, Somerset, is attested by *Johanne Marascallo filio meo*, *ibid.*, no. 6, pp. 58–60. Lastly, in his old age, John Marshal, the nephew of William, made grants to the Norfolk priory of Walsingham not just for his father, John, but also his mother, *Alice*. The fact that he commemorated his mother by name must mean that she was no casual prostitute, but a

Between John's coronation in May 1199 and the end of 1201, William Marshal was generally to be found in the king's company, whether in England, Normandy, Gascony or Poitou. In April 1200 at Westminster, in August of the same year at La Réole in Gascony, and in May 1201 at Cirencester, John favoured the Marshal with numbers of charters of grants and confirmations; one, a confirmation of the advocacy of Notley Abbey in Buckinghamshire, a Giffard foundation, was made 'out of the love we have for our beloved and faithful man, William Marshal, Earl of Pembroke, and because of the good and loyal service he has done us'.[10] There is no doubt that the Marshal, together with his colleagues Geoffrey fitz Peter, now Earl of Essex, and William Longespée, Earl of Salisbury, were seen by John at this stage in his reign as the main props of his rule, and lavish gifts followed. More established court magnates, such as the Earls of Leicester, Chester and Surrey, received rather less. Between 1199 and 1201, the Marshal reached the peak of his life as court favourite, raised by his lord to be the most powerful magnate in the southern Marches of Wales, or at least he would have been if he had ever stayed there long enough to exert himself.

Losing Normandy

The *History* is generally reticent about the times in the Marshal's career when he was touched by failure, and though the author goes into some detail about John's great defeat, he has little to say about the Marshal's part in the loss of Normandy and the king's other northern French domains. That William played an important part is however clear from what other sources have to say. When he returned to Normandy with the king at the end of May 1201, William would not have considered that he was heading into a potential war zone. A year before, King John had apparently succeeded in ironing out a comprehensive peace settlement with Philip of France. He secured recognition of his standing as his brother's heir, as Philip was persuaded to drop his support for Duke Arthur's claim to succeed his uncle Richard. John was even welcomed and feted at Paris in the aftermath of

---

woman of good birth. This brings us to the identity of that Alice. In the early thirteenth century, Alice de Colleville made a grant at Maidencourt, Berks, to Poughley Priory, Berks, for the souls of the brothers John Marshal and William Marshal Earl of Pembroke (putting John first). In this pious grant for the dead lover and his brother, her son's patron, we may have the evidence we need to pinpoint John Marshal's mother, see Cartulary of Walsingham, British Library, ms Cotton E vii, fo. 95v; Westminster Abbey Muniments no. 7242. There are two known contemporary women called Alice de Colleville. One was an early thirteenth-century Suffolk widow, alias Alice of Frostenden (who had married a Robert de Colleville), see *Blythborough Priory Cartulary*, ed. C. Harper-Bill (2 vols, Suffolk Record Society II, III, 1980–1981) II, pp. 151–2. The other, and more likely, candidate was wife to a Sussex landowner, William de Colleville, around 1200 (John Marshal was a Sussex landowner and sheriff of Sussex from 1190 to 1194), see *Curia Regis Rolls* I, p. 200; III, p. 193.

10 *Rot. Chartarum*, p. 74.

the treaty, which was sealed by the marriage of his niece, Blanche, daughter of the King of Castile, to Louis, King Philip's son. The young couple were dowered with the troublesome province of the Norman Vexin, so defusing another potential source of conflict.

But things went very badly wrong the next year. For all that John was prone to misjudgements, the fault in this case did not lie with him, but with Philip. The French king had been humiliated and cowed in several years of warfare with King Richard between 1195 and 1199, but it must have become clear to him that John, of whom he had already made a fool in 1193, was not the equal of his fearsome brother. Though defeated in his first attempt to gain Normandy in 1200, Philip was watching and waiting for his next opportunity. After all, he had the teenage Arthur at his court always ready to bring out to lend legitimacy to any invasion of John's lands.

The trigger for John's downfall in France was the ambition of the ill-omened family of Lusignan in Aquitaine. The king went to France in 1201 to confront trouble in the strategic region of the Angoumois in Aquitaine, whose ruler, the Count of Angoulême, had as heir a sole daughter Isabel, then not much more than 12 years old. Seeing the danger of such an unattached heiress, John had promptly secured a divorce from his first wife, the Countess of Gloucester, and married the girl himself in August 1200. In doing something so decisive, however, he antagonised the Lusignans, who had already negotiated a marriage between their leader Hugh and Isabel.

King John was not wrong to get involved in the business. A Lusignan–Angoulême marriage would have been fatal for his rule in Aquitaine and John had to frustrate it. However, he then failed to reconcile the Lusignans to their defeat, and by March 1201 they were already in insurrection in Poitou. As John's officers and army re-established his dominance in Poitou, the Lusignans, as a last resort, appealed to King Philip as the overlord of John over his 'want of justice' in the affair. It gave Philip exactly the opportunity he was looking for. In April 1202, John – by refusing to answer in Philip's court – was formally dispossessed of Aquitaine and declared no longer Philip's vassal. His continental lands (apart from Normandy, which Philip awarded himself) were then granted in July to Arthur of Brittany. In July 1202, Philip's army crossed the frontier of Normandy and began his final determined campaign to extinguish Angevin rule in France.

Where was William Marshal in all this? He had rejoined the royal court by the end of March 1201 as it moved south to Canterbury, and he remained with the king as he sailed with his army from England. He travelled with the king on his Poitevin campaign. After that, the trail grows cold, as we can no longer plot his movements from the witness lists to the king's charters. His biographer did not think the Marshal was at John's great victory of Mirebeau in 1202, for he was said to have been in Normandy when despatches of the king's victory reached him. The king's lightning strike from Maine succeeded in capturing Arthur and all his main southern rivals, a master stroke that should have ended the war. Indeed, on hearing the bad news, Philip's forces in the duchy temporarily called off their campaign, news that his biographer says William deliberately caused to be leaked to the French camp around Arques for that very purpose. Great must have been William's frustration when King John entirely mishandled the aftermath of Mirebeau and reignited the conflict.

From various sources, we know that from 1201 John was using the Marshal in a local capacity to defend the northern borders of Normandy and the Pays de Caux, where indeed most of his Norman estates were. Here, he operated with some success until 1203 along with the Earl of Surrey, himself a great landowner of the region, and the king's half-brother, William Longespée, who had married the Marshal's first cousin, Ela of Salisbury, and received the earldom to which she was heir. The Marshal remained high in favour throughout this period. The William le Gros who was made seneschal of Normandy early in 1203 would seem to have been his nephew of that name, promoted no doubt through William's influence.

An attempt has been made to link William Marshal with the death of Arthur of Brittany at Rouen in 1203. There is an odd and wilful determination among historians who want to stigmatise William Marshal as an accessory to a murder that probably did not in fact happen. But apart from a dubious passage in the *History* that refers to an undatable dispute between the king and the Marshal, which seems to have been on a quite different subject, there is no evidence that he was anywhere near Rouen when the death is supposed to have happened. It is, in any case, an event that is impossible to fix in time. A clerk in England in 1203 dated a document 'in the second year from Arthur's imprisonment', following the common practice of using notable events rather than Anno Domini to date charters. So it must have been commonly believed that Arthur was still alive and in prison well after July 1203, or the clerk would have been more circumspect. If so, it contradicts the date of April 1203 to which the untrustworthy Margam Annals assign the death.[11]

In 1203, John's continental domains began to fall apart as his vassals in Normandy and Anjou turned against him. Philip of France was able to exploit the situation to the full. The *History* has little to say of 1203; it has a distinct aversion to tales of failure and defeat. It does mention the Marshal's embassy to King Philip, besieging the town of Conches in the southern march of the duchy, seeking but failing to open discussions about a truce. It portrays the king and Marshal having a frank discussion, as men of the world, about the worth of a victory that depended on turncoats. King Philip shrugged: traitors were, he said, like rags you use in the toilet and then throw them down the latrine. So pointed a conversation might well have occurred and the French king's words been preserved in the Marshal circle.

---

11 M.D. Legge, 'William the Marshal and Arthur of Brittany', *Bulletin of the Institute of Historical Research*, 4 (1982), pp. 18–24. For the charter date, in a formulary of John's reign, *Lost Letters of Medieval Life*, ed. M. Carlin and D. Crouch (Pennsylvania, 2011), pp. 30, 31.

The author entirely fails to mention the Marshal's leading part in the last serious bid King John made to turn back the French tide sweeping downriver from Paris. The great fortress of Château Gaillard towered on its rock above the right bank of the river Seine on the Norman frontier, a formidable obstacle in the way of any approach to Rouen. A determined siege of the castle began in August 1203, with French forces digging in on the opposite bank and constructing a great wooden bridge across the Seine using boats as pontoons, on which were erected four siege towers that could command the lower defences. Hearing of this at Rouen, King John entrusted the Marshal with command of a relief force that would attack the bridge by river and land, marching and sailing upriver by night to take the siege lines unprepared. The Marshal was to lay waste the siege lines and massacre the camp followers, while troops in the galleys would assault the pontoon bridge.

But coordinating the assault proved more than the attackers could manage. The land force led by William arrived just before dawn and began its murderous work among the unarmed camp followers, who were driven screaming on to the bridge, but the river transports were delayed and the French were able to repulse both attacks in turn. Without the riverborne reinforcements, William Marshal's force was driven off with many casualties by his great rival, William des Barres, a famous captain who was to the Capetian court very much what Marshal was to the Angevin one.[12] The failure of this relief march was the last serious attempt John made to defend Normandy. Though the castle held out till March the next year, John had already left Normandy long before it fell. Accompanied by William Marshal and the rest of his court, he sailed for England on 5 December 1203. The writer known as the Anonymous of Béthune mentions William indeed as one of those earls who crossed with the king's ship.[13]

Fall from grace

William Marshal remained with the king at his court in England over Christmas, and when he returned to Normandy six months later as an ambassador to King Philip the duchy was almost totally in French hands. The loss of Normandy was a difficult time for the English magnates, many of whom held some land in the duchy that they would lose if they did not do homage to the new ruler. The English magnates of John's reign were well aware of earlier times when England and Normandy had separated, as in their fathers' days when the Count of Anjou

---

12 The account is to be found in *Oeuvres de Rigord et de Guillaume le Breton*, ed. H.-F. Delaborde (2 vols, Paris, 1885) II, pp. 177–90, from the *Philippis* of William le Breton, King Philip's household chaplain, who was an eyewitness of some of the action at Château Gaillard. Painter refused to credit William le Breton's account on the rather specious grounds that he only introduced the Marshal's name in a poetic way to enhance the glamour of des Barres' triumph, but the account is very particular on the identity of the English leader, and names the Marshal on three occasions.

13 Anonymous, p. 97.

conquered the duchy from King Stephen. Then most had had to give up either their Norman or English lands, following the ruler from whom they held most.

The same thing happened in 1204, but unlike 1144 the position was to be permanent, and indeed there are indications that some Norman landholders anticipated the separation would be long-term. A number of Anglo-Normans divided their estates at this time, giving away the Norman portion to brothers or younger sons. William Marshal seems to have taken an optimistic view of the problem. It is undeniable that he loved Normandy, land of his youth and best years. Now as a man approaching his sixties, he would have been very reluctant to quit it. In 1200, he was still estate building in Normandy, and by an exchange with Roger d'Abenon annexed to his castle-lordship of Orbec in central Normandy, Roger's considerable patrimony, in return for lands of his in England.[14]

The Marshal must have had abundant time to consider his response to the crisis. It would not be surprising if his urging of John to make peace, which we hear of as early as 1203 before they left Normandy, was not at least partly influenced by his desire for a stable situation in which he could reach some accommodation about his Norman lands. In May 1204, John sent him to Normandy as part of an embassy to Philip to seek terms. The other earl with him was Robert of Leicester, one of the greatest landholders in Normandy and a man with much more to lose than the Marshal. The mission was not a success, but both earls used it as an opportunity to negotiate on their own account. King Philip, in return for a substantial sum of money, gave them both a year to meet his demand that all Norman landholders must do him liege homage or lose their lands.

The Earl of Leicester never had to face the decision. He died before the end of 1204. No direct compensation was offered to the Marshal for his potential losses in France but there is evidence that King John wanted to give him some inducement for his continued support, offering the possibility of gains in Wales. John made one direct grant to him in April 1204 of the lordship of Goodrich Castle in Herefordshire to add to his possessions in the southern March, and in August allowed him the privilege of a market in the town there.[15] This could by no means outweigh the loss of an honor the size of Longueville, but in November, or early in December 1204, William Marshal was in west Wales once again. With a 'mighty host' (probably at royal expense), he successfully recovered from the Welsh the Castle of Cilgerran (an event we hear of only from the Welsh annals).[16] Cilgerran

---

14 *Rot. Chartarum*, p. 65.

15 *Ibid.*, p. 124; *Rot. Clausarum* I, p. 4.

16 *Brut y Tywysogyon: Red Book of Hergest Version*, ed. T. Jones (Cardiff, 1955), p. 186; *Annales Cambriae*, ed. J.W. Ab Ithel (Rolls Series, 1860), p. 63. These annals do not date the seizure of Cilgerran, and Painter calculated that it happened in summer 1204 (linking it with the Marshal's meeting with the princes of Gwynedd and Powys in July at Worcester, as the king's agent); but the subsequently discovered 'Chronicle of Wales' tells us that in fact, the Marshal seized the castle 'at the turn of the year about Advent', see T. Jones, 'Cronica de Wallia', *Bulletin of the Board of Celtic Studies*, 11 (1946), p. 32. The meeting at Worcester cannot therefore be linked directly to any campaign. The Marshal was with

had been part of the earldom of Pembroke in the 1130s but had fallen into Welsh hands. In 1200, John had been unable to give it to the Marshal with the rest of the earldom because the princely house of Deheubarth would not give it up, so he compensated him with two lordships in Dyfed. John had now let the Marshal loose with a licence to take what he could by force. He had heard no doubt that Maelgwyn ap Rhys, the hitherto dominant prince of Deheubarth, had been defeated in war with his nephews in the course of the summer, and the Welsh of that region were now divided and weak.

Again, we must ask why the *History* does not mention this campaign, particularly because it was so obviously a success. The only answer that makes sense is that which applies also to the failure to mention John's brilliant successes in the Beauvaisis in 1197, his creation of William as earl in 1199 and the trip to the Pembroke and Ireland in 1200: the author will not willingly recall anything that reflects well on King John. He therefore edits out all mention of the acquisition of the earldom of Pembroke and the king's subsequent grants. It is a remarkable fact that Pembroke does not feature at all in the *History*, despite being the seat of William's earldom after 1199, except when King John embarked there for Ireland in 1210.

Before the year given to him by King Philip was up, in spring 1205, the Marshal was back in Normandy on another, more informal embassy to King Philip. Before he had left England he discussed his plight with John, and he was generously allowed a licence to do homage to the King of France. The act was performed in March or April 1205, and the Marshal received back Longueville and his castelries of Orbec and Meullers. The one difficulty was that Philip would not be satisfied with less than the Marshal's exclusive liege homage for his Norman lands.

William returned to England to face the consequences. He may be forgiven for thinking that there would be no aftermath. His rise had been so effortless since 1186 that 20 years of continuing success had blinded him to the possibility of disgrace. But his determination to hang on to his Norman lands went beyond reason. If it is a sample of the Marshal's capacity for independent political judgement, then it is a sign that he had not yet become as accomplished a magnate as he was a courtier.

There were undeniable precedents for the position in which he chose to put himself. The best known were the counts of Meulan, who had been vassals both of the King of England and King of France since the eleventh century. In 1157, the then count came to a generally acceptable arrangement that he owed his liege, or principal, homage to the King of England. If the counts then followed the King of England in war against the King of France, they did not lose their French lands,

---

the king at Winchester on 6 October 1204, but there is no evidence of his being at court again until 16 December, at Clere, Hants. It is likely that the campaign in west Wales occupied a good part of the brief intervening period; the *Annales Cambriae* stress the Marshal's speed, appearing before the castle walls and taking it at the first onset, before the *teulu* (household guards) of Maelgwyn in the garrison could even arm themselves.

some of which were to send their normal quota of knights to the King of France for the campaign.[17]

This was the position that the Marshal was attempting to secure for himself in 1204–1205. It is the position that the legal treatise known as Bracton pictures him in while describing the situation of Anglo-French magnates later in the thirteenth century.[18] But King Philip was not so easily fobbed off, and by the written terms of the 1204 settlement between him and William, which still survives in Paris, William was obliged to accept that he was Philip's liege man in Normandy.[19] This meant that he might not fight Philip in France without losing his lands. One cannot acquit the Marshal of wilful blindness here. He could not but be well aware of the plight of the then Count of Meulan, Robert, an old acquaintance of his from the days in Young Henry's household. He had in fact indulged in some sharp profiteering at the count's expense in the crisis of 1204. He took from Count Robert his Dorset manor of Sturminster when he was in dire straits for money.[20] Count Robert had ended that year living on royal charity in England, but this was a warning lost on the Marshal.

John's reproaches towards the Marshal were not long in coming. It is unlikely that John had seriously thought about the consequences of the Marshal's actions in Normandy, or at least had been persuaded that William had obtained preferential terms from Philip. When the Marshal returned, he found that John had been acquainted with the exact terms of the oath he had taken, and the phrase that William was to be Philip's liege man in France had angered the king. The Marshal protested that this did not harm King John's interests, but John was not so easily reassured. It is not necessary to see the Marshal guilty here, as Painter did, of deliberate deception of the king, just over-optimism. But he was certainly being obtuse and rash in seeking his own advantage, and unjustified in hoping that he would muddle through unscathed in a conflict with the king.

There is good evidence, indeed, that the Marshal was growing reckless in his behaviour to the king, and had already tried his patience. As we've already seen, William was never shy as a young man in pressing his claims for reward on his master and prosperity seems to have made no difference to his self-assertion. The *History* says that he had remonstrated with John for his lack of vigour in defending Normandy even before the king abandoned the duchy, though its unsupported evidence can't be entirely trusted.[21] But independent sources tells us he indulged in at least one very public dispute with John in the summer of 1204, which the *History* does not notice, but the royal court at the time most certainly did. William

---

17 D. Crouch, *The Beaumont Twins* (Cambridge, 1986), pp. 64–79.
18 *De Legibus et Consuetudinibus Anglie*, ed. T. Twiss (6 vols, Rolls Series, 1878–1883) VI, pp. 374–6.
19 *Acts and Letters*, no. 84, pp. 163–4.
20 *Curia Regis Rolls* III, p. 124.
21 *History* II, lines 12721–49.

had confronted the king privately with the demand that he override the proper process of law and award him the Meulan manor of Sturminster in Dorset over the heads of the two countesses who disputed its ownership with him. When John suggested mildly that the Marshal wait for a few weeks until the case could be brought before his full council, the Marshal had become stubborn, demanding a decision on the spot, and repeatedly refused to back down, until other courtiers intervened and mollified him. John had been annoyed enough to direct his clerks to file a report of the incident in the justice rolls.[22]

In June 1205, William came to an open breach with John. The king was determined on an expedition to recover his position in Poitou, and William was summoned with the other magnates to go. He refused. A loud quarrel followed in council, with both men appealing to the judgement of the barons. John accused William of conspiracy with the King of France; William said the king was inciting him to break the terms of his agreement with Philip. The other barons preferred not to get involved, but the argument went on. Many of the younger household knights, who were a feature of John's personal following, were hot against the Marshal, but none was so confident that he would risk proving his case in battle against him. The barons, particularly Baldwin de Béthune, Count of Aumale, the Marshal's old friend, whose daughter Alice was now betrothed to the Marshal's son William, patched up a reconciliation, but there was no denying the fact that the Marshal had miscalculated, and for the first time in his career as a magnate he was out of royal favour. A new political life had begun for him.

In the cold, 1205–1207

The Norman and Angevin kings of England had some obnoxious ways of dealing with courtiers who had offended them. The Angevins were the more sophisticated. Putting aside the unprovable and dubious allegations about his disposal of Arthur of Brittany and the deliberate starvation of the Briouze family, the time of King John was not notable for political murder. John was not given to executions among his barons. Indeed, on one occasion he even expressed dissatisfaction with a baron who had (legally) executed a treacherous dependant. He was not a particularly bloody tyrant, however unpleasant and insecure a man he was. The Normans had fewer scruples. John's great-grandfather, Henry I, the Conqueror's son and a man much praised of late for his sophistication as a ruler, had personally hurled a traitor to his death from a tower in Rouen. But as the ground approached, Henry's victim at least had the consolation that his learned executioner had disposed of him

---

22 *Ibid.* The Marshal got his way. On 23 August 1204, Sturminster was committed to his household knight, Thomas of Rochford, and in the next month the sheriff of Dorset was directed to deliver the manor to him along with lands that had belonged to the Norman baron, William Martel, *Rot. Clausarum*, pp. 6–8.

in the same way as the Ancient Romans dealt with treason to the Republic: precipitation, from the Tarpeian Rock on the Capitol.[23]

The world of Henry II and his sons was less bloody, but this does not mean that it was a pleasant experience to be on the wrong side of the king. To offend the king, as several bishops and lay magnates did, was to court exile and financial ruin. Becket, of course, lost his life, although Henry II was not directly to blame for that. Becket's colleague and adversary, Bishop Arnulf of Lisieux, gives a better picture of how the Angevin method was meant to work. First, privileges were withdrawn, and the court became noticeably unfriendly. Royal bailiffs suddenly became harsher in their exactions, lands were occupied and lawsuits began to go against him. His power drained away as men learned that the king had withdrawn his favour. Who would follow a man who could not further his career? Therefore, his canons, and even his nephews, turned against him. A stony silence met petitions. In the end, Arnulf could cope no more and resigned his see after five years of humiliation. Harried out of Normandy, he ended his days in the Abbey of St-Victor in Paris, awaiting from the king a promised pension that was slow to come.[24] Even he was luckier than Robert Bloet, Bishop of Lincoln under Henry I. His archdeacon, Henry of Huntingdon, records something of the same method employed against him and how, worn out at the end, he collapsed and died at the king's side.[25]

Barons, too, met the same method. But we know less of their roads to disgrace, for their problems were usually less well documented. We do know that the Marshal's father, John, encountered royal disfavour from 1158 onwards. His part in the hounding of Becket was perhaps intended to buy him back some tranquillity. Now with William Marshal, we see at last a baron under a cloud. It was not the deepest and darkest of clouds, but it was undoubtedly a chilly and uncomfortable place to be. The *History* depicts the king retiring to his chamber after his encounter with the Marshal: 'He thought hard, after he had eaten, how he could get even with the Marshal, and how he could find a means to distress him.'[26] But if this was so, the king was circumspect.

The fact is that though there was a breach between the two men in the summer of 1205, it was not as severe as the *History* wishes us to believe. After his death, John was universally acknowledged to have been a bad thing, as indeed he still is, and for good reason. To be in opposition to John was to be on the side of the angels. So the author of the *History* deliberately disguised the closeness between John and its hero in the first years of the reign. When the two men disagreed, it

23 C.W. Hollister, 'Royal acts of mutilation: the case against Henry I', *Albion*, 10 (1978), pp. 330–40, cautions against regarding Henry I's brutality as psychotic: he regards it as necessary in the context of his times.
24 *The Letters of Arnulf of Lisieux*, ed. F. Barlow (Camden Society, 1939), pp. lii–lix.
25 Henry of Huntingdon, 'Epistola de contemptu mundi', in *Historia Anglorum*, ed. T. Arnold (Rolls Series, 1879), pp. 299–300.
26 *History* II, lines 13249–52.

was an opportunity to persuade the reader that the Marshal was a hero of the moral resistance to the ogre-king, by playing up the severity of the break. But William was never that. He had made his fortune by loyalty to the king, and it was too late to change tack for him in 1205, even if it had been a practical course to take. Nor was there ever much danger of the Marshal sinking beneath the weight of the king's displeasure. He was only in a situation of real discomfort in 1208, and that was largely his own fault.

It may well be that John was more correct in feeling threatened by the Marshal than the Marshal was to feel under threat from him. By 1205, once the great Earl of Leicester was dead and his estates dismembered, the Marshal sat at the head of one of the greatest political affinities in the king's realm. It may be for this reason that when the king challenged him, the barons around the Marshal kept their peace and would not take sides. When no one would name the Marshal as a traitor, the king demanded the Marshal's eldest son, by then 15 years old, as a hostage. The Marshal could only give the boy up, trusting in his own reputation for loyalty. John also began to whittle away at the Marshal's privileges, as well as his peace of mind. At Michaelmas 1205, just after the argument with the king, William lost the county of Sussex, which he and his brother had enjoyed since 1190.

John was not prepared for an outright breach, if, that is, he intended one at this point. Perhaps he may have considered that he had warned the Marshal from further trifling with him. Not only that, but it may well be that the king preferred it that William now remain where he could be observed by his agents, at court or in his various residences about England or the March. The Marshal in fact remained at court for most of 1205, not in favour, but not in too obvious disgrace either. Although the flow of grants to him ebbed considerably from what it had been in 1204, it did not wholly subside. In the summer of 1205, after his dispute with the king, he had the wardship of the land and heir of the baron Warin fitz Gerold.[27] He was still in a position of trust. Indeed, in November he was detailed with three other earls to escort King William of Scotland south to a meeting with John at York.[28] He was probably at court for Christmas. He remained there in 1206 until the king departed from England into Poitou in June. The *History* tells us that the king still had confidence enough in him to particularly charge the Marshal and his 'other best knights' to keep the realm in his absence. No insistence was made that he should go with John this year. We are told that the Marshal made sure to send many of his English knights and sergeants with the king, so to that degree the *History* admits that the Marshal had been chastened.

After April 1206, all trace of William Marshal disappears from royal acts. He did not appear again at court when the king returned to England at the end of September after a notably successful campaign in Gascony and Poitou. It is far from clear why he did not come back to the court. No source mentions a new breach

27 *Rot. Clausarum* I, p. 39.
28 *Rot. Patentium*, p. 56.

in 1206 between the king and the Marshal. Indeed, before he left, the Marshal obliged the king with a gift of wine and a loan of 100 marks (£66 13s. 4d.), which the king promptly repaid.[29] On Boxing Day 1206, the king also obliged the Marshal by allowing him to resume the lands of one of his Norman tenants who had quit England for good.[30]

There does not therefore seem to have been any obvious increase of tension between the men that would account for William's removal from court. But remove himself he did. For some of the time at least, the Marshal was in his castle of Chepstow on the border of Wales. The only clue we have as to what was going on at this time is that the *History* does say that William approached the king after he came back from France and sought his permission to go to his lands in Ireland, a request he made more than once, apparently, until the king graciously allowed 'our beloved William Marshal' such a licence in February 1207.[31] If affairs had come to a crisis, then there is little trace of it to be gleaned from the records, or even the *History*. The crisis is more likely to have occurred in that rather impenetrable object, the Marshal's head.

The Marshal did not always bear up well under mental strain. He had departed the Young King rather quickly in 1182 after their breach, even though there was no question of any arrest or physical threat, and the Young King was still willing to employ him in the tournament field. We can therefore suggest that in 1207, the Marshal was running away, as he had run away in 1182. He was not a coward in any sense of the word. But the mesh of petty harassment in which he may have seen himself as caught was demeaning to him. The *History* is determined to picture the king and its hero as at loggerheads from 1205 to 1207, and that might indeed have been the Marshal's own view, if only with hindsight, because the two men were to go on to fight out two political duels in 1208 and 1210. But other indications tell us that the level of tension was still low in 1205–1206. However, we can still admit the possibility that the Marshal was jaundiced enough to want to be anywhere else but on the same island as the king.

King John's plan for Ireland

John had arrived in Dublin as Lord of Ireland in 1185. Had things worked out differently, he might have been crowned King of Ireland, for his father had papal permission to do so, and a gold crown was sent to Henry II from Rome for the purpose later that year. Although John's first expedition to Ireland was not a great success, politically or militarily, it was not perhaps as catastrophic as some have concluded, for his father was willing to finance another the next year. But it was cancelled as other problems loomed in France. After that, John continued to take

29 *Rot. Clausarum* I, p. 72.
30 *Ibid.*, p. 75.
31 *Ibid.*, p. 81.

a distant but proprietorial interest in Ireland. Though he didn't go there, he had endowed several of his intimates with large Irish grants, and he did not take kindly to his arrangements being challenged. William Marshal had already found this out to his cost in 1190 when he found John's butler, Theobald Walter, installed as a cuckoo in his Leinster nest. A result of that incident may have been the Marshal's scrupulously correct and cautious attitude to John as his overlord for Leinster throughout the 1190s.

John found an auxiliary in promoting his Irish interests among the old colonials in an Anglo-Welsh baron by the name of Meilyr fitz Henry. Meilyr had arrived in Ireland as a young knight with Earl Richard fitz Gilbert in 1169. His cousin Gerald of Wales memorably described him as a squat, dark and powerful man, as ferocious in battle as he was short in stature. He was very much a man of the Marshal's generation, but his experience had been in the embattled English colony of Ireland, not the mannered and political world of the tournament circuit and the royal court. In terms of lineage, he could very much look down on William Marshal. He was a grandson of King Henry I and so the second cousin of King John, a difference in standing that may not have assisted relations between William and Meilyr in Ireland.

Meilyr had great success over three decades in accumulating considerable estates across Ireland, in Munster and Meath, as well as the lordship given him originally by Earl Richard in Uí Fáeláin (County Kildare) at the northern edge of Leinster. Capable, well connected and greedy, he was the perfect candidate in 1199 when John wanted to appoint his first justiciar of Ireland as king, to manage and further his interests from Dublin. Since Meilyr crossed with John to France in 1200, we can imagine that the two men had a chance at some point to discuss quite how the king wanted Ireland governed. We find that Meilyr was not entirely happy with the direction the king wanted to pursue: he appears to have objected to the way things were going once the king's plan became clear to him in 1201. But he backed down and in the end sold his colonial soul to the king. The potential gains were too great to be ignored.

John wanted to do more than manage his own royal estates and dues. Ever scheming, he had plans to develop Ireland in ways that the Irish barons were going to dislike intensely. His vision was a radical and, at first sight, unrealistic one. He would reshape Ireland into a facsimile of England, with a bureaucracy ruling from a Dublin that would rival Westminster and Rouen, and all the Irish, native and immigrant, under the same crown. From the beginning of his lordship in Ireland, he indeed made a point of reserving 'the rights of the crown' in new grants he made there, notably over high justice and Church appointments. Now these would be asserted over the greater lordships. The king would enforce there the rights he had in England: the exclusive right to try criminal cases in his courts, management of the currency through mints and an exchange, and the appointment of bishops. But Ireland had to that date gone down the route that had already been followed in Wales, where marcher barons had established themselves in miniature realms of their own (such as Pembroke and Netherwent), where they administered their own law and waged war with the neighbouring Welsh princes on their own terms. The King of England's writ did not run in Wales, but John was determined that the same would not be true of Ireland, where he already had the beginnings of a royal centre in Dublin and its surrounding district.

In 1204, John ordered Meilyr to commence building there what would become one of the greater fortresses of the Angevin dynasty, intended to house a royal arsenal, treasury and Exchequer. Before the end of the year, Meilyr had received orders to centralise the minting of coin in Dublin and suppress any other currency in Ireland. He was also to institute the same register of judicial writs as operated in England: a declaration that English common law now applied to Ireland. In 1206, another significant order obliged Meilyr to create royal sheriffs and shires for the first time in Ireland outside Dublin, in the Briouze lordship of Limerick.

The people who might stand in John's way were the lords of the three great honors that had been established in Ireland since 1170. In 1199, these were Walter de Lacy, Lord of Meath, John de Courcy, Lord of Ulster, and, of course, William Marshal, Lord of Leinster, the greatest of them all. To achieve his aim, John had to deprive them of the liberties they had long assumed to be theirs by right of conquest, liberties that were as yet unquestioned in the March of Wales across the Irish Sea. John began his campaign in 1200, not long after the Marshal returned from his first visit to Ireland. So when John went on the next year to promote William de Briouze to be lord of a new great lordship in central Ireland based on Limerick, it was on the very same terms he had imposed on other lesser men in the past.

William de Briouze was at the time his very close friend and supporter, a substantial landowner in Normandy, Sussex and the Welsh March. Some credited him with being one of the moving spirits in getting the Norman barons to agree to accept John over his nephew Arthur on Richard's death. He was, in theory, a perfect choice as an accomplice: a loyalist and a man of high and impeccable lineage (much more so than Marshal, Courcy and Lacy), whose uncle Philip had some previous claim on the region of Munster. John was clear in making the grant of Limerick and the Irish Kingdom of Thomond to Briouze that it was limited. It did not include the city of Limerick itself, relations with the native lords, appointments to bishoprics and abbeys or anything else the king might claim as his own right. In this way, John raised the stakes of royal jurisdiction in Ireland and opened hostilities against the existing lords.

Into this unsuspected trap blundered William Marshal. Leinster was a convenient place for him to retreat in 1207, and that perhaps was its main attraction for him. He might go there, knock heads together and feel better. A final consideration may well have been his wife's views on the matter. The *History* suddenly brings Countess Isabel forward in the events of 1207–1208 as a force in her own right. It is as if it cannot hold her part in her husband's affairs down any more, and she bobs to the surface of the narrative. It is perfectly possible that she worked on her husband at this time for them both to return to the principal part of the inheritance she had from her father, and which was on loan by marriage to the Marshal. When he died, and if she did not remarry, Leinster would one day be her own again. As we have seen, she had already had the opportunity to govern it in person between 1200 till perhaps as late as 1203. Much of the impulse for what happened next might well have come from Isabel. It may even be she had sensed the drift of the king's policy, and was urgent that her husband go out to meet it. By 1206, John had staked a claim to control the whole process of law in Ireland, successfully overthrown de Courcy in Ulster, and was already now moving against the Briouze lordship of Limerick, which was no longer necessary to his purposes. Ingratitude was one of John's least attractive qualities. Isabel might well have begun to wonder exactly what the king's plans for her land of Leinster involved.

The Leinster crisis, 1206–1208

In light of his ambitions for Ireland, it is a little odd that the king was willing to let William Marshal go there, for all that the *History* says he was reluctant to do so. It is possible to overestimate the disfavour the Marshal was held in by the king at this time. In none of the subsequent events is there much evidence that John seriously contemplated depriving the Marshal of any part of his own lands, or of his liberty. He did not even levy a fine on him to clear his ill will after 1205, though he did demand his eldest son as hostage. The boy William had, however, been fostered out some years before to the court of Baldwin de Béthune, Count of Aumale, the Marshal's friend, so he was not being torn from the bosom of his family by this move, as the *History* pretends. There is no doubt that the king was annoyed with William and suspicious of him, but clearly the suspicion never reached the level where the king felt he must break the Marshal or himself go down. Nor for that matter would the coming difficulties of 1207–1208 shake the Marshal's public goodwill towards the king. So it may well be that in letting Marshal cross to Ireland, the king had some idea that he might actually further his schemes, as the good and loyal servant William had for the most part proved himself to be.

The king remained tolerant of the idea of William Marshal in Ireland throughout the winter of 1206–1207. John of Earley and Henry Hose, two of the most intimate of his followers, had been allowed protections by the king while they were with their lord in Ireland (for both were tenants-in-chief and, like their lord, needed the king's licence to go abroad). But that winter, the political state of Ireland became unexpectedly turbulent, as Meilyr fitz Henry took even the king by surprise in conducting an unseasonal military campaign that abruptly deprived Briouze of Limerick – without his orders, as the king claimed. That event coincided with a sudden reverse in his attitude. King John claimed to have had second thoughts about letting loose the Marshal. The *History* tells us that it was at this point at the beginning of Lent, in March 1207, that King John sent to the Marshal, withdrawing his permission to go over the sea, unless he surrendered his second son.

If this demand was actually made, we could suggest that this was no more than a cheap scheme by the king to frustrate the Marshal. Doubtless, the king expected the Marshal to give up the crossing, since it was no longer in his interests to have

William in Ireland. It makes a good and dramatic story, but the problem is that the author may have misread one of the documents in the Marshal archive that was his source, and dated the demand for Richard a year early. It may actually have been made the next year in different circumstances. The king's sudden change of mind early in 1207 might be no more than his being querulous and unhappy at losing the Marshal's counsel at this point.[32]

Whether the demand was made or not, the Marshal promptly left, even after being privately told that the king really would rather he did not sail for Ireland and regretted giving him permission to sail. It was tactfully communicated by one of his friends among the royal household knights, a brother of one of his own knights, who had been sent for that purpose. But he had the king's leave, and for good or ill, as he said, he was going. Considerable evils did follow for him. As soon as the king heard he had gone, he relieved William of control over the castle and shire of Gloucester, the key to his influence in the west. The keeping of the forest of Dean and its castle of St Briavels was also taken back into royal hands. The king removed from the Marshal the keeping of the royal castle of Cardigan and gave it instead to the lesser marcher baron, William de Londres.[33]

Whatever personal motive he had, there were also practical reasons for the Marshal to go to Ireland, good enough for him to want to brave royal displeasure. Leinster was a problem of lordship he had only just touched on so far in his career. He doubtless went off to Ireland intending to wield a vigorous new broom, without any encouragement his wife may have given him. He and his wife had, since 1200, been promoting schemes to reorganise her inheritance. But there was also the new problem of John's aggressive justiciar, Meilyr fitz Henry. William had left Geoffrey fitz Robert as seneschal when he left Leinster in 1200, and we know from several references that Geoffrey was active in improving his lord's estates over the next few years, settling disputes and promoting a scheme to bring Osraige (Ossory) under firmer Marshal control. It was Geoffrey, it seems, who set up a new borough next to the large and ancient religious community of St Canice of Kilkenny and raised or improved a castle opposite the monastery at the river crossing, so promoting what was to become a new Marshal capital for Leinster.[34] In this, the Marshal had

---

32 Despite what the *History* says, Richard Marshal – in 1207, probably around 12 or 13 – may not have been demanded of his father until over a year later on 4 June 1208, when the Marshal was commanded by writ, being once again in England at the time, to hand the boy over to this self-same Thomas of Sandford, *Rotuli Litterarum Clausarum* I, p. 118. Richard appears still in the king's hands in 1212, when he was committed again to Thomas as a compromise guardian, *Rot. Clausarum* I, p. 132. It is possible that the author elicited the idea of the king's demand from the original writ (which the Marshal archive would have preserved) but accidentally or wilfully misread the date, or it may be that he was right and Richard Marshal was required from his father in 1207, but orally.

33 *Ibid.*, p. 81; *Rot. Patentium*, pp. 70, 71, 74; *Pipe Roll of 9 John*, p. 210.

34 Geoffrey's agency in founding and promoting the borough before 1204 is seen in *Acts and Letters*, no. 55, pp. 123–6, esp. p. 126. He played a similar role at Carlow, according to later evidence, *ibid.*, no. 127, pp. 219–23, esp. p. 223.

the support of Bishop Hugh of Ossory, whom he had befriended on his first visit to Ireland. Countess Isabel, it seems, had been assisting the bishop's reform of his diocese and promotion of the Church of Kilkenny as his seat in her period of regency in Leinster, which her husband had sanctioned.[35]

But by 1204, anxiety over Leinster had shifted from necessary reforms to threats to the integrity of Isabel's inheritance. Geoffrey was superseded as seneschal in or around May of that year by an even closer member of the Marshal retinue, William's nephew and knight, John Marshal.[36] It was a move that shows Leinster was moving up the Marshal's agenda, and if so it must be because his agents there were already concerned about the threat King John was posing to the old order in Ireland. John Marshal may have been delegated to deal with the growing problem of Meilyr fitz Henry, the king's justiciar.

Meilyr, with the connivance of King John, had already increased the problem he represented to the Marshals by arranging in 1200 with an old Irish colleague, Geoffrey de Coutances, to exchange with him the Leinster lordship of Loígis, to increase his grip on the northern borderlands of the province.[37] Then, just before John Marshal arrived, Meilyr took the step that brought him into direct conflict with the Marshals. His pretext was the death of the lord of Uí Failge early in 1204, a Leinster lordship that was conveniently between Meilyr's older lands of Uí Fáeláin and his new lands of Loígis. Meilyr claimed wardship of the lands and heir on the king's behalf, but without any royal warrant to do so.[38] It was a naked land-grab, and King John's willingness to encroach on the rights of the great lords of Ireland had made it possible.

35 *Acts and Letters*, no. 82, pp. 159–61. Reform of the episcopal estates in Osraige was 'with the agreement and consent of Countess Isabel', which indicates in this case the scheme was her idea rather than just an idea carried out by her husband with her agreement, as the act has to have been issued before 1207 and can be plausibly dated to the period of her regency.

36 *Rotuli Litterarum Patentium*, pp. 40, 42, 50. We catch a brief glimpse of John Marshal's activities in Leinster in September 1205, acting on his uncle's behalf in a settlement between Cartmel Priory and St Thomas's Abbey, Dublin, *Register of the Abbey of St Thomas, Dublin*, ed. J.T. Gilbert (Rolls Series, 1889), pp. 337–8.

37 *Rot. Chartarum*, pp. 76–7. King John craftily arranged this by buying out Geoffrey's claim on Loígis with new lands in Connacht, in return for which Geoffrey gave Loígis to Meilyr. Though the king had not technically given away lands from Leinster, he had made the transfer possible, and indeed claimed to 'have given' Loígis to Meilyr. No mention was made of any Marshal consent to this bargain, only Geoffrey's. It's a classic example of John's legal chicanery at its worst.

38 See the reconstruction in M.T. Flanagan, 'Defining lordships in Angevin Ireland: William Marshal and the King's justiciar', in *Seigneuries dans l'espace Plantagenêt: Actes du colloque de Bordeaux-Saint-Emilion (3–5 mai 2007)*, ed. F. Boutoulle (Ausonius, 2009), pp. 41–9, and the recent illuminating study by Colin Veach as principally presented in 'King John and royal control in Ireland: why William de Briouze had to be destroyed', *English Historical Review*, 129 (2014), pp. 1051–78, and see also his *Lordship in Four Realms, the Lacy Family, 1166–1241* (Manchester, 2014 esp. ch. 5).

John Marshal was busy in Leinster for well over two years before his uncle arrived. Although we do not know the degree of his success, he could not have done so well as to reassure his lord and uncle that he could leave Leinster to look after itself. Another crisis over a Leinster wardship followed on the heels of the problem with Uí Failge, when in 1205 there died Theobald Walter, John's childhood friend whom he had illegally endowed with Leinster lands in Osraige in the 1180s. Meilyr apparently moved to seize Theobald's Leinster lordship, on the pretext that Theobald was a royal tenant-in-chief elsewhere so all his lands came under the king's control on his death until his child heir came of age. But King John did not sanction this action, and in 1206 the Marshal still had sufficient clout at court to secure a royal writ telling Meilyr to back off and let his bailiff take over Theobald's lordship.

Late in February, or early in March 1207, the Marshal arrived in Ireland with his wife and all his *mesnie* to a mixed welcome. His arrival made something of a stir. The *History* tells us that some of his men rejoiced to see him in Ireland; others, notably Meilyr fitz Henry, were less than enthusiastic. Meilyr in fact wrote to the king urging him to call the Marshal back if he were to preserve his interests intact. The *History* does not go deeper into this malevolence towards its hero. It assumes that Meilyr and his sympathisers, like all the Marshal's enemies, were motivated by simple malice. We, however, must try to look deeper.

The Marshal's career had not so far put him in a situation where he had to manage powerful men who wanted nothing from him, and indeed were actually hostile. In Ireland in 1207, he went among men who had to be ruled by him, but were reluctant to be ruled. It cannot be said that he had much success at first; indeed, in 1207, he experienced the ultimate humiliation for a well-intentioned lord: a rebellion against his authority by his dependants. This is the importance of the Irish problem for William Marshal. It tested his capacity as no other episode of his life was to do. He had to fend off the king with one hand and preserve his lordship in Leinster with the other. He himself realised the nature of the crisis he had weathered, for after 1208 he single-mindedly devoted himself to the reconstruction and pacification of Leinster. Here, we find the first signs that the man had some streak of greatness in him; that he was more than a successful sportsman and courtier. In the Leinster years, we discover why the Marshal came in the end to rule England.

A comment made by one of one of Meilyr's close relatives, Gerald of Wales, gets us close to the view of some of Marshal's Leinster tenants about him. In a rather lofty analysis of Irish affairs offered unsolicited to John in the manner of an old friend and companion, Gerald snorted about 'the newcomers to Ireland, who owe their position more to luck than any ability and their success to other people's endeavours than their own'. It was people such as William de Briouze and William Marshal to whom he was referring; latecomers usurping the fruits of the heroism of Gerald's family, of people such as Meilyr fitz Henry. Gerald growled about the arrogance and 'haughty insolence' of these courtiers. He also pandered to the king's notorious paranoia by more than hinting at the 'arrogance and autonomy' of these unnamed men, suggesting that 'they may well presume to usurp the rule of Ireland as rumour has it they will!'[39]

Another window into the old colonial mind may be found in the poem once known rather romantically as 'The Song of Dermot and the Earl', but more properly and prosaically known now as 'The Deeds of the English in Ireland'. It is a French verse work that describes the conquest of Leinster by Earl Richard and his men in the 1170s. The prominence nonetheless given in it to younger men such as Philip of Prendergast (who had joined the Marshal's *mesnie* by 1189), Meilyr himself and the Cogan brothers, combined with the complete absence of any mention of Countess Isabel, the Marshal or the men he settled in Leinster points to a date of composition in the 1190s or early 1200s.[40] It was a poem composed for the edification of an embattled but self-confident community of aristocrats.[41] It was a statement of its difference and superiority as demonstrated by its heroic past achievements. The Anglo-Welsh of Leinster were pleased to hear themselves called the *Irreis* (the Irish) by their poet, not because they regarded themselves as part of the Celtic fringe, but because it described their identity as a group of warrior colonisers in the toughest and remotest outpost of Christendom.[42] The Welsh origins of many of them gave them further solidarity: St David was their particular patron (the dominant cult of Deheubarth), and kinship further linked them through inter-marriages between the royal house of Deheubarth, and the Anglo-Welsh kin groups known to Gerald as the 'Geraldines' and the 'Stephanides'. They were men apart, and, naturally, they were superior to the soft *Engleis* across the sea.

The existence of such a feeling could account for much of the animosity that Meilyr was at one point able to foment against the Marshal within Leinster itself. Meilyr was, in particular, bound to see William Marshal as an intruder. He had fought his way across Leinster with the *mesnie* of Earl Richard, and rose after his death first in partnership with his kinsman Raymond le Gros, then on his own account under John's regime. He was the grandson of Henry I of England, son of a royal bastard engendered on Nest of Deheubarth, daughter of King Rhys of Tewdwr, and reputed to have been the most attractive woman of the early twelfth century. It is doubtful that he could ever have been impressed with the best knight in all the world, who now occupied the earldom of the already legendary Richard Strongbow, his sometime lord.

Meilyr had not just moved against him in Leinster, he had unwisely also taken action against Walter de Lacy, Lord of Meath, perhaps seeing him as an obstacle to dealing with William de Briouze's collapsing lordship in Limerick, for Lacy had

---

39 *Expugnatio Hibernica*, ed. A.B. Scott and F.X. Martin (Dublin, 1978), App. B, pp. 261–5 (my translations).

40 The new edition by Evelyn Mullally calls the work *The Deeds of the Normans in Ireland* (Dublin, 2002), just to complicate matters further. She corrects its dating to the 1190s (p. 37).

41 M.D. Legge, *Anglo-Norman Literature and Its Background* (Oxford, 1963), pp. 303–4.

42 *Deeds of the Normans*, p. 129 (line 2968).

married one of Briouze's daughters. Just about the time William Marshal arrived
in Leinster, Lacy flexed his military muscle and drove Meilyr out of the castle he
held of him in Ardnurcher and expelled him from the lordship of Meath. So William
Marshal arrived to find that the arrogance of Meilyr and the unpopularity of the
king's measures amongst the more powerful of the magnates of Ireland now gave
him some leverage. Only two months or so after his arrival, a body calling itself
'the barons of Leinster and Meath' addressed a letter to the king. We only know
of it from the king's outraged answer. But this tells us that the Lacy family, who
dominated Meath and Ulster, and the greatest knights of Meath and Leinster
(including the Marshal's retainer, Philip of Prendergast) had combined to protest
directly to the king about the actions Meilyr had taken, allegedly on his behalf.
The particular grievance they chose to pursue was Meilyr's peremptory action in
taking over the Fitz Gerald lordship of Uí Failge back in 1204. The king's words
alone give us the full savour of his reaction:

> I was astonished at the request you made of me in your letter. You seem to
> want to issue a new statute (*nova assisa*) in my land without me. In my days
> and the days of my forefathers it was unheard of that a new statute should
> be decreed in a country without the consent of its prince. What you ask is
> neither right nor has any precedent. You want my justiciar of Ireland to give
> something which I have ordered confiscated back to someone without my
> instructions! I tell you that you must withdraw the demand you made on
> my justiciar about Uí Failge. He is to reply to no man about what he has
> been ordered by me to confiscate, without my instructions. You may very
> well tell me that you aren't being remiss to your lord, and just seeking his
> justice. Know then that I will look to my *own* rights in the proper place and
> time with God's help![43]

The Marshal is significantly absent from the letter's address. But his hand must
have been deeply in it, for he was the greatest magnate of those parts, and most
of the men named were his tenants. The land in dispute was an area he had to
control, and his rights as Lord of Leinster had been challenged when Meilyr had
grabbed it. The proxy petition to the king against Meilyr's holding Uí Failge can
only have been a Marshal ploy, assisted by his Lacy colleagues in Meath and Ulster.
He was the 'someone' to whom the barons wanted Uí Failge returned.

The Marshal may have underestimated the petition's impact on the king, even
though he knew that John was an insecure man, apt to suspect conspiracies. The
king would have known who was behind the petition and his reply to it is laced
with undisguised anger. He had not wanted William in Ireland; now he was there,

---

43 *Rot. Patentium*, p. 72. I have removed the royal plural in this translation, as it obscures
the very real emotion the letter conveys. The letter's final sentences are difficult to
translate, perhaps because John's rage made him incoherent to the scribe who was taking
down his words.

what he had feared might occur seemed to be happening. The result was an order to the Marshal to return to England, sent, the *History* believed, at the prompting of Meilyr. We do not know the precise date of this order, for it does not survive in the royal records, but it must have been sent during the late summer, for the *History* records that the Marshal landed back on the mainland at Michaelmas (29 September). With him came a large number of the barons of Leinster, including the justiciar himself. They had all been summoned to John, as seems probable, to discuss the petition concerning Uí Failge that had so upset the king, but which he had promised to consider in due course. But there was more at issue, for the king decided that the time had come to move more decisively to secure his overall aim of exalting royal power in Ireland, as indeed his letter to the barons of Meath and Leinster implied he would.

A little over a month later, the whole crowd of them was attending King John at his palace of Woodstock. The king then proceeded to stage a convincing and damaging victory over the Marshal. The Irish barons who had come were heaped with gifts and promises. Meilyr was already in the king's pocket, but at Woodstock the king secured the public adherence of two prominent members of the Marshal's affinity: his nephew, John Marshal, and his wife's brother-in-law, Philip of Prendergast, both well-established and long-term members of the Marshal *mesnie*. The king bought Philip by substantial grants in Munster, near Cork. John Marshal accepted a week later a grant of the title 'marshal of Ireland' and the district of Kilmeane (Co. Roscommon) for the service of five knights. Meilyr, Philip and John were lovingly and pointedly named by the king at this time as the three men in Ireland whom he held in the greatest trust. Others of the barons of Leinster who had supported the petition against Meilyr also turned their coats in return for grants or confirmations: William of Barry, Richard Latimer, David de la Roch, Eustace de la Roch, Adam of Hereford, Richard of Cogan and Gilbert of Angle. Two Pembrokeshire barons who were present (Robert fitz Martin of Cemaes and Robert fitz Richard of Haverford) also had grants.[44] Again, the Marshal's absence from these dealings is significant. These were his barons and retainers who were being courted in front of his eyes. These men, there to support his dignity before the king, had metaphorically kicked the legs from under him and covered him in dust as they stampeded into the king's camp. The *History*, of course, fails to mention these events.

What the *History* does dwell on at this point is what the men of the Marshal's *mesnie* who had been left in Ireland were doing. Doubtless, this was to point out to those in the know the contrast with the men who followed the Marshal to England. The *History* could not afford to be too specific on what the unfaithful did. Many of the men who deserted the Marshal before the king at Woodstock and Tewkesbury in November 1207 were still alive and powerful in the later 1220s. What was more, John Marshal was to return quickly enough to his uncle's affinity

44 *Rot. Chartarum*, pp. 171–4.

and serve him well (it may even be that his delay of a week after the court at Woodstock before taking his grants from the king might have been caused by a pause to consult his uncle). It would have been unwise for the author to dwell on the doings of the Marshal's men and barons in November 1207 in England. Besides, what was happening in Ireland was a good story: a tale of valour and loyalty.

The Marshal and his men suspected that some attempt would be made against his lands when he left Ireland. For that reason, he left most of his *mesnie* of knights behind him. At this point, Countess Isabel took centre stage, a place in which she is not often seen. However, she was a key figure in Ireland: granddaughter of King Diarmait and daughter of Earl Richard Strongbow. Her presence might rally to the Marshal side some of the sentiment that still clung to the name of Strongbow. The *History* was written by a man who had little time for women, and who was writing for men who shared his apparent indifference, but there were times when his prejudices were overridden by reality. The *History* gives the countess the chief place in the council of the Marshal's men held before his departure. It was her doubts as to King John's intentions that they debated. She had been prominent in an earlier council, held before they all left Chepstow for Ireland. She had not wanted her son Richard delivered to the king. We can fairly conclude from these fleeting but telling appearances, and from the charter evidence, that she was in reality no mere cipher in her husband's affairs. She was a great lady in a long tradition of powerful Norman aristocratic women; her advice and consent were both needed and sought, and as we have seen, she had taken the rule of Leinster into her own hands in 1200 for a considerable period.

The countess was left to defend her husband's (and her own) interests in Ireland, although she was pregnant with her third son, Gilbert.[45] This abandonment may have been by her own insistence, rather than for health grounds. An advanced state of pregnancy had not stopped her travelling with her husband to Normandy in 1190. Two leading knights of the *mesnie* were detailed to serve as bailiffs under her in Leinster: Jordan de Sauqueville and John of Earley. Earley was left in charge of Osraige and the southern half of Leinster, then known as Uí Chennselaig, the original tribal kingdom of her grandfather (the modern counties of Kilkenny and Wicklow); Jordan took the northern half up to the confines of the royal lands of Dublin, based on the older centre of Kildare. Earley was less than happy about the responsibility, but took it at his lord's insistence, having as under-bailiff a fellow knight, Stephen d'Evreux. Stephen was the Marshal's cousin and we can see him as a key link at this time with the Lacy family. His family had been major tenants of the Lacys in Herefordshire since the eleventh century. The Marshal seems to have counted on him to steady and guide John of Earley. In all, another eight knights of his retinue, and the banner-bearer, William Mallard, were left with the

---

45 It may be significant that Gilbert was dedicated to the Church apparently from birth, it might conceivably have been as a consequence of a vow undertaken in this family emergency, that he would be given – like the prophet Samuel – to God if the Marshals came through the crisis successfully.

bailiffs. According to the *History*, only Henry Hose was detailed from the *mesnie* to escort the Marshal to England (John Marshal and Philip of Prendergast were Marshal followers but were at this time great men in their own right, and royal vassals).

The Marshal's last act before he departed was to summon an assembly of the barons and knights of Leinster to his chief fortress of Kilkenny. John of Earley urged him at this time to take hostages from among them for their good behaviour. Rather grandly, the Marshal refused, though there is reason to think that he later changed his mind about being so mild to his men. Besides, many of the barons were travelling to the king with him, and he may have thought the measure superfluous, particularly since the greatest of them had put their names to the petition against Meilyr. Their turnabout at the meeting at Woodstock with the king must have come to him as something of a shock.

The terms of his final address to his men of Leinster at Kilkenny may or may not be what he actually said, although I am inclined to think them an honest attempt by his biographer to reconstruct the speech. However, they are most evocative of his situation in 1207. He made a dramatic entry, Isabel on his arm:

> Lords! See the countess, whom I here present to you; your lady by birth, the daughter of the earl who freely enfeoffed you all when he had conquered this land. She remains amongst you, pregnant. Until God permits me to return, I pray you to keep her well and faithfully, for she is your lady, and I have nothing but through her.[46]

The accent is entirely on his wife, the Lady of Leinster, then pregnant and in need of protection. He had nothing to say about his own claims on the men of Leinster whether on his own, or more particularly, his sons' account. He was declaring in clear terms that he felt that he had no hold on his Irish tenants; he could count only on his *mesnie*. The only force that could constrain the barons and knights of Leinster was that feeling of difference that we have already observed in the 'Deeds of the English in Ireland'. It had grown up in the 1170s under Earl Richard Strongbow, and the Marshal's wife, Earl Richard's daughter, was the only channel by which he might tap it for his advantage.[47] The assembly mumbled the

---

46 *History* II, lines 13532–44.

47 One must note at this point the bizarre comments of Duby on this speech (pp. 157–8). In his interpretation, in leaving her behind, the Marshal's chief fear was that Isabel would run off with someone else and leave him empty-handed; the knights of the *mesnie* and the men of Leinster were being enjoined to keep her under close guard. He is said to have feared that she would surrender herself to some public display of dalliance with another man that would force him to divorce her and render himself penniless (he would seem to have Louis VII and Eleanor in his mind here). One can only say that if this were his secret motivation in the speech, then the events that subsequently came about must have surprised him: did the rebels of Leinster later fight to get into Kilkenny merely in order to seduce the poor, pregnant woman?

required responses of loyalty, but the jaundiced writer scoffs, 'the wicked will do or say anything'.[48]

Before he went, Meilyr 'the false' (as the *History* takes care to call him, recalling that the Marshal was in fact his lord) planned a campaign against the Marshal to be carried out as soon as he and the old earl were gone, a proxy war in which neither of the principals was directly involved. Meilyr's kinsmen and retainers assembled and, a week after the departure of the Marshal and their lord, they descended on New Ross, where the Marshal was developing a port and large borough.[49] They butchered a score of his men and burned down his granges, riding away with a haul of plunder: 'and so commenced in Leinster raids and open war'.[50] In the meantime, the Marshal received a cold welcome at court, and had to watch Meilyr and the defaulting Irish treated with pointed kindness and consequence. Meilyr followed up his advantage. He persuaded the king to allow his return to Ireland and to send letters recalling to England the three bailiffs the Marshal had left to protect his interests: John of Earley, Jordan de Sauqueville and Stephen d'Evreux.[51] They were sent around the beginning of January 1208, carried by Thomas Bloet, one of the king's brightest young household knights, a man with Irish interests himself and younger brother of one of the Marshal's own knights, Ralph. Early in January, Meilyr himself accompanied Thomas and the letters to Ireland.

Thus far, things had gone remarkably well for Meilyr. Apparently, his was one of the few boats that were able to brave the stormy crossing to Ireland in the four months after Michaelmas 1207. But on his arrival in Ireland, as the *History* points out with a fine irony, uncomfortable reality caught up with him. Subsequent events prove the truth of W.L. Warren's observation that there was only a limited amount that the king could do to influence events in Ireland. His power there was more theoretical than real, unless he came himself with a large army. Because of the storms, the Marshal's men had not received the king's instructions, and so they had had several months to work uninterrupted at the defence of their master's

---

48 *History* II, line 13550.
49 The *History* calls this place *la Novele vile* (i.e. 'Newtown'). Meyer thought it might be Newtown-Barry, Co. Wexford, but that place cannot be linked to the demesne of the Lord of Leinster. The Marshal's foundation of New Ross, Co. Wexford, however, would be as likely to be called 'the New Town' in its early days, and pillaging it would be a very good way to score a direct hit on the Marshal's prestige. New Ross was already in being when the foundation charter of Tintern Parva was issued (*Acts and Letters*, no. 95, pp. 175–8), and it is likely that the Marshal and his advisers had begun its construction during the visit of 1200.
50 *History* II, lines 13573–4.
51 Enrolments of these letters do not survive, unfortunately. We do know that they were sent, however, for there is a reference in February 1208 to John of Earley's contumacy in ignoring them. They were said to have been dispatched 'two months and more' before 20 February. The *History* also indicates that they were sent at some time in early January 1208. See *Rot. Clausarum* I, p. 103.

interests. They had been able to make some resistance to Meilyr's men and had one of his favourite knights in prison.

When he arrived, Meilyr contrived a meeting with the opposition and, with a triumphant flourish, he caused Thomas Bloet to hand over to the Marshal's men the letters recalling them. They drew aside to have them read out and pondered their significance, knowing their lands would be forfeit if they did not comply. John of Earley gave it as his opinion that they would be dishonoured if they gave up the position of trust in which their lord had left them. Stephen d'Evreux thought that the king might do as he pleased with their English lands, rather than they be shamed before God in giving up their charges. All agreed to stay put come what may, and Jordan de Sauqueville proposed outflanking Meilyr by negotiating assistance from Hugh de Lacy, Earl of Ulster, with whom the Marshal had been working against Meilyr the previous year. They returned to Thomas Bloet and said firmly that they would not do that for which they would be scorned.

'Let us not complain of the game if we lose land and honour; better that than to lose land, honour *and* the love of our lord.'[52] This, according to the *History*, was what Earley said, and indeed he may well have done so. They were brave sentiments, the sort that men of the age respected. The men stating them were remarkable men, and as knights of the *mesnie* in a position of particular closeness to their lord. However, it would not do to think that such warlike loyalty was typical of the age. Others were not so selfless. Philip of Prendergast, their former colleague, had returned with Meilyr to Ireland, and he was captured on the other side in the subsequent campaign.

The Marshal, in the meantime, was without news from Ireland, and closeted with an insecure king who feared him. It was, as the *History* says, his 'hour of great danger'.[53] From January to March 1208, he was in the most difficult position he was ever to know at court. We do not need the *History* to tell us at this point that he behaved with a coolness that was remarkable. It was the sort of politic reticence that kept his men in awe of him. The Marshal was with the king at Guildford on 25 January 1208, a fortnight or so after Meilyr, Thomas Bloet and others had made the crossing back to Ireland. No news could filter back, for, as the *History* tells us, the crossing was too stormy until early in February. Lack of real news did not hinder the king's malice against William, however. The *History* gives a vivid portrayal of the harassment kept up by the king against his former favourite. In a fit of ill-natured petulance, the king sidled up to him and asked whether he had news from Leinster. The Marshal said he had not. With a snigger, the king announced to the Marshal that he had heard that there had been a siege of Kilkenny. The Marshal's *mesnie* had been caught in the open, and in attempting to relieve the place and free the countess Stephen d'Evreux and Ralph fitz Payn had been killed outright

---

52 *History* II, lines 13727–32.
53 *History* II, line 13585.

while John of Earley had been mortally wounded and had died later. The whole court was as astonished as the Marshal, for everyone must have known that there could have been no such news. The king, however, in his fevered desire to torment the impassive Marshal, was willing to say anything to get a reaction. The reaction that he did get did not suit him. In the sudden silence that must have surrounded the men, the Marshal said, 'What a pity about the knights, sire, for they were your men too, which makes the business all the more regrettable.'[54] The king (blushing and ruffled perhaps) said, 'I will think about it.'

The incident is one of those in the *History* that has the ring of truth, despite what seems at first sight to be something of contrivance in it. It opposes a most uncourtly king to its courtly hero and has the king ignominiously worsted by his own undisguised malice. But there is other evidence of such petty harassment. The king at this time had his officers take in hand all the lands of John of Earley and Stephen d'Evreux, whether held directly from him or others. He was, however, particular to confide such lands to the lords from whom they had been held. This was only proper, according to ideas of the time, but it also gave him an opportunity to boast of what he had done. A letter was duly sent to William on 20 February (which must have been before news of Meilyr's defeat had reached England) to inform him what had been done, particularly to John of Earley, whom everyone knew to be as close to the Marshal as one of his sons:

> I want you to know that I have delivered to you the lands I confiscated from John of Earley, which he held from you [probably a reference to Earlytown, Co. Kilkenny]. I took away his lands because more than two months ago I instructed him to come to me and he did not do so. I very much want you to produce both him and the others I summoned before me, as is right and proper. I need them here for my own business, and I will keep their lands until they surrender to me.[55]

After the beginning of Lent (23 February in 1208), ships began to reach the mainland from Ireland. The news they brought was uncomfortable to the king. Meilyr had gone down before a coalition of the Lacy family and the Marshal's adherents in Ireland, but not without a great fight. It was a war that had raged across Leinster and Munster, and which, according to the Irish annals, had been very savage. Meilyr at one point had the countess under siege in the new castle of Kilkenny. But in the end, he was driven off, his lands and castles had been seized and the justiciar himself had been captured. He had submitted to Countess Isabel and given his son as a hostage for his good behaviour. Philip of Prendergast and the knights of Leinster who had sided with Meilyr had also come to terms, likewise surrendering their children, or younger brothers if they had no offspring, to the countess.

---

54 *History* II, lines 13846–51.
55 *Rot. Clausarum* I, p. 103.

The king was very much afflicted by this news, according to the *History*. Yet he managed to bring himself, nonetheless, to be philosophical about the defeat of his minister. In part, that was because William gave him a way out. King and Marshal met at Bristol some time in the first week of March. The Marshal kept up his front, giving no clue in his behaviour that he had heard the news and, when the king asked him, pretended ignorance. The king had the dubious pleasure of breaking the good news to the Marshal, yet seems to have carried it off with some nonchalance. He had resumed the courtly pose whose shattering some weeks previously had so startled the court. The Marshal, too, was courtly in reply. He muffled his delight and replied temperately: 'Sire, I thank Our Lord. But I had no idea when I left Ireland that there was a man there who wanted to make war on me!'[56] The king smiled, he may even have taken the remark as a joke. The Marshal was happy to pretend ingenuous frankness, for in pretending he allowed the king enough face to be able to retrieve his position. The court scented the new mood and suddenly the Marshal was again the object of deference and respect.

On 18 March at Marlborough, where in fact William may well have been born, the king and he came to a formal agreement. The Marshal was to surrender Leinster to the king and receive it back on new terms, limiting his jurisdiction in some respects from what it had been: a strategic concession to allow the king to claim a victory of sorts.[57] William had in fact conceded the basic principle he knew the king had wanted, the same rights as king within Leinster as he had within Wiltshire. The king was willing, however, to concede that the Lord of Leinster had the right to the wardship of his vassals, even if they held lands elsewhere, so compromise was in the air. Some weeks later, Walter de Lacy did the same. Three days after the agreement, Meilyr was briskly told to give Uí Failge back to the Marshal.[58] The Marshal's dangerous time had come to an end. No difficulty was made about the Marshal's return to Ireland in the summer of 1208, although it may have been at this point, rather than the previous year, that he was asked to hand over his son, Richard, as security for his good behaviour (see above). Meilyr's subsequent disgrace was permanent. He was still in office in June 1208 (the Marshal was then still in England). But by early 1209, Meilyr had been replaced by John's loyal friend and clerk, John de Grey, Bishop of Norwich, for whom the appointment was very convenient, as England was under an interdict and most of the other English bishops had fled to Scotland or France.[59] Meilyr lived on for another 11 years, but he was

---

56 *History* II, lines 13923–6.
57 A superior version of the agreement to that recorded in the royal enrolment (*Rot. Chartarum*, p. 176) has been found in the records of Christchurch Dublin, and is now published in *Acts and Letters*, pp. 479–81.
58 *Rot. Patentium*, p. 80.
59 Meilyr was still justiciar on 19 June 1208, when the king sent 'his beloved and faithful' Ailbe, Bishop of Ferns, Meilyr fitz Henry, his justiciar, and Philip of Worcester to negotiate with the Irish kings, *Rot. Patentium*, p. 84. The pipe rolls do not record the crossing to Ireland of his successor Bishop John de Grey of Norwich and his followers (in eight ships) until what seems to be early 1209, *Pipe Roll of 11 John*, p. 58.

not left in peace. His great castle of Dunamase in his Leinster lordship of Loígis was taken from him at some point, probably after his defeat by Countess Isabel's forces, and then retained by the king, nor was his son and namesake allowed to succeed to his lands, on the alleged grounds of his illegitimacy.[60]

As for William Marshal, when he returned he may have wanted to do no more than retire for a period to Ireland. It may not have been a place of great tranquillity in the early thirteenth century, but he had as good a cause to be as disenchanted with the court as such rarified and ironic spirits as John of Salisbury or Peter de Blois. Aged now over 60, the Marshal needed a rest. So he returned to Kilkenny, a retirement plan of restructuring his Irish lordship and imposing himself on his wayward tenants seeming to be his main concern. Unfortunately, the Irish Sea was no barrier to the shockwaves of the growing political crisis of John's reign in England, which would seek him out even in Kilkenny.

60 *History* II, lines 14123–5. Dunamase was in the king's hands in 1211 (after William Marshal was forced to hand it over to the king in 1210 at Dublin, *History* II, lines 14319–72), but in 1216, after John's death, when Marshal was in power as regent, it was restored to the lordship of Leinster, as Flanagan points out, 'Defining lordships', pp. 54–5.

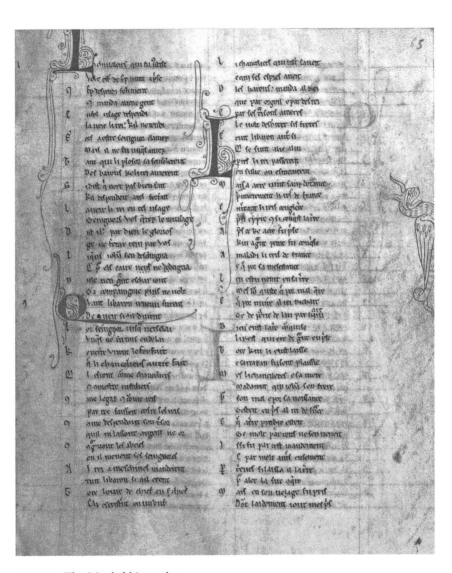

FIGURE 1 The Marshal biography

A folio from the only surviving medieval manuscript of the History, dating to the second half of the thirteenth century. It is itself a copy of one of the author's original drafts. It is probably a product of an urban workshop. The copyist takes care to get the number of lines right by checking off the beginning of each couplet with the proper initial before returning to copy out the rest so as to limit the risk of missing a line

FIGURE 2 The Resafa cup

A silver armorial cup was discovered at Resafa in Syria in 1982. It had been manufactured early in the thirteenth century for the Coucy family, great barons of the Remois in Northern France, as can be worked out from the heraldry with which it is engraved (pictured here), and had subsequently been taken to the Crusader states. It is a rare survivor of the display of plate which every great family commissioned for use in their halls, and is the sort of item great lords might offer as gifts or prizes in their tournament culture. The heraldry includes that of William des Barres, the Marshal's rival, and the range of identifiable shields may indicate that it was in fact commissioned for a tourney event in Picardy

FIGURE 3 Cartmel Priory

Cartmel priory church is the one survivor of the Marshal's pious works. Although he founded it for the good of his soul in 1189 on a royal estate he had enjoyed since 1186, it is unlikely he often visited it. The fabric of the present priory church is mostly later than his time

FIGURE 4 Seal of Walter fitz Robert

This remarkable seal impression depicts the baron, Walter fitz Robert, a member of the great Anglo-Norman house of Clare. It can be dated on stylistic grounds to the 1150s and is a detailed representation of a lord as he would have appeared on the tournament field of William Marshal's day: marked out from common knights by a display of the heraldry of his dynasty displayed prominently on shield and horse trappers. Note the streamers fixed to the back of his helmet and wrist designed to whip out in the wind of his passage in the great charge of the tournament

FIGURE 5 Pembroke Castle

The great round keep of Pembroke Castle (on left) was probably commissioned by the Marshal to mark his acquisition of the fortress in the autumn of 1200. It was built on a huge scale, perhaps inspired by several great donjon towers being built across Northern France in the late twelfth century

FIGURE 6 Chepstow Castle

The double-towered gatehouse (on right) has been recently dated to the time of the Marshal acquisition of Chepstow castle in 1189. Its surviving doors were fashioned of timber that can be dated on dendrochronological grounds to have been felled between 1159 and 1189, while the gatehouse itself was associated with a coin of the mid 1180s. The likelihood is that it was built in 1189 or very soon afterwards. It tells us that the Marshal disposed of a remarkable amount of capital in the year he married Isabel of Striguil

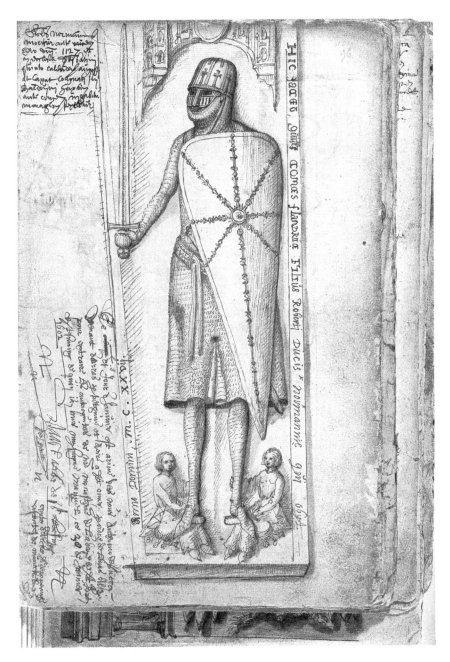

FIGURE 7 Tomb: William Clito, Count of Flanders (died 1128)

This drawing is of the lost tomb effigy of Count William, eldest grandson of William the Conqueror. It was once in the abbey of St Bertin of St-Omer, and can be dated on stylistic grounds to the 1170s. It depicts the count in the up to date armour of the very time that William Marshal rode the tournament fields of Northern France, the same as described by Ralph Niger in 1187 (see pp. 199-200). Note the visor plate fixed to his helmet, just the sort of face protection that we know William Marshal pioneered

WILLIAM MARSHAL
first Earl of Pembroke (died 1219)

FIGURE 8 Tomb: William Marshal (Temple Church)

The tomb traditionally identified with William Marshal in the Temple Church in London is one of the earliest examples of a military effigy used as a ledger stone to cap a burial. Earlier custom was to depict a dead nobleman in civilian dress, but within the Marshal's own lifetime the Church began to relax restrictions on the burial of noblemen within churches in the guise of knights in part because of the impact of the idea of crusading knighthood

FIGURE 9 Magna Carta 1216

This is the reissue of Magna Carta sanctioned by the council held in November 1216, following the coronation of King Henry III. It was sealed by William Marshal and the cardinal legate, Guala Bicchieri. This copy is the one sent north to Durham cathedral, where it survives still in the archives. Though the Marshal seal has become detached and was lost, a cast of it was taken

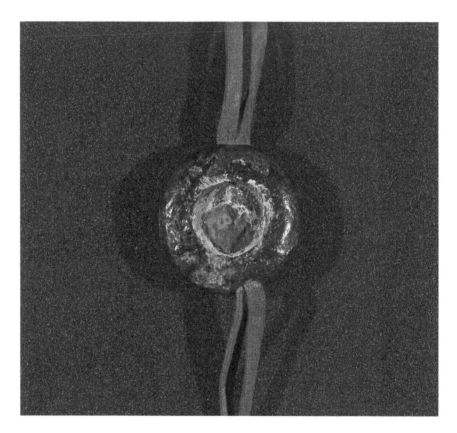

FIGURE 10 Seal of William Marshal

Of all the manifestations of the Marshal's personality, his eight surviving seal impressions are some of the most peculiar. We know that he used the same seal throughout his career as a knight, at the very least from 1189, never changing the matrix or updating it to reflect his status as a magnate, an earl or as Regent of England. It is not just modest, but tiny in relation to those of his fellows. Since he cannot have done it though parsimony, it must be that he preferred to keep it in modest courtliness, or possibly even because it was a gift from his beloved Young King when he created him a knight banneret in 1179

6

THE DUEL WITH KING JOHN

The Marshal lived in Ireland for the best part of the next four years, but it was hardly in retirement. He made reforms in Leinster. He made a point of settling many of his retainers in lands near Kilkenny: Mallardstown (from William Mallard, a prominent sergeant of his) and Earlytown (from John of Earley), Co. Kilkenny, still recall some of his grants. Other grants came the way of his loyal knights: Ralph Bloet, William le Gros, Thomas of Rochford, Nicholas Avenel, Stephen d'Evreux, Jordan de Sauqueville and Henry Hose. It was in Ireland that many of his political affinity became his tenants for the first time.

The older colonists of Leinster who had opposed him had a thin time by contrast. The Marshal received them on his return to Leinster with withering coldness. David de la Roch, one of the rebels and one of the barons of Leinster who had sold out to King John and Meilyr in 1207–1208, was made a butt of routine humiliation by the Marshal affinity for many years thereafter. Once, Peter fitz Herbert, a Marshal ally in the south-west, publicly snubbed him by refusing to sit next to him at a council in England. Philip of Prendergast's treachery was particularly shocking, as he had been welcomed into the Marshal affinity in 1190 and occupied a leading position there in England and France, presumably because of his Irish expertise and influence. His sons remained with third parties in England as hostages for his good behaviour until at least 1215.[1] Tellingly, William Marshal disciplined him the same way as King John disciplined his barons, and indeed the Marshal himself, a strategy for which John was much criticised. If the Marshal could take punishment, he was also capable of giving it out, for he had learned well from his masters.

The Marshal had returned to Ireland to conduct some punitory raids on the Irish as part of a reconciliation plan worked out with the king. He may well have done

1 *Rot. Patentium*, pp. 123, 144.

so for he was pledged to expand his lordship of Kilkenny westward to the borders of Munster and exert greater control over Uí Chennselaig and the diocese of Ferns, areas of Irish lordship; we know for certain of a bitter campaign in the west of the island in 1212.[2] In an epitaph composed on the Marshal, which was preserved by Matthew Paris, he was made to say, 'I am he who was a Saturn to Ireland, the sun to England, a Mercury to Normandy and a Mars to France.' Meaning, in the first case, that he had been 'a brutal subjugator' (as Matthew Paris put it) towards the Irish.[3] That the Marshal was none too keen on the Irish is evident enough. He was an accommodating enough patron to the English bishops in Leinster: the Archbishop of Dublin, the Bishop of Glendalough and the Bishop of Ossory. The last, in particular, had significant grants and concessions from him. If there were differences with the other bishops, they were at least allowed amicable settlements.

On the other hand, the Bishop of Ferns, a Cistercian by the name of Ailbe (Latinised as 'Albinus') Ua Máel Muaid, got nothing from him but harassment. In part, this was political retribution, for Bishop Ailbe had been a close ally of John since before he was king and before the Marshal came to Ireland. His loyalty was to John, and we may imagine he was enthused by John's programme of removing Irish bishops from the influence of the Irish magnates. But there is a certain enthusiasm in the Marshal's persecution of Ailbe that indicates a more personal motivation. The Marshal's lands in Ireland were under interdict by the Archbishops of Dublin and Tuam before the end of John's reign as a consequence of his treatment of Ailbe. The case shuttled between the royal court and Rome until the Marshal contrived to evade Church jurisdiction early in 1218. Nonetheless, when he died, the Marshal was under excommunication by Bishop Ailbe for violently seizing and withholding two episcopal estates. Matthew Paris appears to have either met the bishop – who was often in England – or someone else who had, and felt a certain sympathy for him; he believed the excommunication to have been 'not undeserved'.[4]

In his Irish policies, we can at last see the Marshal as ruler, rather than as courtier and soldier. His lordship of Leinster had come to grief in 1207, when many of his vassals rebelled against him. There can be little doubt that this crisis disturbed him, for he acted with typical decision and, we may say, harshness once he had the upper hand. One cannot help recalling the way his father had dominated north Wiltshire in Stephen's reign. William chastised and terrorised those who came within his sphere and who opposed him. His men, monks and burgesses were settled on the land in order to secure it. Amicable agreements secured the goodwill of his powerful neighbours, the Lacys. Whatever naivety he may have had at the outset of his career as a magnate, the Marshal had lost it by 1208.

---

2 *Ibid.*, p. 80; *Annals of Loch Cé*, ed. W.M. Hennessy (2 vols, Rolls Series, 1871) I, pp. 247–8.

3 *Chronica Maiora*, ed. H.R. Luard (7 vols, Rolls Series, 1884–1889) III, p. 43: '*Fuit enim Hibernicis nocivus edomitor*'.

4 *Ibid.*, IV, pp. 492–3.

The Irish War of 1210

The Marshal's first confrontation with King John ended with the reconciliation of March 1208, but it was not by any means the end of his problems with the king. John's ambition to exalt royal power in Ireland remained on his agenda, and not long after William's return to Leinster its consequences fatally entangled not just William, but also his allies, the Lacy brothers. The catalyst was the fate of John's former favourite, William de Briouze, whom the king had decided to cast off in 1207, in a brutal act of ingratitude. The king – in his legalistic way – was later to dictate a memorandum to posterity to justify his persecution of Briouze between 1207 and 1210, and it reveals him at his mendacious, pedantic and self-righteous worst.[5]

Ignoring the fact that he had himself set up Briouze by making him a poor bargain in his grant of a lordship in Thomond in 1201, as well as glossing over the deceitful and peremptory actions that threatened to dispossess Briouze of Limerick and the lordship in 1206–1207 and the subsequent proxy war he let loose on Briouze through Meilyr fitz Henry, John tells us that he was in fact the offended party. John claims his grievance against William de Briouze lay in William's ceasing to pay the 5,000 marks maybe in late 1203 for the possession of the Irish lordship, despite negotiating several extensions on the debt. Nor, said the king, had Briouze paid anything for the farm of the city of Limerick, other than a £100 loan he had offered the king in his last stay at Rouen in 1203. The long-suffering king finally began decisive moves intended, he said, to bring about discussion and a resolution of the grievance.

A conference at Gloucester in April 1208 between the king, Briouze and his friends led to the surrender of some of his lordships until the debt was paid, but John showed his vindictive pettiness by adding 1,000 marks to the debt because of the expenses he had to go through to bring Briouze to the table. His vindicatory pamphlet fails to mention that particular peevish act. But Briouze failed to surrender his sons and those of his tenants, as had been agreed. In September 1208, after William Marshal had settled his own difficulties with the king and returned to Ireland, a by now desperate Briouze gathered a force to try to liberate his Welsh castles from their royal garrisons, defying the king in rebellion since he had no other leverage to use. Failing in that, he sacked Leominster, Herefordshire, but finding no wider support in England or the Marches he fled as an outlaw with his family to Ireland.[6]

The king's pamphlet against Briouze confirms that William Marshal was one of those who received Briouze and his family in Ireland, sheltering him for a short

---

5 See for this document and its chronology now, D. Crouch, 'The complaint of King John against William de Briouze (c.September 1210)', in *The England of King John and Magna Carta*, ed. J. Loengard (Boydell, 2010), pp. 168–79.

6 For the best interpretation of this complicated affair, see now Veach, 'King John and royal control, 1051–1078', *English Historical Review*, 129 (2014), pp. 1051–78.

period in the winter of 1208–1209, when he took him in on Briouze's landing at Wicklow. Marshal may well have felt bound to do so because of what he owed to the Lacy family, into which Briouze had married his daughter and with whom Briouze eventually found a more permanent shelter.[7] There, Briouze and his family sheltered for the best part of two years, with the active complicity of Marshal and the Lacys, who made no response to royal writs demanding his arrest. John could do no more at that point, as he had already experienced the uncomfortable ability of the Irish magnates to resist his will. The Lacy brothers were further bolstering their ability to resist the king in the aftermath of John's first attempt against them. In the course of the year 1209, they were the first of John's barons to open negotiations with King Philip of France, offering their military support for an invasion of England.[8] It was a scheme that King Philip had been pursuing fitfully since 1205; it was his decisive and final answer to the threat of the Angevin dynasty that had so humiliated his father and him. He would follow them to England and destroy them utterly.

In June 1210, King John landed in Ireland, and changed the nature of the conflict there. For Marshal and Briouze, the game was up. Even before the king embarked in Pembrokeshire for the crossing, both men crossed over to join the king and sought a settlement. There was a public showdown at Dublin later, where the king presented charges against Marshal, but the slight degree of his danger can be seen in the fact that leading courtiers such as Geoffrey fitz Peter were not afraid to stand up and offer themselves as pledges for his conduct. Although the king reserved some harsh words for what he considered the Marshal's lukewarm support, and took three hostages from his *mesnie* and the Castle of Dunamase, there was no trial or conviction.

The two Lacy brothers were banished even though Walter offered to submit. Hugh de Lacy fled to a new life in the south of France. Briouze's fate was rather less happy even than theirs. The king offered him a settlement on exorbitant terms, but rather than accept it Briouze holed up in Wales and attempted to run an insurgency, which seems to have had pitifully little support. Following the king's great success in his military tour of Ireland that summer, and the arrest of his wife and family as they attempted to cross the Irish Sea to flee to Scotland, Briouze sought refuge at King Philip's court. It was there that he heard the news of the tragic death in imprisonment that winter of 1210–1211 of his wife and eldest son, deaths that John's enemies were all too happy to claim were not accidental.

The dissident barons leaving England for the Capetian court would soon bring other circumstantial stories of John's unnatural vices: his supposed murder of his nephew Arthur, his unrestrained sexual assaults on young and noble girls at his court, and his open irreligiosity. It was propaganda that would all assist Philip's

---

7 The Marshal's own excuses for his actions are hardly convincing: he claimed not to know that Briouze was at odds with the king; he also claimed he had been obliged to shelter Briouze because Briouze was his lord – a claim nobody has successfully fathomed.

8 C. Veach, *Lordship in Four Realms* (Manchester, 2014), pp. 138–40.

case that John must be replaced as king of England, and if by anyone, why not his own son, the Lord Louis, husband of a granddaughter of King Henry II, and thus – in the irregular succession custom of England – a valid candidate for the throne?

The road back to favour

King John ended 1210 undoubted lord of the British Isles, and stronger than he had been since the crisis of 1204, despite the continuing interdict. In August 1212, however, the glory of that success had dimmed, despite further dramatic successes against the Welsh of Gwynedd. The king got wind of a plot among certain of the northern barons to assassinate him, and it seems to have come as a dramatic blow to his confidence. He became – we are told – rather more responsive and accommodating to his barons, a party of whom were now prominent at the court of King Philip. He began to address their complaints, which it seems were not unknown to him.

In Ireland, William Marshal began to experience a change of mood from the royal court. The loyalty of which he was such an icon was now a quality of such value that it overrode even John's personal distaste for the old earl. In 1211, William was named as one of the guarantors of the king's treaty with the defeated Prince Llywelyn of Gwynedd. William had just helped by loyally assisting the justiciar in the suppression of a rising by the native Irish. Rather artfully, late in the summer of 1212, when the crisis had broken, he had bolstered the king's peace of mind by getting the Irish barons to write to the king pledging their support. He knew all too well the king's paranoia and how vulnerable it might make him to manipulation, as he had himself been the victim of it. He himself wrote, offering to come to England to help in person and volunteering advice on the king's problems with the Pope. He chose his moment well, as the king's reply most feelingly tells us:

> I have thanked by letter my barons and men of Ireland for their good and faithful service and for the oath of fidelity they lately swore to me; but I do not doubt that it was by your counsel and motivation, as much as that of the carrier of the letters, that the assurance was made. By your good will I have all other men well-disposed in this business, so I am the readier to give you my thanks. I add to these thanks for your willingness to come to me in England, but I cannot allow you my permission at the moment. The bishop of Norwich [the Irish justiciar], who time and again by letter and messenger praised your loyal counsel and assistance, cannot spare your presence, so necessary to him in Ireland at the moment. I ask you to stay there, helping the bishop to maintain my interests, so that at a later time I might renew my eternal gratitude to you [sic]. I send you a copy of letters my English magnates made for me, and I ask you to seal a similar letter, along with my other barons of Ireland . . . You should better provide for your boy, who is with me and lacks horses and a robe. I will provide what he needs at my

own cost, if you agree, and I will hand him over to one of your knights (perhaps John of Earley, or one of his men). If you want it otherwise, let me know by letter that he is to stay with the court and that you will answer for what I pay in the boy's expenses. I will provide it in any case, and have the money from you when I can. Do not believe what was said to you about my wanting to send the boy into Poitou. I never had any such intention. I never even heard of such an idea until the justiciar told me about it.[9]

The letter is a rare insight into relations between John and one of his great magnates at a critical point. The fact that these sentiments were written at all tells how much store the king was suddenly willing to put by good relations with the Marshal. Here, John was putting his need and gratitude for William's support on the record. He was giving the Marshal a stick with which he might be beaten later. He even carefully adds the little domestic details of young Richard Marshal, the son currently being held at court (now a young knight and in need of horses and the requisite garments). The letter seeks to create, or at least project, a warm family atmosphere between king and magnate. The king denied rumours that he had meant to take the boy to Poitou without his father's permission in the campaign that had earlier been planned for that year: perhaps a last attempt to needle the Marshal, from which he now wanted to distance himself. We know that initially in the summer of 1212, John had suspected the Marshal's complicity in the plot and he had demanded Richard Marshal from his father at that point.[10] Harsh words may well have been said then around the court that must now be unsaid.

Everything was arranged as the letter suggested. Richard Marshal was delivered to John of Earley, who himself began to benefit from the Marshal's return to favour just as he had suffered when his lord was out of favour. He was entrusted with the county of Devon and named marshal of the royal household (according to the *History*).[11] The king's mood towards his barons had indeed softened considerably as a result of the shock of the conspiracy. The Marshal was one of many who was to benefit from the king's sudden need for friends. He did as he was asked in the king's letter and organised the petition from the barons of Ireland, which the king

---

9 *Rot. Clausarum* I, p. 132.
10 *Rot. Clausarum* I, p. 122: the king ordered a naval demonstration off North Wales to discourage Welsh adventurism at this point, but also warned that his commander 'must ever be vigilant that no harm be worked against you from the lands or jurisdiction of Earl William Marshal', see comments in J.C. Holt, *The Northerners* (Oxford, 1961), p. 83 and n. The *History*'s assertion that the king held both the Marshal's sons at this time is dubious (lines 14526–78). He had certainly taken Richard in 1208, but must have returned him, asking him again in the summer of 1212. In the meantime, he had probably held the younger William at court, but in the summer of 1212 he must have already released William to be married to Alice de Béthune, which may be why Richard was demanded instead that summer, see *Acts and Letters*, pp. 22–3.
11 In fact, this episode may have been a confirmation of the royal chamberlainship that John's grandfather and father had held.

wanted, in support of the king against the Pope, with whom he was edging towards a peace settlement.

It was in May 1213 that the king decided that he needed the Marshal more in England than in Ireland. He was especially needed because there was a widespread refusal among the English barons to turn out for military service. A summons brought the Marshal (and allegedly some 500 Irish knights) to Kent, now threatened with seaborne invasion by King Philip. The *History* remarks with approval, tinged with a little astonishment, on the judicious conduct of its hero: 'He took no heed of what had gone before with the king, nor his cruelty, because ever he loved loyalty.'[12] The good Marshal, the impassive and detached courtier, seems even to have been beyond the comprehension of his faithful knights at times.

After his return to England, the Marshal was continually busy working at upholding the failing fortunes of his king. His support for John never faltered, and with the Earl of Chester he seems to have grown in importance to the king as others dropped away. The spate of rewards to him from the king increased in the same way as they had during the previous golden years of high favour between 1199 and 1204. The fortress and port of Haverford within Pembrokeshire was made over to him by a grateful king in October 1213. He was restored to his position of dominance in South Wales. The king gave him back the keeping of Cardigan, and added Carmarthen and Gower. This advanced the Marshal's fortunes in Wales beyond even what they had been in 1207. During the Marshal's period of disgrace, John had placed his loyal, and hated, officer, Faulkes de Breauté, in control of royal interests in the southern March. This position was now to be the Marshal's, in augmentation of his already considerable lands in the region. It is no exaggeration to say that he emerged from his period in the wilderness stronger than he had been at the peak of his influence with King John in 1204, virtually justiciar of the March.

For a while, things went very well for the king. A naval victory by the English fleet at Damme in 1213 removed the immediate threat of invasion. What was more, the king took the line with the Pope that the Marshal (and many others) had advised in 1212. He submitted, and as a result found himself the favoured son of Innocent III. There were general promises made of reform to the barons, which for a while placated them. It seemed that John's fortunes had turned. He optimistically prepared for the reconquest of Normandy and his other lost lands. He sailed for Poitou, his great army including a large force of Marshal knights, led by young Richard Marshal in his father's stead. John had insisted on it, to his father's undisguised unhappiness. Unfortunately for John, the shattering defeat by King Philip of his ally and nephew, the Emperor Otto IV, at Bouvines in July 1214 crippled his ambitious plan. He returned to England discredited and morose, at the mercy of the barons whom he had for so long oppressed financially and politically. In the ever-memorable words of Professor James Holt: 'the road from Bouvines to Runnymede was direct, short and unavoidable'.[13]

---

12 *History* II, lines 14588–90.
13 *The Northerners*, p. 100.

Magna Carta

William Marshal was now, at the age of 67, a venerable figure, held in deep respect not just for what he was, but for the living link he represented with the great days of the Angevin hegemony of north-western Europe. He made a prestigious and effective chief negotiator for the king. His imperturbable loyalty was a most necessary anchor for the party we can now call the royalists.[14] We are at a loss for his actual thoughts about the rights and wrongs of the situation (although John of Earley might well have known them). The *History*, for good reason, refuses repeatedly to talk about the royalist and rebel barons' motives. It would have been difficult for its author to do so. His chief patron, the second Earl William Marshal, had fought against John in the war, while the elder William, his father, had been for the king. Far better for the poet to gloss over the whole question.[15]

The king and his officers and advisers were shaken by Bouvines, and two days after the news of the battle reached John messages were already speeding out from him to his men, getting them prepared for the worst. Gradually, disaffection spread south from the core of opposition in the north of England. Many barons, even loyal ones, did not meet payments they owed the king. Even so great and iconic an Angevin bureaucrat as Earl Saher de Quincy of Winchester embraced rebellion. Troops were recruited by the king from Poitou and dispatched to England. Royal castles were hastily provisioned; siege machines constructed. England was a disturbed anthill of military activity in a way it had not been since the so-called 'Leicester War' of 1174, when the earls had risen and the Scots and Flemings invaded (the Marshal was by now one of the very few surviving magnates who had been an actor in the events of that year). There can be no doubt that John expected the worst in the autumn and winter of 1214, and was getting prepared for it, even though the barons' demands were not formally put to him until January 1215 at London.

William Marshal, alone among the lay magnates, stood surety in the London negotiations for the king's good intentions when John persuaded the meeting to postpone discussion until after Easter (19 April) 1215. William was delegated by the king (along with the Archbishop of Canterbury and other bishops) to meet the northern barons at Oxford on 22 February. But the meeting was arranged at short notice, and might never have happened. On 27 April, William and the archbishop were again deployed to meet with the barons who had finally lost patience and had gathered in arms. They were to receive the demands of the rebels, but, when they brought them back, John would have none of them. At Brackley, Northamptonshire (the chief residence of the dissident Earl of Winchester) on 5 May 1215, they sealed letters of defiance to the king (as William Marshal had himself done in 1173 on defying Henry II). When the barons heard John would not

---

14 The term 'royalists' (*regales*) was applied to Stephen's supporters in the civil war of his reign. *Realx* (king's men) was the name applied to men of the royal *mesnie* in the reign of Henry II, and it was the cry of the Marshal's men at the Battle of Lincoln in 1217.
15 Painter, *Marshal*, p. 180, makes this same point.

negotiate, they broke camp at Brackley and marched to besiege the royal castle of Northampton. Their banners were unfurled on the march, a signal that open war was now in progress.

At this point, the Marshal ceased being a negotiator and was sent off to rally royalist support; perhaps, as Painter suggests, he was sent to raise his affinity in the south-west. It is likely enough that the security the Marshal affinity offered him was at least part of the reason why the king operated from the southern March and the south-west in the years of the war. In the meantime, the war abruptly ended, almost in an act of farce. The barons unexpectedly turned south and, with the connivance of the citizens, seized London. This was a fatal stroke against the king, for London was already regarded as the capital of the kingdom, and most of the machinery of government rested in Westminster. The king and the few remaining royalists retreated on Winchester, and prepared to surrender on terms, for there was nothing else to do.

When the Marshal returned to the king's side, it was to resume the role of middleman once more. The king was already beaten, for the seizure of London had led to mass defections to the barons. William Marshal was prominent in the negotiations that led up to the sealing of Magna Carta at Runnymede on 15 June (although it is highly unlikely that he was the joint author of the charter, as Painter wished to believe). What is more, it was he who was sent to London to announce the king's surrender to the barons' terms.

The *History* has nothing to say on the Magna Carta War (other than to assure the reader that its hero took no part in the baronial seizure of London). Partly this may well be because the charter and the brief baronial victory of June–July 1215 did not have much significance when viewed from the author's standpoint in the mid-1220s. Partly also it may be because of the position of the younger William Marshal in June 1215. As a demonstration of his importance, some sources already attribute to the younger William the style of 'earl' long before his father's death. He was now in his mid-twenties, a baron in his own right, a married man who now himself employed a notorious *mesnie* of hard-bitten knights and who had raised his own banner. He would soon be a widower. His first wife, Alice, daughter of the elder Marshal's friend Baldwin de Béthune, had been packed off to Flanders and her relations there during the emergency of that summer. She returned under safe conduct from the king in autumn 1215 after the failure of the Magna Carta settlement. She was dead probably by the next year, perhaps through complications during a pregnancy. His foundation of a chantry for her soul was most likely made in London in 1216, before Young William abandoned the Capetian cause.[16]

---

16 *Pipe Roll of 17 John*, pp. 40, 43; *Chronica Maiora* II, p. 605. This was not by accident; contemporary society credited men as 'earls' more loosely than was done in subsequent centuries. Henry, the bastard son of Earl Reginald of Cornwall, calls himself earl in his charters at this time, although indeed he was never created earl by the king. Matthew Paris calls the same Henry earl, showing that the practice was general. For Alice's movements, *Rot. Patentium*, p. 156; *Acts and Letters*, nos. 164–5.

The Young Marshal, for unknown reasons, took the baronial side at some time in May or June 1215, and was named by Matthew Paris as one of the 25 barons who were to monitor the king's performance of his obligations.[17] He was to be an adherent on the rebel side until after the king's death. The *History* attempts to pass over the Young Marshal's flirtation with rebellion. This indicates some later sensitivity and embarrassment about it in Marshal circles. We can only guess what his father thought about it, but some of the guesses that can be made are seductive. Might the old Marshal have been so devious as to actually encourage his son to go with the barons, to act as his informant and insurance in case the king went down beneath his troubles? The compiler of the Worcester annals certainly believed that the elder and younger Marshals were in collusive communication, even though on opposite sides, late in 1216.[18] It is an entertaining but unprovable suggestion, though even Painter found it irresistible (however, he was sure it was never a conscious scheme on his hero's part). Bearing in mind the Marshal's other exploits in duality (particularly his tightrope walk between John and Richard in the early 1190s and John and Philip in 1205), I would not have put it past him at all; indeed, there is reason to believe that he was repeating a stratagem he had used many years earlier. If the elder and younger Marshals were in clandestine concert in 1215, then the situation was very like that between the two Marshal brothers, John and William, in 1190–1194: one Count John's man, the other Richard's.

Magna Carta, as a means of averting open war between royalists and rebels, was an unfortunate failure, and from the perspective of the Marshal biographer in 1224, less than a decade later, it had little significance. But the Marshal himself might not have been so dismissive of the document. He had been closely involved in the negotiations that crafted it. He and his like may have been the reason why some of the briefing papers that survive concerning it were presented in French. Over the next couple of years, his behaviour reveals that William had some faith in the settlement he had agreed with his friends in the rebel party, and that would be a conviction that was to have an incalculable effect on British history.

We do have a contemporary verdict on Magna Carta, written up by a Flemish political commentator who visited England at this time (a man called by historians 'the Anonymous of Béthune'). The settlement clearly fascinated him, and he spends some time giving his (unfavourable) opinion on it. He singles out three particular issues about Magna Carta he had picked up on his travels and conversations in England: disparagement, forest offences and limits on the size of fines. The king's arranging of unsuitable marriages for their women had been a major complaint of

---

17 The Young Marshal was named as one of the rebel barons in London early in June 1215, see J.C. Holt, *Magna Carta* (Cambridge, 1965), app. VII, no. 1, pp. 342–3.
18 *Annales de Wigornia*, in *Annales Monastici* IV, p. 406. The Patent Rolls record a protection for the Young Marshal to visit his father in April 1216 under the escort of the Master of the Temple in England (the Marshal's particular friend). *Rot. Patentium*, p. 175. Whatever the ostensible reason given to John for the meeting, it could not have been other than a family strategy conference in the light of news from France of Louis' problems.

the barons in 1100, and features heavily in the charter, a complaint that goes with the king's unfair exploitation of wardships. The rapacity of the king's foresters was another issue. In 1100, Henry I had clearly been challenged on the same subject, but made minimal concessions. Restraining the king's ability to fine and tax his subjects at will had been a major concern in 1100, and John had made it more pressing still.

Power without restraint was tyranny, and this was no longer to be allowed John, by setting actual ceilings to what he could ask. From now on, he had to ask his magnates for their consent. It was only slightly moderated by imposing similar restrictions on the barons themselves. The Anonymous did not, however, take notice of the clauses that immortalise Magna Carta: that no free man may be brought to law without the 'lawful judgement of his peers' and 'to no one will we sell, to no one will we deny or delay right or justice' (cc. 39, 40). These clauses decisively limited royal power ever afterwards in England. The Anonymous did notice – and found shameful – the clauses that appointed 25 barons to monitor the implementation of Magna Carta and keep the king in check. This too had a long-term impact. The repeated baronial coups over the next two centuries were likewise to appoint committees to limit the king's power to act and tie him to their agenda.

By September, mutual lack of trust between the parties was causing any hope in the settlement to crumble into warfare. The Marshal remained with the king until the end of July, attending a make-or-break conference at Oxford, to which the barons had come armed to indicate their impatience. It was at this time that the king abandoned the charter and secretly sent to the Pope asking him to annul it. Pope Innocent's subsequent condemnation of Magna Carta – which reached England in the first days of September 1215 – was decisive for its short-term future: the king, he said, had accepted it 'by force and fear'; it was 'demeaning and shameful, but also illegal and unjust'. The barons must 'voluntarily renounce this settlement, making amends to the king and his people for the losses and wrongs inflicted on them'.[19] The pope may have recognised that John was the problem and the barons had a case of sorts, but all he could do was offer his mediation. The barons would hardly accept that, and so full-scale civil war broke out.

The Barons' War

War against the king was already in progress in the north in August, while the barons in the south were still talking to the king. Thereafter, the Marshal's military skills were what was needed, and he moved, or was sent, to the southern Marches. The Welsh had perceived John's weakness. An opportunist alliance was forged between the Marshal's old adversary Maelgwyn ap Rhys, Llywelyn ab Iorwerth, the dominant prince of Gwynedd, and the younger members of the Briouze family. From the summer of 1215 through the winter of 1215–1216, the Marshal had the

---

19 *Selected Letters of Pope Innocent III concerning England, 1198–1216* (London, 1953), no. 83.

difficult task of organising resistance to Welsh incursions to the west, while monitoring rebel movements to the east. Indications are that there was not very much that he was able to achieve in the face of this war on two fronts. He could do little more than sit tight and try to hold what he could, while the Welsh overran the north of Pembrokeshire, Carmarthenshire and Gower. King John, in the meantime, had rather more success. He penned the rebels in London while he had considerable success in picking off outlying garrisons. He took the formidable castle of Rochester in a meticulous and brilliant siege.

The rebels did at least make one significant move. In November 1215, Earl Saher led an embassy to France, which appealed to King Philip of France for aid, and offered the Crown of England to his son, Louis. It was an invitation greeted at the Capetian court with great satisfaction, and Louis enthusiastically embraced the cause. Some reinforcements were sent to London, though Louis did not immediately appear. At this point, in the spring of 1216, John attempted to persuade Philip not to send his son to England. The Marshal was one of the ambassadors selected to reason with Philip, and so, for the last time in his life, he crossed to France. The embassy was a failure, and the Marshal and his colleagues returned early in April to report to the king. Within two months, Louis himself appeared in England, to the consternation of the royalist party. With the aid of King Alexander of Scotland, the royalists were driven out of the north, down to the Trent and Humber. Apart from Dover and Windsor, the south-east went over to the French. In many ways, it was a situation not unlike what happened in 1066. The *History*'s sentiments at this point would have done justice to one of Harold's defeated thegns.

> Many fine casks and barrels of wine were drunk by the rascals of France. They were so full of themselves that they said England was theirs, and the English had abandoned their lands to them, having no right to them.[20]

This seems to have been a sentiment stemming from the Francophobe element in the Marshal's English *mesnie*. Doubtless, it was also a sentiment shared by a wider group within England. It was generally believed that French arrogance was the reason why the Young Marshal ultimately abandoned Louis' cause.[21] But this view of matters does not square with the Young Marshal's determination to make the best of his position at Louis' court. He had his right to be Louis' marshal in England recognised by the prince, and attempted to get Louis to restore to him the castle of Marlborough, which his grandfather had lost in 1158. His failure to do so might well have been the true reason for his disenchantment with the French.

The king slowly retreated into the west, basing himself at Corfe Castle and abandoning much of the east coast. The Marshal, too, was back in the southern March in June, waiting on events and watching. The royal party in England had

---

20 *History* II, lines 15102–8.
21 *Chronicon Thomae Wykes*, in *Annales Monastici* III, p. 47.

shrunk. Even the king's half-brother, the powerful Earl of Salisbury, had gone over to Louis. Apart from the Marshal and the Earl of Chester, only the Earls of Derby and Warwick remained attached to John's cause, and neither of them disposed of a political affinity of any great weight. Things remained dire in October 1215, when John suddenly decided on a sally into the north to reinforce the loyal garrisons of Lincoln and Newark and drive a wedge between Louis and the Scots. Although the campaign was a partial success (that is, apart from difficulties in crossing the Wash), John fell ill at King's Lynn and it rapidly became clear that he was dying. The realisation that King John's turbulent reign was in its last days changed everything, and the shock of the news was to propel William Marshal into an entirely different sphere, for he was within weeks himself to be ruler of England.

7

THE SAVIOUR OF THE ANGEVIN DYNASTY

The Marshal coup

Enteric (or gastric) infections killed far more men in medieval warfare than did battles. William Marshal had already witnessed the dying agonies of John's eldest brother, the Young King Henry, in 1183, and by now he had probably seen other similar deaths. The poor state of medieval hygiene rapidly spread bacillary contamination through water and food. King John's killer was probably a bacterial infection (shigellosis), which within a day or so of infection inflamed the intestines, causing diarrhoea with blood loss, terrible cramps, fever and an inability to retain body salts and nutrients. Since medieval people were unable to rehydrate the body other than orally, the function of the major organs was compromised and death followed when they shut down, usually within less than a week of the symptoms appearing. Apart from fever and debilitation, victims might remain lucid and conscious nearly to the end, as the Young King Henry had. In the Middle Ages, this was important: it allowed the dying person to go through and participate in the appropriate deathbed rituals.

John kept up the business of government at Newark to the bitter end, his clerks issuing letters and writs under his seal even on his last day. A physician was summoned to attend him, in this case Adam, abbot of the nearby monastery of white canons at Croxton. Coincidentally, Croxton was an abbey that had been under John's direct patronage as Count of Mortain since 1189. Adam seems to have been one of the few senior clerics at the king's deathbed, as he took responsibility for conducting the king's confession and last rites, though the Bishop of Winchester was also there. The medieval sequence of the last rites involved first a public confession by the dying man of his sins. We know this did in fact happen as William Marshal's nephew and banneret, John Marshal, was present in the room and gave his recollection of it to the Marshal biographer. He reported King John as expressing particular contrition for his treatment of Marshal. He also said that John was in considerable pain from internal cramps throughout.[1]

Following the confession and act of penitence, the dying man was supposed to offer restitution for what sins he could. King John seems not to have done that, leaving it to his executors to do it for him after his death (particularly in relation to the crusading oath that, like his eldest brother, he had taken but not fulfilled). He didn't confess in those solemn moments to any of the supposed murders of which he was accused by his enemies, which is rather telling testimony that he had not arranged either his nephew's death, nor that of the Briouzes.[2] John had a brief last testament drawn up, which was supposed to have been sealed by eight of the men present as witnesses, but it is some evidence of the confusion of the moment in the death chamber that the clerk failed to get them to do so. It still survives at Worcester Cathedral, where it was carried along with his corpse, and it proved in due course to be a very useful document for William Marshal.[3]

John did not remain lucid in his final hours, but is reported by the Marshal biography as suffering distressing hallucinations and as raving in fever before at the last subsiding into unconsciousness (the shutdown of his kidneys would have allowed toxins to build up rapidly in his body). Ralph of Coggeshall (whose source was a Cistercian monk of Savigny called John, who had arrived at Newark in the night just after John's death) says the king's final moments were so harrowing that the household knights the monk met refused to talk about it.

King John died in the middle of the night of 18 October, as a gale raged around the town and shook tiles from its roofs. Many of the townsmen later claimed that horrifying phantoms had been seen in the streets at the time of his death, for such things were to be expected at the death of kings. His body was promptly disembowelled, prepared and wrapped by Abbot Adam, and at dawn a mass for the dead was said before the corpse by the freshly arrived monk, John of Savigny. The swollen and diseased intestines and the internal organs were sealed and taken for burial at Croxton. The body was then escorted by his household south-westwards in the direction of Worcester, where the king had requested burial.

The *History* squirms around and deliberately obscures what happened next. To begin with, its author lies outright in depicting an affecting scene as the king publicly apologised on his deathbed for all the ills he had done the Marshal, begged his forgiveness, and recognised at the end his worth and loyalty. What was more, he

---

1 *History* II, lines 15144–206.
2 That doesn't mean John didn't have regrets about the fate of the Briouzes, for which he was ultimately responsible. It has been pointed out that a week before his death, as he first sickened, he made a grant to one of William de Briouze's daughters with licence to found a religious house for the dead members of her family, it became a priory of nuns at Aconbury in Herefordshire, *Rot. Patentium*, p. 199, see H. Nicholson, 'Margaret de Lacy and the Hospital of St John at Aconbury, Herefordshire', *Journal of Ecclesiastical History*, 50 (1999), pp. 629–51.
3 S.D. Church, 'King John's testament and the last days of his reign', *English Historical Review*, 125 (2010), pp. 505–28, gives some new insight into the document.

supposedly entreated those present to entrust his nine-year-old heir, Henry, to the Marshal's keeping. This did not in fact happen.[4] The king's testament now travelling with him to Worcester did no more than set up a large committee of 13 'ordainers' (among whom was indeed William Marshal) who were to take responsibility for the defence of England against the Capetian invasion and the rebel barons. But the will shows some evidence that even in the king's last hours, a Marshal coup was under way.

The will confided England to Cardinal Guala, the papal legate, three bishops, three earls (Pembroke, Chester and Derby), three English barons and two foreign mercenary captains. Of these 13, only Bishop Peter of Winchester and John of Monmouth (and very possibly Walter de Lacy) are definitely known to have been at Newark with the dying king. The 13 were selected specifically by the king and those of his council present to represent a balance between three groups with different interests: the Church, the loyalist aristocracy and the king's formidable mercenary captains.

The three barons selected are the most significant names, however. They show how a Marshal party was already present in the death chamber. The three named included one of John's most loyal henchmen, William Briwerre, long a Marshal colleague at court; a marcher associate of Marshal's, John of Monmouth, who was actually in the chamber; and Walter de Lacy, the powerful Irish baron and long-time Marshal ally, who was also present. Their links with William indicate that he already had a means to influence the future regency even before the king had died. If so, it was through his nephew and seneschal John Marshal, who was there too at John's deathbed, no doubt urging the Marshal case and despatching messenger after messenger through the stormy night to his lord and uncle where he was based in Gloucester Castle. Since John Marshal was the biographer's informant as to John's deathbed, we hear his voice as to what he wanted the world to think happened there.

So it was that William Marshal was well primed to make his bid to take control of England in the week after the king's death. He rode directly from his base at Gloucester to meet the funeral cortège as it approached Worcester, a significant move that the *History* does not disguise, though it doesn't comment on its significance. He promptly appointed himself master of ceremonies for the funeral, which probably took place on 25 or 26 October. On his own authority, Marshal trawled royal treasuries for the necessary silks to cover the royal coffin. He person-ally authorised the grant of part of the neighbouring castle to the cathedral as a

4 The Anonymous (p. 180) also mentions the king on his deathbed entrusting his son and kingdom to the Marshal, but it is likely that the author (in the same way as the author of the *History*) was simply extrapolating from what happened later at Gloucester. The generally reliable Barnwell chronicler (II, p. 233) has the Marshal, Guala and the Bishop of Winchester entrusted with the king and kingdom 'by the common counsel' of the magnates, If this were so, then at least one well-informed contemporary did not see the late king's provision as the source of the Marshal's regency.

gift for the dead king's soul.[5] He did so despite the fact that it was Earl Ranulf of Chester who had just the previous fortnight recaptured Worcester for the king and garrisoned the castle; it was said with the connivance of the younger Marshal, still nominally fighting for the other side.

Following the funeral, the assembly moved down the Severn to Gloucester. On 28 October, the legate, bishops and loyalist barons (in the absence of the Earl of Chester) met in council at Gloucester, to which the boy Henry was to be brought from Devizes. Marshal did not await the boy king's arrival with the others, however. His biography tells us he rode out with an armed retinue to secure the boy at Malmesbury, and he can only have done it to pre-empt any rival claim. Marshal pushed for the boy's immediate coronation and himself dubbed the nine-year-old a knight before the ceremony. The day after that, he accepted the position of regent from the assembled court, but he had in fact already seized it. The Chester party was not too happy that their earl had been outmanoeuvred. A bid was made to dislodge Marshal from the Regency within a couple of months, with Chester's representatives at Rome arguing that Marshal was feeble and too old to rule England, but the victory at Lincoln on 20 May 1217 would in the end quell opposition to William Marshal's regime, which was to remain in power till April 1219.[6]

Such were the austere facts of a political coup by which William Marshal took power. Though it seems he found people willing to go along with him in the circumstances, he in fact seized power, and did not take it up reluctantly as his biographer would have us believe. His biography's careful picture of his fears and hesitancy at Gloucester and deference to the rival claims of Chester are deliberate misrepresentation. He became regent because he saw himself as the only man capable of uniting England behind the boy king, whose childish dignity and pathos is said to have reduced him to tears, and indeed it might well have for William was a man whose heart was easily touched by children and he was undoubtedly a devoted father to his own. He was already de facto regent well before the coronation, and not appointed protesting his unworthiness after the ceremony, as the *History* claims. If there had been such a scene of doubt and conventional reluctance, it had happened earlier, when his nephew's messengers had arrived on blown horses from Newark with news of King John's death.

In council after his elevation with his three closest friends and knights, William Marshal found John of Earley exalted at his lord's promotion. Earley was full of the honour of the deeds that needed to be done; the desperation of their situation; the need never to surrender. He proposed retreat to Ireland to carry on the fight there, if Louis took England: 'never will a man have earned such honour in the land!' The Marshal caught his mood: 'Your advice is true and good. If everyone abandons the boy but me, do you know what I shall do? I will carry him on my

5 *Roll of Divers Accounts for the Early Years of Henry III*, ed. F.A. Cazel (Pipe Roll Society, new ser., 44, 1982), p. 36; *Cartulary of Worcester Cathedral Priory*, ed. R.R. Darlington (Pipe Roll Society, 1968), pp. 174–5.
6 *Royal Letters* I, p. 532.

back, and if I can hold him up, I will hop from island to island, from country to country, even if I have to beg for my bread!'[7] We can never be wholly sure if the *History* reports what were the actual words of the Marshal, but these somehow ring true.

The revival of Magna Carta

The Marshal and his royal ward quitted Gloucester on 2 or 3 November and moved to King John's favourite residence at Tewkesbury, moving thence to a great council of royalist magnates and bishops at Bristol. The royal clerks began to work out precisely what official position the Marshal should occupy. At first, they thought that he should be called 'justiciar of England',[8] but decided that that would not work. Hubert de Burgh, King John's loyal aide and then castellan of Dover, had been the late king's justiciar since 1214, and his importance meant that the new government wanted to keep him in the post. Besides, King John's former ministers were to argue that their appointments remained valid until Henry III came of age. So a new title was created for the Marshal.

On 12 November 1216 at Bristol, William was called by the king's clerk *rector noster et regni nostri*, literally 'our governor and the ruler of our kingdom'. Perhaps 'keeper' or 'guardian' would be a better translation of the word *rector* than 'regent', but 'regent' expresses better the power that the Marshal now wielded. His authority lay behind all royal acts. Within days of the coronation, the majority of letters or grants issued in the king's name went out 'by the earl', and were attested either by him alone, or with the legate. Many administrative acts went out in his own name, although how many is uncertain, since they were not registered by the chancery.[9] The Marshal's seal was appended to royal letters, for the Young King had none of his own until the end of 1218. Payments owed the king were often made to William Marshal in person, rather than to the Exchequer. For nearly three years, the Marshal was the mainspring of what government there was.

The Marshal's task was now to pacify England. In general, he was lucky: Matthew Paris – and modern historians seem to be in agreement – expressed the sentiment that people were more well-disposed to Henry 'for it seemed to all that it was not right to put the evil of the father upon the son'.[10] That was not enough of itself to safeguard the boy king's inheritance, however; that was up to the moves his guardians would make on his behalf. One of the first acts that William Marshal

---

7 *History* II, lines 15688–96.
8 See *Patent Rolls*, 1216–1225, p. 2: *iusticiarius noster Anglie* on 2 November at Gloucester.
9 A copy of one such Marshal precept, addressed to the sheriff of Lincoln instructing him to assist the younger Marshal in collecting a scutage from the men of the fees of Earl David and Gilbert de Gant, survives on an Exchequer Remembrancer's roll, TNA: PRO, E368/3 m. 3d. Another, addressed to the barons of the Exchequer, is a receipt for 20 marks, which the abbot of Tewkesbury had paid him in person, and which he wanted the barons to note on their accounts, TNA: PRO, E368/1 m. 7d.
10 *Chronica Maiora* III, p. 2.

took was inspired. We cannot say for sure if it was his suggestion, or that of the legate, his partner in power, or of the November council at Bristol, but out of that meeting came the decision to reissue a version of Magna Carta in the name of King Henry III, sealed by the seals of the Marshal and the legate Guala. The Marshal is likely to have been the force behind it, however. After all, Guala was the representative of a papacy that had condemned the original document. Who knew better than the Marshal the mood of the barons of England, his colleagues of many years? Not only that, but through his son, the younger William, he had a direct contact with the rebel party, so he knew what would influence them. By sealing and reissuing Magna Carta in its first days, the new Regency government had hijacked the cause of reform, and made any baron who continued to fight for Lord Louis no more than a Capetian mercenary.

The Magna Carta agenda became in fact the central plank of the Regency's legitimacy. The 1216 reissue was not much different from the original, though clauses had been modified to preserve royal rights. Most obviously missing was the clause the Anonymous of Béthune had found so outrageous, the one that confided oversight of the terms to the council of 25. But since real power was going to be in the hands of the barons for a decade and more to come, that was hardly necessary any more. The 1216 reissue no longer anathematised John's mercenary captains; not surprisingly, since they were now the military mainstay of the Regency. Curiously, there was no response from Louis of France, though we know that he obtained a copy of the 1216 reissue. But Louis issued no rival Magna Carta of his own, a revealing indication of the emerging differences between the English and French monarchies. The Capetian monarchy did not treat its nobility as a partner in dialogue, nor bargain with it.

Even after the end of the emergency and the pacification of England, the Regency of William Marshal did not set Magna Carta aside. By the end of 1217, Magna Carta had become the touchstone of its legitimacy. In November of that year, the Marshal and his advisers were still sufficiently energised to draw up a new version, the one that became in fact the text that was taken into English statute law. It was issued on 6 November 1217 as two documents, the 'Magna Carta' itself, and a lesser charter called the Charter of the Forest, a supplement that finally addressed the vexed issue of royal forest administration, which had been infuriating the barons since at least the reign of Henry I.

Magna Carta was to be issued again by several kings over the next century and more, not least by King Henry III in 1225 when he finally came to adulthood, but it was William Marshal and his council who provided the final form of the text, and consigned it to the ages. In so doing, they embedded in English political life what had in fact been its most striking feature in the previous century, the dialogue between king and political community that had informed the exercise of kingship under Stephen, Henry II and even Richard I. It had been a dialogue King John had brutally suppressed, for which he was rightly judged a tyrant. He paid the tyrant's cost, but it was William Marshal who redeemed it, and set the English monarchy and its peoples on a new and very distinctive course.

The Battle of Lincoln (1217)

The Marshal and his colleagues offered easy terms to those willing to submit to the king, and by offering a general restitution for ills. During the winter of 1216–1217, the balance of power between the two sides hardly quivered. The greater men among the rebels did not show any sign of reconsidering; the Marshal did not have the resources to take much action. Louis, on the other hand, did not have any success against the great castles holding out for the king. In February 1217, he returned to France to consult with his royal father, but had small comfort from the visit. Philip was under great pressure from the Church and would not assist him in any useful way.

When Louis returned to England late in April, he found that the situation had worsened considerably. Before he had left, the royalists had been able to make some headway in the Cinque Ports. The Young Marshal and the Earl of Salisbury had taken advantage of his absence to return to the royalist camp. If there had been any collusion between elder and younger Marshals, the need for it had now passed, perhaps. The *History* says that the two men simply fell in with the Marshal's raid on the Sussex Castle of Knepp (the centre of the confiscated Briouze lordship), then in the hands of Roland Bloet, brother of one of the Marshal's knights. It fails to mention the fact that they had been on the opposite side until then. These two were the most prominent of the *reversi* 'the returners' (as royal records call them). The rolls recording the king's correspondence register an ever-increasing number of protections and safe conducts to men who were returning to their allegiance.

But the kingdom would not be regained by the Marshal sitting still and waiting for Louis to go away. There must be some successful military demonstrations to regain the initiative and a measure of prestige. The *History* records the subsequent campaign in great detail, its author occasionally stopping to tell us that he was reconstructing the complicated military manoeuvres from written descriptions sent him by his informants. Attempts were made to move along the Channel coast and hamper Louis' communications with France, and a number of important castles fell. In the north Midlands, the Earl of Chester continued John's campaign of the previous autumn of harrying the rebels there, in order to stop the northern barons linking with Louis. Ranulf was not quite as strategically minded as the late king or the Marshal, however. He chose to combine business with his own personal concerns and attacked the Earl of Winchester's Castle of Mountsorrel in the Soar Valley in Leicestershire. It was a castle from which the Earl of Winchester's predecessors had ousted Ranulf's grandfather.[11] In the circumstances, this did not really matter. It was enough that the rebels were being pressed and kept off balance. In the event, the siege of Mountsorrel set off a train of events leading to an outcome that was more than gratifying to the Marshal.

11 See E. King, 'Mountsorrel and its region in King Stephen's reign', *Huntington Library Quarterly*, 44 (1980), pp. 8–9.

Louis of France was persuaded by the Earl of Winchester that a column should be sent to the relief of Mountsorrel. A substantial force was provided, the French in it captained by Thomas, the Count of Perche. When they arrived there, it was to discover that the royalists had already retreated. The rebel forces therefore moved eastwards, pillaging as they went. They headed for Lincoln Castle, long under desultory siege by a mixed force of northerners and French, but hitherto defiant under its remarkable female castellan, Nicola de la Haie. They did not know that the Marshal had concentrated the main royalist army at Northampton, behind them, and was in pursuit.

Taking what forces he had, and scraping together what he could from local garrisons, the Marshal assembled at Newark a force that the *History* totals at 406 knights and 317 crossbowmen. These figures sound convincing, because they are not the large, round numbers that literary sources usually employ. It may well be that the author had access to the muster rolls of the army. It was the Marshal or his agents who were supposed to keep these rolls, so this is not unlikely. On 19 May 1217, this modest-sized column left Newark for the 25-or-so-mile march to Lincoln. Still ringing in their ears was the Marshal's pre-battle harangue. This was a custom beloved of Roman generals and still practised from time to time in the medieval world. As the *History* records this speech, it was short, simple and unaffected, well-adapted for the circumstances. His men were to remember their honour, families and lands. They were not to be backward in deeds that day, for they were fighting for the Holy Church. He stated their task and circumstances simply: to destroy the French who had come to take their lands, or be destroyed themselves. The French were God's enemies and they had foolishly divided their forces; now God had given the opportunity to finish them. It was a most effective piece of rhetoric mixing land, possession and peoples in a volatile, dangerous cocktail. Before they left, the legate had given them a plenary absolution for their sins to that day. Those who died fighting the excommunicate rebel force would go direct to Heaven.

The *History* says they spent the night at Torksey, having passed down the Trent. Torksey was a borough and port on the river Trent, some 10 miles to the west of the city of Lincoln. Roger of Wendover (prior of Belvoir in Lincolnshire in 1217) says they camped at Stow, but his evidence is not irreconcilable with that of the *History*, for it is possible that the Marshal's camp was on Till Bridge Lane (the Roman road approaching Lincoln from the north-west) at a point near to both Torksey and Stow. As the contemporary Barnwell chronicler recognised, the Marshal's clear intention was to avoid approaching the city along the Foss Way from the south (which would bring them to the side of Lincoln where the French and rebels were encamped), but come down to it along the ridge towards its north-west corner, on which was the castle, still held by its loyalist garrison. The French had stationed their siege machines and main force in the city, not being sure of the loyalty of the citizens.[12]

---

12 See the unsuperseded analysis of the strategy behind this, in F.W. Brooks and F. Oakley, 'The Campaign and Battle of Lincoln, 1217', in *Associated Architectural Societies Reports and Papers*, XXXVI, pt 1 (1922), pp. 297–301.

The day of the battle was a Saturday, 20 May 1217. After a mass and another harangue by the Marshal, the army broke camp and moved at dawn (around 3.45 a.m. in the Trent Valley on that day, there being no British Summer Time in those days).[13] Then, the army began to move, in very good heart, as if to a tournament (as the *History* says). It was a march of about 10 miles to Lincoln, and the stiff pace tired their horses. According to Roger of Wendover, it was still early in the morning when they reached the city. The army should in fact have easily reached Lincoln by 6.00 a.m. Roger of Wendover placed the beginning of the battle halfway between the first and third hours, which, if we take him literally, means 6.25 a.m. He also says that 'like all good businessmen', the royalists had finished their work (including the pursuit, no doubt) by the ninth hour (that is, 3.45 p.m.).

The royalist army was seen some time before it reached Lincoln by besieged and besiegers alike. The French forces retired within the city gates, deceived as to the inferior numbers of the royalists. Louis' force in fact consisted of over 600 French and English knights. By now, the sun was well up, and both armies must have paused to assess the situation; the royalists needed to take time to recover from their march. Sometime later in the morning, no doubt after a council of war, the Marshal – perhaps reluctant to fight a pitched battle – sent his nephew, John Marshal, forward to the walls to talk to the enemy commanders. He had advised others often enough to avoid battle, and it perhaps went against the grain to fight one himself. He may have hoped the French would simply withdraw. As the Marshal's nephew and a leading baron, John would have been a suitable envoy. Both the *History* and an anonymous poem on the battle say that John's embassy was attacked by the French. This would seem to have been because after talking to the French, he had compromised his mission by an opportunistic meeting before the walls with Geoffrey de Serland, one of the royalist commanders of the castle garrison, who had slipped out to pass on news of the state of affairs in Lincoln to the relief column and to tell him that there was a castle door open by which the Marshal's men could enter.[14]

13 This is a detail revealed by an anonymous contemporary lyricist in the line, 'the sun was touching the earth with its first beam', *The Political Songs of England*, ed. T. Wright (Camden Society, VI, 1839), p. 25. I must thank the Royal Greenwich Observatory for its help on these points.

14 This seems to be the significance of *History* II, lines 16449–54, which indicate that John Marshal was the herald sent by the Marshal to challenge the French, after they had withdrawn into the city. The same mission is mentioned by the anonymous contemporary poem on the battle ('an embassy is sent to the city to call the irreligious to the way of peace'), *Political Songs*, ed. Wright, p. 25. Wendover II, p. 215, confirms part of this story, saying that on the Marshal's approach, the commanders of the castle 'secretly sent a messenger by a small gate (*posticum*), which was at the back end of the castle . . . who informed them of what was happening within the walls and told them also that they could now get into [the castle] by the postern, which because of their arrival was now open'.

The account of the *History* is more than a little confused at this point. It relied on the memoirs of several men for the events of that day, and more than one was willing to take credit for finding a way into the city: 'Those who gave me my matter don't agree, and I cannot follow all of them; I shall lose the right road and won't be believed.' At any rate, it seems clear that Faulkes de Breauté was sent to follow up Geoffrey de Serland's advice, enter the castle and distract the French within the city by deploying his crossbowmen on the broken walls of the castle to harass their engineers. However, Faulkes was unable to assault the French through the castle's main gate into the city. Both John Marshal and the Bishop of Winchester claimed at this point to have found an alternative and unguarded route into the city. Although the entry of the bishop into the castle is not attested by any other source, it need not be doubted. But the bishop seems to have embroidered his story somewhat, claiming that he was able to leave the castle and penetrate into the city of Lincoln itself and find an open gate by which the Marshal's army could enter.

The identity of this all-important gate has been disputed in the past, but scholars are now in agreement that what is being referred to is in fact the city's west gate immediately north of the castle.[15] The *History* says that it had been blocked by masonry some time before the siege. This is by no means unlikely: it would have been in the interests of the besiegers of the castle to limit movement so near the castle walls. Knowing of the existence of this undefended gate, and that it was possible to unblock it, probably as noon approached, the Marshal sent troops forward into the city. Other contemporary writers disagree and imply that the north gate was forced by storm, but in fact, once the Marshal's forces were within the city, the north gate was indefensible and other royalists might well have entered by it once the rebels pulled back to the cathedral. Wendover talks of Faulkes de Breauté distracting, and perhaps panicking, the French as they withdrew by heavy fire from the castle.

The Marshal, who must have realised that this was to be his last battle, was rather too forward for the comfort of his colleagues and *mesnie*. Once the way was found, he would not wait for scouts' reports, but rode forward until reminded that he had forgotten to put on his helmet. But then, he was now perhaps 70 years of age and may have felt he had something to prove. He had the satisfaction during the battle of seeing off with several smart strokes Robert of Roppesley, one of King John's young *mesnie* who had turned traitor and refused to return to the royalist side. The Marshal also had the strength to take scatheless several blows on his helm, which were strong enough to dent it. The royalists, though outnumbered, pressed in on the French and rebels with great success. In many ways, the fight was like the first action in which the Marshal had participated in the streets of the suburbs of Neufchâtel-en-Bray: a constricted street fight with no possibilities for a decisive charge. Although having the advantages of numbers, the French were unable to

---

15 D.A. Carpenter, *The Minority of Henry III* (London, 1990), pp. 37–8. On the identity of the gate, see F.W. Tout, 'The Fair of Lincoln', *English Historical Review*, 18 (1903), pp. 248–50; J.W.F. Hill, *Medieval Lincoln* (Cambridge, 1948), p. 204.

rout the royalists: it may have been a matter of lack of morale; it may have been dismay at the sudden inrush of the royalists and their quick seizure of their artillery; or it may have been the crossbowmen of Faulkes de Breauté harassing them from the castle.

A stand before the west end of the minster (probably in the present Exchequer Gate) was organised by the French commander, Count Thomas of Perche. But that too failed to halt the royalists as the young count was accidentally killed. A splintered lance penetrated the eye slit of his helm and he fell dead. The Marshal was present at his fall and was upset by it. He and the count were first cousins. After the count's fall, the French began to give way and were pressed down the hill towards the southern gate of the city, the Stonebow. They must at some point have broken under the pressure. The *History* gives a vivid picture of the French and English rebels being pushed down the hill in several streams, trying to rally as they went. The royalists had the advantage of fighting downhill now. The *History* talks of a last stand of the French on the flat ground at the bottom of the hill – perhaps at the Stonebow gate in front of the church of St Peter at Arches – which was routed when the Earl of Chester's men dashed out of the side street running south-west from Claxledgate to Stonebow. In the middle of the afternoon, the French and rebels began to run, and fled across the bridge into the suburb of Wigford across the river Witham. There was a jam as the crowd of routed men struggled to get through the barrier at the hospital of the Malandry, the West Bargate, which closed off the road out of Wigford, as it passed through a bank and over a ditch. The pursuit continued as far as Holland Bridge, near Horbling, a causeway that carried the Boston–Grantham road across the Holland fen, 25 miles south-east of Lincoln. This reveals that the routed troops headed in the direction of Spalding or Peterborough. Many of the rebel foot soldiers were caught and killed by the local peasantry.

Only three of the horsemen involved in the battle died (including the Count of Perche). Great numbers of rebels were captured, however: 46 barons and 300 knights, including the Earls of Winchester, Hereford and Lincoln. John, the Marshal's nephew, took prisoner himself seven bannerets and their followers. Nor was the Marshal himself remiss in sweeping up profits from the victory. The Yorkshire baron Nicholas de Stuteville must have surrendered to him in person as he was cornered somewhere on the hill of Lincoln. The price of defeat for Nicholas was 1,000 marks ($\pounds$666 13s. 4d.) to be levied on his estates in Yorkshire and Cumberland. The Marshal was as business-like in his later days as he was when he was a young knight making a living on the tournament circuit. Taking advantage of his position as regent, he had the Stuteville contract for the ransom entered on the Exchequer Fine Rolls, as if it was a government transaction and could be pursued through its judicial sanctions. The Stuteville ransom can only have been one of many by which the Marshal turned his office to profit.[16]

---

16 D.A. Carpenter, Fine of the Month, May 2007, www.finerollshenry3.org.uk/content/ month/fm-05-2007.html.

The departure of Louis of France

Great victory for the boy king though Lincoln was, it was not enough to persuade Louis to leave England immediately; he wanted terms by which he could decamp to France with a minimum loss of face. Early in June, he opened negotiations with William Marshal, settled with his army at Chertsey on the Thames below Staines. A subsequent meeting between plenipotentiaries of both parties actually managed to reach a settlement. Great men were present: four elder abbots of the Cistercian order and the Archbishop of Tyre, probably dispatched by King Philip to assist in extricating his son from an increasingly sticky situation. Unfortunately, Louis balked at the failure to include his chief clerical adherents in the amnesty promised to the barons. Negotiations broke down and Louis chose to sit tight in London until he heard news of his wife's efforts to send reinforcements to him across the Channel. The Marshal moved to prevent this, assembling his army at Sandwich late in August. The Cinque Ports, which had frequently opposed John, were willing to accommodate the Marshal and the young Henry III.

The subsequent sea battle off Sandwich was a conclusive victory for the royalists. The Marshal had not taken ship; his men had persuaded him that he was too valuable to risk to the uncertainties of a shipboard battle, and he had gone along with them (not unwillingly, according to Matthew Paris).[17] We may well believe him: such a battle would have been a new experience for the Marshal, and he had reason not to be fond of maritime travel. The victorious admirals in this case were the justiciar Hubert de Burgh and Richard of Chilham, the bastard son of King John; the Marshal and the boy king watched the distant fight from the clifftops. There could be no argument with such a judgement of God. Louis began negotiations for his withdrawal at once.

There was at the time a view that the Marshal should have closed in on London and worked for the capitulation of the remaining French force. That he did not do so opened him in later days to accusations of double-dealing from which it was difficult to exculpate him. Since the Marshal's policy from the assumption of the regency had been to deal gently with the rebel party as long as it was willing to talk, it is hard to see what else he could have done. Temporising had been successful to date and a change of tactic would have seemed unnecessary. Besides this, it really would have been as embarrassing as his later detractors suggested had he taken prisoner the son and heir of King Philip, his lord for his Norman lands. The fact that he had a fleet move to block the Thames estuary hardly indicates (as Painter suggested) that he was torn between two courses of action: the militant and the pacific. It was simply a means to improve his bargaining position, for bargaining was what he intended doing.

17 *Chronica Maiora* III, p. 28.

The terms he was willing to accept were very easy; in fact, they were much the same as the two sides had agreed in June.[18] Prisoners were to be released free of further ransom payments, and lands restored to Louis' English followers. The Scots and Welsh allies of Louis were to give up their gains. An indemnity of 10,000 marks (£6,667 6s. 8d.) was to be paid against Louis' expenses in England. All that Louis had to do was to leave with his men, and undertake to assist in the future restoration to Henry III of the lands in France his father had lost. Needless to say, the last condition was never fulfilled, despite the Marshal's particular care that the indemnity was paid in full.

Such easy terms towards Louis (although not to the repentant rebels) did not endear the Marshal to future generations. Matthew Paris records that Henry III in later days peevishly berated the Marshal's son, Walter, for what he was pleased to call the old Marshal's treachery. From the same source comes the story that Philip Augustus announced with relief, after hearing of the disaster of Lincoln but that the Marshal still lived, that he had no fears for his son.[19] It is likely that Matthew was recording a genuine feeling of disenchantment later current in royal circles about the Marshal's doings at this time. Matthew Paris is also a little uncharitable to the Marshal's memory at other times, recalling with disgust his treatment of the Bishop of Ferns. Such a courtier as the Marshal could hardly have expected a completely favourable verdict from posterity once he was no longer available personally to harry his accuser with offers of a duel. Indeed, he hardly deserves complete absolution; there remains too much that was ambiguous in his political career for that.

Making government pay

The Marshal enjoyed 19 months of power after the departure of Louis from England. In those months, his government achieved some degree of success in settling the kingdom. Before the Marshal resigned, the Exchequer was restored (although the sheriffs were reluctant to account to it), and some old debts began to be reclaimed; taxes were levied and collected (although not at the high rates of John's reign); and the justices began their circuits once more. The government had at least regained the appearance of being in control, although it is clear that the regent and his council had not been able to restore the strength of the Angevin monarchy that John had inherited. The sheriffs and castellans of the civil war were not easily displaced and had learned to think of themselves as supreme in their localities. At the centre, moreover, it was government by the magnates for the magnates.

18 The terms agreed in June still survive in a draft copy, as does the eventual treaty of September 1217. The textual problems are considered by F.M. Powicke, *King Henry III and the Lord Edward* (2 vols, Oxford, 1947) I, pp. 25–9.
19 *Chronica Maiora* III, pp. 25–6; IV, p. 157.

The full restoration of government was not the Marshal's achievement; it belonged to Hubert de Burgh after the Marshal's death. The Marshal's regency served its purpose in winning the war; it did the job with determination and – in the case of its use of Magna Carta – with some imagination, but after that it fell into drift. Nonetheless, after all the qualifications have been made, the Marshal provided a prestigious figurehead and a politic and affable presence at the head of affairs. In the period of slow recovery from civil warfare, his charm and (by now) venerable presence were invaluable.

Where we get closer to the Marshal at this time is in those affairs that touched his *mesnie* and estates. He did not neglect to promote the interests of both himself and his affinity while he was regent. This remark is not meant as a criticism of his conduct; what he did was no more than any other man of the time would have done in his circumstances. He was neither rapacious nor impolitic in his use of the greatly amplified powers of patronage that his position gave him. No doubt he was quite sensitive to the necessity of restraint when his power depended on the consent of the barons who had raised him to the regency. He was still one of them; no degree of royal charisma touched him at all. He was not such a regent as England had ever had before: no royal sibling or consort.

One area of policy that concerned the Marshal deeply was – naturally – Ireland, where he had gone through fire between 1207 and 1210. He had not forgotten the way he and his fellow marchers had been imposed upon by King John, and now he had the chance to do something about it. The Regency made a point of restoring Reginald, the heir of the devastated Briouze family, to his lands and possessions, including Limerick, thus undoing the family's dispossession by the late King John.[20] William served his own interests also in Ireland, and wasted no time about it. A letter was sent to the Irish justiciar from the council at Bristol in November 1216, abruptly restoring their liberties to the great honors of Ireland, and so erasing the intrusion of royal jurisdiction within Leinster. But that aside, Marshal could not escape the logic of his own government. The same letter announces that a copy of Magna Carta was to be sent overseas from Bristol to Dublin, for the Regency had determined that its provisions were to apply in Ireland, though they did not do so in Wales or Cheshire.[21] King John had his victory there, for he had established that Ireland was included within the English legal system.

The Marshal certainly served himself, although he did not take quite as greedy a share of the pie as others might have. Perhaps the most satisfactory acquisition he made was the castle and town of Marlborough, recovered from the rebels in 1217. This was quite likely where he had been born, and he had certainly spent much of his childhood there, for it had been the centre of his father's activities until Henry II had taken it back into royal hands in 1158. He might well have

20 *Patent Rolls*, 1216–1225, pp. 72–3, 112.
21 *Foedera, conventiones, litterae et cuiuscunque generis acta*, ed. T. Rymer; new edn, ed. A. Clark and F. Holbrooke (Record Commission, 1816) I, pt 1, p. 145.

reflected that he deserved some compensation for the losses he had to suffer in west Wales, where Cardigan, Cilgerran and Carmarthen had to be abandoned to the Welsh.

Nearer home, his lands had been much battered by the Welsh Lord Morgan ap Hywel (or Morgan of Caerleon, as he frequently called himself in Anglo-French fashion). The house of Caerleon was a curious survival of native lordship in south-east Wales. The lords of Caerleon were descended from Caradog ap Gruffudd, who had been client king of Glamorgan allied to the Conqueror until his death in 1081. His kingdom had then disappeared and his son been impoverished, but in 1136–1137 under his grandson, Morgan ab Owain, it had been restored. King Morgan had dominated Gwent under both Stephen and Henry II until his death in 1158, his power based on the castles of Caerleon and Usk.[22] The family had great prestige in Wales and played up their connection with the Roman fortress in which their castle was built, feeding on the Arthurian legend associations invented by their neighbour, Geoffrey of Monmouth. Indeed, archaeological excavation has established that the Welsh royal residence at Caerleon still included standing and roofed Roman buildings at this date, a great propylon, or monumental arch, and a baths complex. The Welsh may have imagined they were occupying one of Caesar's own palaces.[23]

Subsequent princes of the line had not fared so well after King Morgan. Earl Richard Strongbow had reduced and taken Usk in the 1160s and later had dispossessed the Welsh temporarily of Caerleon. Nonetheless, the lords of Caerleon remained a power, fitfully allied with the king and marcher interests. Morgan of Caerleon's father had been a major prop of Henry II's power in the southern March. Hywel ap Iorweth had gravitated into the political orbit of Llywelyn ap Iorwerth, Prince of Gwynedd. He and Morgan his son fought with Llywelyn for Louis' interests in the civil war, but unlike Llywelyn did not lay down his sword after the departure of the French. He was hot to recover land that he claimed the Marshal had occupied. This may be a reference to lost Usk or some part of the Welsh portion of Netherwent.

A damaging war ravaged the Marshal lordships in Gwent in 1217. Hywel and two members of the Bloet family, Roland and Walter, fell in the hostilities along with several other Marshal knights. Even the capture of Caerleon by the Marshal's bailiff (probably John of Earley) around the end of September 1217 did not end the hostilities. The Marshal soon afterwards had the Countess of Gloucester's Castle of Newport and the lordship of Gwynllŵg committed to him.[24] The reason for this was that Morgan ap Hywel's last fortress was the Castle of Machen in upland

22 D. Crouch, 'The slow death of kingship in Glamorgan, 1067–1158', *Morgannwg*, 29 (1985), pp. 20–41.
23 R. Howell, 'Roman past and medieval present: Caerleon as a focus for continuity and conflict in the Middle Ages', *Studia Celtica*, 46 (2012), pp. 11–21.
24 *Rot. Clausarum* I, p. 330.

Gwynllŵg. If he controlled Gwynllŵg, he could pursue Morgan into the hills legally, rather than trespass into another marcher lordship. In the end, under pressure from Llywelyn, Morgan reluctantly submitted to the adjudication of a council at Worcester in March 1218. This took Caerleon from him, and he did not recover it in the elder Marshal's lifetime. Ten years later, Morgan recovered only part of his inheritance under new terms, to be held as a vassal of his the younger Marshal. In the meantime, the Marshals had deliberately demolished the remains of the Roman palace in which the Welsh kings had held court.

The Marshal was also able to secure for himself half of the English lands of the Count of Perche, who had been slain at Lincoln. The counts of Perche, great magnates on the French side of the southern Norman March, had accepted lands in the south-west of England to seal an alliance with King Henry I, and had remained one of the small number of French counts with English interests ever since. Following the fall of Count Thomas of Perche at Lincoln, his several demesne manors were given to the Earl of Salisbury. This earl would not part with them after the settlement with Louis. The Marshal did not insist, and by a quiet arrangement allowed Longespée to keep two, while he took two for himself (including, oddly enough, Newbury, Berkshire, where his father had abandoned him as hostage to King Stephen over 60 years before).[25] The Marshal and Longespée may well have cloaked their seizure under the tenuous claim of kinship to Count Thomas, for the Marshal was the count's first cousin and Longespée's wife was also a relation. Geoffrey II of Perche had married the Marshal's mother's sister (who was sister also of Patrick, Earl of Salisbury). The two earls were also successful in filching the royal manor of Shrivenham, Berkshire, which had been held by the counts of Perche at the king's pleasure. They bought out Count Thomas's heir, the Bishop of Chalons, in December 1217.

The Marshal was reluctant to use royal manors in his patronage of other men. The royal estates had been too badly enfeebled by the war. Some short-term patronage was available in the confiscated lands of rebels, but by the settlement of 1217 these had to be given back. For a while, his son enjoyed the lands of two earls, Winchester and Huntingdon, and those of a baron who claimed to be an earl, Gilbert de Gant, but their submission deprived him of this princely estate. He was compensated by several large cash payments 'for his support in the king's service'. By this time, the younger Marshal was supporting a sizeable *mesnie* of knights in his own right, and some enlargement of his income was very desirable to him. In February 1218, this was provided in a grant of the profits of the royal exchanges in the greatest cities in the kingdom. John Marshal also did very well out of confiscations. He had a grant of the master forestership of the kingdom (apart from the forests that had been appropriated by several magnates); he also had the keeping of Devizes Castle. The Marshal otherwise provided for his men in grants of wardships, escheats, fairs and markets, such as those granted to John of Earley,

---

25 Carpenter, *Minority of Henry III*, pp. 91–2.

Jordan de Sauqueville, Ralph Musard and Ralph Bloet (as well as himself, his son and his nephew).

Resignation, death and afterwards

In Westminster, around the end of January 1219, the Marshal suddenly became ill. A severe bout of internal pain seems to have rendered him entirely unfit for business until the second week of February. He was now, or was approaching, the age of 72. Until this sickness, he had been a hale old man, a stranger to illness. It may not have been at once apparent that he was dying, for he was able to resume business. The doctors were allowed some scope to practise their arts on him. On 7 March, he was strong enough to ride to the Tower of London, attended by Countess Isabel. Here, he must have come to the bitter realisation that he was dying. He became bedridden in his weakness.

In the middle of the month, William was placed in a boat and rowed upstream to his manor of Caversham on the Thames opposite Reading. Caversham and his family's ancestral castle and centre at Hamstead Marshall were his two favoured English homes. It is not surprising that he wished to be taken to one of them to die. It was an easy journey and he had made it in less than a day when he had used the manor as a staging post in his journeys about the kingdom over the past three years. This time, the journey was made rather more gently, and spread over three days in easy stages.

Caversham had certain advantages for the theatre of death that was to unroll there. It was across the Thames from the royal abbey of Reading, which could host the boy king who accompanied the dying regent's retinue. And indeed, the Marshal continued to transact business from what he might not yet have finally decided was his deathbed at Caversham. For nearly three weeks after his arrival, a steady output of letters left Caversham, mostly under his name rather than those of his fellows in government. The king was settled across the river at Reading with his tutor, the Bishop of Winchester. Nevertheless, the pain continued and his appetite was quite gone. To an untutored historian, the description of his illness sounds like a wasting form of bowel disease, perhaps a cancer, since it was not associated with any flux. The reader may treat the observation for what it is worth.

It was not until the week before Easter (7 April) that the Marshal resolved to pass on the reins of government. A council summoned by the Marshal sat around his bed for two consecutive days (8–9 April) and deliberated what was to be done. Brushing aside the claims of the Bishop of Winchester, the Marshal commended the 11-year-old king to the legate's care. Suppressing the acute pain by which he was racked, the Marshal took the boy by the hand. He earnestly, and pointedly, prayed God to cut short the king's life if he followed the example of any criminal royal predecessor (*alcun felon ancestre*): it seems that he was uncourtly enough at the end as to (almost) criticise King John openly. The king and the court left him then and moved away to Wallingford.

The Marshal had yet another month of life before him after taking leave of the king. The story of those days has been often told and well, a tribute to the quality of the *History*'s verse at this point: I will have more to say about it in a later chapter. There is only need to refer here to the steadfast attendance of his son and his knights, the tearful farewells to his wife and daughters, and his reception into the order of Knights Templar. But to the end, he remained Earl of Pembroke, distributing robes to his knights just before he died. He deliberated his last testament in council with his men the day after he laid down the regency, and before he became a Templar. Few texts of baronial testaments survive from before the late thirteenth century, so the description of the Marshal's will is particularly valuable.

The Marshal first provided for the division of his lands. Until her death, all the lands he had by marriage would return to his wife alone, but he could determine with her their future division. Like his father, he meant to provide for his two eldest sons; there was no hint here that the practice of primogeniture had as yet any hold on the aristocracy of England. The *History* does not say precisely how this was done, but we know from the later history of his family that Leinster, Pembroke, Striguil and the ancestral Marshal lands in England went to the eldest son, William. Richard, the second son, had the Marshal's Norman lordship of Longueville, but also the Giffard honor of Crendon in England. The Marshal chose to continue the integrity of the Giffard lands in Richard, and did not intend to use his testament to remove forever the problem of his divided allegiance by splitting his lands at the Channel.

Gilbert, now around 12 years old, was already a clerk in minor orders and so there was no problem in providing for him. Some provision was made for Walter, who was still no more than 10 in 1219. He had his father's acquisition of Goodrich and other manors. The youngest of them, the ill-fated Ansel, who died less than a month after succeeding his brothers in the Marshal inheritance, was initially to be ignored. His father perhaps was willing to let him make his own way in the world, as the earlier Ansel Marshal, his brother, had done in the 1170s. However, the intervention of John of Earley with the Marshal secured Ansel lands in Ireland worth £140.

Only one daughter, Joan, was unmarried at this time, and she was temporarily provided for by £30 of land and a cash sum of 200 marks (£133 6s. 8d.). There were also legacies to his monasteries: 50 marks (£33 6s. 8d.) to Notley Abbey and each of his foundations in Ireland, and 10 marks (£6 13s. 4d.) to the cathedrals of Leinster (did he include Ferns, one wonders). He left his body to be buried at the Church of the New Temple in London, and the manor of Upleadon, Herefordshire, was his gift to the order. A few days later, the earl's almoner, Geoffrey the Templar, drew up the testament in written form and it was sealed by the Marshal, his wife and son. It named as executors Abbot David of Bristol, John of Earley and Henry fitz Gerold. It was then carried off to the legate, the Archbishop of Canterbury and the Bishops of Winchester and Salisbury, who were to be the supervisors of the testament, and who confirmed its contents. It seems that they also nominated the archbishop's steward, Elias of Dereham, to assist the executors named in the testament.[26]

The Marshal died about midday on 14 May 1219; the windows and doors of his chamber flung open; his silent men and several prelates about his bed; supported by his son, his eyes fixed on the cross. So ended in the fullest of medieval pomp his remarkable story. His body would then have been washed and embalmed, and laid out behind a processional cross in the sanctuary of the Chapel of Caversham between the stalls of the Augustinian canons of Notley. It would have been these priest-canons who would have kept the vigil for him all that night with the grieving family and household and sung the first post-mortem mass for his soul at dawn on 15 May 1219. The corpse was moved to Reading Abbey and presumably rested there on the night of 16 May 1219. His wife – who would enjoy the relative freedom of widowhood for less than a year before she herself died – courteously made a grant of rents to the abbey that had welcomed his corpse. The continuator of William of Newburgh notes that the bier was received with a solemn procession and laid in the choir for a full mass of the convent.

The next day, it was carried on to Staines, where it rested overnight. On 18 May, escorted by numerous earls and barons, the Marshal's body reached Westminster Abbey, where the continuator of William of Newburgh says a vigil and mass was held. The funeral took place (probably on 20 May 1219) at the New Temple Church, the day after the body lay at Westminster. It was performed by the Archbishop of Canterbury and the Bishop of London.

What is generally reckoned nowadays to be the funeral effigy of the Marshal (early in form and with legs straight, resting on a dog, for faithfulness) is still to be found in the Temple Church. It was heavily restored by the Victorians and badly damaged by a German incendiary bomb in the Second World War. The case for the identification is by no means proven, and its present situation bears no relationship to where it originally stood, for it was moved in the extension of the church later in the reign of Henry III.[27] Nonetheless, if it is him, the Marshal is

---

26 For Walter Marshal's share of his father's lands at Goodrich, Sturminster Marshall and Bere Regis, see *Close Rolls, 1227–1231*, pp. 527, 539, 552. For Elias of Dereham as co-executor, see his statement in the Exchequer in 1244, TNA: PRO, E368/15.

27 I must thank Sandy Heslop for his advice on the style of the monument. There were originally 11 such medieval effigies in the Temple, as stated by the sixteenth-century London antiquary John Stow, whose memory went back to Mary's reign, *A Survey of London*, ed. C.L. Kingsford (2 vols, Oxford, 1908) II, pp. 50–1, but he incorrectly identified the Marshal's (talking of it as cross-legged). His contemporary, William Camden, saw a tomb of the elder William Marshal that he said he could identify by an epitaph, J. Weever, *Antient Funeral Monuments of Great Britain* (London, 1631, repr. 1767), p. 224 (but again the 'cross-legged' effigy was specified). It was a cross-legged effigy that was being shown to tourists in the Temple as the elder Marshal's still in the later seventeenth century, *The Journal of William Schellinck's Travels in England*, ed. M. Exwood and H.L. Lehmann (Camden Society, 5th ser., I, 1993), p. 58 (*s.a.* 1661). It looks indeed as though one of the later Marshal effigies was interpreted as that of the father, perhaps on the grounds that he was believed to be a crusader, and so his effigy must have crossed legs.

laid out on his back in his distinctive gear as a knight, unhelmeted, his moustachioed face framed by his mail coif. His eyes are open in the light of the day of resurrection. It was a style of commemoration that grew up in his own lifetime, for it was only his generation of knights that first had the self-confidence, and indeed temerity, to appear armed in church, both alive and dead.

The *History* records several posthumous tributes said of the Marshal, all laudatory. He died certain of his salvation, for he had planned for it as carefully as he planned any of his military campaigns. If treasure invested in the fabric of churches and the prayers of monks and priests could bring him everlasting life, then indeed he had cause to be optimistic. His men at least believed that he rejoiced with the elect of Heaven: 'we believe that his soul is in the company of God, because he was good in this life and his death'. Such indeed was their partisan view. Matthew Paris and others were less sure. The Marshal had died excommunicate by the Bishop of Ferns, who was obdurate in refusing to lift the ban, even at Henry III's insistence. When, many years later, building work at the Temple necessitated the opening of the elder Marshal's tomb, the corpse was found to be in a very poor state, its remains nauseatingly decayed despite the attempts at embalming and its being stitched into a bull's hide packed with salt. Men saw this as the result of the Irish bishop's curse. Matthew Paris was less sure where the Marshal's soul resided than was John of Earley.

8

THE MARSHAL AND HIS SOCIETY

The courtly world of the Marshal

The Marshal was a paragon of the military virtues of his day. We do not just have to take the word of his biographer for that. He was tutor-in-arms to the heir of the kingdom of England for a dozen years, prized captain of three successive Angevin monarchs and a (generally) successful commander in the field. These things we know from sources other than the *History*, so we need not doubt what it says. The Marshal was a great practitioner of what his day and age called *chevalerie*; but what he meant by the word and what we read into it are two different things. Several modern writers have had much to say about the Marshal not just as a soldier, but as an example of what they see as an early pattern of 'chivalry' and 'knight-errantry'.

The problem about applying the word 'chivalry' to the Marshal is that he would not have recognised our use of it. To him, the French word *chevalerie*, as it is used in his biography, meant what we would say in English was 'knightliness': the skills of horse riding and management of arms that he and his colleagues employed to make a living. He might have gone a little further too, and used it to mean the camaraderie and solidarity that knights shared in camp, in the hall and on the sports field. 'Chivalry' was for him what the knights did. What might have raised the Marshal's eyebrow was if we took *chevalerie* to mean a code of mannered and highly moral conduct suitable to the aristocratic male. That was a meaning of the word that his sons' generation was developing.

The Marshal would have called the code of superior manners that he was educated in as a boy not 'chivalry', but courtliness (*courtoisie*). This was, in fact, a code of behaviour and it was taught the young in the households where they were placed. It was written about not just by clergy, but by the barons of the day. It was the sort of behaviour that a man adopted in order to be a successful member of a royal or princely court, so there were pressing reasons why the young should acquire it. Social ease and confidence might translate into a career. Twelfth-century knights and clerks alike had to attract attention from the great person whose court they sought a place in. Attention might get them patronage. On the other hand, they were not alone in seeking attention; other equally ambitious rivals were after the same thing. Those rivals could be dangerous enemies, so a 'courtly' person not only tried to stand out from the crowd, he also deployed all his skills to avoid making enemies and keep as many useful friends at court as he could.

There is no doubt that the knights and barons of William Marshal's generation were self-conscious courtiers, out to get promotion and favour from the king: they made a career out of it. Like most careerists, they crafted their speech and behaviour to make the most of their opportunities. In effect, they were trapped into this sort of behaviour. If all you could expect was what you could earn by pleasing the great in their courts, you had to modify your behaviour to be acceptable and charming. This was why this form of behaviour was called *courtoisie* or *cortesia* by twelfth-century people: it was how you must behave in the public assembly, the court.

But courtliness was not chivalry, and for this reason. Twelfth-century writers, laymen and clerks alike tell us that courtliness might be encountered in clerics, women and even (to their surprise) in peasants. It was not a form of behaviour that applied to any one social group, though obviously it was more likely to be exercised in the aristocratic hall than anywhere else.

There has been a long debate, going back to the first writers on chivalry, as to the extent to which courtliness was taught to the uneducated layperson by the Church, a view most recently and intelligently discussed in the work of Professor Stephen Jaeger. He was the first writer to treat courtliness as a social code to be found universally in medieval courts as far back as the tenth century, if not further. The successful clerics at the German imperial court he studied positively oozed charm, imperturbability, modesty and accomplishment. In their ambition to get an edge over their rivals, they turned to the study of the moral philosophers of Ancient Rome: Cicero was for them a favourite source of advice. However, these German clerics were not missionaries of courtliness to a benighted world, as Professor Jaeger takes pains to say. Their skills were aspired to by any medieval person who wanted to get on, and there were other ways of acquiring basic instruction in manners, not least from courtly knights and barons to whom parents sent their children to acquire just those skills, as happened to William Marshal in the 1160s.[1]

By the time William Marshal was growing up, such skills were being routinely taught to young knights who wished to succeed in the competitive courts of the Angevin royal family. Certainly, some eminent writers of the later twelfth century were consciously reflecting on what it was to be a courtier: John of Salisbury, Walter Map, Gerald of Wales and Alexander Neckam were all Anglo-French clerks who wrote on their experience of the court. But Marshal would not have turned to

---

1 For his most recent essay on the subject, C.S. Jaeger, 'The origins of courtliness after 25 years', *Haskins Society Journal*, 11 (2009), pp. 187–216.

these men for instruction, even if he could have read Latin. He would, however, have recognised what they were describing, for they dwell on the cost to an individual of trying to live in such a competitive and strained environment.

Peter of Blois, an unhappy inhabitant of the court of Henry II, remarked on what it was that ambitious courtiers had to smile through at court: 'I could only marvel at one particular magnate, and how he was able to tolerate the petty nuisances of being a courtier; a man who had been for many years a soldier and accustomed to the command of others.'[2] Perhaps he was thinking of William Marshal. We might well remember in that regard those strained conversations the *History* reports that its hero had with King John, as the king maliciously attempted to prick the Marshal's infuriating composure. It may have intimidated and infuriated John, but other princes were pleased by it. At Epernon in 1179, the Marshal was the celebrity guest at the pre-tournament receptions hosted by dukes and counts. Why? Because 'the Marshal was polite (*corteis*) and behaved reasonably (*raisnables*), and did not put on airs (*ne s'en faiseit pas trop halt*)'.[3]

The *History* tells us a good deal about courtly behaviour, because it was produced in a rarified courtly environment. Disguise had much to do with it. A courtly man disguised his accomplishments as well as his true feelings, and he was reluctant to put himself forward, until pressed. William Marshal dominated the tournament fields of the 1170s, but, his biographer says, he was reluctant to boast (*vanter*) of his martial excellence. When he was asked by a party of ladies to sing while they were idling away the moments before a tournament, William was reluctant, but when he finally sang his performance was of course tuneful and accomplished. As for anger and precipitate action, the Marshal resisted them. He realised that curbing his aggression for the time being and waiting for an appropriate time to pursue a grievance was better than striking out when he was at a disadvantage.[4]

Marshal was moderate in all things, apart from ambition. This moderation of the career courtier in word and action was a defence. It was dictated by the fact that he was not alone in his ambitions. The *History* calls these rivals for patronage and recognition 'losengiers', a word of uncertain origin but much employed in twelfth-century literature. As far as the author was concerned, their defining feature was blind malice against his hero. In fact, as we have seen in the conspiracy in the Young King's household in 1182, they were nowhere near so elemental and evil. They were simply no more than what Sarah Kay neatly describes as 'the real and

---

2 Peter of Blois, *Epistolae*, in *Patrologia Latina: cursus completus*, vol. 207, no. 14, col. 46.
3 *History* I, lines 4358–60.
4 *History* I, lines 3971–6, 3984–7: when outmanoeuvred by two knights at a tournament, 'he did not put up a very great defence for his heart and mind told him that he would have them again for all their force. He did not put up a great struggle because he knew them by sight and by their first names, he knew their surnames and whose company they were in . . . when it comes to the reckoning both of them will be given such a deal that they will have the worst of it'.

ineradicable threat to courtly society: other courtiers'.[5] Since colleagues at court were liable to be his worst enemies, as their ambitions jostled with his own, the wise courtier tried to make himself as small a target as possible.

The features of William Marshal's behaviour we have examined through his biography have much in common with the clerical courtiers who hung around the royal courts seeking preferment. They simpered and smiled, were witty and clever, and tried to avoid making enemies. They made themselves amusing and popular by telling good stories. The Marshal's contemporaries at the royal court, Gervase of Tilbury and Walter Map, in fact made big collections of amusing, marvellous, spooky and sometimes frankly horrifying tales: they used them as currency in the marketplace of the royal hall, and then recycled them by publishing them to enhance their literary reputations. Good raconteurs were noticed and valued, and they made fewer enemies. William Marshal could spin a yarn with the best of them. He had a whole cycle of stories about his daring and dangerous father, which are now fossilised and embedded in the first part of his biography. There is, as we have seen, a self-deprecatory edge to the stories that survive of his early days as a knight. He knew how to laugh at himself for effect.

Women were actors within the world of courtliness, as they were not within the masculine world of chivalry. The *History* does not ignore women; it even credits Countess Isabel with an important role in her husband's council (a role that the charters both of herself and her husband go some way to confirm). It is notable, though, that the author entirely ignored the period when Countess Isabel ruled Leinster after 1200, for maybe as long as three years, and indeed pretended it did not happen. The *History* does not venerate women in any particular way. It says William Marshal had a good deal of respect for his sisters; he made a point of visiting them on the rare occasions that he was in England in his early career. He was also deferential and polite to the noblewomen before whom he performed his deeds in the tournament. Women came within the bounds of his courtliness, for, if they were not possible patrons themselves, they had husbands who were. He was, besides, a well-disposed man and on one occasion, at the firing of Le Mans, he had his squires assist an old lady whose house was burning down with all her goods inside. Perhaps he did not see the irony that it would not have been necessary at all if his colleagues had not set light to the city in the first place.

But this does not amount to the sort of behaviour nineteenth-century French scholars chose to call 'courtly' or 'chivalrous' love, an exaggerated deference to the noblewoman amounting almost to idolatry. The Marshal saw nothing to admire in the woman he caught eloping with a clerk. He was as stringently moral on that occasion as the most priggish cleric would have wanted. There is nothing in the *History* of the sensuality and playfulness of Andrew the Chaplain or Béroul, the Marshal's contemporaries. Their 'advanced' notions were far beyond the

---

5 'The contradictions of courtly love and the origins of courtly poetry: the evidence of the *Lauzengiers*', *Journal of Medieval and Early Modern Studies*, 26 (1996), p. 227.

conventional morality of the Marshal and his men. The suggestion that the Marshal might have committed adultery with the Young King's wife is greeted with genuine horror and outrage. The Marshal prided himself on his sound principles.

To the author of the *History*, therefore, women are (like the Marshal's own mother) assets and objects of material promotion; delightful, gentle and beautiful it is true, but still pieces in the game of ambition. The *History* has a limited time to spare for women. Not one comes through as a developed character in her own right, not even Countess Isabel. It paints a man's world, a world of violence, comradeship and high politics. The only traces of the world of romance are the adjectives borrowed to depict women from the vocabulary of the stock romance. Few women had any business in the real world of the Marshal's *mesnie*, and they were a positive menace to its emotional life. There, men fed their need for security and companionship by fixing their affections on the iconic figure of the Marshal, their impassive lord and father, sinking their insecurities in the brotherhood of serving him. The chasm in their lives that his death opened up could not be filled, although the *History* itself was an attempt by his bereft men to summon up a wraith of the Marshal, so that not all of what had once been was lost to them.

The sexuality of the Marshal can therefore be open to homoerotic interpretation, and the language of his biography, and indeed his own charters, makes no bones about his emotional fixation on his young lord, his only true lord, Henry the Young King. They lived a close and homosocial life, and there seems no reason to doubt that his relationship with the king was the most fulfilling in Marshal's emotional life. There would be little point in speculating as to whether his feelings towards the younger man tipped towards the homosexual. To begin with, the emotional language of the biographer was not the Marshal's own and is no reliable indicator of the depth of his feelings for his lord. We may fairly assume, however, that William's relationship with his royal lord and patron was the most passionate emotional bond he ever formed with another human adult, for it was evident to everyone around them that they were *carissimi*, a Latin word that can mean 'the closest of friends', or indeed – in other circumstances – lovers.

We cannot really approach the sexuality of William Marshal apart from registering its consequences, and they are undeniably heterosexual. The most significant snippet is, however, the evidence that he did indulge before his marriage in a relationship on the fringes of the court that produced a son, a boy he acknowledged and called by the family name of Gilbert. He most likely encountered this lady, an Englishwoman, in his extended stay in England between 1174 and 1176, for he was in France and the Holy Land for almost all the subsequent period till his marriage. We don't know her name, but we do know she subsequently married a member of a gentry family of the name of Essex. She later had a half-brother for Gilbert called Roger, who went into the law and was to have a career as a royal justice, possibly assisted by his Marshal connections. The bastard Gilbert Marshal, however, was given properties in at least two Marshal manors – significantly, neither of them manors his father had obtained from Countess Isabel. His father married him to a lady of a knightly family of Buckinghamshire, though

Gilbert may not himself have followed his father in the profession of arms. He survived his father, though not his legitimate brothers, and as far as can be told he was, like all but one of them, childless.

The *preudomme*

It was not William Marshal's ambition to be a chivalrous knight, as we might say. What he aimed at being was the ideal of masculine conduct he would have encountered in his education. It was an ideal quite independent of clerical and classical ideals. It could be summed up in one word (and often was); the word was *preudomme*. The word appears as already an old one in the earliest surviving French literature of the first decades of the twelfth century. It was an amalgamation of three French words, *preuz*, *de* and *homme*. Perhaps the nearest analogy might be the old-fashioned Irish turn of phrase: 'broth of a boy'. A *preudomme* was a '*preuz* of a man'. The quality of being *preuz* was derived ultimately from the Latin adjective 'probus', a word that might mean variously: 'tried and tested', 'upstanding' or 'mature'. By the first time we meet it, around the year 1100, the word *preudomme* already defined an ideal type of man: one that other men looked up to and respected. It was the existence of this ideal type that was so useful to William Marshal and his like in their struggles in the court.

But first, how was this ideal type defined? In the *Song of Roland*, the earliest significant literary work in the French language, a product of the time of the Marshal's grandfather, the idea of the *prozdom* turns up frequently. In the *Song*, men are called *prozdom* when they assist their lords with good counsel (lines 26, 604) and when they strike manfully against their enemies (lines 1288, 1557). In one case *proz* (mature) counsel is opposed to *fols* (reckless) counsel (lines 1193, 1209) and elsewhere it qualifies names and deeds that confer prestige (lines 221, 597). The composite *prozdom* of the late eleventh century was therefore a man of mature sense and wisdom, an experienced and effective soldier, and a valued supporter of his prince. To be called a *prozdom* was to receive the respect and deference of your fellows at court and on the field of battle. In the *Song*, the most obviously *proz* of men was Count Oliver, *li proz e li gentilz* ('the upstanding and well-born man'), the companion of Roland. He had the courage and skill in arms to command respect in a military aristocracy, but also he was a man of good counsel, more so than his friend Roland. He revealed the qualities of the complete *prozdom*. He knew the hearts of men; he knew that Roland's aggression and misjudgement made him a danger to himself.

Oliver was restrained in language, sound in judgement and objective in any situation. When the French saw the Saracen army approaching them at Roncesvalles, it was Oliver who made an accurate assessment of the enemy strength and deduced the chain of betrayal that had brought them there. It was Oliver who pragmatically advised Roland to summon assistance, and was of course ignored. Before he died, Oliver has the chance (lines 1723–6) to rebuke a repentant Roland for his rashness (*legerie*) and to praise moderate judgement (*mesure*) over recklessness (*estultie*). To that extent, the *Song* is an anthem in praise of the complete *preudomme*. It is because of this sort of use of the word that the great French medievalist Marc Bloch was quite convinced that the *preudomme* was the contemporary and popular synonym for what we call the 'courtly' man.[6]

We can be quite sure that William Marshal had the ideal of the *preudomme* before his eyes when he entered the world of the court: we know for a fact that his father (called *preudome corteis e sage*) was the model of conduct most in his mind when he was a young man.[7] Cicero did not figure in his curriculum as a squire. The word *preudomme* would have been frequently in his own mouth, and he would not have got far at court had he not himself been recognised as one. The qualities of the *preudomme* continued to be defined and refined throughout his lifetime. When a clerical writer in north-eastern France wrote a vernacular tract about lay conduct around about the year the Marshal died (a work the anonymous clerk called the *Ordene de Chevalerie*), it was the *preudomme* he fixed on as his ideal. His *preudomme* was described in terms familiar from the *Song*. The *preudomme* was wise (*sages*) and not indiscreet (*fols*). Although the tract then went on to relate the *preudomme* to the precepts of biblical Wisdom literature – indicating that the author was working in the twelfth-century Latin clerical tradition of moralising on knighthood – the author nonetheless did have a worldly ideal before him.[8]

The *preudomme* was a consistent and persistent ideal of aristocratic virtue throughout the twelfth century: he was the practised, intelligent soldier and man of affairs. The clerical writer might wish to moralise on the *preudomme*, and even appropriate the word to describe God and his saints, but it was a worldly ideal that he was borrowing. According to the Marshal's colleague, Master Stephen de Fougères – writing in the vernacular in the later 1150s – the *prodome* was the acme of the inhabitants of the royal court, the sort that sordid flatterers and backbiters tried to overthrow. King and bishop alike must be *prodom* in their dignity, integrity and concept of public duty.[9] It was with Stephen that the lay ideal of the courtier was first united with the theory of the schools in the Angevin realm.

So how was the quality useful to the courtier? Once a man such as William Marshal was recognised as a *preudomme*, he had a social defence denied to the cleric at court. A *preudomme* was a man who ought not be treated in any way that compromised his dignity and honour. Secure in his personal prestige, a *preudomme* might exert his autonomy and at times defy even the king in a way that a clergyman (unless he were a candidate for sanctity) could not. A theme both in medieval literature and in the history of medieval government is the tension between the king's responsibility for public order and peace, and the aristocracy's claims to be

---

6 Bloch, *Feudal Society* II, pp. 305–6.
7 *History* I, line 27.
8 *The Anonymous* Ordene de Chevalerie, ed. and trans. K. Busby (Utrecht Publications in General and Comparative Literature, 17, Amsterdam, 1983), pp. 105–19.
9 *Le Livre de Manières*, ed. R.A. Lodge (Geneva, 1979), cc. 21, 42, 86.

able to resort to violence in matters of its honour and its own interest.[10] In the *History*, we find the reported view of William de Tancarville, Chamberlain of Normandy and 'father of knights', that England in the 1160s was no longer a fit place for knights, presumably because the balance there had shifted to the king's view of order. No tournaments were allowed in England under King Henry II. But the *preudomme* might not just claim an autonomy in the use of violence; his autonomy would be asserted in his use of language to his prince.

A perfect instance of this is in a story to be found in the Marshal biography. It does not concern the Marshal, but rather an Angevin knight called Joubert de Pressigné. Joubert was sent by Henry II to negotiate with the mercenary captain Sancho de Savannac to release William Marshal, who was being held hostage for the Young King's debts. Instead, Joubert committed Henry II to paying the debt, which the king discovered when Sancho turned up at court and asked for the 100 marks he was owed. Henry turned on Joubert: 'How is it that this man is asking me for his money, and for what reason?' 'I'll gladly tell you why: in your name I told him in no uncertain terms that you would underwrite the debt. That is what I said, that was my understanding, and I fully admit that I said what I did.' Joubert considered that his honour and the king's demanded generosity, so he wilfully exceeded his instructions, despite the risk. What is more, the king accepted what he had done, and paid up.[11]

The Marshal, under stress, was free in his use of words towards his lord. In short, he was a great complainer, both when he was a knight and when he was a magnate. These complaints could be trivial or they could be more serious, but both the biography and other sources tell us that the Marshal was relentless once he did begin to complain. An example comes in 1188, when the Marshal was a retained household knight of the elder King Henry, and felt he had not received sufficient reward for his endeavours. So he complained. We know he complained because – courtesy of Professor Nicholas Vincent – we have now the text of a letter written by King Henry to the Marshal summoning him for the campaign of the summer of 1188, in which he intended to retake from King Philip the castle of Châteauroux in the province of Berry.[12] The Marshal, however, was exasperated with his lord, and had not apparently been shy in telling Henry repeatedly that he was frustrated. As the king pointed out in his summons to the Marshal: 'You have ever so often moaned (*planxisti*) to me about the small fee with which I enfeoffed you': in his need in 1188, the king was willing to offer him more, marriage to the

---

10 R.W. Kaeuper, *Chivalry and Violence in Medieval Europe* (Oxford, 1999), pp. 94–8.

11 *History* I, lines 7144–53.

12 The taking of Châteauroux in Berry occurred on 16 June 1188 as a result of differences between King Philip and Count Richard of Poitou, Henry II's son, over Toulouse, see W.L. Warren, *Henry II* (London, 1973), pp. 619–20; R. Benjamin, 'A Forty Years' War: Toulouse and the Plantagenets', *Historical Research*, 61 (1988), pp. 279–80. Henry II returned to Normandy from England 10–11 July 1188, Eyton, *Court, Household and Itinerary of Henry II*, p. 289.

heir of Châteauroux, no less. But before the Marshal got this promise (which proved ephemeral), he must have been complaining to the king's face for at least two years.[13]

The Marshal was a man who would not be quiet, and he had no self-consciousness or modesty about asserting his rights when he believed they were being ignored. The Marshal was quite as assertive about his dignity. These were occasions when his standing as a *preudomme* was publicly threatened or questioned. His response was invariably to stand up and justify himself vociferously and aggressively, and, in his biographer's view, successfully. We see this at Nottingham in 1194 when William de Longchamp confronted the Irish barons with the king's wish that they do homage to him. Richard had just crushed the last adherents of John in England, and seems to have wanted to assure himself of John's Irish vassals' loyalty. Although some barons agreed, the Marshal refused. He had paid homage to John, he said, and to swear it for the same lands to King Richard was, in his view, *felonie*. He also refused to dispute the point with Longchamp, because he said that would make him a *losengiers*.[14] Fortunately for him, King Richard was amused and let the question drop.

A later incident was similar, but its consequences were more serious, as we have already seen. This was when, in June 1205, the Marshal had his first major rift with his great patron, King John. He had returned from France after doing homage to King Philip for his Norman lands, claiming that he had John's consent in doing so. This gave the Marshal's enemies among the household knights – two are particularly named – the chance to accuse him of *traïson* and *felonie*. The king immediately sought a judgement from his barons, who demurred; the *History* says that they were moved by the Marshal's plea that condemning him would lead to their own persecution in due course. Whether this happened or not, it seems that the king then consulted with his military household, which contained a party hostile to the Marshal. But when it turned out that the only way to bring him down was to fight a duel, the young knights backed off, leaving the king baffled and vengeful.[15] The consequence for the Marshal was exile from the court and years of Angevin-style persecution.

13 N. Vincent, 'William Marshal, King Henry II and the Honour of Châteauroux', *Archives*, 25 (2000), p. 15: 'Persepe te michi planxisti quod de paruo feodo te feffaui'. Mid-twelfth-century literature preserves similar attitudes: William of Orange is depicted as complaining to Louis the Pious that 'for all that I have served and defended you, I have not acquired so much as a halfpenny, so that no one calls me a knight at court', translated from *Le Charroi de Nimes*, ed. J.L. Perrier (Classiques français du moyen âge, 1982), lines 253–5.

14 *History* II, lines 10312–30.

15 For the full incident, see *History* II, lines 13052–248. The Marshal's son, in 1220, came out with the declaration that his father had done homage to Philip 'having with him letters of the king of England', see *Cartulaire Normand de Philippe-Auguste, Louis VIII, St-Louis et Philippe-le-Hardi*, ed. L. Delisle (Société des antiquaires de la Normandie, 1852), p. 43. The author of the *History* (writing five or so years later, while the issue is still very much a live one) implies much the same with his story of John's words of permission to the Marshal in April 1205 to do homage to Philip.

There were differences between clerical and lay culture, and they were rooted in the need of the knight not just to be a courtier, but also to be seen to be a *preudomme*, a man of vigour, discretion, loyalty and honour. When these qualities conflicted with the king's will, then the layman had but two choices: to sacrifice his honour, or put his career in deep jeopardy. All too often, perhaps, the layman whose career was under threat compromised: he blustered and wheedled, he intrigued and betrayed, and so became a *losengiers*. This would be why weary and satirical clergy, such as Peter of Blois, expected little of people at court. Writing around the year 1184, he said that the natural disposition of a courtier was to conspire, to succumb to envy, to accept bribes, and to imagine an insult when none was intended.[16]

But the braver and more daring spirit might turn and defy his lord. The *History* is a text that is well aware of the dilemma of the knight or baron at court. Its hero was a man who was prepared to defy his lord when he was in the position where his self-image as a *preudomme* could not sustain the demands the king put on it. Kings such as Henry II and Richard, who well understood this inner conflict, might well then accept this act of autonomy, and not see it as treason. Kings such as John, whose imperial will was more important than his servants' principles, reacted otherwise, to his courtiers' cost and his own eventual ruin.

William Marshal was not therefore a chivalrous man. But he is an important character in our growing understanding of how the idea of 'chivalry' grew. Over the past 20 years, his name has become more and more prominent in studies of the subject, and that is only as it should be. His biography proves that some at least among the knights and barons of his day did work hard at their public faces. They were courtiers and the more accomplished of them acted in a contrived and courtly way. The courts in which they acted out their careers were, to that extent, places of mannered sophistication. The contemporary clerical sources tell us the same, and also tell us that the royal and princely courts of the twelfth century were dangerous and edgy little worlds, and not at all comfortable for their inhabitants.

Ambition and the need for security were the motivating forces that kept courtiers in attendance on their lord and shaped their behaviour. In the Marshal's time, there was not any 'code' of chivalry to be a manual to instruct the aspiring knight in how to conduct himself; something like that does not appear fully formed until the 1220s at the earliest, and by then William Marshal was dead. Nonetheless, before the Marshal died, a number of writers were at work writing extensively on the subject of what it was that made a knight exemplary. Before the Marshal died, the Flemish writer Ralph de Houdenc had produced a detailed treatise called the 'Romance of the Wings', which was a major step towards just such a codified body of behaviour. But Ralph was only one of a number of clerics during the Marshal's lifetime who attempted to produce a moral template for the good knight. The most specific of them was Bishop Stephen de Fougères (died 1178), whom the Marshal would have known when he was a young courtier in

---

16 *Epistolae*, in *Patrologia Latina: cursus completus*, vol. 207, no. 150, col. 440.

Normandy. In his 'Book of Conduct', written before he was a bishop, probably late in the 1150s, Stephen set out his criteria for praiseworthy behaviour in many walks of life. This is what he said of the knight:

> Born of a free father and a free mother, a man is invested as a knight to pursue a strenuous life, so he should be intelligent, and should not be corrupt and full of vice. If he is sensible he should be both tough (*hardiz*) and of honest conduct (*proz*). He should bear himself gracefully towards the Church and all folk. The knight should concentrate on the idea that he should spend the days of his youth in being loyal, more so than a monk should be steadfast in his vocation. The knight takes up the sword in such a spirit that he should neither commit a crime nor lie, nor should he contemplate deceit; he should assist Holy Church, he should attend it and live only on what is his rightful estate.[17]

The bishop was undoubtedly putting together in his book sentiments that he had dwelt on in sermons given to the royal court and to other congregations. The Marshal would have heard sentiments just like them delivered by Stephen and by other clerics. So Marshal knew from the pulpit that a knight must be honest and true, protect the Church, the poor and the weak, and be well mannered. He would have whole-heartedly agreed with these sentiments, for in his way he did pursue them. Stephen was merely preaching the way of the *preudomme* with a light ecclesiastical and moral gloss. However, it was on the field of the tournament, in the siege and in battle, rather than at court, that the 'chivalrous' nature of the Marshal was most open to question, and here we find his conduct to be at its most pragmatic and self-interested.

The tournament mentality

What is the 'chivalry' the Marshal displayed in the tournament field? From around the age of 21 to the age of 37, William Marshal was an habitué of the tournament. The *History* lists 16 tournaments in which its hero participated between 1167 and 1183. The rise of this sport to respectability was very much a feature of the Marshal's own lifetime. Meetings of knights for the purpose of military games are first mentioned in France in the late eleventh century, but little is known of these early tournaments. They were probably informal meetings of vigorous, military-minded free men, but not yet patronised by the higher aristocracy. They acquired early on a bad reputation as undisciplined riots. Kings and popes moved to ban them, in the latter case because they were a distraction of Christian energy from the crusade. For a good century and more, they occupied the same place in the view of the establishment as drug-fuelled raves or Stonehenge solstice-worship does now. Henry II of England would not allow them to be held in his kingdom but, as the *History* indicates, permitted them in the Marches of Normandy and in Anjou.

---

17 *Le Livre des Manières*, cc. 148–51, pp. 81–2.

It was during Henry II's reign that the tournament became a more respectable aristocratic pursuit. This was partly because the fact of being a knight had become more generally regarded, in northern France and England, as a social distinction rather than a military calling. But also, as Duby points out, the organisation and sponsorship of great tournaments was a means for the great duke or count to pose as a leader of the nobility. In Stephen's reign in England, we first hear of a magnate, Hugh de Mortemer, being killed at such a meeting. In Normandy in 1166, as the *History* tells us, William de Tancarville thought it a desirable thing to lead his *mesnie* around local Norman tournaments. By the time William Marshal was the master of the Young King's *mesnie*, tourneying was all the rage and it occasionally found great patrons around Northern France; Philip, Count of Flanders, being the chief of them.

Most of the tournaments were small affairs, a score or two of knights divided for the purpose of the game into two informal teams. Such meetings were advertised by word of mouth and chiefly attended by local knights and people such as the Marshal, professionals who drew much of their income from captures and ransoms. At the height of the season in France, in late autumn, a determined knight might get to one every two weeks. In such circumstances in the later 1170s, William Marshal and a Flemish acquaintance, Roger de Jouy, decided to milk the circuit for everything it was worth. They came to an agreement that they would team up and split the profits from the captures they made on their own account over the next two years. They were meticulous; they had to be, since the money they earned in this way made no small difference to the degree of aristocratic display they could flaunt. The Young King's kitchen clerk, Wigain, undertook to keep a tally of their captures (probably rather a relief for him to be doing something other than totalling the consumption of capons), which survived the decades to be seen by the Marshal's biographer. In 10 months from the opening of a season in Pentecost to its close the next Ash Wednesday, Wigain's tally amounted to 103 knights. On his deathbed, the Marshal recalled with mingled regret and pride that he had taken as many as 500 knights prisoner on the field.

If the Marshal was right, one can only marvel at the obstinacy of the knights who were willing to place themselves in front of his lance; confirmation of the old belief that there is one born every minute. The Marshal had some cause to feel the bitterness of this knowledge. His biographer let slip the intriguing detail that he had not been universally successful in his early career as a tourneyer. At a tournament near Eu, on the borders of Normandy, late in 1178 or early in 1179, the Marshal met up again with an adversary from his earlier days, Matthew de Walincourt. Matthew had been a renowned knight, serving at various times from the late 1160s to the 1180s in the household of Count Baldwin V of Hainault and Count Ives of Soissons.[18] The Marshal had a grudge against him because, when

---

18 *La chronique de Gislebert de Mons*, ed. L. Vanderkindere (Recueil de textes pour servir à l'étude de l'histoire de Belgique, 1904), pp. 111, 142; W.M. Newman, *Les seigneurs de Nesle-en-Picardie, xie–xiiie siècle* (2 vols, Philadelphia, 1971) II, pp. 111, 114, 137, 157.

he was a young and unrecognised knight, Matthew had defeated him and refused to restore his horse to him, leaving him in financial difficulties. The Marshal took great delight at Eu in depriving Matthew of his horse on two occasions, and, on the second, he refused point blank to restore it to the older man. Matthew had deprived him when he was an unknown youngster and he had sorely felt the loss of a horse, despite the intercession of great men on the Marshal's behalf. Now the Marshal had done the same to him. In that tournament, he captured 10 knights in all, and took away 12 horses, a handsome increase in his fortune.[19]

Tournaments were not necessarily 'chivalrous' places. The Marshal might on occasion be generous with his winnings, but he was in the field principally to win and to rake in profits. Contemporary clerks picked up rumours of the sharp practice in which some tourneyers indulged to make money. The English clerk Alexander Neckam, who was studying in Paris while the Marshal was riding the tournament fields of Northern France, heard some sleazy tales of what went on there. He heard of the practice, indulged in by hardened and unscrupulous knights, of secretly tipping off collaborators on the opposing tournament team as to who were the naive and inexperienced knights on their own side. When the boys were taken prisoner, the cheats on both sides would cynically split the profits made on their victims' horses and armour. Such was the pool-hall morality of the tournament in the 1170s. 'Slavetrading' and 'shameful betrayal' was what Neckam called it.[20]

Did the Marshal make his fortune as one of the racketeers of the tournament? Neckam might have thought so. The sort of deal reached by William Marshal and Roger de Jouy led to something like the situation he described. The Marshal and Roger were on different teams in the great tournament at Lagny in 1180, yet despite being on different sides they would have taken a share in each other's profits. Was what they were doing sharp practice? It can be said in their defence that it does not follow that either of them tipped off the other about the weak players in his team, and it is certain that the Marshal did not. If he had been guilty of that degree of duplicity, it would not have helped the Marshal's reputation as a *preudomme*, who must be loyal to his friends and followers. No such knight would have achieved the social eminence and respectability the Marshal achieved: it would have been material too rich for the *losengiers* to ignore when they tried to subvert his reputation.

On the circuit

The Marshal in the 1170s was a great and renowned sportsman at the centre of his world. He was never more at home than in the rich and brilliant flagship tournaments of that glittering decade, when his master, the Young King, and several other wealthy dukes and counts were pouring huge sums of money into the circuit

19 *History* I, lines 3181–374.
20 *De naturis rerum libri duo*, ed. T. Wright (Rolls Series, 1863), p. 312.

and giving a new meaning to the term 'largesse'. They drew hundreds of participants from all over France and England; some even came from Scotland. It is on these affairs that the *History* gives us the greatest detail. On such occasions, great magnates from all over the Anglo-French world would converge on the chosen field, lords from the area comprehending Scotland, England and the Marches, Flanders, Hainault, Anjou, Poitou, Normandy, Brittany, Champagne, Burgundy, Picardy and the area then called 'France' – which we now call the Île-de-France, the region ruled directly by the Capetian king.[21]

Few subjects of the emperor, no Italians, Navarrese or Spaniards are mentioned in the *History* in connection with a tournament, but we know from the work of Occitan poets that the sport was all the rage on either side of the Pyrenees in the 1170s, with its own great patrons, and it may be that it formed a distinct circuit that drew knights south rather than north. The northern fringe of the core area of the Marshal's tournament in the 1170s seems to have been marked by the popular one regularly held near Louvain in the duchy of Brabant (modern Belgium) mentioned by Walter Map.[22] Nonetheless, areas outside the tournament's French heartland likewise felt the enthusiasm for it in the 1170s, and it was an annoyance for knights resident in England that the sport was banned in their homeland.

The *History* gives us a lot of incidental information about the sort of sites picked for the tournament. The greater ones occupied a large amount of space. A broad and level valley bottom was one sort of favoured site. The *History* records four venues that fit that sort of description, at Anet and Eu on the borders of Normandy, at Maintenon in the forest of Yvelines and at Joigny in the Île-de-France. The popular venue between the Norman border town of Anet and the upstream village of Sorel, which comprised six kilometres of river meadow along the river Eure, was used for tournaments in spring 1178 and June 1179. There was another sort of terrain that was acceptable.

The site between Ressons-sur-Matz and Gournay-sur-Aronde, 15 kilometres north-west of Compiègne, was rather different from the floodplain sites. It was a series of flat-topped hills between two marshy valleys, but it was nonetheless very popular with organisers. Ressons-Gournay had indeed a very long history as a tournament venue. It was in regular use as early as 1169, when the tournament there degenerated into a real battle because of a personal difference between Count Baldwin of Hainault and Count Philip of Flanders.[23] The *History* also mentions its use in the summer of 1176, in November 1182 and again on Saturday 15 January 1183.

21 See for my deeper consideration of the sport, D. Crouch, *Tournament* (London, 2005), from which much of the following is drawn.
22 *De Nugis Curialium*, ed. and trans. M.R. James (rev. edn, Oxford, 1983), p. 164; M. Keen, *Chivalry* (London, 1984), p. 84.
23 Gilbert of Mons, *Chronicon Hanoniense*, in *Monumenta Germanicae Historiae: Scriptores*, xxi, p. 518. It was still in use in the 1240s: see *La Manekine*, ed. H. Suchier (Paris, 1884), lines 2665ff.

There seem to have been three criteria for choosing such sites. They had to be reasonably level, to allow complicated and unhindered mounted manoeuvres: this in itself limited the possible venues. Second, and for the same reason, they should preferably be on floodplains or hill-pastures with a minimal amount of hedging and fencing. This sort of terrain would also have been less liable to sustain agricultural damage. The Marshal's French contemporary, the cardinal-bishop James de Vitry, criticised tourneying knights for trampling hedges, and for swearing at and harrassing agricultural labourers who were at work within the limits of the tournament ground. He was not exaggerating, for the *History* talks of the participants riding through and breaking down vine stocks in the Lagny tournament of 1179.[24]

The last reason for choosing a particular tournament ground was probably traditional, perhaps going back to the sport's earliest, countercultural days in the eleventh century. Of the eight large sites described by the *History*, six were on marches where the jurisdictions of great princes met: two on the borders of Normandy at Eu and Anet. This would seem to recall a time when tournament gatherings were suspected by princes and raised issues of law and order: to pick a site in contested borderlands would be to try to sidestep their jurisdiction, and to use territory more accustomed to war conditions.

The *History* gives a good deal of further information about how tournaments were organised. Indeed, it is our chief source for the staging of the twelfth-century event. On the day before a great meeting, there might be receptions and parties hosted by particular celebrities, such as those where the Marshal was lionised before the great tournament of Epernon in the summer of 1179.[25] The action might begin that very evening with displays and introductory combats (*començailles*) between lesser individuals seeking notice, before the review parade and the day opened with the grand onset (the *estor*) between the teams with the princes and counts who were their leaders. These evening preludes were also called the 'vespers' of the tournament, in a faintly irreligious allusion to the sequence of the clerical day: vespers being the evening office before the new liturgical day began. At Joigny, a light-hearted Marshal joined in the preliminary jousts in order to make a present of a captured horse to a singer who asked for one in a flattering song composed in his honour.

The tournament ground across which the main action happened – called by the interesting name of 'piquenpance' by Stephen de Fougères, although the *History* always calls it the 'place' – was not by any means a featureless plain. To begin with, as at Anet in 1178, the tournament action spilled into the town streets, which it should not have for they were out of bounds beyond the lists. At the second tournament at Anet in 1179, some Picard knights took refuge in a barn and defended

---

24 *The Exempla of Jacques de Vitry*, ed. T.F. Crane (New York, 1890), pp. 62–4; *History* I, lines 4832–40.
25 *History* I, lines 4319–45.

it as a miniature fortress until they surrendered to the Marshal, while in the same tournament French knights took possession of an abandoned and ruined castle mound to fight off their pursuers.

There would be roped-off boxes called *lices* (or 'lists'), which seem to have acted as team bases, where squires were stationed to secure the ransomed horses (sometimes with their riders still on them) that had been taken into custody, as at the meetings at Anet and Eu in 1178/79. These and other roped areas on the field were known as *recets*, and were safe areas into which knights could not be pursued and where they could rest and recover. Places to rest and tie up their wounds were very necessary for horse and man alike, for the day's action would go on until late afternoon. As the day ended, the knights would ride around looking for captured friends, or looking to arrange ransoms. Disputes would be brought before respected princes to settle, and the most eminent men present would award the prize of the day to a team or individual who had drawn particular attention; usually the Marshal, according to his biographer.

The greatest tournaments had a patron who would publicise, host and organise the gathering, feast his great guests and offer token prizes to the best knight on the day. In the case of Philip of Flanders, on one occasion he equipped with some generosity the Young King and his men who appeared at a tournament in the county of Clermont without the ironmongery of war. The tournament patron, whether Count of Flanders, Duke of Burgundy or the lesser Counts of Clermont, Beaumont-sur-Oise or Dreux, clearly expected to gain something from this considerable outlay. No doubt, Duby is right to suggest that it was done as much to assert their dignity against the growing power of the French monarchy, by providing bread and circuses for the knights, as for pleasure. But one should not avoid the more simple cause of the patronage of tournaments: its usefulness in promoting the status of great magnates against each other, as much as the king.

The Marshal owed his position and favour with the Young King to his infection of the boy with the lust to tourney. Duby's description of the Marshal as the 'team manager' of the Young King's tourneying *mesnie* has a certain validity, although player-manager would be nearer the truth. The king's continuing favour to William depended on unbroken success, and the Marshal did his best to provide it. He exerted himself to attract into what was a basically Anglo-Norman *mesnie* the most distinguished knights of Flanders, France and Champagne: it would expand to over 100 knights for a big occasion, each drawing 20 shillings a day as a fee. Such men could name their own price to enlist under Norman colours for the season. This was very much a transfer fee market. We know that lords might well use the tournament to spot likely talent.[26] When, in 1183, the Marshal had informally parted from the king, a number of dukes and counts promptly offered substantial inducements for him to join their service. We have seen the evidence that he did in fact accept Count Philip's offer before his recall to his estranged lord.

---

26 See the examples marshalled in Keen, *Chivalry*, p. 89.

As a sport, tourneying was a most dangerous activity: in the level of violence the participants suffered, it was rather like horseback American football with sharp sticks and no referees. There were some elements of it that make the sporting analogy as irresistible to me as it was to Duby. There were teams dressed in the same colours and there was a decided team spirit about the game, with captains, team chants (the *enseigne* or 'war cry') and regional loyalties. In a great tournament, as at Lagny in 1180, teams were grouped into their nominal place of origin by nations: English, Bretons, Flemings, Normans and so on. In other ways, though, the analogy is inadequate to describe more than the underlying spirit of the tournament. There was no formal objective to be achieved, just individual honour to be won. The winning side was the one that chased the other from the field, or that which amassed the greater number of captives at the end of the day's fighting. Also, the individual went in for it for more than the satisfaction of team spirit and cooperative endeavour; he went into it to fill his purse.

Few rules governed the tournament field, apart from the feeling that it was generally bad form to slip away from your captor once his attention had been drawn away, or steal the horses taken by another man. The most regulated part of the business was the taking of ransoms. A man once taken must undertake to pay a ransom, but that done he could be allowed to rejoin the field if he felt up to it. The *History* is very hot against bad sportsmanship where it involved ransom, and very particular that it be paid. On the other hand, it is willing to balance this punctiliousness with admiration for the knight, as William Marshal is said to have been at Joigny, who tempered industry with largesse. At Joigny, the Marshal took numbers of prisoners as usual, but is said to have distinguished himself by grandly giving away his winnings.

Men conducted themselves on the twelfth-century tournament field with the same brutality and ruthlessness as they did on the battlefield, nor did they necessarily use blunt and unpointed weapons.[27] Since the main justification for the activity was that it offered an authentic training ground for war, we must not be surprised at this. In his earliest excursions on the field in 1166, young William Marshal acquired characteristic tourneying injuries: damaged hands and a battered skull. Many tourneyers must have suffered broken noses when their helms were beaten back into their faces. As the biographer tells us, at one early tournament William's helmet was hit so hard it was turned 180 degrees on his head, and stayed back to front for all he could do. In the tournament of Pleurs, William famously had to lay his head on an anvil for a smith to prise his battered helm off his head. One of the few differences between war and tournament was that in the sport, a death on the field was thought to be a tragic misfortune.

27 See, for example, the description of a tournament in the romance *Garin le Loherenc*, ed. A. Iker-Gittleman (3 vols, Classiques français de moyen âge, 1996–1997) I, lines 1453–5 (datable to 1160 × 1180).

The *après tournoi*

The greatest thing for William Marshal about the tournament circuit was it not only gave him a chance to excel in armour and on horseback, with all the profit that followed from his prowess, but it also gave him an unparalleled chance to do what we would call 'networking'. It was vital for any unlanded knight to be seen and get known on the circuit. Both Marshal's physical and courtly skills were deployed to charm, amuse and befriend his colleagues on the circuit, and to identify likely patrons. The pressing need for a man such as him to network was proved in 1183, when he needed a new employer, and to find one he resorted immediately to the tournament meetings of Northern France, where he found himself the happy object of a bidding war.

The entire occasion of a tournament was arranged with socialisation in mind. The team would usually turn up a day in advance of the meeting, and an organised *mesnie* would have sent ahead its chamberlains and ushers to secure appropriate lodgings in the town base to which it was assigned. Above the doors of their quarters would have gone up a shield bearing the device of the king or his banneret who was to occupy the house. It's unlikely that the wealthy Anglo-Norman team would ever have had to pitch tents in the fields outside, as latecomers had to. Most likely, the Young King would have been welcomed by the civic fathers, hats doffed, competing to hold his stirrup while he dismounted, the sort of scene contemporary writers describe. All the eminent lords present that evening would offer drinks receptions, and the shields over their doors advertised where the events were happening, for those who were confident enough of their acquaintance to seek an entry into their company. Gatecrashers were common.

The French writer Jean Renart gives a vivid account of the gossip and exchange of news when friends met at such an upstairs reception, looking down on the torchlit streets crowded with sightseers and servants and commenting on the knights they spot. Knights would move from reception to reception looking for acquaintances. Heralds would race through the street announcing the arrival of a particular champion, hoping for some coins for their flattery. A great lord such as the Young King would have been accompanied by boxes of linen, napery and plate, which his household staff would unpack as they set up a lavish dinner for his favoured guests. Many tourneyers travelled with female companions, not always their wives. So the dinners would have been accompanied by singing, dancing, flirting and, quite often, followed by sex. All sorts of trades followed the tournament circuit: farriers, physicians, provisioners, horse dealers and smiths. The oldest profession was undoubtedly represented too.

This was the Marshal's world, and his biographer rejoices in the eminence he had obtained in it by the mid-1170s. This is his description of his networking at the Épernon meeting of 1179:

> The high-ranking men who had gone to the tournament were lodged throughout the town. It is the custom that in the evening they go and visit

one another at their lodgings; this is a fine custom and their conduct is courteous and polite when they seek to talk together, get to know one another and acquaint one another with the affairs which each has in hand.[28]

Every prince who was present acknowledged William as a friend and he was invited to the receptions they were holding. In this way, the Marshal was affirmed as a man who had a claim to high status in his small and mobile world, even though he was still then but an unlanded knight. Such was medieval celebrity.

The night after the grand tournament, the entertainments were even more lavish, for great dinners were held at either tournament base at the expense of the tournament sponsor. His (or her) honour depended on the quality of the entertainment and food offered. The exhausted and often injured participants seemed nonetheless to find the energy to enjoy themselves. All awaited the verdict of the sponsor and the onlookers as to who had been judged the most distinguished knight in either of the two sides. It might be announced in a figure dance offered by the ladies present, who would bear the prize teasingly through the throng until arriving at the designated champion. The prize might be a mere token – an animal or (as in one case in the Marshal's career) a big fish. But some sponsors offered elaborate items of the jeweller's or goldsmith's art commissioned especially for the occasion. The Marshal won the prize on more than one occasion, as his biographer boasted, thus publicly consolidating his reputation.

It was in the afterglow of the meeting that quite ambitious entertainment might occur. Some meetings in the heat of summer staged their dinners under brilliantly lit marquees in the meadows, the field outside occupied by field kitchens and troupes of musicians. The tourneyers, washed and changed into livery robes, would process in pairs to their places with their ladies. After the main courses, while dessert was being served, would come specially staged entertainments, where knights might demonstrate a different sort of prowess. There survives a poem performed after a tournament in the 1180s by the great tourneyer Huon d'Oisy, castellan of Cambrai. It's a remarkable and good-humoured fantasy depicting an imaginary tournament when the wives and lovers of the knights present took the field, with little jokes about each individual lady. Huon was a prolific and accomplished poet and musician, as were many of his colleagues. The Marshal biographer mentions that William was quite happy as a young man to sing to entertain the ladies, and indeed that he had a fine voice. He does not tell us whether William was also a poet and composer; one assumes that he did not have that skill, for the biographer would have been sure to mention it if he had. But nonetheless, he would have danced away those nights under the opening stars, and stood up at the call of his friends to perform the lays he had memorised, for the basic truth about William Marshal and his career was that he was a youth who was forced to sing for his supper.

28 *History* I, lines 4329–38.

9

THE MARSHAL AT WAR

The tournament being what it was, we can expect even less of the chivalry of Sidney Painter on the battlefield. Here was a place of real seriousness. Indeed, it was the field of war that gave the aristocracy the only warrant for its privileges in the stock view of contemporary writers. They fought for Christ and for justice while the clerks offered intercession with God. The peasants who worked to provide the necessities for both had to console themselves that they were the foundations of the two shafts that held up the sky.

The Marshal and his class had ways of alluding to their reason for existence. On surviving impressions of the Marshal's seal, he appears represented, as do almost all of his lay contemporaries, garbed as a knight on horseback. The common image of aristocracy in the late twelfth century was a military one. Since William the Conqueror had his new seal cut after conquering England, it had been thought increasingly suitable for a great man or ruler to be depicted as a horse-soldier. It did not happen all at once. There was a different, older idea that a lay lord should be shown in civilian dress, the military display confined to the sword that was to represent his power to discipline the evildoer. Some seals and all tomb-effigies preserve this more pacific and judicial aristocratic image until the Marshal's time. His own reputed tombstone was therefore something of a new departure in noble monuments.

But in general, from the early twelfth century onwards, it was the arms and accoutrements of a knight that automatically identified the aristocrat. The association of ideas had advanced so far by 1200 that just to be a knight was recognised as qualifying for inclusion in a superior social group. In the Marshal's own lifetime, this idea had advanced to the point where a knight, however poor, could still expect to be addressed as *sire* or *messire*, a form of public deference extended in the first half of the century only to earls and barons.

Since the great aristocrats had for many generations made war their profession, this conjunction of ideas is by no means odd. The oddity lies in the newer idea that the knight was himself noble just from taking the rite of passage of dubbing; this particular association of ideas was a novelty, and it appeared in the Marshal's own lifetime. It is in the Marshal's days that it was first stated that the right of investing a young man as a knight should be forbidden to the magnates and belong only to the king: if knighting had become a rite of passage not just into manhood, but into an upper social level, then some believed that the king should monitor it.[1]

It was partly through people such as William Marshal that knighthood became of itself a quality of nobility. Younger sons of barons, such as he was, would have bridled at the thought that they were not as noble as their father. If they took up the profession of arms, it did not alter their status, and their presence would enhance the status of the men of meaner origins they associated with in the *mesnies* in which they were employed. As we have seen from the Marshal's career, it was finding employment that was the trick; even he found himself without employment on occasion. But war was an all too regrettably common state in the twelfth century, and the Marshal found no difficulty in attracting men of the right calibre to his banner when he in turn became an employer of knights. Like all magnates, he kept a household contingent of knights: in his case, he was escorted everywhere by between eight and twelve of them. But in times of warfare, this riding retinue was expanded much further.

Although his earldom was supposed to provide the king with over 60 knights' service, we do not know if that was the total required of him on campaign. We have the evidence of the text of King Henry II's military summons to the Marshal in June 1188 that he should appear in Normandy before the king with 'whatever knights he could'. This being the only surviving such writ from the twelfth century, the evidence it offers cannot be cross-checked. But the probability is that the Marshal and his colleagues augmented their retinues with a suitable company of knights hired for the occasion, and the number they hired was up to them. These extra knights might or might not have been obtained from among his tenantry for the occasion: it is significant in that regard that his knights in the assault on Caerleon in 1217 included Scudamores and Bloets, families from the southern March of Wales. But we do not know whether or not they were answering a summons from the Marshal to fight in return for the lands they held, or fighting for pay and honour. In Ireland in 1207–1208, many of his tenantry were fighting against him, and his paid retinue was what stood between him and dispossession.

There is no doubt that the Marshal hired other troops on occasion. There were in his day, especially in the Marches of Wales, mercenaries ready for hire. The lord of Raglan in his Gwent lordships held his large manor in return for providing the lord of Chepstow with what was called in the 1170s a 'Welsh knight'. These

---

1 The view is found in *La Chanson d'Aspremont*, ed. L. Brandin (2 vols, Classiques français du moyen âge, 1923–1924) I, lines 156–63. The work is regarded as having been commissioned for the court of Richard the Lionheart. This striking declaration (made in the romance at the behest of Charlemagne) can be interpreted as echoing advanced opinion in Angevin court circles.

'Welsh knights' were the sort of horse serjeants that King Henry II hired in hundreds from South Wales for his 1188 campaign: trained horse warriors who would otherwise have found employment in the *teuloedd* (military households) of Welsh princes and magnates. Mounted warriors who were not knights are in evidence in the Marshal's retinue, although they are called 'squires' in the French sources. In the 1170s and 1180s, as well as later in the Middle Ages, men called squires were not all in training to be knights. Such men might not have been as heavily armoured or as well paid as the knights of the Marshal's retinue, but would doubtless have been quite as professional in their training and service. Infantry too would have been available for hire, but the sources are simply not there to tell us what use the Marshal made of them.

Dressing the part

The sources of the time, and the *History* itself, focus on the knight. They do so for cultural and social reasons. The figure of the knight was more than just a military icon. On his seal (which can be dated as far back as the later 1170s) and on his alleged tomb, we see the Marshal garbed as a knight would have been at the close of the twelfth century, for that was where his social distinction and utility lay. Many of the developments in knightly equipment in the twelfth century must have arisen from the needs of the tournament circuit rather than warfare, and also responded to its fashions and fads.

It happens that we have a unique insight into the knightly gear of William Marshal's circle in a work written by a man he knew, Ralph Niger, one of the chaplains of his beloved lord, the Young King. Around 1187, several years after the Young King's household had dispersed, Ralph wrote a remarkable theological work taking as its framework a thoroughly up-to-date and detailed catalogue of knightly equipment.[2] He describes the knight arming for war, first fixing his spurs to his shoes, and then lacing mail leggings to protect legs, thighs and groin. These were his 'chausses', and by William's day they had become standard equipment. After that, he threw his hauberk over his head and upper garments, which were fitted with mail-mesh mittens, to protect the hands, which were the most likely part of his body to be exposed to mutilation. Ralph is the first writer to tell us that knights in the 1180s were trusting to stouter armour than the fine and flexible mail that formed their hauberk. Under it, they now laced boiled leather armour plate across their chests. They added other moulded leather plates (*genouilliers*) to protect their lower legs and knee joints.

On the knight's head was a mail coif, like a balaclava, and around the chin would have been laced a chain mail muffler, called a 'ventaille', for added protection

---

2 *De re militari et triplici via peregrinationis Ierosolimitane*, ed. L. Schmugge (Berlin, 1977). For a good overview, see especially, F. Lachaud, 'Armour and military dress in thirteenth- and early fourteenth-century England', in *Armies, Chivalry and Warfare in Medieval Britain and France*, ed. M. Strickland (Stamford, 1998), pp. 344–69.

against lance points. Over that, by 1200, it would have been customary to wear a light iron cap, less confining than the older helmets with nasal that remained the fashion until the end of Henry II's reign. But for full protection in battle and tournament, however, the great helm would have been worn, the same that is depicted on the seal of his lord, King Richard. It was an enveloping iron bucket with eye slits and ventilation holes punched in it, laced tightly to his shoulders. The *History* has the Marshal wearing one of these in the 1170s, though they do not seem to have been in full fashion till King Richard's reign. But Ralph Niger's catalogue confirms that such an item, with its faceplate (*viseria*), was a common item of equipment in the mid-1180s. It would have been a natural response to the dangers from fragmenting lances in the grand charge of the tournament.

Once fully armoured, the knight would take up his boiled leather, painted shield, and then assume his arms. The straight double-edged sword, which was by the 1180s a symbol of his knighthood, would be belted to his waist. The contemporary schoolmaster and moralist, Robert of Ho, tells us that knights wore their sword by that time even if they weren't in armour preparing for combat. They did not even take it off at mass, Robert says, because it represented the fact that they were always ready to defend the Holy Church from infidels and heretics. In the tournament, the knight would always have several ash wood spears available, the spares being carried by his squire. They were designed to shatter into three pieces with the shock of an accurate strike against the shield of an oncoming opponent, so as to absorb some of the blow. Otherwise, the knight might be carried backwards out of his saddle.

The mount was not forgotten in these preparations. Armour was being strapped to the warhorse in Western Europe at least as early as the 1140s. Initially, it may have been confined to the destrier of the lord, to offer additional protection to a man whose capture would be the focus of competing knights in the tournament field. Ralph Niger describes a mail or moulded leather head piece, a 'tester', a 'collar' to protect the horse's neck and breast and a 'crupper' to protect flanks and rear. Painted linen coverings were draped over the lord's horse, as can be seen in the surviving seal of the baron Walter fitz Robert (see Figure 4), whose son Robert was William Marshal's co-eval (he was born in 1148) and who fought with him at Lagny-sur-Marne in 1179.

The Marshal at war was then a formidable and, we might also say, colourful figure: robes of yellow, green and red linen or silk, the polished steel helmet, gilded clasps and jewels flashing in the sunlight; one could hardly imagine a more impressive military peacock. The effect of a whole, uniform company of such creatures must have been a quite deceiving sight. No wonder the young Perceval, brought up in ignorance of the world by his mother in a Welsh forest, was made by Chrétien de Troyes to fall in love with such military magnificence at first sight, and mistake the first knights he met for angels.[3] Contemporary writers, such as Jordan Fantosme,

3 *Le Conte de Graal*, lines 125–52.

preserved stirring descriptions of the effect of a twelfth-century army on the observer. It is colour they often pick on, the overwhelming effect of the strong colours – red, blue and white – at a distance. Then there is the added effect of the uniform accoutrements of the disciplined companies (*conrois* or *constabularia*); the shields, the fluttering pennons and thickets of lances, which hypnotised the eye. In terms of visual effect, at least, the twelfth century fielded more formidable armies than had been seen in Western Europe since the time of Theodosius.

The warrior *preudomme*

We can only wonder, in the moralising strain adopted by the older and wiser Guy of Warwick, home from the wars and alone on a tower of his castle as the sun went down, whether all this glamour was justified by the result.[4] Indeed, there is nothing glamorous in the warfare described by the Marshal's biographer. It is a prosaic business of siege, calculated brutality, waste and trickery. The pattern of the warrior most admired by William Marshal was his father, John. It would seem from the *History* that the Marshal instructed his young followers in war in examples he drew from his father's life. To William, his father provided an admirable example of a captain and lord. If John Marshal was so admirable as a soldier, then we have in his son's stories of him the particular qualities that he admired.

Courage, particularly in adversity, was plainly one quality to emulate. Although the *History* does not admire failure, it could at least praise the desperate stand of John Marshal in Wherwell Abbey in 1141, holed up in a tower, engulfed in flame and spattered with molten lead. It was not his fault that he was in such a pass. He was there because the Angevin army he had joined was defeated, and he had for once done the generous thing and covered the retreat of the empress. Such was the reward for the truly self-sacrificing chevalier; he was sacrificed. The *History* preferred that its heroes did not get in such desperate straits. It admired far more the cunning that could turn possible disaster to triumph.

John Marshal was admired for his address in luring the dangerous mercenary Robert fitz Hubert into captivity in his castle, under smiling assurances that he was in fact planning an alliance with him. The *History* chuckles over John's dawn ambush of King Stephen's force, just as it emerged, unarmed, from its base to destroy him, fooled by his deceptive assurance that he had too few men to resist the king. Most praise went to John for edging out of a losing military situation by a strategic capitulation, putting aside his wife and taking instead the sister of his great enemy to form an alliance. William Marshal himself was a by-product of this particular stratagem, son of this politic marriage.

Like father, like son. John Gillingham has described the various deceptions and brutalities that the Marshal perpetrated in his long military career. The Marshal's wars were not usually the sort of full-dress affairs for which tournaments were the

---

4 *Gui de Warewic* II, lines 7568–74.

preparation. 'The kind of war William fought – and by definition this was the kind of war the best knights fought – was a war full of ravaging, punctuated quite often by attacks on strong-points but only rarely by pitched battles.'[5] The *History* describes 17 sieges, but only three or four battles (depending on how seriously Neufchâtel-Drincourt in 1166 is taken as a battle). The Marshal only took the field in three pitched battles in all his long life, and two ended up as street fights, not gallops across grassy plains into trembling companies of infantry.

The *chevauchée* (the word is employed by the *History*) was the principal horror that war inflicted on the land. It was the systematic pillaging and burning of enemy land by a raiding column of knights and sergeants. It enriched one side at the expense of the other, and put pressure on the enemy. Although, as Professor Gillingham points out, there is good evidence that the author of the *History* was well aware of the idea of the war of attrition and the pressure of economic damage on resources, such warfare was also a denial of the enemy's lordship: he could not protect his people and this was a grief to him (as the plundering of Netherwent by the Welsh in 1217 was a matter of grief to the Marshal). There was otherwise no feeling that this, the seedy side of war, was anything but honourable.

Self-control in battle, as much as in the king's hall, was also admired in this age. It was a more sophisticated age than it is given credit for being. Medieval armies lacked the logistical support of the early modern period and depended too heavily on foraging the countryside where they were camped for their supplies, so the largest armies kings and princes could keep in the field were generally only a few thousand horse and foot. Yet twelfth-century armies were highly disciplined and manoeuvrable. Their tented quarters and pickets were laid out by specialist officers, and marshals and constables maintained discipline within them. Their commanders (*guiots*) insisted on having their authority respected, and delegated command over their subordinate companies to captains (*chevetaignes*). Judging by the literature with which they were entertained, twelfth- and thirteenth-century soldiers delighted in picking apart battle tactics and discussing the use of topography to secure military advantage. So well aware were they of the uncertain chances of battle, and so secure were they in their professional pride, that medieval commanders did not feel any sense of inadequacy in avoiding battle unless overwhelming odds were on their side.

In the twelfth century, warfare was the professed occupation of an aristocracy that was also becoming literate and articulate. It was a century that saw for the first time for a long time magnates as well as kings who turned to the pen and the written word for the purposes of propaganda, administration, correspondence and, indeed, amusement. Even the Marshal did not escape the influence of this movement, although, unlike Geoffrey fitz Peter and many of the court of the kings he served, as well as the kings themselves, he was probably not literate to any useful degree. It may be that the Marshal was untypical among his generation in being

---

5 J. Gillingham, 'War and chivalry in the history of William the Marshal', in *Thirteenth Century England* II, ed. P.R. Coss and S.D. Lloyd (Woodbridge, 1988), p. 12.

unlettered, in which case his biography (again, the product of a lettered laity) may have grossly distorted our picture of the barons of his day. There is every reason to see the twelfth century as the first in Northern Europe since the eclipse of Rome in which there was an aristocracy that expected learning among its members as much as military proficiency.

A military aristocracy that also cultivated and admired learning was going to find much to interest it in that earlier age. Professor Gillingham, in his writings, has shown how widespread among the twelfth-century aristocracy were the maxims of Vegetius, the fourth-century writer on warfare. Intelligent, instructed soldiers would fight with more considered and mannered tactics than the popular picture of all-in knightly melees would accommodate. Head-down charges, as we have already seen on the tournament field, were not the way that the leading captains won the day. They held back, deceived their adversaries and probed for a weak point before committing themselves. Only then could the morale of the well-disciplined *mesnie* be used to full advantage. The same was true on campaign. All was feint and movement. A full-scale battle was rarely entered on, for the result might be uncomfortably decisive and irretrievable. Battles, as at Lincoln in 1217, were for desperate men. Otherwise, as when a determined Count Baldwin of Flanders met King Philip of France in 1197 outside an invested city, one did not fight unless the odds were overwhelmingly in your favour. Philip drew off from the belligerent Flemings and left the city to its fate. The *History* did not criticise him for this; it complimented him on his sense. Again, the *History* condemned the Emperor Otto for unnecessarily taking on the retreating French at Bouvines in 1214. If he had just waited, he would have obtained as good a result as if he had met and destroyed the French. As it was, the emperor's decision and its unexpected result cost him his throne and lost Normandy to John for good.

The Marshal knew, partly from his father and partly from experience, the burden of one of Vegetius's maxims as well as if he had read it: 'courage is worth more than numbers, and speed is worth more than courage'. As at Cilgerran in 1204, he knew the value of surprise and the confusion it might cause. To achieve it, he and his contemporaries would march at night, pretend to disperse to deceive the enemy to do likewise, or use the uncongenial winter season to stage unexpected strikes and raids. There was a premium placed on disciplined and reliable recon-naissance to try to minimise the danger of being caught off guard. The Marshal time and again gave lessons on this. Local intelligence and informers were a necessary complement to scouts. As much as could be was done to avoid being taken off guard by the enemy.

This was the way that men fought in the twelfth century if they were wise and experienced, if indeed they were *preudommes*. But by the time the Marshal's biographer was at work, society was not as comfortable as had been the Marshal in his day in this sort of unapologetic violence. The *History* gives us pause for thought about this. The least appreciated feature of its portrayal of the Marshal is the marked reluctance of the author to describe his subject as engaged in more than mannered acts of violence even off the tourney field. He only hints at them. He never says that Marshal killed anyone, though we know from Welsh, Irish and Capetian historical sources that the Marshal was responsible for acts of widespread butchery. Other sources of his own time do not indeed play down this aspect of the Marshal's career. In 1217, he unleashed a massive assault on Caerleon Castle, long held by his Welsh rival, Hywel ab Iorwerth (despite the war in the Marches then supposedly being over), in which Hywel was cut down and his garrison along with him. It was to be well over a decade before Hywel's son was able to reclaim his family's possession of their castle, having to settle in the meantime with receiving back his manors from Marshals as their tenant.[6]

The most graphic portrayal of the Marshal as red in tooth and claw comes from the pen of William le Breton in his eulogy of his late master, King Philip II Augustus of France. He pictures thus the briefing given by King John to the Marshal for the relief attempt on besieged Château Gaillard in 1203:

> King John, pondering his concerns, sought a way to relieve the garrison, but no means was possible in daylight and he was wary of an attack at night. He discussed his predicament with the Marshal in this way: 'O most faithful keeper of my counsels, take a group of 300 elite knights and 3,000 mounted serjeants, along with 4,000 infantry. Add to these Lupescar's mercenary band. As soon as night falls make a sudden descent on Château Gaillard, since there is no moon tonight. Attack on that side of the river from which King Philip has crossed by a bridge. Nearly all his knights have passed over it with the king along with the knight, [William des] Barres, and the Champenois troops, warlike men whose daring is great. On the bank remain Count Robert [of Dreux], [Louis] the king's heir, Hugh de Châteauneuf, Simon [de Neaufle] and Cadoc's mercenaries. These troops are dug in near the bank, by the efforts of engineers, to safeguard the bridge. Camp followers and riff-raff are scattered across the countryside, along with those people who are to be found selling good round the camps. It may well be that you can satisfy my rage on them, as it is my pleasure to unleash slaughter.'[7]

William le Breton's concern is to disparage King John's courage and judgement, and the Marshal – 'most faithful keeper' of the felon-king's counsels – is comprehended in his contempt. He goes on to describe the consequences for the hundreds of unarmed camp followers behind the siege lines at the Marshal's hands:

---

6 For the assault, *Brut y Tywysogyon: The Red Book of Hergest Version*, ed. T. Jones (Cardiff, 1955), *s.a.* 1217 (p. 217) and *History* II, lines 17747–84. For Hywel's death in the campaign, TNA: PRO, E368/5, m. 9d and for a discussion, D. Crouch, 'The transformation of medieval Gwent', in *Gwent County History* II, *The Age of Marcher Lords, c.1075–1536*, ed. R.A. Griffiths, A. Hopkins and R. Howell (Cardiff, 2008), pp. 32–3.

7 *Oeuvres de Rigord et de Guillaume le Breton*, ed. H.-F. Delaborde (2 vols, Paris, 1885)[II] pp. 181–2 (lines 140–6), my translation.

In just this way King John sent his soldiers into the deepest danger, not deigning to accompany them himself. The king is obeyed, and he drags his feet while the rest make no delay in setting out. The troops arm themselves and the ships slip their moorings. Both forces make haste to the castle, one by water, the other land. Unsleeping, they travel through the quiet and darkness of night; giving up their rest so as to hurry into battle . . . The hours are separated by set intervals, and now three times the cockerel is roused to herald the dawn light by its raucous cry. Suddenly the rising sun frees the castle from the gloom of night, and now indeed the Marshal has led his column in haste there by a shorter land route, while the twisting course of the Seine has delayed the voyage of the fleet. The riff-raff, the traders and the unarmed common folk lie about unconscious from their drinking bouts, and they are slaughtered like sheep by the drawn swords of the soldiers. A good few of the crowd of them meet an unexpected end, dead before they can feel the fatal blow. This is the fate of those deeply asleep and dead drunk. Very soon a terrified shouting rings through the camp. The jam at the bridgehead causes the now-roused men to plunge into the river, because the bridge cannot take so many thousands of people at once.[8]

In comparison, the author of the Marshal's biography portrays the Marshal at war in a very different way. As John Gillingham points out, the biographer was not by any means unaware of the existence of this form of punitive warfare, for he portrays Marshal in 1188 urging Henry II to mount an expedition to waste and pillage the French Vexin, with all the inhumanity to the poor and defenceless such warfare would entail, and has the king as a result calling Marshal *corteis* (meaning 'an excellent fellow').[9] But the inhumanity is only implied, not described, in the *History*, and the grief the *chevauchée* causes King Philip is what the biographer dwells on. The author certainly knew what happened on such occasions and we can detect that he was uneasy about touching on it. When Le Mans was in flames at the hands of Anglo-Norman troops that same year, and the Marshal and his company were retreating through the city, the biographer makes a point of describing his hero dismount to assist an old lady save her possessions from her burning house, such a selfless act being the way Marshal customarily conducted himself towards the distressed, we are told, for among his many other fine qualities he was *pitos* (tender-hearted). Indeed, the kindly Marshal was nearly asphyxiated in his act of decency by the fumes given off by the old lady's smoking coverlet, which penetrated his helmet vents.[10]

His biographer's deliberate evasiveness in his portrayal of the warrior Marshal is quite different from the way contemporary *trouvères* describe warfare. For

8 *Ibid.*, pp. 184–5.
9 Gillingham. 'War and chivalry', pp. 1–13, at p. 7, referring to *History* I, lines 7784–7852.
10 *History* I, lines 8749–72.

instance, when Guy of Warwick is caught in an ambush by his Lombard enemies, he and his disadvantaged companions duly carve souls from bodies, heads from shoulders, and shoulders from trunks; they cut through helms and shields with their swords, and run men through their disembowelled bodies. Guy's helm is battered and his blood leaks down his mail hauberk, yet still he fights on undaunted against the odds, grieving as he does for a fallen comrade.[11] Violence thickly crowds the pages of Guy's romance in just the way and indeed in much the same language as has been demonstrated in the somewhat later Lancelot cycle.[12]

But compare this stylised massacre with the biographer's account of William Marshal, similarly ambushed by French knights at the ford of the Sarthe outside the walls of Le Mans in that same year of 1188. With a few companions from the royal household, he slowed the pursuing French down in a suburban street by an elegant display of jousting in which lances were broken, but apparently not heads. Although we are assured the encounter was no game (*gieus*), the author preserves the wonderful picture of the exalted Marshal caracolling his horse in front of the city gate and throwing a bridle through it for his squire to catch, before cantering back down the street to tug the reins of their horses away from other French knights, and so capture them. It is as mannered as a medieval illumination. The only injury recorded in this action was a broken arm suffered by Andrew de Chauvigny as he was captured by Marshal, though it was inflicted not by his captor, but by a rock thrown from the city wall. The damage done was on a huge scale, we are told, but all the corporal damage the author details was to the horses' legs by the broken lance heads scattered around the street. It is all so apparently mild and unlikely, yet the author's eyewitness source for this vivid incident was unimpeachable: it was the Marshal's squire, the then teenage John of Earley, the boy who caught the bridles his master threw back to him through the gate.[13]

The biographer is trapped by his need to show Marshal to be a pattern *preudomme* as such a character was beginning to be understood in the days of the Marshal's sons. He had to appear statesmanlike, measured, rational and civilised: could a man be simultaneously *preudomme* and be depicted as unapologetically violent? The author plainly concluded he couldn't. In the 1220s, the *preudomme* was being judged by his aspiration to a higher ethical standard, which included the moral leadership in society that he shared with the prince. So the *preudomme* did not seek or rejoice in violence, unless the Church sanctioned it. To be seen as such a restrained *preudomme*, as his children wanted William Marshal to be seen, the contrast button of his social performance had to be turned down and the red filtered out.

It was at around this time that the moralist Robert de Blois declared why it was knights should be respected: it wasn't because they carried swords, he says; it

---

11 *Gui de Warewic* I, lines 1229–1382.
12 R.W. Kaeuper, 'Chivalry and the "civilizing process"', in *Violence in Medieval Society*, ed. R.W. Kaeuper (Woodbridge, 2000) pp. 23–4.
13 *History* I, lines 8585–8738.

was because of the moral authority the sword represented.[14] Whether the Marshal himself would have cared much for such a view of where his own prowess lay is another matter entirely. As his troops were massacring hundreds of unarmed and screaming French camp-followers, male and female, on the plain below Château Gaillard in 1203 at his bidding, it seems unlikely to me that Marshal felt his reputation as a *preudomme* was being compromised. It was the abject failure of his relief column that did that, which was the reason why his biographer passed over the entire incident in silence, and also why William le Breton, an eyewitness of the butchery and no fan of the Marshal, was determined that we should hear all about it.

14 J.H. Fox, *Robert de Blois, son oeuvre didactique et narrative. Étude linguistique et littéraire suivie d'une édition critique avec commentaire et glossaire de l'"Enseignement des princes' et du 'Chastoiement des dames'*, (Paris, 1950), lines 72–8."

10
LOVE AND LORDSHIP

Love and loyalty

The sources are such that we can learn a little of what went on in the heads of those long-gone men, the Marshal's knights, and something of the tensions in their mobile, shifting community. First, as we saw in the last chapter, there was the schism between the lay and clerical households: no doubt both sides being cordial and courtly under the eye of their lord and employer, but both feeling the superiority of its own order, each distinct in its rites of passage and education; the knights feeling all the force of their trained hands and horses, the long cloak – the *chlamys* – of aristocracy and the gold spurs on their heels telling of society's recognition of their superior standing; the clerks in their sober garb and shaven scalps confident in quite a different source of power, the power evoked by Gregory VII, St Anselm, Becket and, latterly, Innocent III. Both groups competed in self-importance, both expected by this date to be respectfully addressed as *messire, dan* or *dominus*. As Philip de Novara said, in their sons' childhood there came a choice to well-off parents as to what occupation they should put them. There were only two choices, and both had their particular skills – their *mestiers* – in which they had to be trained from a young age: *clergie* and *chevalerie*. It may be that they arose out of the same social group, but clerks and knights were placed in very different occupations.

This was the natural schism within the household, but there were other tensions brought on by outside pressures. Some of the Marshal's men had acquired lands, wives and responsibilities. True, they owed everything to him, but they had responsibilities too towards others, their own followers and their families. Contemporary literature recognised this difficulty. When a great man fell, his men were not regarded as disgraced if they left him so as not to share his ruin. So Thomas Becket's knights and wards left his household regretfully in October 1164 when it was clear that his confrontation with the king would lead to his ruin.[1] For some, the rival attractions of the royal household, the ultimate source of favour and good things, was too much. John Marshal, William Waleran, Hugh of Sandford, Philip of Prendergast and Alan de St-Georges were some of the Marshal's knights who at a moment of crisis, or over several years, left him for the king's entourage. They became king's men first and the Marshal's men second. Even kinship could not prevent this, as John Marshal proved. Henry Hose simply left him when his father died in 1213 in order to take over his family responsibilities in Sussex. Such things happened in the twelfth and thirteenth centuries. It might have been an age when loyalty was prized, but there were many men even then who respected prag-matism and material ambition rather more than ideals. Loyalty was not absolute at that time, except in theory and in romances. The Marshal himself was perfectly aware of that fact; for that reason, he was willing to tolerate a certain amount of backsliding from his men. There was no permanent breach between him and his nephew John, after John favoured the king in 1207 rather than his uncle. The Marshal had high standards of loyalty, as did others in his circle, such as the three bailiffs of Leinster in 1208, but he was a realist too.

However, there remained a core of faithful friends in the Marshal's household who acted up to the ideal of fidelity. On them, the Marshal had cast such a spell that they were willing to lose everything for him. It is for them that the *History* makes its hero say: 'that man is no loyal friend who is found wanting in help in a great moment of need'.[2] The debate among the knights of his *mesnie* left in Ireland in 1208, which was recalled for his biographer by some of them years later, is a classic exposition on loyalty between lord and man. The leaders of his *mesnie* were threatened by the king with the loss of their English lands if they did not abandon Ireland and appear before the king. These were men who at that time held little or no land from the Marshal. Yet John of Earley nonetheless said that if he lost his lands and even his honour by opposing the king, he would at least still keep the love (*amor*) of his lord. Love, too, was the word for what these men returned to their lord. By their love and honour, as he was to say after the crisis of 1208, they had saved his lands, and he blessed them for it. Long ago as it is, we can still feel something of the warmth that linked the Marshal to some of his men, a bond that was in those days in England often expressed physically by embracing and kissing. If the kiss of peace was denied by the Marshal to erring followers, as it was to Philip of Prendergast and David de la Roch, then it was a matter for bitter tears and lament: a public rejection, like a slap or a father's curse.

Maybe for some of them it was not so much the need to honour the personal bond; perhaps it was the strictures of their fellows they feared, unwilling to risk the ridicule that went with overt materialism. This ridicule was a fearsome and unforgiving thing. In the romance called *Garin le Loherenc* (Warin of Lorraine),

---

1 F. Barlow, *Thomas Becket* (London, 1986), p. 115.
2 'Quer cil n'est pas amis entiers, qui a grant besoing faut d'aie', *History* I, lines 6904–5.

written while the Marshal was a household knight, the consequences for those regarded as betrayers of sworn faith to their lord are given starkly: 'When men in their recklessness dare to attack their own lord: as they have betrayed their sworn faith, so God help me will they be disgraced, and the whole world ought to regard them no more than as they deserve.'[3] The *History* itself shows that this disgrace was a social reality. David de la Roch, one of the Irish barons who opposed the Marshal in 1208, is said to have found it difficult to make friends afterwards. The influential West Country baron, Peter fitz Herbert, publicly snubbed him by refusing a seat next to his at a council. Such social delights, chuckled over by the loyal core of the Marshal's household, awaited the unsubtle opportunist.

The Marshal's household knights were young men, much younger than the Marshal. John of Earley was his junior by a full generation, still in his thirties during the crisis in Leinster that so deeply tested the quality of the Marshal's household knights. The same seems true of all the others; only Alan de St-Georges was near in age to the Marshal, and even he must still have been a good decade younger than his lord. Henry fitz Gerold was literally what the men of that day would have called 'young': a landless, unmarried younger son. Likewise, the young Nicholas Avenel served the Marshal as under-sheriff of Gloucestershire while his father was still alive and he had a career to make for himself.

Some lingering expressions of devotion from his men to the Marshal reach us from the dry folios of monastic registers. John Marshal, the Marshal's nephew, remembered his uncle William, and his aunt Isabel too, in his own old age and commemorated them in a gift to Walsingham priory in Norfolk, seeking the canons' prayers for his late lord's soul.[4] Geoffrey fitz Robert also made a point of commemorating the Marshal and Countess Isabel (then still alive) when he founded the priory of Kells in Leinster, although this was a more perfunctory gesture because the foundation was on the Marshal's land.[5] Rather more interesting in terms of assessing the extent of the *amor* that called forth such gestures is the grant by Alice de Colleville to the canons of Poughley in Berkshire. As has been explained, there is good reason to think that Alice was the lover of William Marshal's brother, John, and the mother of John Marshal, his nephew. She commemorated both brothers' souls (naming the elder John first) in the grant.[6] It was a poignant gesture by someone who may by then have been a rather lonely old lady, living out her days in retirement in the Thames Valley, a farewell to her youth and, perhaps, lost love and young friendship.

---

3 *Garin le Loherenc*, ed. A. Iker-Gittleman (3 vols, Classiques français du moyen âge, 1996–1997) II, lines 7838–45.

4 Cartulary of Walsingham, British Library, ms Cotton Nero E vii, fo. 95v. John, although a bastard, remembered his father and also his father's lover, his mother, whose name he gives as Alice; from this it seems that, whatever her morals, she had been a gentlewoman and makes the identification with Alice de Colleville the more likely.

5 *Irish Monastic and Episcopal Deeds*, ed. N.B. White (Irish MSS Commission, 1936), pp. 300–1.

6 Westminster Abbey Muniments no. 7242.

But John of Earley is the man through whom we can get nearest to what these followers thought. When he first met the Marshal, he was little more than a boy sent abroad to a foreign land by a mandate from a remote king, into the care of a stranger. The Marshal must have made him welcome and been pleasant to him. Why not? He too had had the same experience: dumped abroad for an education with strangers. The two were from the same part of the world, their fathers' chief seats within the same county, Berkshire. John was fatherless, William Marshal not yet a father, but a man, we know, who thought much of fondness to the young, praising King Stephen, who had indulged him as a boy. The Marshal was indeed good with children, and we can say with some certainty that he earned his own sons' love. He was besides a man that a boy could respect.

We can guess that the Marshal and John might well have fallen into each other's arms, their interlocking, emotional needs a strong bond between them. When in 1194 John of Earley had become a knight, and a man of considerable means in his own right, he did not quit the Marshal's household. He lived on, with no other desire apparently but to serve his one-time guardian, in political and emotional servitude. By following his lord to Ireland in 1207, he risked losing his patrimony, and lose it he did. In the fullness of his malice, King John actually wrote to the Marshal taunting him with the fact that Earley was now landless, and his service to the Marshal had made him so.[7] The king knew how to hurt most cruelly. On another occasion, to unbalance the Marshal, he pretended to have news that Earley and others of his men were dead in Ireland, defending the Marshal's interests. To this tormented king, the bond between the Marshal and his men was a way to twist and torture the Marshal's composure, to undermine his courtly tranquillity, though it is to be doubted that he could have said to what constructive end he did it.

John of Earley took no reward for his service, other than a manor in Leinster, and that only because it may have been a convenient place near to his lord's chief castle of Kilkenny. It was all for the great love and honour (*de la grant amor e de l'onor*) between the men. When the Marshal was brooding over the problems of accepting the regency in 1216, John of Earley advised him not to take it up, although others of the *mesnie* were keen that he should, seeing possibilities of great advancement. John saw his purpose in following the Marshal differently from some of his colleagues. At the Marshal's deathbed, he was still there to attend his lord's needs. And after death, he served him still, not just as the executor of the Marshal's testament (a task that was still engaging his energies several years later), but as one of the promoters of the project that produced the *History*. He poured out his memories for the author to work into a fitting monument to his lost lord, and not just his memories; his money, too, supported the biographer as he worked. The *History* may well be a distorted and partial work, but we should not forget that it is distorted by this almost incomprehensible love of a man for his lord and, we might properly say, father.

---

7 *Rot. Clausarum* I, p. 103.

But this would not be the right point to leave the Marshal and the subject of his lordship over men. We must also consider the Marshal and people who were not his men, or at least men who were outside the charmed circle of his household and affinity. Enough has been said about his relations with the barons of Leinster to realise that there was another side to his lordship, the sharp edge of his sword. Philip of Prendergast found he had only the Marshal's formal forgiveness after his unsuccessful conspiracy in 1208. His son David was still a hostage for his good behaviour to the Marshal seven years later.[8] Once he had Meilyr fitz Henry at his mercy, the Marshal made sure that neither he nor his family would bother him again. He took his castles and ensured that Meilyr would have no more than a life interest in his lands.

This is symptomatic of the other side of the coin of lordship to that represented by the Marshal's *amor* towards his true men. William Marshal knew, as his stories of his father demonstrate, that the world was a hard place, and that a lord's duty was to be a welcoming fortress to the men who were loyal to him but turn a flinty face to the others. The *History* is full of evidence of this. It sorrows over the rebel plundering of New Ross in 1207 and the Welsh devastation of the Marshal's lordship of Netherwent in 1217, but is indifferent to the wasting and burning carried out by the Marshal himself on his many campaigns. The duties of a lord were nicely framed by Geoffrey of Monmouth, who wrote in the heyday of the Marshal's father's career in the late 1130s. A good lord must be a great oak to his men, spreading his sheltering branches over them. But to others, he must be a name of such terror that the fear of him keeps off ill will from the men under his protection.

The Marshal as a lord was therefore a harsh man, except to the intimates of his household and his political friends, the very people who had the *History* written as a monument to him. The *History* therefore tells only half the story. The Marshal's ideas of justice add to this picture. Eustace de Bertrimont, his longest-serving retainer, contributed to the *History* his memories of an incident in 1183, on the Marshal's return to the Young King's household. While resting by the road, the Marshal and his friends were passed by a couple riding hard, a man and a woman. The woman's complaints of her weariness attracted the Marshal's attention. He stopped the pair and interrogated the man. It transpired that he had eloped with the woman, the sister of a prominent Flemish castellan; what was more, he was a runaway monk. This shocked the Marshal, but he was willing to let the pair continue since the woman did not appear to be under any constraint. But an idle inquiry about how the two were to live changed his mind about intervening. It turned out that the man had a sum of money that he intended to put out at interest. The Marshal, under threat of violence, promptly confiscated the money and sent the couple packing into poverty and degradation, as we must imagine.

The audience of the *History* was expected to approve of this. Knights must applaud the confounding of a lecherous clerk who corrupted a noblewoman; clerks

---

8 *Rot. Patentium*, p. 144.

must approve of the frustration of the scandalous scheme by a colleague, already compromised by sexual incontinence, of living on the profits of illegal usury. What *we* notice is: that the money thus acquired went straight into the Marshal's pocket, to be used for his own purposes of patronage; that some years later the Marshal himself was exploiting the Jewish debt market in Normandy; and that the roadside justice he did to this couple was summary and merciless and had no warrant. Another man as outraged would have apprehended the pair and delivered them to the agents of the local archdeacon, the officer with the approved power to try and to punish them.

We know very little about the Marshal as judge in his own court. When he sat as a royal justice, it was always with other, more experienced men, which does not encourage any faith in his reputation. But there is one example of what went on in his own court that gives some hints as to the measure of the man's justice. Soon after he married Countess Isabel, the Marshal made a particular point of holding a court of his honor of Striguil, as any new lord would, to receive the homage of his new tenants and, just as important, what they must pay him on his entry into possession for charters of confirmation of their lands. He was, as we know, short of money. One tenant, Payn of London, did not turn up to do homage for the land he held in Barrow, Suffolk, nor did he send an agent to represent him. The Marshal had him summoned in court the proper three times, and, on his non-appearance, sent his men to take possession of the land. So far, he was completely within his rights and was indeed acting wisely. No lord could safely allow tenants to evade their obligations. However, when Payn's son William appeared before him to reclaim the land by a payment and to begin a dispute in the Marshal's court with the man he said should have done the homage instead of his father, the Marshal refused him a hearing. This was outrageous behaviour; it was refusing a tenant justice, and in 1194 Payn and his son went to the king to complain and commence a suit against the Marshal himself.[9] We do not know the result of this suit, which probably means that it was settled by a compromise in due course. But it does not show the Marshal's ideas of lordship in a good light. His only motive in refusing justice to Payn of London was to keep the land he had taken back for his own purposes.

The essential hypocrisy of the Marshal is not something that we can avoid. It was as a courtly dissembler that Matthew Paris remembered him after his death. William de Longchamp (a man who never mastered the skills of the court and therefore may well have prided himself on being blunt and plain-speaking) accused the Marshal in the presence of the king of being two-faced: a difficult accusation for any courtier to avoid. The Marshal, as we have seen, happily elevated his own interests into justice. Time and again in his differences with the king, his justifications of his position are merely paper masks for his self-interest. But to be two-faced was something that his own society and background forced on him.

---

9 *Rotuli Curiae Regis*, ed. F. Palgrave (2 vols, Record Commission, 1835) I, pp. 62–3.

He grew up in the household of a father who served his own interest in a particularly brutal way in a chaotic and dangerous period. This father, whose memory he apparently respected in later life, used William's infant life as a bargaining counter with the king.

At the courts of his various lords, he had to smile and simper among men, some of whom were his deadly enemies and who plotted his downfall. His composure is a matter of record. He rarely revealed his innermost feelings, however chatty he might have been to his young knights about the amusing exploits of his own youth. It was proverbial in the twelfth century that a man who talked too much was storing up trouble for himself, and it was by such proverbs that the Marshal had been educated in court-craft.[10] It was not until he was on his deathbed that he spoke to his son, John of Earley his *carissimus*, and others of his intimates, of the spiritual awakening that he had undergone in the Holy Land, and only then did he produce the grave cloths he had bought over 30 years before. We can only guess in these circumstances how important were his relations with his family and his intimate followers. But to me, they were all important. Courtly tranquillity and composure must have taken its toll of his peace of mind as much as the unrelenting pursuit of his own advantage. Family and friends must have seemed the one stable, warm part of his life. No wonder he was so little inclined to forgive the likes of Philip of Prendergast, whose treachery had compromised not just his dignity and affections, but the security of his lands. Lucky for Philip that ideas of propriety had advanced to the point where the Marshal would not execute him, as his wife and *mesnie* wanted.[11] Instead, Philip was excluded from the Marshal's inner circle, which to the Marshal and his men might have seemed a satisfyingly cruel form of emotional extinction.

Lordship and affinity

Around the fringes of the Marshal's retinue was a penumbra of men whom it would be difficult to call 'followers' because they did not follow him on any regular basis. But they were of great importance to his exercise of power in society. Some (the Irish barons) were his dependents, holding land in his lordship and technically owing him knight service, but others were in a more hazy relationship to him; you might call them 'friends' or 'allies' depending on the degree of emotion or pragmatism that you could detect in their relations. The Marshal did have an enviable capacity for making friends, something that stood him in good stead in his political career.

10 Such a saying appears in the 1170s in Chrétien de Troyes, *Le Conte de Graal*, ed. F. Lecoy (2 vols, Classiques français du moyen âge, 1972–1975) I, line 1652, but it is to be found in conduct literature going back to the Roman empire and indeed beyond.

11 Such things did still happen, however. Roger de Lacy had executed in 1193 the constables of Tickhill Castle, his sworn men who delivered the castle to Count John against his orders. His action was not illegal, but called down great opprobrium on his head, Howden *Gesta*, II, p. 233.

He was a courtly man in a courtly age. Great magnates in the twelfth century ideally conducted themselves with affability and humour at court. The most politic among them massaged each other's egos with care and consideration. A fair sample is the speech of the Earl of Chester in 1216 at Gloucester when men were split as to whether he or the Marshal should assume the regency. The Earl of Chester had been beaten by the Marshal in the struggle for power and had to be soothed. The Marshal, who wanted the job, had to save Chester's face; he was old and feeble and could not do it. A younger man such as Earl Ranulf perhaps . . .? But no, said Earl Ranulf, that cannot be, 'You are so good a knight, so fine a man, so feared, so loved, and so wise that you are considered one of the first knights in the world. I say to you in all loyalty that you must be chosen. I will serve you, and I will carry out to the best of my power all the tasks that you may assign to me.'[12] Here is as good a specimen of the dance of the courtly magnates as you are likely to meet with. No naked ambition, no disagreeable and aggressive moves. All is arranged by gentle nudges and affectionate phrases. Powerful men have to defer to each other; to disagree and offend unnecessarily would be dangerous, it would commit them to expensive and damaging hatreds.

But there were warmer and more sincere relationships, even at court, just as there were more openly hostile ones (such as the acid relations with William de Longchamp in Richard's reign). Perhaps chief among these was Baldwin de Béthune, the younger brother of the Picard magnate, Robert, advocate of Arras. The two were intimate when they were both landless young hopefuls in the riotous household of the Young King. It was Baldwin who organised William's reinstatement into the household after his disgrace in 1183, and who corresponded with him while in exile. His career paralleled William's. Like William, he achieved a county through marriage, in his case Aumale on the Norman frontier, with other lands in Yorkshire. In 1205, he stood up for William fearlessly at Southampton before the enraged King John. To seal their long friendship, William and Baldwin betrothed, and eventually married, William's eldest son to Baldwin's eldest daughter. The *History*, naturally, has much to say about Baldwin's valour and loyalty to its hero; he is all but the second hero of the work.

There were other magnates who were close to William Marshal. The most potent of all was Geoffrey fitz Peter. Geoffrey, like William, was the son of a royal official in the West Country, in his case Peter, the royal forester of Ludgershall in Wiltshire. It is not unlikely that William and Geoffrey's fathers were connected in some way, for John Marshal had held Ludgershall throughout Stephen's reign. William and Geoffrey had entered Henry II's household at much the same time and risen together in royal service, though by different means. Both were given great heiresses in 1189 by King Richard, and were created earls within minutes of each other by King John in 1199. Geoffrey attests several of William's early acts, perhaps those transacted within the precincts of the royal palace or when they

---

12 The translation is by Sidney Painter.

were co-justiciars in King Richard's absence. A later charter still exists by which William conceded to Geoffrey his share of the profits of the market of Aylesbury, Buckinghamshire, to which they both had a claim.[13] Their relationship was doubtless less warm than that between William and Baldwin de Béthune; one tends to imagine Geoffrey – whether justly or not – as an obsessive businessman with not much time for personal relations. But to have his passive goodwill was no small thing in early Angevin England. King John is said to have confessed his fear of Geoffrey on hearing of his death in 1213: 'Now at last I am king!' When such a fearful man stood beside the Marshal in his difficulties with the king in 1210–1211 and put his name forward as guarantor for him, the Marshal might be easy in his mind.[14] Because he had such friends, the Marshal might, on occasion, stand up to the king in a way that few others dared. The watching presence of his powerful friends at court could make the king tractable and cautious.

The Marshal's attachment to other, lesser magnates has a more local political direction to it. From the Marshal's powerful friends at court, he wanted general goodwill and support. From the Berkeley family, on the other hand, he wanted acquiescence and collusion in his local ambitions. The relationship between him and the family of Berkeley had nothing to do with any land they held from him; the bonds were much stronger since they were rooted in local power and mutual security.[15] The Marshal and the Berkeleys were partners in the informal business of powermongering. There is a record of the strength of the links between them. In 1220, his son William wrote to the justiciar of England saying of Thomas of Berkeley, the brother and heir of Robert, who had married his niece, that 'for many years [Thomas] has been so allied and obliged (*obligatus et confoederatus*) to me, that he could not leave my interest or council'.[16] The Berkeleys were by far the greatest barons in Gloucestershire, the county that William controlled as sheriff for long periods in Richard's and John's reigns. They were patrons of the Abbey of Bristol, and Bristol was a town in which they retained a considerable interest. Since William Marshal controlled Bristol Castle between 1199 and 1205, the Berkeleys had to come to terms with him. Indeed, the brothers Robert and Oliver of Berkeley had the keeping of the town between 1201 and 1203, an impossible task unless they were already in the Marshal's camp. The Berkeleys were a very necessary political accessory for the Marshal: they controlled large numbers of manors and a hundred; they had a powerful stone castle dominating the road from Gloucester to Bristol; and, what was more, a large following of their own

---

13 *Acts and Letters*, no. 37, pp. 99–100. Geoffrey attests three charters of William all dating to the 1190s.
14 *Rot. Patentium*, p. 98.
15 Robert of Berkeley attests the Marshal's solemn foundation charter of Cartmel priory in 1189 × 1190. Many of the Berkeleys of Berkeley and Roger Berkeley of Dursley appear with the Marshal's following in a charter of 1200 × 1205, Berkeley Castle Muniments, Select Charter 85.
16 *Acts and Letters*, no. 119, pp. 206–8.

knights. Their support was the keystone to the Marshal's structure of power in the West Country.

The Berkeley family, and also the earls of Salisbury – linked by kinship – were the more obvious and noticeable members of the Marshal's affinity. There were others who are less obvious, but whose behaviour in the period of 1214–1217 indicates that they, too, were local allies of the Marshal: John of Monmouth, Countess Isabel's cousin and lord of the town from which he took his name; Walter of Clifford, another baron of the southern March; and Walter de Lacy, a great man in Herefordshire and Ireland. They were all men of local power in their own right. Their affability to the Marshal, a more important man than they were, is the evidence that we must look to the West Country of England and the southern March if we are to begin to understand the Marshal's power. For it was here that the pattern of his own possessions dictates that he would have needed to form a local political connection, his 'country', as magnates were already calling their spheres of interest.[17]

The knights in the Marshal's retinue, for the most part, were also bound to him by local interest. The analysis in the previous chapter of the Marshal's following of knights revealed that two-thirds of them had no traditional ties with him based on homage, faith and service between landlord and military tenant. There was therefore little of the automatic and hereditary demand on his followers for their support. It was a personal loyalty, depending only on the shifting needs of the two men involved. When the relationship had served its purpose, it ended and the men parted, often amicably, such as Henry Hose and Nicholas Avenel, who disappeared from the Marshal *mesnie* to look after their own family interests, without a backward glance.

What we see in the Marshal's household is one of the first demonstrable examples of a great magnate's political connection based on different ties: self-interest, protection, place-seeking and the centripetal force of local domination. This sort of connection is older than the later medieval period in which it is considered the political norm. Indeed, as far back as Stephen's reign, we can see great magnates who responded to the troubles of the time in England and Normandy by widening their circle of followers beyond those with whom they had tenurial links. Waleran of Meulan in the Normandy of the late 1130s fitted together an 'affinity' (the word was actually used by Robert de Torigny about his following) of lesser barons, which dominated central Normandy until his disgrace in 1153. The same thing was done in the 1140s in the southern Marches and south-west Midlands by Earl Roger of Hereford (a political forerunner of the Marshal). Both Waleran and Roger used written compacts to attempt to secure their power; Waleran even contracted to pay one of his recruits a considerable annual money fee in return for his support. Such

---

17 Magnates of the twelfth and thirteenth centuries talked of their *terra* ('country') or *potestas* ('jurisdiction') when looking for words to express their local dominion. Later medieval historians occasionally treat the idea as a later development.

written instruments were refined by the fourteenth century into routine links between magnate and knight. Work is steadily revealing that the Marshal was not alone in exploiting such links in his time. Even an heir to five generations of local landed power, such as Henry, Earl of Warwick (who joined the beleaguered royalists in 1216), made efforts to widen his influence beyond his military tenants, who were too often going their own way, seeking the protection of others.[18]

The strengths and weaknesses of the old and new social orders are seen to the full in the Leinster crisis of 1207–1208. The Marshal brought his loyal *mesnie* with him to Ireland, but they were not enough to guarantee his success. In Ireland, as we have already seen, the Marshal's poor relationship with his tenants was nearly fatal for his successful lordship over Leinster. Since many of them were indifferent, or even hostile to him, he had to oppose to them such alliances as that made with Walter de Lacy, lord of neighbouring Meath, and his brother Earl Hugh of Ulster. In Ireland, we see the conflict between the old feudal order and the new world of the affinity made corporeal. The Marshal needed the Lacys's non-feudal support because he could not trust his feudal tenants, and they would not be won over into into his affinity. The victory of the combination of retinue and affinity over the tenantry in Leinster was an allegory of the age, a quixotic joust.

Other magnates in the Marshal's position in past days would have deployed grants of lands to assuage the hostility to the newcomer, but he could not do that; he did not have the resources for a free-for-all. It was the king who was able to give rich rewards; therefore, it was to the king that many of these Irish tenants turned in 1207. They threw over the Marshal, setting the link of homage and service at nought. They were properly chastised for their mistake. After the crisis of 1207–1208, it is heartening to see how many of the greater men of the province once more dutifully attest his Irish charters: Thomas fitz Anthony, Philip of Prendergast, William fitz David, Walter Purcel, Maurice of London, Ralph de Bendeville, Gilbert du Val, Richard of Cogan and William of Naas. It may be that after 1208, they were scared to stay away. They had learned that if lordship could not be bought, it might be imposed.

If there was not much land to grant, how did the Marshal appeal to the self-interest of the men he selected; how did he reward? We do not know if the Marshal paid money fees to knights of his *mesnie*, although we do know that his sons did settle life rents on some of their men. What evidence there is suggests that the Marshal did to his men what his lords had once done for him: supported them by grants of robes and, doubtless, other knightly accessories. The Marshal was also prepared to do a little to satisfy the more traditional expectations of his knights. Society had still not got over the expectations raised by the great binge of land patronage under the Norman kings. William held sufficient possessions (particularly

---

18 See now for the structure of aristocratic power in England in this period, D. Crouch, *The English Aristocracy, 1070–1272: A Social Transformation* (New Haven, 2011), esp. ch. 8.

in Ireland) to offer some of his followers perpetual grants of land, still the prime reward desired by such men. In this way, what were originally 'bastard feudal' connections might be technically 'legitimised'. So it was that the young knight Thomas Basset, son of the baron Alan Basset of High Wycombe, was given in heredity 10 pounds' worth of land at Speen in Berkshire by the Marshal 'for that he might be retained, and of my *mesnie*'.[19] Speen was the sort of estate that the Marshal was able to give away; it was the Marshal's own acquisition and was not part of the ancestral estates he still reserved for himself, the demesne, as it is often called for brevity's sake. By this date, demesne was sacrosanct to land-starved magnates; it must be husbanded and passed on to their sons and daughters.

One of the chief methods of rewarding the knights of the retinue is only mentioned in passing by the *History*. This was the frequent delegation to the Marshal's followers of administrative duties. Yet, despite the silence of the *History*, it is clear enough that the Marshal's knights were often to be found presiding over various portions of his widespread domains, or engaged in a number of distinctly civilian duties as their master's agent. The *History* only mentions the occasion in 1207–1208 when the Marshal departed from a rebellious Leinster to an unknown fate at King John's court. Then he had divided responsibility for his great lordship between John of Earley and Jordan de Sauqueville as bailiffs, who were to be assisted by a council of the more loyal barons of the province: Geoffrey fitz Robert, Walter Purcel and Thomas fitz Anthony. Of those three men, Geoffrey had already been a seneschal of Leinster and would one day be so again; Thomas fitz Anthony would also serve a turn as seneschal. Of the Marshal's household knights, another two held that particular seneschalcy: John Marshal and William le Gros, his nephews. Leinster was a situation of considerable power and trust. The men who occupied its seneschalcy tell us as much; almost all were men close to the Marshal either in blood or in affection.

But seneschalcies and other such offices in the Marshal's gift were also rewards as well as duties, and what was going on in contemporary households tells us that they were prized rewards circulated around the intimates of the household. In a way, such positions were predecessors of the cash fees received by household knights of later centuries, an alternative method of reward to land grants. The Earl of Warwick, for instance, circulated his chief stewardship from one to another of his several household knights every year or two. To grant seneschalcies to one's intimate knights was part of the reward for their service in the Marshal's day, when it was less easy to come by land to give away. From descriptions of other, particularly

---

19 *Acts and Letters*, no. 13, pp. 66–9. For Thomas Basset (died 1230), see the table of relationships compiled by S.L. Waugh, *The Lordship of England* (Princeton, 1988), p. 212. There is a possible confusion between the Thomas Basset of this grant and his uncle, the more famous Thomas Basset of Headington, but the younger Thomas is a more likely candidate for retaining in a household at this date. I must thank David Carpenter for discussing this with me.

ecclesiastical seneschalcies, we know that their holders might collect handsome fees. The lord would pay his seneschals an annual cash sum from the profits of the lordship. In 1189, the keeper of the honor of Striguil under the king was collecting £20 a year, enough money to keep two knights in their essential needs for a year. Sums of money might be demanded for holding the courts of the lordship and of its constituent manors, others for putting new tenants in formal possession of their lands, or for receiving homage to the lord. By this date also, stewards would be expected to produce accounts for their period in office: revenue received and paid out.

So it is that Jordan de Sauqueville, joint-bailiff of Leinster in 1207–1208, was to be found in 1216 as seneschal of Pembroke. John, son of John of Earley, was acting in 1219 as the seneschal of the Marshal's marcher lordship of Netherwent, perhaps on his father's behalf. Stephen d'Evreux was the Marshal's seneschal in the ancestral Marshal lands in Wiltshire in 1199; in 1214, he was acting as attorney at Westminster for the Marshal's son.[20] Nicholas Avenel acted for the Marshal as his under-sheriff of Gloucestershire from 1192 to 1194 and 1199 to 1201, doing the routine work in the shire and travelling to Westminster to account for his master before the Exchequer. He was succeeded by another Marshal knight, Thomas de Rochford, until 1204. One at least of the Marshal's knights, William Jardin, who first appears in the Marshal's service in England as his attorney at Westminster in 1194,[21] was allowed a particularly long term of office. He seems to have acted as seneschal of Crendon for the best part of its tenure by the Marshal.

There were indeed other seneschals apart from these delegated household figures, more 'professional' figures, if the adjective can be applied in that day and age. Richard of Husseburn, a well-known clerk, occupied the seneschalcy of Netherwent at some time in John's reign.[22] In Normandy, William's seneschal in his honor of Longueville for many years was William d'Héricourt, not a knight, for he is listed separately from the knights when he appears in a charter of 1198. Such men would have been a necessary leaven to the delegated, household seneschal: administrative careerists to add their specialist knowledge to the Marshal's affairs. The two types of seneschal existed quite happily alongside each other, for all knights who were landholders were obliged to know the essentials of estate business and law, and indeed by this time many knights themselves employed such men on their own affairs.

Another notable fact about the Marshal affinity was the large part that kinship played in it, even though William Marshal had few surviving close male relatives after 1194 (other than his brother the Bishop of Exeter, who died in 1206). Male kinsfolk were a ready way of enhancing the retinue. As far back as 1180, William had recruited his landless brother Ansel to his banner in France, once he was able

20 *Memoranda Roll 1 John*, p. 62. The scribe seems to have garbled his name to . . . *smundus de Deuereals*; *Curia Regis Rolls* VI, p. 51.
21 *Rotuli Curiae Regis* I, p. 63.
22 Cartulary of Llanthony, TNA: PRO, C115/K2/6683 fo. 287r.

to offer him a place.[23] His brother John had joined him in 1189 and with his brother came his nephew, the illegitimate John Marshal, his brother's son. The young John Marshal found a home in his uncle's *mesnie* when his father died in 1194, and in 1199, when King John was lavishing gifts on his uncle, John Marshal shared in the family's luck, securing an important heiress and a Norfolk barony of moderate size. Another nephew was that Anselm 'the earl's nephew' who appears with him in Ireland on one occasion among his clerks.[24] He was Anselm le Gros, made treasurer of Exeter by his other uncle, Bishop Henry Marshal, before 1205, and later promoted to be Bishop of St Davids. Anselm and his brothers derived from an otherwise unmentioned marriage of a sister of the Marshal to a Gloucestershire knight, William le Gros, sometime steward of Earl William of Gloucester.[25] Anselm's brother, William le Gros 'the firstborn' (he had a younger brother of the same name), found a place in the Marshal's household. It seems likely that he was the William le Gros who was briefly seneschal of Normandy for King John in 1203–1204, probably as a favour to the Marshal.[26] William le Gros, however, was later more prominent as a leading knight in the household of the younger Marshal, rather than that of the father.

23 Ansel Marshal's fate after 1180 is unknown. There is some evidence that he was before or after that date a knight in the retinue of his first cousin, Count Rotrou IV of Perche, a charter of whom he witnesses late in the reign of Henry II, Archives départementales de l'Orne, H 2621 (a reference I owe to Dr Kathleen Thompson). For Count Rotrou and his Wiltshire connections, K. Thompson, *Power and Border Lordship in Medieval France: The County of Perche, 1000–1226* (Royal Historical Society, Studies in History, New Series, Woodbridge, 2002), pp. 76–8, 86–108.

24 *Acts and Letters*, no. 30, p. 87.

25 For Anselm's career, *St Davids Episcopal Acta, 1085–1280*, ed. J. Barrow (South Wales Record Society, no. 13, 1998), pp. 11–12. For William le Gros, steward of Earl William of Gloucester before 1160, see *Earldom of Gloucester Charters*, ed. R.B. Patterson (Oxford, 1973), p. 165. An undated Norman act of Earl William of Gloucester curiously has as witnesses the names 'William le Gros' and later, among the earl's junior officers, 'William *Mairscallus*', which might possibly indicate that there was a time when William Marshal had picked up Gloucester office through his brother-in-law, see Cartulary of St-André-en-Gouffern, Archives départementales du Calvados, H6510, fo. 22v, William le Gros is mentioned as the father of the two Williams, Anselm, Robert and Hamo le Gros in a Bradenstoke charter drawn up in the presence of Earl William, see Cartulary of Bradenstoke, British Library, ms Cotton Vitellius, A XI, fo. 167r–v. He also seems to have been the father of a daughter, Margaret, whom he married to Ralph de Somery, another baron of the honor of Gloucester, before 1194. The marriage contract survives and was witnessed by William Marshal and his knights, see Brooksby cartulary, Bodl. Libr., ms Wood empt. 7, fo. 97r. The le Gros family held a knight's fee from the earl at Old Sodbury, Gloucestershire, where William le Gros (II), Anselm's brother, erected a borough around 1218, now called Chipping Sodbury, with royal (that is, his uncle's) approval, see now for the family, N. Vincent, 'The borough of Chipping Sodbury and the fat men of France', *Transactions of the Bristol and Gloucestershire Archaeological Society*, 116 (1998), pp. 42–59.

26 *Rot. Patentium*, p. 33.

In 1189, the Marshal was joined by Philip of Prendergast, an Irish and Pembrokeshire baron who was his new wife's brother-in-law (Philip had married Earl Richard Strongbow's illegitimate daughter, Matilda). Another of Isabel's relatives by marriage was prominent in the Marshal's household: Geoffrey fitz Robert. Geoffrey was one of William Marshal's Wiltshire knights. Soon after 1189, the Marshal married him to Basilia, a matron in her late forties and the recently widowed sister of Earl Richard Strongbow. Geoffrey was thus the uncle of Countess Isabel. Stephen d'Evreux was another of the Marshal's knights who was credited with kinship with him (the *History* calls Stephen the 'cousin' of the Marshal), although the exact relationship between the two is impossible to work out.[27]

It is not unusual to find kinsfolk in some numbers in the households of the great: a family expected to share in the good fortune of its members. The same is as true in the household of a bishop or an abbot as in that of an earl. It was a great man's duty to promote his brothers, nephews and cousins, and suitably marry his nieces and female cousins as much as his daughters. William Marshal, a man fortunate in his relations, had benefited from this universal mechanism in society as a boy, and was to play patron to his relatives in his turn. This was not to say, however, that lords got more reliable service from their kinsfolk than from their other followers. Gerald of Wales and Arnulf of Lisieux both had cause to complain of what they had suffered from their ingrates of nephews, whom they had nurtured and promoted through the Church. William Marshal had to suffer the apparent treachery of his nephew, John, in the crisis of his fortunes in 1207–1208, despite the fact that John owed everything to his uncle. But John would not risk his future by crossing the king in the matter of his uncle, so he temporised.[28] No doubt, if he had been in the same position, the elder Marshal would have found what he considered an appropriate justification for such an act. The *History*'s silence on the defection, however, is eloquent testimony to what the Marshal and his more loyal followers thought about John Marshal's actions. Kinsfolk may well have been expected to be able to offer their lord more of the *amor* that a lord expected from his men, but society's expectations were not always fulfilled. In truth, family relationships were as far from idyllic in the twelfth and thirteenth century as at any time in recorded human history. It was just that it was an age that had higher expectations of feeling and duty.

27 Stephen d'Evreux was the son of John d'Evreux and grandson of Walter d'Evreux, followers respectively of William de Briouze (II), Lord of Brecon, and Walter de Lacy, Lord of Weobley. One of these elder d'Evreuxs might conceivably have married a Marshal woman, although it is quite as likely that an earlier Marshal might have married a d'Evreux woman, for the family succession, see now, B. Holden, 'The making of the middle March of Wales', *Welsh History Review*, 20 (2000), pp. 217–18, 218n.

28 It is fair to point out here that Stephen d'Evreux, his cousin, was more loyal than the Marshal's nephew. Stephen, like John of Earley, had his lands confiscated. Stephen's Castle of Lyonshall, Herefordshire, was taken over by the king's officers in 1208 and later entrusted to the men of Walter de Lacy, Stephen's overlord: *Rot. Patentium*, p. 91.

The Marshal and money

Money was important to the Marshal and his exercise of lordship and patronage. He, no less than other magnates, copied the king and operated a financial office. Some of his colleagues, such as the Earls of Leicester, Chester and Gloucester, had long had elaborate annual sessions before their chief men and themselves sometimes called, like the king's, 'exchequers'. Here, the seneschals and bailiffs of the various estates came to have their accounts audited. The Marshal probably had a less elaborate system. Like his brother John, and his cousin the Earl of Salisbury, William Marshal had a 'chamber' that took in money and issued receipts at some important castle or other centre.[29]

Since we know that the Marshal had close relations with London financiers, recruited London clerks and based at least one of his clerks in the city, it is not unlikely that an office of some sort was kept up in the earl's houses at Charing (where we know Master Joscelin, his deputy-marshal, was based). Joscelin may well have administered there an institution later called a 'wardrobe', a storehouse and accounting office for the purchase and distribution of goods in the city for the Marshal's household. The 'wardrobe of Earl William Marshal' was specifically referred to by royal clerks in July 1217. Payments destined for the king had been made into it at Gloucester.[30] At that time, the 'wardrobe' of the Marshal was itinerating with him (for London at that time was still in the hands of Louis of France), but some branch of it may well have been settled at London both before the French had arrived and after the city was recovered. It is very significant in this respect that in 1219, when the Marshal was contemplating his last distribution of livery robes to his knights, he ordered that if there were not enough, more should be sent for downriver to London. There, then, a small outpost of his household may well have worked, storing up the ultimate source of the Marshal's power: the silver pennies that paid his knights and servants, bought their robes, horses and arms, and the silks, furs and precious vessels that displayed his dignity and grandeur to the world.[31]

The Marshal and money is an interesting subject. We tend to think of medieval barons as rather unworldly in that respect, urged on by a hungry class of dependants to profligate generosity: the 'largesse' for which the *History* so extravagantly praises the Young King Henry. But the Marshal had been poor and knew the inconveniences of poverty. He had no great store of money in 1189 when he arrived in London to marry the heiress of Striguil. To Painter, that made him a jolly knight errant, generous and profligate. The Marshal, like a pattern feckless aristocrat, found his way to the city magnates who were very willing to assist him. But at this point,

---

29 For the financial office kept by Osbert, chamberlain of John Marshal, see *Pipe Roll of I John*, p. 226; for the chamber of Earl William of Salisbury, see *The Cartulary of St Augustine's Abbey Bristol*, ed. D. Walker (Bristol and Gloucester Archaeological Society, Record Series, 10, 1998), pp. 39–40.

30 *Patent Rolls, 1216–1225*, p. 83.

31 A gold cup belonging to the Marshal was mentioned in a schedule of debts drawn up for his executors. *Roll of Divers Accounts*, ed. F.A. Cazel (Pipe Roll Society, 1982), p. 34.

reality intrudes on the romance. His quickness and ruthlessness in levying a relief on his new tenants (that we hear of from sources other than the *History*) demonstrates that he was not so foolish as to want to rely on the moneylenders for any long period. By the end of the century, we find that he was the one who was exploiting the moneylenders. In Normandy in 1201, William Marshal had a grant from King John of a Jew, Vives de Chambay, and enjoyed the profits of his moneylending.[32] It seems likely that he was free enough with money in his earlier days, but like many men his hand grew closer as he had more to grasp. In London, he and his sons enjoyed long and profitable dealings with the city magnate, and later sheriff and mayor, William Joinier.[33] His links with the city of St-Omer in Flanders brought him into close relations with William son of Florent, a merchant of the city. He used William as his financial agent in raising the money to pay off the indemnity to Louis in 1217. Since Flanders had long been the destination of most of England's greatest export – wool – it may well be that the Marshal and this Flemish merchant were already engaged in mutually beneficial relations: disposing of the sacks of wool from his Welsh and Irish estates. The Marshal became a wealthy man. He himself advanced sums of money to King John in 1206 and had been in a position to loan money to support a campaign against the Welsh in 1194.

Such indications of his canniness are intriguing reminders that the Marshal did not live in a heroic society, whatever the *History* might try to persuade us. Earlier in the twelfth century, the highest of Norman aristocrats, Waleran, Count of Meulan, did not find it beneath him to take an active interest in the wine trade that passed through his lands on the way to England and the herring fleets that used his ports.[34] Such great men did not market their own produce, but in forming close relations with the men who had the skills to do it for them they entered a world that some of them did not seem to find uncongenial. The world of commerce had its own excitements and dangers, and for the magnates with resources to exploit it was one way to accumulate the sacks of coins that made so much else possible. The Marshal was alert enough to his commercial interests to indulge in town development to improve his lordship of Leinster, with boroughs developed or improved at Kilkenny, Carlow and New Ross.

If nothing else, the Marshal's friendly relations with merchants, burgesses and his own household clerks should remind us, if we need reminding by now, how two-dimensional was the *History* written to commemorate his life. Generations of romantically inclined historians have long overstressed the military element in aristocratic life (for which the *History* is in no small part to blame): it is as if we judged today's upper class only by their doings at Badminton, Klosters, Henley or on the golf links. It is arrogant to assume that the twelfth-century aristocracy was less complex than ours, simply because it is so remote from us.

---

32 *Rot. Patentium*, p. 3.
33 Cartulary of Waltham, British Library, ms Cotton Tiberius C IX, fo. 91r; *Calendar of Charter Rolls* I, p. 124.
34 D. Crouch, *The Beaumont Twins* (Cambridge, 1986), pp. 185–9.

11

THE MARSHAL'S MEN

One particular side of William Marshal's career deserves a good deal of attention: his relations with the men who looked to him as lord. The subject is an important one: it touches on the very nature of aristocratic and royal power in the Marshal's lifetime. A bigger consideration than that, however, is that the *History* gives us a unique source by which we can examine the relations between the Marshal and his knights. Historians have only recently begun to look at the general nature of the power wielded by the aristocracy in the period 1150–1250. It is now clear that the way he exerted lordship in his own day was something new. William Marshal lived at a time when structures of aristocratic power were beginning to change.

Recent writings on the English aristocracy of the late twelfth and early thirteenth centuries have sketched out a scheme of change. The scheme is by no means generally accepted, but a brief sketch runs as follows. For three generations after the Conquest of England, the English magnates had based their followings on the tenants of their lands, bound to them by a miscellany of links conjured up by the phrase 'knight service'. From 1066 through to the reign of Henry II, magnates either relied on families endowed in the first great surge of landed patronage in the reign of the Conqueror, or they raised up new families by further land grants. But during Stephen's reign, the flow of land grants began to dry up: magnates no longer had the spare land available to endow new men. As the flow dried up, so relations between magnates and their traditional followers became brittle, and often snapped. John Marshal, William's father, is himself an example of this. During Stephen's reign, he raised himself to power by retaining a host of knights. He could not do so by giving them land, but by offering money and protection. In time, a more powerful neighbour, the Earl of Salisbury, compelled him by superior military power to give up his independence and enter into a dependent relationship, but a relationship that was not a traditional one based on land, even though it was sealed by a very traditional marriage alliance.

The 1180s and 1190s, the very time when the Marshal was promoted into the baronage, was a time when the lesser knights of England were becoming more mobile in their allegiance. New magnates with access to court patronage could exploit this, and attract men to them who were looking for the rewards that their traditional lords could no longer offer. The Marshal (who inherited little in the way of a landed following) was one of the first great magnates in England that we know created a political connection not based on landed links and traditional allegiance, but on political interest and more subtle forms of reward, an 'affinity' as the Marshal's contemporaries were already calling it. He laid the foundations of his power in society on the rubble of an older society (though it is unlikely that he realised it). In the study of the Marshal's following, which is the basis of the next two chapters, we can find much to explain this change. The exercise of recreating the Marshal affinity is no small step towards finding a new view of medieval England.[1]

We are not short of evidence. The *History* has a lot to say on the subject, although, as you might expect, what it says needs to be treated with care. Methodical as he was, Sidney Painter stopped short of the work necessary to balance and complement what the *History* says. This would have involved tracking down and analysing the surviving originals and copies of the Marshal's writs and charters. There are at least 98 of them, with several charters more that were drawn up in the earl's presence. Most are charters of grant or confirmation to individuals or to religious houses; a few are letters of various sorts. Fifty of the charters have that important appendage, a witness list. This was a list of men present when the Marshal gave his instruction that a charter should be made by his clerk, the men who could later stand up in court and swear to the facts of the matter should anyone question the charter's authenticity. The men who are in the witness lists of the Marshal's charters between 1189 and 1219 should theoretically be the men who were his trusted companions, the members of his *mesnie*.

One of the most important things that a study of William Marshal's household achieves is its validation of the way medieval historians have reconstructed baronial followings from a study of charter witness lists. Comparing the evidence of the charters with the people who are named as members of his *mesnie* in the *History*,

---

1 The decline of the older 'honorial' style of magnate following was the theme of a key debate by D. Crouch, D.A. Carpenter and P.R. Coss, 'Bastard feudalism revised', *Past & Present*, 131 (1991), pp. 165–203. I have since sketched out a complex developmental model to fit the period 1150–1250, in D. Crouch, 'From Stenton to McFarlane: models of societies of the twelfth and thirteenth centuries', *Transactions of the Royal Historical Society*, 6th ser., 5 (1995), pp. 179–200. For a comparable case of magnate power to that of William Marshal, see the study of Henry II, Earl of Warwick, in D. Crouch, 'The local influence of the Earls of Warwick, 1088–1241: a study in decline and resourcefulness', *Midland History*, 21 (1996), pp. 1–22. The continuing importance of honorial 'feudalism' well into the thirteenth century is, however, stressed by D. Carpenter, 'The second century of English feudalism', *Past & Present*, 168 (2000), pp. 30–71. For my developed view, D. Crouch, *The English Aristocracy 1070–1272*, ch. 8.

we can say (thankfully) that the charter witness lists mirror exactly what the *History* has to say: the same people appear in both. Such a study has to be pursued with discrimination. Just because a name appears once or twice in the lists means little. It is when a name appears on several occasions in different documents datable to different years that a long-term relationship can be deduced. So we see the name of Geoffrey fitz Robert featuring in 12 of the 50 lists, the earliest datable to 1186 × 1188, and eight between the period 1199 and 1211. What other deduction can we make but that Geoffrey was close to William Marshal? The *History* tells us that he was exactly that, close enough for William to marry him to his wife's aunt and to employ as his seneschal of Leinster. Between the charters and the biography, therefore, we have a unique insight into the composition of a great baron's following at the turn of the twelfth century.

There are some odd omissions in the *History* that the charters make good. The *History* tells us little about the Marshal's non-military followers: the minor estate officers, the lesser household members and, with but one exception, the clerks who surrounded the Marshal. But these men are to be found in the witness lists of his charters. Their absence from the *History* tells us a lot about the prejudices of its author and his patrons. They had no time for clerks, not even those who served the Marshal loyally for two decades. The only one of these who is ever mentioned is the clerk, Philip, who is pilloried by the author for suggesting to the Marshal in the days before he died that he sell the robes that the Marshal had in stock to distribute to his knights, and use the money for the good of his soul.

Here again, we find that streak of anticlericalism and antagonism between the household clerk and knight that was so marked in the following of the Young King decades before. The *History* in its omissions and sly prejudices preserves this malign spirit for us to examine. Yet oddly, it preserves it by the means that clerks used, and in a way that tells us that this divided world was decaying. The *History* was composed and written by a layman. The Marshal, bred for the battlefield and the court, never really needed to know the skills of reading and writing, and certainly not Latin, which was the language of business in England and France. Other young aristocrats, particularly those destined to succeed to lands and a place in local or national life, had different needs. They needed to cast accounts, or at least be able to understand the accounts their servants made for them; they needed to be able to read the stream of writs successive English kings, particularly after Henry II, poured out from their chanceries.

Some barons learned to enjoy a book for its own sake. A good example was the Marshal's wife's first cousin and his neighbour in the Wye Valley, Gilbert fitz Baderon, who is said to have kept a library of French and Latin works in his Castle of Monmouth. He is said to have lent one of these to the poet Hugh of Roteland, in a literary conceit to explain the origin of one of Hugh's romances.[2] We know that

---

2 Hugh of Roteland, *Protheselaus: Ein altfranzösischer Abenteuerroman*, ed. F. Kluckow (Göttingen, 1924), lines 12707–14.

the Marshal learned to put a value on a good education. We know this because both his elder sons were put to their letters and both had reputations of being well instructed in the liberal arts, which meant that they had been educated in Latin as well as French. The third son, Gilbert, was formally educated to a rather higher standard again. We know the name of his private tutor, a Master Henry of Ho. Unlike his elder brothers, Gilbert Marshal was despatched in his teenage years to an institution of higher education, one of Western Europe's greater schools, most likely at Paris, for he emerged with a degree of *magister artium*. He was ordained only to the minor order of acolyte, sufficient to allow him to hold ecclesiastical benefices, which he began to acquire in the mid-1220s. His minor orders did not bar him from succeeding his brother Richard in 1234, nor indeed from taking on a sexual partner in his student days, by whom he had a daughter he acknowledged, called Isabel.[3] It is a little ironic that the only son of William Marshal who presented him with a grandchild was the one he and his wife had intended to be a celibate clergyman.

The knights

The chief part of the Marshal's immediate following, when it came into being around 1189, was his retinue of knights. Judging by the spirit in which the *History* was written, his knights would have been the first to agree with that observation. They gave him much of his political weight in society, and their attendance at his side gave him dignity. His contemporary, Gerald of Wales, portrayed such medieval attitudes in the lame but evocative Latin wordplay: 'Earls [*comites*] get their name from "accompanying" [*comitando*], for it is right that they be accompanied by many men.'

The Marshal had already had some experience of keeping his own following before 1189. In 1180, he had been lent by the Young King Henry a sufficient following to form up under his own banner on the field of Lagny. These knights were not his to keep or support from his own resources; they were a temporary gift from his master to enhance his favourite servant's dignity. But the important thing was that after 1180, the Marshal might raise his banner as a lord of men and recruit what following he was able. Certainly we know that before the Young King's death, at least two young men were attached to his banner rather than the king's. One was his squire, Eustace de Bertrimont, a Norman first mentioned in 1183. He was a landless soldier who was to live all his life in the Marshal's household. He was never among the first ranks of his intimates, and his lack of weight in society might well explain this. The other was a certain Henry Norreis ('the Northerner'), from his name an Englishman. This man, by his unwise trumpeting of the Marshal's fame, roused a good deal of animosity against the Marshal in the court of the Young King. It is not necessary to see him as the Marshal's herald, as Duby did, merely as an ill-judging squire and sycophant.

3 For the education of Gilbert Marshal, see *Acts and Letters*, pp. 26–7.

Henry II's favour added new members to the Marshal's household. In about 1187, the young John of Earley came into his household, where he then filled the part of the Marshal's squire. He was a wholly new addition to the Marshal's growing dignity: an aristocratic ward. John was born about 1172 and his father, William of Earley, had died at the end of 1180. William of Earley had been a titular royal chamberlain and had considerable estates in Berkshire and Somerset, enough to be considered a lesser baron rather than a knight. On his deathbed, he had devoted certain estates and churches for the foundation of a priory at Buckland, which he committed to John's great-uncle, Thomas of Earley, Archdeacon of Wells, for Thomas to set up the new monastery. The other Earley lands remained in royal keeping until 1194, perhaps farmed out to Archdeacon Thomas's care until he died around 1191. John, as an underage tenant-in-chief of the Crown, would also have come into the king's hands; by 1186, he was a young man of about 14 years, just the right age for fostering into a noble household. The king gave him, but not his lands, to William Marshal until he came of age. As we have seen, the Marshal had another ward in Heloise, the heiress of Kendal, around this time. From these arrangements, William had an access of dignity from the keeping of young aristocrats and future tenants-in-chief, but there were more practical benefits. According to the usual arrangement, the Marshal should also have had the right to marry off his wards. He could have given John of Earley to one of his family, or sold his marriage for a suitable sum. We might know a lot more about the Marshal–Earley relationship if we knew what he did with the marriage, but all we know of John of Earley's wife is that she was called Sybil. Her name suggests a Marshal family connection, but we cannot prove it.[4]

Even before 1189, there is evidence that the Marshal had the resources to have household knights. In his earliest known charter, two significant names appear, the young Wiltshire knights William Waleran and Geoffrey fitz Robert, at the time (c.1187) young men in expectation of the succession to family estates, but also landless. Both men were to follow the Marshal loyally from the reign of Henry II into the reign of John. The appearance of the Marshal's charters in some numbers after 1189 gives us a picture of the size of his household. Careful winnowing and comparison of evidence gives us a total of 18 knights who can be linked to the Marshal for long periods of time. (A detailed analysis of the Marshal's following is to be found in Appendix I.) From this group would be drawn his riding retinue: the *History* tells us that 10 knights accompanied him to Ireland in 1207; charters suggest a group of seven knights around him was not unusual. The 'pool' of 18

---

4 Sybil was a Marshal and Salisbury family name, as borne by the Marshal's mother and daughter. It is interesting to speculate that he somehow married John of Earley to a Marshal before 1194. Both William and John Marshal had by that date produced children, though illegitimate. What if Sybil, wife of John of Earley, had been a Marshal bastard? This would go a long way to accounting for the remarkable attachment of John to William Marshal throughout his life. For William Marshal would have been his wife's uncle or even his father-in-law.

knights does not include certain others who appear no more than once or twice in his charters, or not at all (Ralph Musard and Thomas Basset, for instance), but who were clearly linked to the Marshal. Both Ralph and Thomas joined the Marshal in John's reign.

Certain clear patterns emerge when we look at these knights as a group. First, a majority of them had no 'feudal' connection with the Marshal. Twelve out of the 18 (that is, two-thirds) were not his tenants. As I have said already, this is not a particularly surprising fact for the day and age we are dealing with. By the end of the twelfth century, the bonds formed by land grants between lords and their followers back in the post-Conquest period had loosened. In some areas, they loosened sooner than others. In Leinster, as I have already said, the Marshal could still count – and indeed insist – on the attendance of his tenants at his court. In England, too, there is evidence that he expected his men at least to come to his court when summoned. But it is equally clear that very few men indeed from his honors of Striguil and Crendon in Wales and England sought out places, or were given places, in his retinue. Only one of his Crendon tenants joined his circle, Jordan de Sauqueville, but, according to his son's version of events, Jordan did not find his way into the Marshal's graces because he was his tenant. Jordan had besieged the Marshal with petitions because the king's officers had made encroachments on his manor of Fawsley while Crendon was in royal wardship.[5] Jordan was an opportunist who was allowed to leap on the Marshal bandwagon when Crendon came into his hands. Either the Marshal had just liked Jordan's face, or had restored Fawsley as an act of policy to give him a friend in Buckinghamshire at no great expense to himself.

The tenants who do appear in the Marshal's entourage on a regular basis were all very significant men. The most important was Ralph Bloet. The Bloets could not be ignored by any lord of Striguil. It was not just that they were the principal tenants of the honor of Striguil in Wales and England. Ralph Bloet's brother William had married a sister of the late Earl Richard Strongbow, and Ralph and William both had acted as keepers of the honor and the castle of Chepstow before William Marshal obtained Earl Richard's heiress. It was Ralph who would have formally delivered Chepstow Castle to the Marshal or his attorneys in the summer of 1189. The extensive English lands of the Bloets were a useful piece in the jigsaw of influence he was building up in the south-west of England. Their manors lay in Gloucestershire, northern Hampshire, Wiltshire and Somerset, precisely the areas in which the Marshal was developing ambitions to raise an affinity. Ralph's other brother, Walter, was castellan of Raglan and a great man in northern Gwent. Ralph, too, was an important character in the Marches of Wales. He had married Nest, a sister of Iorwerth ap Owain, the Welsh ruler of Caerleon and the hereditary enemy of the lords of Chepstow.

---

5 H. Round, 'Tales of the Conquest', in *Peerage and Pedigree* (2 vols, London, 1910) I, pp. 285–6.

TABLE 3 The Marshal's knights

John of Earley	c.1187–1219		Berks., Som.
William Waleran	c.1187–1202		Glos., Wilts.
Geoffrey fitz Robert	c.1187–1210	(died 1211)	Wilts.
William Jardin	c.1196–1219		Beds., Suss., Bucks.
Jordan de Sauqueville	c.1200–1219		Bucks.
Ralph Bloet (III or IV)	c.1189–1219		Glos., Hants., Som., Wilts., Gwent.
John Marshal	c.1194–1219		Norf., Wilts.
Hugh of Sandford	c.1196–1205		Berks., Bucks.
Henry Hose	c.1199–1213		Berks., Hants., Suss.
Henry fitz Gerold	c.1199–1219		Berks., Oxon., Wilts.
Alan de St-Georges	c.1189–1204		Suss.
Roger d'Abenon	c.1189–1200		Surr., Hants.
Philip of Prendergast	c.1189–1207		Pembs.
Thomas of Rochford	c.1189–1206	(died 1206)	Glos., Herts.
Thomas de Colleville	c.1189–1200		Yorks., Lincs.
Nicholas Avenel	c.1189–1204		Devon., Glos., Som.
Stephen d'Evreux	c.1199–1219		Glos., Herefs., Worcs.
Eustace de Bertrimont	c.1182–1214		Beds., Suss., Bucks.

Nest Bloet was a woman whose importance was more than local. She had been Henry II's mistress at some time in her adventurous career early in the 1170s and produced a son by him, Morgan, named after her brother, the last Welsh king of Glamorgan. She remained remarkably influential in royal circles, especially with King John. She placed several of her legitimate sons in his household, and had a number of grants and favours from him. The cooperation of the Bloet family was an absolute necessity for the Marshal, and it is likely he sought them out rather than they seeking him. Ralph appears in his entourage as early as his Cartmel charter of 1189 × 1190. He died around 1199 but his son Ralph took his place in the Marshal's entourage, and another son, William, entered the household of the Marshal's eldest son; he was the Young Marshal's banner-bearer at the Battle of Lincoln in 1217.

Even before he inherited his brother's honor in 1194, the Marshal's entourage had begun to reflect a geographical bias. From his father, William Marshal must have learned the importance of controlling a distinct area, for John Marshal had been spectacularly successful in accumulating lands and followers on the north Wiltshire Downs and in the Kennet Valley in Stephen's reign. The need for a magnate to have a country of his own was not necessarily for security's sake. In the 1190s, it was not possible for the Marshal to accumulate the sort of lordship that his father had pieced together in the disturbed circumstances of half a century before: a discrete castellanry designed for military security. Nor did he have the spare land to raise up new men in an area he wished to control. But what he could do was to define an area for his ambitions and work on existing landholders there, overawing and cajoling them with his influence at court. They in turn might seek him out for protection and advancement. The *History* preserves a naked and unashamed statement of this political necessity. At Gloucester Castle in 1216, Ralph Musard, a Gloucestershire knight who had long been in the Marshal's political sphere, advised the Marshal to accept the regency: 'You will be able then to advance your men, and others besides.'[6] Ralph's advice was preserved to act as a foil to the more modest and less mercenary sentiments of John of Earley; but nonetheless lords must reward, and Ralph Musard was not offering advice that household knights and political adherents would have found in any way unethical or shameful.

What more natural for William Marshal than to pick on the land of his childhood for his country. In 1189, when he arrived in England, he already had some of the basic blocks to hand. His wife brought him lands scattered throughout the south-west counties. His brother joined up with him, and he was the first cousin of the Earl of Salisbury; both were men powerful in the same area. He obtained Gloucester Castle and the keeping of the county; he had the promise of the substantial support of John of Earley when he came of age; and he acquired the support of the Bloets. Add to this the magnate alliance of the Berkeleys, which he made during the 1190s, and you have a decided geographical bias to the Marshal affinity. Right from the beginning, his recruitment of knights reinforced this West Country trend. Stephen d'Evreux had a castle in Herefordshire and estates in Gloucestershire; William le Gros, the Marshal's nephew and Lord of Sodbury, and Ralph Musard were also Gloucestershire knights; William Waleran, Geoffrey fitz Robert and Ralph Bloet were from the Wiltshire area; Henry Hose and Alan de St-Georges came from Sussex; Hugh of Sandford, Thomas Basset, John of Earley, Jordan de Sauqueville and William Jardin were all from the Thames Valley; and Nicholas Avenel was from Devon or Somerset. No wonder that in founding Cartmel priory in the far north, he used canons of the family mausoleum of Bradenstoke, or that in founding the Abbey of Duiske in Leinster, he solicited Cistercians from the Wiltshire Abbey of Stanley; from Chepstow to the Thames Valley, everyone would soon have realised that William Marshal had come to England determined to make a political mark in the one corner of the kingdom he might call home. In a way, he was the typical hometown boy made good, come back to dazzle the folks with his wealth, a species not otherwise unknown in the twelfth century.[7]

Apart from the insignificant Eustace de Bertrimont, there was not a Frenchman among the Marshal's followers. No wonder the *History* introduces a sour anti-French note now and again. The household on which the author drew for his sources was wholly English. When they recalled for his biographer what had happened in 1183, those of his household who contributed their views were quick to blame the Norman knights of the Young King's household for their master's disgrace: he was

---

6 *History* II, lines 15433–42.
7 Compare Orderic Vitalis's story of the English royal justice of Henry I's reign, Ralph Basset, who came back to Normandy and expended his new wealth on a luxurious castle on his small ancestral estate, to the disgust of his neighbours.

overthrown, they were convinced, because he was an Englishman raised to high favour by the king over Frenchmen. There is defensive antagonism in this: the Marshal's knights resented the French. Perhaps they were fed up with being told how superior the French were in military capacity to the English. There is a smug delight in the tales of the Marshal's tournament days that it was an Englishman who had created for the Young King a *mesnie* that bore down all others in competition. In the description of the campaigns of 1217, there is great outrage at the 'pride' and 'bravado' of the 'French rascals' who presumed to invade England and despoil the English of their lands. A century and a half earlier, the followers of Harold Godwinson could not have been more outraged at the arrival of William of Normandy. Whether the Marshal had shared their prejudice is another matter. The bare facts of his itinerary in the 1190s demonstrate that he loved Normandy. At Lincoln, he treated with great respect the claims of the Normans in his army to have what they contended was the traditional honour of the first blows of the battle, even though he then awarded the privilege to the Earl of Chester's men. The mocking jibe put in the mouth of his old master, the Chamberlain of Tancarville, about England being a poor place for a military man, might well have been the Marshal's own, made palatable by being put into the mouth of the quirky and disagreeable old Chamberlain.

The clerks

Most great magnates tended to acquire particular friends in the Church. The Marshal was no exception. This sort of man was occasionally part of his clerical household, the way the Berkeleys and the Béthunes occasionally came into the orbit of his lay household. They added a certain tone to the Marshal's reputation in the world, a respectability and profundity of counsel. He opened a long and profitable relationship with Hugh le Rous, later Bishop of Ossory, on his visit to Leinster in 1200–1201. Bishop Hugh returned the visit in 1203, staying with the Marshal at his Berkshire seat of Hamstead Marshall. He assisted the Marshal with his Cistercian foundations of Tintern Parva and Duiske, and the Marshal obliged him with guarantees of the liberties of his diocese, an annual rent of gold pieces at Kilkenny and confirmations of churches the bishop claimed as within his estate. He and the Marshal exchanged lands at Aghaboe (Co. Laois) in furtherance of the earl's schemes to bolster his lordship to the west of Kilkenny. This was quite a contrast to the Marshal's venomous relations with another episcopal neighbour, Ailbe, Bishop of Ferns, a man less amenable and courtly and, worst of all perhaps, Irish.[8] The Marshal was particular friends besides with two English abbots, Edward of Notley and David of St Augustine's, Bristol. Notley was a Giffard foundation within what was called the 'advocacy' of the Marshal, and Bristol Abbey was within his political

8 *Acts and Letters*, nos. 80–2. For the Marshal's relationship with Ailbe of Ferns, see R. Hill, 'Ecclesiastical letter books of the thirteenth century' (Oxford BLitt thesis, 1936), p. 232.

sphere. Edward of Notley was involved at one point with the Marshal's plans to reorganise the church in Leinster,[9] and was at his deathbed, offering comfort. Abbot David was a latecomer to the Marshal's circle, probably during the time after he became regent, but he was particularly trusted. In February 1218, he was said to be in Ireland, specifically on the Marshal's business, not his abbey's.[10] He was to be one of the executors of the Marshal's last testament.

We do not know much; in fact, we know almost nothing about relations between William and his clerical brother, Henry. Since Henry Marshal owed all his promotions in the Church to his brother's fortunes at court, we can hope that relations were good between them, but there is little evidence of any relationship at all. Doubtless, this was because Henry died more than a dozen years before his brother. If he had survived him, he might have made a significant contribution to the *History*; we might perhaps have had his memories of the Marshal family history and William's early days. But he did not, and so as a result the work is fuller of inaccuracies than it might probably otherwise have been. The one known point of contact between the two brothers was their joint patronage of their nephew, Anselm le Gros. William had him in his household for a while and Bishop Henry, before he died, promoted Anselm to the treasurership of Exeter Cathedral.

From the beginning of his career as a magnate, the Marshal had a large clerical staff. Some of these were called 'chaplains', the others 'clerks'. Since the chaplains always precede the clerks in witness lists, it is likely that they were in priestly orders and the clerks in the less restricting and burdensome orders of deacon, subdeacon or even lesser ones. Details are lacking, but it is probable that the chaplains of the Marshal's household were there to say mass and take confessions for the itinerant retinue, as ministering priests. They formed the Marshal's 'chapel': not a building, but his travelling entourage of spiritual advisers, with their vestments, portable altars and sacred vessels, and whatever collection of missals, psalters and relics the Marshal kept. The clerks, on the other hand, doubtless did the job of keeping central accounts and conducting correspondence; although in orders and capable of holding church preferment, they were men who were 'clerical' in a modern, as well as a medieval, sense.

In general, throughout the twelfth century, an earl or great baron would employ as many as a dozen clerics of whatever description at any one time, sometimes more. They did not follow him continuously. We are told of Waleran, Count of Meulan (who died in 1166), that he always had four working chaplains in his employ, two of whom he would keep by him in his travelling household. The other two would be left by the count to go about their own affairs or be detached on other missions.[11] Doubtless, the Meulan clerks would have alternated at their master's court on a sort of rota. Some clerical households had formal chiefs,

---

9 Edward of Notley formed one of a commission in Leinster to investigate the possession of the church of Wicklow, Cartulary of Llanthony, TNA: PRO, C115/77, fo. 287r–v.
10 *Rotuli Litterarum Clausarum* I, p. 377.
11 *The Beaumont Twins*, pp. 153–4.

chancellors, to oversee the lesser clerks just as the seneschal d'hôtel controlled the lay household. A number of great French potentates, and in England the Marshal's contemporaries, Earl Ranulf of Chester and Count John of Mortain, employed such officers, and so did the Marshal's son after 1224, but not the Marshal himself so far as we can tell.

None of the Marshal's household clerks was as important to him as the great prelates who might have called themselves his friends. But that is not to say that his clerks were not trusted or intimate with him. A few of them served him for quite as many years as his longest-serving household knights. It would not be reasonable to think that (whatever the tensions within his household) the Marshal, seasoned practitioner of courtliness and amiability, slighted one section of his entourage for another; indeed, we will see how he furthered some of his clerks in much the same way as he furthered his knights. Two charters, dated at either end of the Marshal's career as a magnate, tell us most about the size of the Marshal's travelling clerical household. In 1189 × 1190, a charter shows him accompanied by three clerks and a chaplain. In 1214, he was at his house at Caversham, Berkshire, with, again, three clerks (one of whom, Philip, named himself as scribe of the charter) and this time two chaplains (on another occasion, one of these same two, Nicholas, was called 'the earl's chaplain'; the other, Walter, 'the countess's chaplain').[12]

Throughout the Marshal's career, there were nine clerks who can be closely associated with him. In terms of attestations, the clerk Michael of London witnessed 15 charters, more than anyone else apart from John of Earley – and was in his service from at least the first year of King Richard to the crisis of King John's reign: nearly 25 years. He followed him through England, Normandy and Ireland. On one occasion, Michael is named as the scribe of one of the Marshal's charters. He performed a range of services for his master besides draughtsmanship. He represented him as his attorney at Westminster in 1199 and 1201, whether before the barons of the Exchequer or the royal justices.[13] It can be proved that others of his clerks were in the Marshal's following for long periods: William de Lisle, Master Joscelin and Michael of Kendal all appear in his acts in the reigns of both Richard and John. The clerk Philip attested with the Marshal eight times, but only in John's reign. It is interesting to speculate on the reason the *History* singles him alone out of the clerical entourage of its hero for criticism. It may be that because he was a relative newcomer, his intervention at the Marshal's deathbed rankled more with the knights of the household.

There are fewer chaplains than clerks evident in the Marshal's household. Two appear with him in Richard's reign, Eustace and Roger. The one who served him

12 *Acts and Letters*, nos. 21, 23. For the earl's and countess's individual chaplains, see 'The Charters of the Cistercian Abbey of Duiske', p. 28. The countess also had her own clerk, Robert, who was murdered in Gloucestershire in or soon before 1219, *Excerpta e Rotulis Finium in turri Londinensi asservatis*, ed. C. Roberts (Record Commission, 1835–1836) I, p. 34.

13 *Memoranda Roll of I John*, p. 6; *Curia Regis Rolls I*, p. 421.

longest was Eustace de St-Georges, who was in his entourage from the mid-1190s to the time of the Marshal's long residence in Ireland from 1207 to 1212. At the end of that period, he seems to have transferred his function to that of clerk. In his later years, the Marshal and his wife still relied on two chaplains, Walter and Nicholas, whom we find in his entourage from the time of the Irish expedition.

A certain Roger appears as the Marshal's almoner on one occasion. The post may have been an additional hat for Roger the chaplain. Much later, the Marshal had as his almoner Brother Geoffrey, a Templar knight. He was following a fashion of the times. Hugh of Avalon, Bishop of Lincoln (died 1200), and John, as count and king, also had Templar almoners. The almoner gave out, from day to day, food from his lord's table to the poor at his door, and perhaps also small sums of money; the fiscal expertise of the Templars might account for their appointments to great households in this capacity. Brother Geoffrey was not above clerical tasks, however, and was the man who wrote out the Marshal's last testament in April 1219. All magnates saw the giving of alms as a pious duty in the twelfth century, and a chaplain-almoner was to be found in the household of the Marshal's colleague, Robert, the last Count of Meulan, who we are told had the needy fed outside his gates at the same time as he ate in his various halls.[14]

We know next to nothing about the backgrounds of the Marshal's clerks. His chaplain Eustace de St-Georges might well have been some connection of his knight Alan de St-Georges, but that is about all we can say. Three of them, at least, had had a good education in one of the more significant schools of England and France, for the clerks Joscelin, Michael and Pentecost took the title 'Master' (*magister*). We know a little more of the way the Marshal rewarded his clerks' service. Master Joscelin (son of Hugh), for instance, was in 1196 (doubtless because of his lord's influence) given by the priory of Longueville the lease of its lands in the Marshal's manor of Caversham for a term of 15 years, in return for paying an annual rent of five marks (£3 6s. 8d.). The Marshal himself, one of his knights and the seneschal of Crendon stood as sureties for Joscelin's good behaviour.[15] Joscelin was also given by his lord, before 1199, some of his houses in the Earl of Pembroke's estate at Charing, at the end of the Strand where it met what was then called King Street (now Whitehall) between the city of London and the palace of Westminster. The Marshal reserved for himself his right to lodge in these houses with his men when he was attending on the king. Since Joscelin for many years before and after 1201 deputised for his lord at the Exchequer, carrying out his duties as marshal, the grant of houses just up the road from Westminster was a great advantage for him.[16] There

14 *Chartes de l'abbaye de Jumièges*, ed. J.J. Vernier (2 vols, Rouen, 1916) II, pp. 207–9.
15 *Newington Longeville Charters*, ed. H.E. Salter (Oxford Records Society, III, 1921), p. 54.
16 *Pipe Roll of 3 John*, pp. 42, 243, 265. This shows Master Joscelin as a member of the Exchequer in 1201, present among the barons when an important letter was opened before the Justiciar; it also tells us that Joscelin had acquired the name 'Joscelin Marshal' from his long occupation of the office. By 1211, Joscelin had been succeeded in the deputy-marshalship by one William Toke, see *Curia Regis Rolls* VI, p. 188. He was dead by 1216,

is some evidence besides that Master Joscelin was rector of the church of St Matthew, Friday Street, in the city of London, which he had served for him by his own chaplain.[17] We know for certain that he was also rector of the Marshal's church of Tidenham in Gloucestershire, just across the river Wye from Chepstow.[18]

The Marshal's clerk, Michael, also had London connections. Indeed, in 1216, he was called 'Master Michael of London'. In 1204, he was acknowledged as the owner of some land in the north of the city in the parish of St Stephen, Coleman Street. Since he had it by inheritance, it is very likely that he was a Londoner himself.[19] It is an intriguing thought that the Marshal might have enlisted his services when he came to London in July 1189 to be married, and had to fill up a number of vacancies in his new household in a hurry. In 1216, Master Michael was said to have been the owner of certain houses in Bristol that he had bought from Margam Abbey.[20] Another of the Marshal's clerks, Philip, was given preferment by his lord in the Marches. He had a half share of the rectory of the wealthy church of Llantrisant in the lordship of Netherwent. The Marshal paid a substantial annual sum to the canons of Llanthony for them to withdraw the claim they made on Philip's church.[21] The curiously named Marshal clerk Master Pentecost (of Inglesham) had the rectory of the Marshal church of Easton Royal in Wiltshire at the time when his lord decided to concede the church to Bradenstoke priory. The Marshal had Pentecost's life interest in the church assured by the Bishop of Salisbury.[22]

There were other members of the household apart from chaplains, almoners and clerks, who might be considered to be 'clerical' in the loosest sense. These were the chamberlains. The most prominent of them was the chamberlain, Walter Cut, from his name an Englishman and from his position in witness lists probably also a clerk, although not a high-ranking one. He seems to have been in the Marshal's service only in Richard's reign. But his colleagues and successors might be found among the four men also called chamberlain in his entourage at one time or another: William, Geoffrey, Osbert and Gilbert. By this date, chamberlains had tended to assume a specialised function in the households of the great as keepers and receivers of their lord's money. It is sometimes found that chamberlains were also clerks, for literacy was a desirable quality in the job. The chamberlain would

see H.G. Richardson, 'William of Ely, the king's treasurer', *Transactions of the Royal Historical Society*, 4th Ser., XV (1932), pp. 85–6.

17 *Acts and Letters*, no. 45, pp. 107–8. Some time later, Joscelin chose to settle his rights there on the Abbey of Flaxley (alias Kingswood) in the Forest of Dean, where he wished to be buried. The association of Joscelin with Friday Street, where the Marshal probably stayed before he married in Richard fitz Reiner's mansion, may indicate that – like his colleague, Michael – he was a Londoner who came early on to the Marshal's attention.

18 *Curia Regis Rolls* VI, p. 29.

19 *Pipe Roll of 6 John*, p. 98; *Rotuli de Finibus et Oblatis*, p. 198.

20 *Rot. Clausarum* I, p. 294.

21 Cartulary of Llanthony, fo. 287r.

22 Cartulary of Bradenstoke, British Library, ms Cotton Vitellius A XI, fo. 104v.

have kept the Marshal's financial office, his 'chamber'. It is interesting how, like 'chapel', the various early offices of the great household took on the names of rooms in the contemporary mansion complex. The chamber (*camera*) was the private room of the lord, the furnishings of which the chamberlain (*camerarius*) once kept. It needs to be observed how promptly the Marshal recruited such a man as Walter Cut to his side. This hardly betrays the attitude of the ingenuous knight and single-minded devotee of the tournament field that Sidney Painter and Georges Duby would have had us believe he was in 1189.

The hidden household

A puzzling absence from the Marshal's retinue is that of falconers and hunters. The master hunter or master forester, always of knightly rank, was a figure that several great magnates began to employ on a regular basis in their households in the Marshal's generation (notably the Earl of Chester and the Count of Meulan). The Marshal certainly possessed enough parks and forests on his estates in England, Wales and Ireland to be able reasonably to employ such a prestigious figure, but he did not, as far as we can tell. Odder still is the utter lack of any mention of his hunting or hawking, the most ancient of aristocratic enthusiasms. Can we suspect him here of unconventionality? Did his preoccupation with the hunting of men on the tournament field spoil him for these scientific pursuits?

There were others of whom we are never likely to hear anything: the porters who packed and carried the boxes and satchels that bounced up and down on the sumpter horses that made up the Marshal's train. There must also have been waggoners or carters employed by the Marshal. We do hear on at least two occasions of Humphrey the Marshal who must have supervised the mechanics of William's itinerant household. We hear nothing of the workers in his hall – his cooks, ushers and menial attendants – only, as the Marshal neared death, of the knights, squires (*valet*), servants (*servant*) and all the others of his household (*maison*) who wept as he prepared for death. Absent also is much mention of the messengers who carried his letters about the country, keeping in fitful touch with the various components of his great estates. We only hear of one, Richard, who was murdered on his master's service near London by a group of highwaymen for the sake of his purse and robe just before 1219.[23] Nonetheless, we know from studying other households that such men existed, and would have swollen his touring retinue to the number of maybe 40 or 50. By such numbers, as well as by the glitter of gold and the sheen of silk and fur, the Marshal was known to be a great man.

23 *Curia Regis Rolls* VIII, p. 142.

12

LA BONE FIN VA TOUT

Spirituality

The *History* does not in general worry too much about the Marshal's spiritual state. He was a good man, and God loves good men. The Marshal's soul only occupies the author's attention at the point he and his paymasters would have considered appropriate: his deathbed. Nonetheless, it is surprising, and unaccountable, that he does not mention any of the Marshal's several expensive religious foundations, save one. Curiously, the one foundation inspired by the Marshal that the author does see fit to place in his narrative is one that cost him little. After the sea-battle in the Channel in 1217 that destroyed the French fleet, the Marshal expressed a wish that a hospital might be built at the port of Sandwich. It was to be dedicated to St Bartholomew on whose feast day the battle had been fought. However, it was neither built on Marshal lands nor with Marshal funds, but with the prize money taken from the French. I can only guess that the hospital's foundation escaped the editor's knife because it made a neat full stop to the story of the battle that saved Henry III's throne. The Marshal's other religious foundations were but unnecessary digressions to the author.

But pious grants aside, the text of the *History* is nonetheless saturated by remembrances of God, even between deathbeds. We may take this as an accurate reflection of the degree of open religion displayed by the Marshal's circle. There was no mocking (except of the household clerks), nor was there indifference. 'God for the Marshal!' was the cry of the Marshal's men. God was ever-present and was particularly to be called on in a crisis, or, at the lowest level, invoked in oaths ('By the Sword of God!' was a fittingly military one used by the Marshal). The narrative has occasional asides that demonstrate a strong sensibility of the workings of God in the world: 'My lords, it is no nonsense that God is wise and courteous; ever he gives aid and succour to the man who believes in him'.[1] This is how the *History* comments on the first tournament of the Marshal's career in 1166, which gave him the capital to quit the Tancarville household. When the Marshal knighted the Young King, the author says: 'Great honour did God to the Marshal that day'.[2] *Damnedex* (the Lord God) was a good lord to his true vassals and rewarded them as a good lord ought. And if the Lord God was a little slow to answer the Marshal's prayers, there were counsellors near him who could make intercession. The Virgin Mary and the Three Kings of Cologne were approached to assist in vindicating the Marshal of the charge of adultery with his master's wife. The devil, too, might be invoked in the heat of anger and battle fury. It was to his mercies that the Marshal committed Richard when he had him defenceless at his lance's end in 1189.

The Christian powers sit a little oddly beside the other supernatural force to be found in the *History*. Fortune and her wheel were also credited with affecting the Marshal's fate, as when the Young King died. This streak of fashionable classical paganism may well reflect the Marshal's own perception of his fortunes. It is an image that is prevalent in the writings of the courtier-clerks of his day, and Fortune's instability and coquettishness would have been constantly in the mouths of the Marshal's colleagues. The power of luck and the Fates must have bothered the Marshal, as it would any courtier, for it must often have seemed that his fate depended on the whim of some supernatural agency beyond his control.

The piety of the Marshal, so far as it is open to analysis, seems to parallel that of another seasoned warrior of his day, his younger contemporary, Philip de Novara. His 'Four Seasons of the Age of Man' is a prolonged and dour sermon on mortality. Even as he deals with childhood, he urges parents to instil as much of piety in their children as infants can bear. To him, youth was a time of direst danger to the soul. Youths (that is, unmarried or childless knights up to the age of 40) were heedless and luxurious by their nature, yet they were at a time of life when their inexperience and foolishness might lead them to be carried off without warning. In what state of soul would they then meet God? For Philip, the business of middle and old age was to send ahead riches 'to that other strange isle' to which all must come, that is, to the world beyond this one. Alms and good deeds must make amends for the folly of youth. For Philip, as for John Wesley and any libertarian, it was a good thing to acquire riches, but only because it increased one's ability to do good to the poor and the Church. The old man might then approach the end of his life with more assurance, and regard with equanimity the fading of his faculties. Such a preoccupation with mortality was very much present in the Marshal's biography.

William Marshal was still a 'youth' when he first made the acquaintance of sudden death, when his uncle was stabbed to death before him in Poitou. His own survival from this incident was by no means assured, and this may have led to reflection.

---

1 *History* I, lines 1363–6.
2 *History* I, lines 2097–8.

However, the only evidence we have is that it led to distinctly malevolent feelings towards the alleged inspirers of the deed, the Lusignan family. The death of the Young King in 1183 is a different matter. Neither the Marshal nor anyone else could have expected the grim scenes that terminated the Young King's life within a fortnight. 'Caitiff death' had stolen away his lord, and we can well believe the description of the grief and despair of his men that broke out in the chamber. What we cannot know directly is what effect the scene had on the Marshal. How accurate is the poignant dialogue between the two men, lord and servant, as the king died? It is certainly affecting. The younger man sinking, but lucidly dictating his testament to his clerks; the Marshal at his side, undertaking the trip to Jerusalem for him, but still talking of recovery. Were the Young King's last words really for him? We cannot know. What we do know is that the deathbed scene did persuade him to set aside his career and travel to the East, with all the risks that decision involved. We know also from his own deathbed reflections that he had decided in the Holy Land that he would die in the Templar order, and that it was in the East that he purchased the rich silken pall that he intended would one day cover his own dead body. It lay untouched for 30 years in one of his castles or monasteries in Wales until John of Earley was sent to fetch it to the death chamber at Caversham. It was the appearance of this cloth, a little faded, that made him talk of these long-ago thoughts before his curious knights.

The Marshal was around the age of 35 when the Young King died. In the reckoning of his time, he might still be called a 'youth', but he had come to that time of youth when 'middle age' was fast approaching and thoughts were more settled and composed. According to the course of life described by Philip de Novara, he was due for a spiritual crisis, and this is what seems to have happened in 1183. There may have been other contributing causes than catching the dying breath of a master rather younger than himself. His career had not been particularly salubrious for the past 10 years. He had recently learned exactly how unstable were the foundations of a life at court. No wonder, then, that the *History* could not find much material for his time in the Holy Land, despite his two or more years there. William Marshal remained a curiously private man in an age without much privacy for the great. It appears he did not care to share with his later household what he did and thought in the Holy Places; it was between him and God, his chief lord.

Supporting the Church

His household was also not favoured with his thoughts on the foundation of his various religious houses in England and Ireland. He founded three: an Augustinian priory at Cartmel in around 1190; Cistercian abbeys at Tintern Parva (*de Voto*) and Duiske (or Graiguenamanagh) in 1200. He also founded a hospital for the poor at Kilkenny, at the bridge near his castle gate, for the poor were always to be found at the rich man's door. The foundation of Tintern Parva (Little Tintern) was also called forth by a spiritual crisis. As we have seen, it occurred when he was in peril of not just his own life, but those of his wife and small children. The ever-mobile aristocrat of the Anglo-Norman world was as much at the mercy of his nerves on embarking on a sea voyage as a modern businessman on boarding a jet. No doubt, there were then too people to reassure them that sea travel was statistically the safest form of travel in the twelfth century. And if there were such people, they would have been right, in theory.

Fatal wrecks were by no means common in the Marshal's time, but some unnervingly well-known characters had foundered at sea: William Atheling, the son of Henry I, and Richard, Earl of Chester, who both went down with the White Ship in 1120. A storm in the Channel had carried away several well-known courtiers in 1165. King Richard had just escaped drowning on the Dalmatian coast on his return from the crusade in 1193. As his own ship yawed and plunged in an autumn gale in 1201, it must have seemed to the Marshal a very cruel joke of that ineluctable force of the Fates that he was threatened with drowning at the very height of his fortunes while going to take possession of his wife's great domain of Leinster. But he was not completely helpless; in such circumstances, others had successfully bargained with God. The Marshal made his vow in the Irish Sea, and the measure of the horror and relief he must have felt can be seen in the promptness with which he began the foundation. He had his wish to do so confirmed by the king within weeks of his return to England. An abbot and monks were in place by 1203, a colony drawn from the original Tintern in his Welsh lordship of Netherwent.[3] It is very likely that he made his wishes known to his monks of Tintern as he passed back from Ireland through Netherwent en route to the court of King John.

The foundations of Cartmel and Duiske were more leisurely and considered. Both seem to have been intended to mark his acquisition of new lordships: polite acknowledgements to God of the grace with which he had favoured William Marshal with more possessions. Cartmel was founded in the first year of William's enjoyment of his wife's inheritance, but it was not founded on his wife's lands.[4] Cartmel was his alone, and the gift was in effect a direct one from him to God, owing nothing to his wife's inheritance, although conditional as all English foundations were on the king's approval. It was executed in a public assembly, the presence of Geoffrey fitz Peter indicating that it was done within the precincts of a royal palace. Although the king did not participate, his brother, Count John, issued a confirmation of the deed as lord of Lancaster. William's relations were

---

3 A copy of the foundation charter survives and seems likely to belong to the time of William's second arrival in Leinster in 1207, *Acts and Letters*, no. 95, pp. 175–8.

4 The date of the foundation charter of Cartmel can be ascertained by its being after the Marshal's marriage to Isabel late in July 1189 and before his departure to Normandy in March 1190. All the witnesses, especially Geoffrey fitz Peter, would have been found in England at this time. The mention of William's 'heirs' (rather than his sons and daughters) is interesting. This indicates that his wife must have been expecting a child, but had not yet produced, and we know that the Marshal's eldest child, the second William Marshal, was born in Normandy in the early summer of 1190.

present: the Earl of Salisbury, his cousin; John 'the king's marshal', his elder brother; and Philip of Prendergast, his wife's brother-in-law. Also present were nine men who can be identified as the Marshal's knights, and four of his clerks. Among the throng was John of Earley, whose memories of this pious scene did not (curiously) make it into the eventual biography of his lord.

The foundation of Cartmel was a considered act and the foundation charter preserves much of the thought behind it. He had done it, he said, 'for the widening of the field of Holy Religion' and 'for the soul of the lord King Henry II, and for the soul of the Young King Henry *my lord* [my italics], and for the soul of King Richard; for my soul and the soul of my wife Isabel, and those of my ancestors and successors and our heirs'. Debts were being paid. Principally, the debt was to God, who had given him a wife, wide estates, royal favour, and now, it seems, was promising an heir. But there was also a debt to the sad shade of the Young Henry, whom few remembered. A local debt may also have been involved. We know from another source that the personnel of the new priory (already in place at Cartmel when the foundation charter was written) was drawn from Bradenstoke priory in Wiltshire, where the Marshal's father was buried. But the Marshal was firm in stating that his new house was to be completely independent of Bradenstoke, it was to be his alone, and it must always be a priory and never promoted to an abbey (for if it had been, the king would have had a claim on its advocacy).[5] The Marshal was also as punctilious as ever about future relations between himself and his heirs and Cartmel. He was its patron and to him belonged the formal right of choosing the prior of Cartmel, in consultation with two canons sent to him by its chapter. There seem to have been few contacts between the Marshal and Cartmel thereafter, which is not surprising in view of its remoteness from his centres of interest. However, he did transfer to the priory a church and village in Leinster at some time after 1199, the later confirmation of which survives.[6]

The foundation of Duiske, some 11 years after Cartmel, was a not dissimilar exercise. He must have decided to do it before he left for Ireland in 1201, and had already got the approval in principle of the abbot of Stanley, another Wiltshire house, who was to provide a colony of monks. The storm en route that precipitated a twin Cistercian foundation at Tintern Parva was an accidental windfall for the white monks; the Marshal increased the stakes with God so that his survival was more desirable to him. He would have announced his foundation of Duiske on his arrival in Leinster, and indeed he secured the assistance of Hugh le Rous, the future bishop, before he left again for England. But Tintern Parva took priority over the next few years, understandably perhaps. An abbot and monks were already in place at Tintern Parva while purchases were still being made to provide an

---

5 The royal claim on abbeys is mentioned in relation to contemporary problems between the Marshal's friend, Geoffrey fitz Peter, and Walden Abbey in Essex, see *Liber de fundatione abbathiae de Walden*, in *Monasticon Anglicanum* IV, pp. 145–8.

6 *Acts and Letters*, no. 22, pp. 79–80.

endowment for Duiske in the period 1207–1212.[7] The cemetery of Duiske Abbey was consecrated by the Bishop of Ferns in June 1204 while the Bishop of Ossory was in England, and this indicates that the monks of Stanley had a cell there then working at the foundation, but it was a slow process.[8] Even in the 1207 foundation charter, there is an air of a thing half-done about the business. The Marshal had written into the foundation charter his approval of any future grants or sales to the abbey that might come its way.[9] The chief difference between the foundations of Cartmel and of Duiske is the prominence in the latter of his wife. It was on her lands that the abbey was erected and so the Marshal has written into the deed her approval of the foundation. When he died, she would enter into the untrammelled enjoyment of her lands, and then any grant he had made would be at her mercy.

One thing that both the Duiske and Cartmel foundation deeds have in common is a concluding passage cursing in his own name and in God's any man who dared to trouble the new houses. In an age that had developed effective church courts to protect pious donations, such curses had become uncommon and dated. That they appear in both deeds is remarkable and allows one to picture the Marshal, thinking back to what was done in his younger days, instructing his clerks to be sure to have a good curse written into the acts to put off ill-wishers. It might well have been his idea of how things should be done properly. It certainly tells us something about how he thought God worked in the world.

Apart from these major acts of patronage, the Marshal's other grants to the Church were limited. Most are not grants at all, but confirmations of what his predecessors had given. The range of his patronage was narrow and in many ways as old-fashioned as the maledictions of his charters. The orders he patronised – the Cistercians and the Augustinians, and even the Templars – were the orders patronised by his father's generation. The patronage of the high nobility at this time was beginning to be diverted into the first purposely founded chantries: chapels of one or several chanting priests singing daily masses for their benefactors' souls, a direct response to the growing concern with the dead's protracted residence in Purgatory. Some of the earliest of them were founded within the English royal family, in memory of the Young King Henry, but it does not seem that William contributed to this industrialisation of masses for his dead lord's soul. What major grants were still being made were being directed towards the orders of Sempringham, La Grande Chartreuse, Grandmont and Prémontré, who were tapping a continuing taste for asceticism that the friars of St Dominic and St Francis would exploit to great effect soon after the Marshal's death.

---

7 'Charters of the Cistercian Abbey of Duiske', p. 16: a deed quitting land to William Marshal, Earl of Pembroke, and his monks of Stanley, which is attested by John, abbot of Tintern Parva.

8 *Ibid.*, pp. 23–4.

9 *Acts and Letters*, no. 32, pp. 89–93.

I know of a total of 27 chapters of regular or secular clerks that had charters from the Marshal: the chapters of Winchester, Lisieux, Dublin, Ossory and Glendalough; the Benedictines of Gloucester, Lyre and Pembroke; the Cluniacs of Longueville; the Tironians of Pill; the Augustinians of Bradenstoke, Cartmel, Dunstable, Kells, Llanthony, Notley, St Thomas of Dublin and Waltham; the Cistercians of Duiske, Dunbrody, Foucarmont, Valmont and Val-Notre-Dame; the nuns of Maiden Bradley and Markyate; and the crusading orders of the Temple and Hospital of Jerusalem. However, most of these charters record not grants, but concessions of grants that his predecessors had made.

Despite this impressive dispersal of parchment, in fact the Marshal gave very little to the clergy. It is even possible that he may have had more from them: sums of money paid to him to secure confirmations of privileges. Apart from his three foundations, the Marshal made real grants to only six churches. Most of these were unimpressive: tithes to Pembroke (Monkton) and Longueville priories; a few acres and houses at Caversham to Notley Abbey; and a church each to the chapters of Christchurch, Dublin, and Bradenstoke, Wiltshire. Curiously, the most striking outright grant to a church other than a foundation was of 10 ploughlands to the Cathedral of Glendalough in Leinster.[10] If there is any preference to be gleaned from the Marshal's Church patronage, it is a thoroughly conventional one towards the Augustinians and Templars, both of whom were much favoured by the courtiers of his father's day. His first foundation was an Augustinian one at Cartmel, and he also favoured its mother house, Bradenstoke, where his father and brother were buried. The Marshal's good friends were Abbot Edward of Notley, an Augustinian house of the congregation of Arrouailse, and Bishop Hugh of Ossory, an Augustinian canon before he was elected bishop. His chief clerical executor was Abbot David of the Augustinian house of Bristol. The stolidity and respectability of the Augustinians seems to have stirred some answering chord in the Marshal. He was a most conventional man.

Dying to the world

This most conventional of men died as such a man must. 'A good end counts for everything' is the proverb that Philip of Novara quotes again and again. All life should be a preparation for the final act, and the Marshal had been thinking of his death and planning for it for fully half his long life. He had done as Philip said a man must, and sent ahead his fortune to the strange isle, the Avalon to which he must one day sail. Two abbeys of monks and a priory of canons were the ports from which he sent his wealth to the other world, and for generations they and others would send after him cargoes of prayer and intercession. So it was with composure that he made the first stage on his journey. Once he knew that his last

10 For these grants, see *Acts and Letters*, *passim*.

illness was upon him, he sent away the futile, self-important doctors, and had himself gently rowed up the Thames and out into the country, away from London and Westminster and the world of affairs that now at the last he found oppressive. Out he went to that very country where his father had manoeuvred and fought in Stephen's civil war. There he settled into his death chamber in the manorial complex at Caversham across the Thames from Reading and nearby Earley, his friend John's home.

His manor at Caversham had for some years been a favourite of his, and he and his wife had built expensively there. They had erected a large and handsome chapel of the Blessed Virgin within the manorial precinct, big enough to host an outpost of the community of black canons of Notley Abbey. The expense was in part because the chapel had to be a suitable place to house a collection of holy relics deposited there, a rival to the handsome display of King Henry I's relics to be found at Reading across the river. It was said the collection had once belonged to Duke Robert of Normandy, the king's brother, which the canons claimed had been deposited at the manor for safe keeping by the duke's mistress, Countess Agnes of Buckingham, Lady of Caversham, in 1106. They supposedly included relics the crusading duke had acquired in the Holy Land, not least the head of the lance that had stabbed Christ's side on the cross.[11] To die at Caversham was therefore to die in company with the saints and to join with Jesus Christ in his own mortal agony.

Though nothing now survives of the Marshal complex at Caversham, and even its site is only approximately known, it has to have had a hall, private chambers and a small town of lodgings within the precinct wall.[12] It made as comfortable a setting as could be contrived for William and his men to await his death. It was a long time coming and he resisted it steadfastly. He showed no fear of death, just the same patience and determination he had shown all his life. But he was treating death as an adversary right till the end, until he had then to admit it was too strong for him. The only real measure we have of his thoughts at this time – for he was still for the most part as guarded as if he were in King John's council chamber – is the sudden loquacity that came upon him when he saw the silken pall that he had sent for from Wales, the pall he intended to cover his bier. Then his eldest son and his men learned for the first time the plans he had made years before for his burial, and some few details of the man's inner life for once escaped the prison of his discretion.

11 The legend is to be found copied from a book that once belonged to Notley Abbey, BL, ms Cotton Titus, C VI, fo.4 v. The chapel was to become celebrated in the time of the Marshals for a miraculous statue of the Virgin it also possessed, N. Vincent, 'King Henry III and the Blessed Virgin Mary', in *The Church and Mary*, ed. R.N. Swanson (Studies in Church History, 39, Woodbridge, 2004), pp. 126–46. Since the Marshal endowed a Lady Mass at the chapel (a Saturday mass in honour of the Virgin), the statue might have been his or Countess Isabel's addition to the chapel's glories on their rebuilding of it in the 1190s.

12 C. Haigh and D. Loades, 'The fortunes of the shrine of St Mary of Caversham', *Oxoniensia*, 46 (1981), pp. 62–72.

It was not just his sons and knights who were waiting all that while. Countess Isabel, too, played a leading part in the ceremonies of the deathbed, though as usual the biographer is not eager to tell us what it was. She was summoned along with their five daughters to his council to hear the Marshal declare that he wished to enter the order of Knights Templar before death. His changed status to monk brought him to the point of farewell with the countess, for admission to a monastic order theoretically terminated the state of marriage, as long as the wife consented.[13] It was with this in mind that the old man 'who was generous, gentle and kind towards his wife the countess' asked Isabel to kiss him 'for you will never be able to do it again', as he said. His wife of three decades obliged, and they wept together, as did everyone else in the death chamber, recognising that the Marshal had taken a major step towards his last journey: parting company with his status as a secular magnate and as a husband. In the end, it was too much. The inconsolable countess and her daughters had to be taken out of the chamber 'for nobody was able to comfort them'.[14]

The biography does not again mention Countess Isabel as attending on her husband. But since his daughters were allowed in to see him up till a few days before his death, it is likely that the countess was often in the chamber, though the biography consistently portrays their eldest son, William Marshal the younger, as taking the principal part in managing the deathbed. The biography, however, does indicate another place in the Caversham manor complex where the countess might very well have been usefully engaged as her husband lay dying. It is likely that her own station during her husband's prolonged deathbed had been in the chapel within the precinct with the clergy, hearing the offices, psalters and masses for her dying husband. The biography hints as much, talking of the ceaseless vigils and exertions she had undertaken over the weeks before her husband died.[15]

At Caversham, the old Marshal lingered, often noticeably in pain and eating little, from the end of March to the middle of May. Ever sensible of the approaching end, he said confession weekly. Though he took on the white cloak of a Templar, he did not yet divest himself of his lordship over men. One wonders whether he was ready as yet to give himself up as lost to life. It is so hard to abandon hope, and with the Marshal we do indeed see that the strongest mind will still turn from the last journey, even though it has accepted that it must soon leave. In the days immediately before he died, he asserted himself with some asperity, scolding his clerk Philip ('Be silent, rascal!'), who suggested that he sell for alms the robes laid in to distribute among his followers at Whitsun. Philip had made the error of reminding his lord of the last and most difficult farewell the Marshal had to make, a farewell to love and lordship. While he lived, he remained stubbornly the Earl of Pembroke.

---

13 As noted in M.M. Sheehan, *The Will in Medieval England* (Toronto, 1963) p. 147 and n.
14 *History* II, lines 18367–87.
15 *History* II, lines 18991–6.

At the end, he sank visibly, quite unable to eat and prey to hallucinations. The day before he died, he startled his attendant knights by declaring he saw two men in white on either side of his bed. They were quick to conclude that God had sent fitting counterparts of themselves to escort their lord on the journey in which they could not accompany him. John of Earley later told the author of the *History* how much he regretted that he had never asked who exactly his lord thought he had seen. The fascinations of the 'near-death experience' are nothing new.

The next day, 14 May, he died in his crowded chamber, a cross held before his face, lying in his son's arms, John of Earley beside him and two abbots signing his absolution. The scene was deeply affecting, and both the Young William and John of Earley took good care that their poet should record those last months of the Marshal's life in every detail, even down to the bread-stuffed mushrooms, which was all that they could get him to eat. As the late Professor Dominica Legge said, in the death scene as nowhere else, the *History* rings true. Here, there is no evasion or explanation. We have been led to the great man's death chamber to see how the good and pious soul that they believed him to be sanctified his life by leaving it as a good lord and a good Christian. There is no moralist's delight in the squalor and wretchedness of the deaths of princes. We had indeed been given a selection of these with which to compare the Marshal's departure: the Young Henry, his father and then John. But unlike them, William Marshal had lived well and died as he should. So he was recalled by the Marshal tenants assembled in Caversham itself some two decades later as 'the noble man of holy memory . . . the Lord William Marshal, not just a good man but the finest of them all'.[16] The good end counted for everything.

---

16 N. Vincent, 'More tales of the Conquest', in *Normandy and its Neighbours, 900–1250*, ed. D. Crouch and K. Thompson (Turnhout, 2011), p. 300–1.

APPENDIX I

The knights of William Marshal

The following is a selective list of the more prominent Marshal knights, as appears from charter attestations and the *History*. Certain men who were attached to the Marshal are not to be found here. Ralph Musard, a Gloucestershire knight, seems to have been a member of the Marshal retinue before the crisis of 1216. Thomas Basset, son of Alan Basset of High Wycombe, Buckinghamshire, was definitely a Marshal protégé, but probably rather late in the Marshal's life.

Other Marshal knights, such as William and Hamo le Gros, Richard Siward, Bogo de Knoville, Bartholomew de Mortemer, William de la Mare and Alan of Hyde, belong properly to a study of the younger William Marshal's household. Charters of William Marshal II in which he is already attended by this *mesnie* some time before his father's death are to be found in *Acts and Letters*, nos. 113, 115, 128, 141, 142, 164, 165.

Knights are listed in order of frequency of attestation.

1 John (II) of Earley. Grandson of John (I) of Earley, chamberlain of Henry I (ob. 1162–1163). Son and heir of William of Earley, Kt, chamberlain of Henry II and founder of Buckland priory, Som. (ob. 1181), and Aziria (viv. 1201), daughter of Ralph de Insula. In royal wardship 1181–1194, custody granted to William Marshal 1187 × 1188. Married Sybil (parentage unknown). Died 1229, before May. Children: John (III); Henry; a daughter, m. Henry de Brehull. Range of dated attestations: 1188–1219.
Sources: *Calendar of Inquisitions: Miscellaneous I*, p. 321; *Pipe Roll of 12 Henry II*, p. 97; *Pipe Roll of 27 Henry II*, p. 5; *Pipe Roll of 6 Richard I*, p. 184; *Buckland Cartulary*, ed. F.W. Weaver (Somerset Record Society, XXV, 1909), pp. 1–2, 26, 30; *Cartularies of Muchelney and Athelney Abbeys*, ed. E.H. Bates (Somerset Record Society, XIV, 1899), pp. 172, 190; *Red Book of the Exchequer I*, p. 235; *Book of Fees II*, p. 547; *Curia Regis Rolls I*, pp. 256–7; E. St J. Brooks, *Knights' Fees in Counties*

Wexford, Carlow and Kilkenny (Irish MSS Commission, Dublin, 1950), pp. 243–6; *Rot. Clausarum* I, pp. 115, 132; *Excerpta e Rotulis Finium* I, p. 184.

2 William Waleran. Son of Richard Waleran of Melksham, Wilts. (ob. a. 1182). Married (before 1206) Isabel, daughter of Roger (III) of Berkeley, Lord of Dursley, by grant of Earl William Marshal. Knight on Wilts. juries, 1202, 1203. Died after 1224. Children: Robert (seneschal of Henry III), William, John. Range of dated attestations: 1188–1202.
Sources: *Rot. Clausarum* I, p. 615; *Three Rolls of the King's Court, 1194–1195,* ed. F.W. Maitland (P.R. Soc., XIV, 1891); *Curia Regis Rolls* II, p. 103, III, p. 2, IV, p. 298, VII, pp. 264, 294; *Pipe Roll of 28 Henry II,* p. 84.

3 Geoffrey fitz Robert. Possibly the Geoffrey fitz Robert *camerarius* who succeeded his brother William in his Wilts. lands *c.*1190. Married (I) 1189 × 1199, Basilia, sister of Earl Richard Strongbow, widow of Raymond le Gros (ob. *c.*1188); (II) 1203 × 1209, Eve, daughter and heir of Robert of Birmingham. Founder of Kells priory and borough 1203 × 1210. Died 1211. Children: William, John (presumably by his second wife for Basilia could not have been less than 42 years of age when they married). Range of dated attestations: 1188–1210.
Sources: *Register of the Abbey of St Thomas Dublin,* ed. J.T. Gilbert (Rolls Series, 1889), pp. 112–13, 125; *Chartae, Privilegia et Immunitates* (Irish Record Commission, 1829), p. 17; *Rot. Chartarum,* p. 28; *Rot. Patentium,* p. 59; *Pipe Roll of 2 Richard I,* p. 123; *Pipe Roll of 5 Richard I,* p. 81; *Irish Monastic and Episcopal Deeds,* ed. N.B. White (Irish MSS Commission, 1936), pp. 300–13; *Calendar of Ormond Deeds, 1172–1350,* ed. E. Curtis (Irish MSS Commission, 1932), pp. 14–16, 134.

4 Jordan de Sauqueville. Descendant of Herbrand, constable of Arques and steward of Earl Walter Giffard (viv. 1086). Son and heir of William de Sauqueville. Died 1227 × 1235. Child: Bartholomew. Range of dated attestations: 1207–1216.
Sources: J.H. Round, 'Tales of the Conquest', in *Peerage and Pedigree* (2 vols, London, 1910) I, pp. 284–9; *Rot. Clausarum* I, pp. 271, 304; *Curia Regis Rolls* VII, p. 100; *Book of Fees* I, p. 464; *Calendar of the Justices in Eyre in Buckinghamshire,* 1227, ed. J.G. Jenkins (Buckinghamshire Record Society, VI, 1942), p. 36.

5 William Jardin. Knight on Bucks. jury 1203. Brother of William of Crendon. Married Cecilia (who later married Gilbert Marshal). Died 1220 × 1223. Children: William. Range of dated attestations: 1196–1219.
Sources: *Curia Regis Rolls* II, p. 217, XI, pp. 189, 231, 500–1; Bodleian Library, ms Dugdale 39 fos. 68r, 69v–70v; *Rotuli Curiae Regis, 6 Richard I to 1 John,* ed. F. Palgrave (Record Commission 1835), p. 63.

6 Ralph Bloet (III) or (IV). **Ralph Bloet (III)** eldest son of Ralph (II). Brother of Walter Bloet of Raglan and Robert Bloet of Daglingworth. Follower and tenant of Richard Strongbow, Earl of Striguil (died 1176). Keeper of the honor of Striguil (*c*.1176–1188). Married Nest, sister of Iorwerth ab Owain, lord of Caerleon (sometime mistress of King Henry II). Died 1198 × 1199. Children: Ralph (IV); Thomas; Roland; William; Petronilla, m (1) William of Feltham; m (2) Diarmait mac Carrthaig, King of Desmond. *Ralph Bloet (IV)* eldest son of Ralph (III). Died 1241 × 1242. Married Eve (parentage unknown). Children: William; Ralph. Range of dated attestations: 1189–1219.

Sources: *Domesday Book* I, fos. 47a, 71d, 96c, 166d; *Pipe Roll of 21 Henry II*, p. 194; *Pipe Roll of 22 Henry II*, p. 193; *Pipe Roll of 31 Henry II*, p. 8; *Pipe Roll of 34 Henry II*, p. 2; *Pipe Roll of I John*, p. 170; *Rot. Clausarum* II, pp. 23, 59; *Lacock Abbey Charters*, cal. K.H. Rogers (Wiltshire Records Society, XXXIV, 1978), p. 18; *The English Register of Godstow Abbey*, ed. A. Clark (2 vols, Early English Texts Society, 1906–1911), pp. 11–12, 134–5; *Durham Annals and Documents of the Thirteenth Century*, ed. F. Barlow (Surtees Society, clv, 1945), pp. 1–2; *Close Rolls*, 1231–1234, passim; *Book of Fees* II, p. 724.

7 John Marshal. Illegitimate son of John Marshal (II). Nephew of the Marshal. With king in Normandy (1203), in Ireland on William Marshal's service (1204), with king at Woodstock and Tewkesbury (1207), Ireland (1210), Runnymede (1215), ambassador to Rome (1215), at Newark (1216), at Battle of Lincoln (1217). Married (1199): Aline, heiress of Hubert (III) de Ryes, lord of honors of Ryes and Hockering. Marshal of Ireland (1207). Died 1235. Children: John; William. Range of dated attestations: 1194–1219.

Sources: References collected in *Complete Peerage* VIII, pp. 525–6.

8 Hugh of Sandford. Son of John of Sandford, marshal of King Henry II? Younger brother of Adam, Richard and Thomas of Sandford. Squire of King Henry II (1189). Married (before 1208): Joan de Chesney, heiress of Missenden, Bucks. With king in Poitou (1205), Durham (1212), La Rochelle (1214). Keeper of Bradenstoke Forest (1223). Advocate of Missenden Abbey. Died 1234. Illegitimate child: Juliana, hermit of Missenden. Range of dated attestations: 1196–1204.

Sources: *Monasticon* IV, p. 492; *Book of Fees* I, p. 105, II, p. 857; *Red Book of the Exchequer* I, p. 144; *Rot. Chartarum*, pp. 188, 201; *Rot. Clausarum* I, pp. 12, 44, 49, 109, 122, 552, 565; *Curia Regis Rolls* VI, p. 358; VII, p. 216; *Cartulary of Missenden Abbey*, ed. J.G. Jenkins (3 vols, Buckinghamshire Record Society, II, X, XII, 1938–1962) I, pp. 21–2, 50–1; British Library, Additional charter 21164.

9 Henry Hose (IV). Son and heir of Henry Hose (III) of Harting, Suss. (died 1213). Patron of Durford priory. Married: Cecilia, daughter of Emma of Stanton. Died 1231 × 1235. Children: Henry, Matthew. Range of dated attestations: 1199–1219.
Sources: References collected in W. Farrer, *Honors and Knights' Fees* III, pp. 83–7.

10 Henry fitz Gerold. Son of Henry fitz Gerold, chamberlain of King Henry II. Younger brother of Warin fitz Gerold (II), also chamberlain. Born 1173. Married (*c*.1203): Ermentrude, widow of (1) Quentin Talbot of Gainsborough, Lincs.; widow of (2) William of Grendon. Executor of William Marshal. Died *c.*1231. Child: Warin fitz Gerold. Range of dated attestations: 1199–1219.

Source: References collected in W. Farrer, *Honors and Knights' Fees* III, pp. 168–74. But see now N. Vincent, 'Warin and Henry fitz Gerald, the king's chamberlains: the origins of the FitzGeralds revisited', *Anglo-Norman Studies*, 21 (1999), pp. 233–60.

11 Alan de St-Georges. Son and heir of Ralph de St-Georges of Didling, Suss., and Agatha, daughter of Ralph fitz Savaric of Midhurst. Married: (1) (?Beatrice) widow of Richard de Guize (*c.*1177); (2) Sybil. Knight (elector) on Sussex juries: 1204; 1206; 1212; 1226. Constable of Knaresborough castle (1214). Died 1226 × 1231. No children, his sister Agatha his heir. Range of dated attestations: 1189–1199.

Sources: *Cartulary of Durford*, British Library, ms Cotton Vespasian E XXIII, fo. 40v.; *Cartulary of Wymondham*, British Library, ms Cotton Titus C VIII fo. 20v.; *Chartulary of the Priory of Boxgrove*, ed. L. Fleming (Sussex Record Society, LIX, 1960), pp. 72, 146–7; *The Chartulary of the High Church of Chichester*, ed. W.D. Peckham (Sussex Record Society, XLVI, 1942/43), pp. 89–90; *Calendar of Patent Rolls, 1358–1361*, p. 535; *Pipe Roll of 23 Henry II*, p. 99; *Pipe Roll of 2 Richard I*, p. 129; *Pipe Roll of 7 Richard I*, p. 37; *Pedes Finium, 1195–1214*, ed. J. Hunter (2 vols, London, 1844) II, p. 91; *Curia Regis Rolls* III, p. 173, IV, p. 157, VI, p. 282, XII, p. 449, XIV, p. 421; *Rot. Clausarum* I, p. 206.

12 Roger d'Abenon. Son and heir of Enguerrand d'Abenon. Married: Adelina, daughter and heir of William Peverel. Died childless 1216. No dated appearances in the Marshal's entourage but all appear before 1199.

Source: References collected in C.S. Perceval, 'Some account of the family of Abernon of Albury and Stoke d'Abernon', *Surrey Archaeological Society*, 5 (1871), pp. 53–8; C.A.F. Meekings, 'Notes on the de Abernon Family before 1236', *ibid.* 122, pp. 157–73.

13 Philip of Prendergast. Son and heir of Maurice of Prendergast. Married (1172 × 1176): Matilda, daughter of Earl Richard of Striguil. Died 1226 × 1229. Children: Gerald, David. Range of dated attestations: 1189–1208.

Sources: *Knights' Fees in Counties Wexford, Carlow and Kilkenny*, pp. 129–41, 145–51; *Rot. Clausarum* I, p. 171; *Rot. Patentium*, pp. 123, 144; *Close Rolls, 1227–1231*, p. 208.

14 Thomas de Rochford. Father unknown, brother of Robert of Rochford. Married (before 1204): Isabel, daughter of Roger of Berkeley. Daughter and heir: Alice, m. . . . de la Bere. Died 1206. Range of dated attestations: 1189–1199.

Sources: Berkeley Castle Muniments, Select Ch. 185; PRO JUST 1/273 m 2d; *Rot. Clausarum* I, pp. 6, 645; *Rot. Litterarum Patentium*, p. 39; *Curia Regis Rolls* IV, p. 298.

15 Thomas (II) de Colleville. Son of Thomas (?). Knight on Yorkshire juries: 1236; 1241. Knight on Lincolnshire jury: 1227. Range of dated attestations: 1189–1199. **Sources:** *Red Book* I, p. 420, II, p. 734; *Curia Regis Rolls* XIII, p. 37, XIV, pp. 145–6, XV, pp. 126, 487, XVI, p. 24, 311.

16 Nicholas Avenel (II). Son and heir of Nicholas (died 1212 × 1214) and Hilaria, co-heir of the barony of Curry Malet, Som. Died after 1220. Son: William. Range of dated attestations: 1190 × 1210.
Sources: Cartulary of Christchurch, Twynham, British Library, ms Cotton Tiberius D VI, pt 1, fo. 46v; *Pipe Roll of 6 Richard I*, p. 238; *Red Book of the Exchequer* I, p. 261; *Book of Fees* I, p. 96, II, pp. 96, 717, 782; *Curia Regis Rolls* VI, p. 142, IX, p. 365; *Rot. Clausarum* II, p. 238.

17 Stephen d'Evreux. Son of John (died *c.*1188). Married Isabel de Cantilupe (sister of William?). Died 1228, before March. Son: William (II) d'Evreux. Range of dated attestations: 1199–1219.
Sources: Lineage reconstructed in B. Holden, 'The making of the middle March of Wales, 1066–1250', *Welsh History Review*, 20 (2000), pp. 217–18. PRO E210/1363; Hereford County Record Office, Hopton Collection no. 107; Hereford D & C Archives, mun. no. 3235; Cartulary of Wormley, British Library, ms Harley 3586, fo. 89r; *Red Book* I, p. 282, II, p. 602; *Book of Fees* I, pp. 439, 440, II, p. 808; *Collectanea Topographica et Genealogica* II, p. 250; *Monasticon Anglicanum* VI, pp. 399–401; *Curia Regis Rolls* VII, p. 51, IX, p. 198, XII, p. 343; *Rot. Chartarum*, p. 156; *Rot. Clausarum* I, pp. 167, 168, 219, 437, 623; *Rot. Patentium*, p. 91; *Pipe Roll 8 Richard I*, p. 91; *Excerpta e Rotulis Finium* I, pp. 168, 442; *Cal Charter Rolls* I, p. 43; *Flaxley Cartulary* I, p. 34.

18 Eustace de Bertrimont. No personal details known. Range of dated attestations: 1183–1219.

APPENDIX II

The Marshal and the Earl Marshal

From his earliest appearances in the *History*, William son of John Marshal is invariably William *li Mareschal*, or often just *li Mareschal*. Yet he did not inherit the office of royal marshal until the death of his brother John in 1194. We cannot dismiss this as a retrospective elevation, however. Other evidence, particularly the government list of the rebels of 1174, preserved by Roger of Howden, tells us that he was called by contemporaries William *Marescallus* (the Marshal) in the lifetime of his brother. In the Exchequer records of 1165–1166, both William's elder brothers, Gilbert (II) and John, are called *Marescallus*. In 1189, his younger brother Henry was also called *Marescallus*. From this, it is clear enough that all the sons of John Marshal (I) took their father's office as a surname.

The transformation of hereditary offices into surnames was by no means uncommon in the twelfth century: there were then numerous families who took the names of Butler, Chamberlain, Steward or Seneschal, or Despencer, who traced their origins to a man who was an actual office holder. Sometimes, the office continued to be hereditary in the family, but quite often it did not; nonetheless, the name continued to be used. The example of the Marshals is more interesting in that it is rather early to find several sons taking their surname from the father's office. I can only think of one comparable example, the Despencer family of Leicestershire. The family descended from Geoffrey, the despencer of Earl Ranulf II of Chester in Stephen's reign. By John's reign, all five of his grandsons were sporting the name 'Despencer'. There may well be other instances, however, of which I am unaware.

The office of marshal was an ancient one. The Latin word *marescallus* or *marescalcus* preserved two ancient Frankish elements meaning 'horse-slave'; it seems very likely that the word was being applied to the unfree grooms of the ancestors of the Merovingian kings of the Franks. The office was well in evidence at the court of the Carolingian kings and emperors, although it was not a high one.

The titles of the Carolingian court were transmitted to the courts of its later imitators, the kings and princes of France. The Normans brought them to England where the royal court contained all the functionaries who had surrounded Charlemagne centuries earlier. According to the *Constitutio Domus Regis* (the Organisation of the King's Household), a treatise compiled early in 1136 for the information of King Stephen, the English court then had a Master Marshal 'namely John' (William Marshal's father). John Marshal headed the department called the Marshalcy (otherwise called the Marshalsea), and received fees and provisions ranking him with the other great officers, the seneschal, the constable and the master chamberlain. His duties then involved the keeping of certain royal records. Besides this, there was his department to oversee. The Marshalcy contained four other lesser marshals, both clerks and knights, assistants called sergeants, the knight ushers and common ushers of the royal hall, the usher of the king's chamber, the watchmen of the court, the tent-keeper and the keeper of the king's hearth. From this information, it seems that the marshal was then responsible for the good order of the court, and the supervision of movements both within and without the palace.

The *Constitutio* assumes that John Marshal actually carried out the functions ascribed to him. Certainly, the evidence of royal charters of 1135–1138 places John in close attendance on the king. But it is very unlikely that any of his sons did so, and unlikely too that he carried out his office about the court and Exchequer after his breach with Stephen in 1138. After that, the office (like the Chamberlainship held by the Earley family) became purely honorary. Thirteenth-century evidence tells us that the later Marshals did indeed occasionally take over the supervision of the hall, but only on great state occasions such as a king's or a queen's coronation. Similarly, the function of the keeping of the records of debts and settlements reached in the Exchequer devolved on to a nominee of the Marshal, a deputy marshal (a clerk called in Henry III's reign 'the marshal of the Marshalcy of the royal court'). The earliest so far known of these is Master Joscelin (occasionally called Joscelin Marshal or Joscelin of the Exchequer), rector of Tidenham, Gloucestershire, and a long-serving clerk of William Marshal (see Chapter 11). The one aspect of the Marshal's office in which he may have kept some active concern was the keeping of the records of service done in the royal army.

The Marshal's office as held by William Marshal, and probably also his elder brother, was an honorific, the work being done by someone else. That does not mean that it was an unimportant honorific, however. The *Constitutio* already reveals that there was the idea at the courts of Henry I and Stephen that certain officers (seneschal, master chamberlain, master butler, constable and master marshal) were raised above others. In Henry II's reign, we begin to find the baronial families who held these hereditary offices were using them as titles in their own right. Thus, the heads of the Hereford family (after it lost the earldom of Hereford in 1155) fell back for its dignity on the secondary title of 'royal constable' (*constabularius regis*). John Marshal (II) on occasion had himself described as 'royal marshal'. The Mauduit family were similarly 'royal chamberlains'. In the thirteenth century, the offices were in the hands of great earls: the Chamberlainship went to the Earls of

Warwick; the seneschalcy to the Earls of Leicester; the constabulary (once more) to the Earls of Hereford. All these earls took the office as part of their style: Henry de Bohun was 'earl of Hereford and constable of England'. Such styles were much sought after. Lacking an English one, the Quincy Earls of Winchester fell back on their constableship of Scotland. The Irish hereditary offices of state were paraded in a similar way.

The Marshal Earls of Pembroke very rarely called themselves 'marshals of England', although their successors, the Bigot Earls of Norfolk, made it part of their routine style after 1245. What did happen, however, was that the Marshal Earls of Pembroke came generally to be called the 'Earls Marshal'. Their surname, title and office were run together in common usage to appear to create something quite new. This was already happening at the time of William Marshal (I). He and all his Marshal successors called themselves consistently 'Earl of Pembroke'. But on several occasions, William was called by others *Comes Willelmus Marescallus*. What this meant was that his title of earl was simply preceding his full name, rather in the same way as the contemporary Earl of Surrey was called *Comes Willelmus Warenne*. To talk of the 'Earl Marshal' rather than the 'Earl of Pembroke' was simply the next step after this, and a personage called the *comes marescallus* certainly appears in the time of William Marshal II. Thus, because of laziness in the thirteenth century, we still have an 'Earl Marshal' in the English peerage, since the late-fourteenth century a title combined with the duchy of Norfolk.

(For this, see, in general, studies in: J.H. Round, *The Commune of London* (Westminster, 1899); J.H. Round, *The King's Sergeants and Officers of State* (London, 1911); *The Complete Peerage* x, appendix G.)

GENERAL BIBLIOGRAPHY

The following is a brief guide to works of use on the general topics covered by each of the chapters.

Chapter 1

For the political background of Stephen's reign, there are a large number of fine studies. R.H.C. Davis, *King Stephen* (3rd edn, London, 1990), gives an insightful, brief and polemical romp through the reign. K.J. Stringer, *The Reign of Stephen* (London, 1993), is also brief and readable, but more measured in tone. J. Bradbury, *Stephen and Matilda: The Civil War of 1139–53* (Stroud, 1996), is a military history of the reign. *King Stephen's Reign, 1135–1154*, ed. P. Dalton and G.J. White (Woodbridge, 2008), offers a variety of essays. Comprehensive recent treatments of the whole reign are D. Crouch, *The Reign of King Stephen, 1135–54* (London, 2000) and E. King, *King Stephen* (New Haven, 2010). For the Angevin side, see M. Chibnall, *The Empress Matilda: Queen Consort, Queen Mother and Lady of the English* (Oxford, 1991). For excellent studies on the general background of Norman and Angevin England, its politics, institutions and culture, see: M. Chibnall, *Anglo-Norman England, 1066–1166* (Oxford, 1986); R. Bartlett, *England under the Norman and Angevin Kings, 1075–1225* (Oxford, 2000).

Chapters 2 and 3

For the reign of Henry II, the only general modern study is W.L. Warren, *Henry II* (London, 1973); this can be supplemented now by the fine collection of essays, *Henry II: New Interpretations*, ed. C. Harper-Bill and N. Vincent (Woodbridge, 2007). For the Angevin age and its culture, invaluable are J. Gillingham, *The Angevin Empire* (2nd edn, London, 2001); M. Aurell, *The Plantagenet Empire, 1154–1224*, trans.

D. Crouch (Harlow, 2007); and R. Bartlett, *England under the Norman and Angevin Kings, 1075–1225* (Oxford, 2000). In contrast to her husband, Queen Eleanor has inspired many studies, see for good guides, J. Flori, *Aliénor d'Aquitaine* (Paris, 2004); *Eleanor of Aquitaine. Queen of France, Queen of England* (New Haven, 2011). For the Kingdom of France at this time, see: E.M. Hallam and J. Everard, *Capetian France, 987–1328* (2nd edn, London, 2001); J. Dunbabin, *France in the Making, 843–1180* (2nd edn, Oxford, 2001). The only published study on the Young Henry is O.H. Moore, *The Young King Henry Plantagenet, 1155–1183* (Columbus, 1925), but this is disappointing on his political career. A recent demonstration as to what can be done with his career is, M. Strickland, 'The upbringing of Henry, the Young King', in *Henry II: New Interpretations*, pp. 184–214. For a detailed study of the last years of the Latin Kingdom of Jerusalem as William Marshal saw it, see B. Hamilton, *The Leper King and his Heirs: Baldwin IV and the Crusader Kingdom of Jerusalem* (Cambridge, 2000).

Chapter 4

For the reign of Richard, there is now one thorough academic study, J. Gillingham, *Richard I* (New Haven, 1999), but see also R.V. Turner and R. Heiser, *The Reign of Richard Lionheart* (Harlow, 2000). For the duel between Philip and the Angevins, the classic study is F.M. Powicke, *The Loss of Normandy* (2nd edn, Manchester, 1961); but see also J.C. Holt, 'The end of the Anglo-Norman realm', *Proceedings of the British Academy*, 61 (1975), pp. 223–65. For a thorough biography of the French monarch, J. Bradbury, *Philip Augustus* (London, 1997).

Chapter 5

Disasters attract crowds of onlookers, and this is as true for John's as Stephen's reign. There are numerous worthwhile studies, beginning with K. Norgate, *John Lackland* (London, 1902); S. Painter, *The Reign of King John* (Baltimore, 1949); J.T. Appleby, *John, King of England* (London, 1960); W.L. Warren, *King John* (2nd edn, London, 1978) and R.V. Turner, *King John* (London, 1994). More recently have appeared S.D. Church, *King John and the Road to Magna Carta* (London, 2015) and M. Morris, *King John: Treachery, Tyranny and the Road to Magna Carta* (London, 2015). For studies of particular aspects of the reign in England and France, *King John: New Interpretations*, ed. S. Church (Woodbridge, 1999) and *The England of King John and Magna Carta*, ed. J. Loengard (Woodbridge, 2010). For Ireland at this time, still valuable is G.H. Orpen, *Ireland under the Normans*, II, *1169–1216* (Oxford, 1911), but there are more recent monographs that break new ground, notably M.T. Flanagan, *Irish Society, Anglo-Norman Settlers, Angevin Kingship* (Oxford, 1989) and C. Veach, *Lordship in Four Realms: The Lacy Family, 1166–1241* (Manchester, 2014).

Chapter 6

For the Barons' War and Magna Carta, see J.C. Holt, *The Northerners* (Oxford, 1961); J.C. Holt, *Magna Carta* (Cambridge, 1965); F.M. Powicke, *Stephen Langton* (Oxford, 1928); C.R. Cheney, *Pope Innocent III and England* (Stuttgart, 1976); D.A. Carpenter, *Magna Carta* (London, 2015). For a military history, S. McGlynn, *Blood Cries Afar: The Forgotten Invasion of England, 1216* (Stroud, 2013); R. Brooks, *The Knight who Saved England: William Marshal and the French Invasion, 1217* (London, 2014).

Chapter 7

For the minority of Henry III, see: F.M. Powicke, *King Henry III and the Lord Edward* (Oxford, 1947); D. Carpenter, *The Minority of Henry III* (London, 1990); N. Vincent, *Peter des Roches* (Cambridge, 1996).

Chapter 8

Courtliness is a subject brought into the historical debate by the celebrated essay on aristocratic mores, C.S. Jaeger, *The Origins of Courtliness* (Philadelphia, 1985). It is contextualised in Anglo-French sources in D. Crouch, *The Birth of Nobility: Constructing Aristocracy in England and France, 900–1300* (Harlow, 2005), the first study to explore the idea of the *preudomme*. For the idea of chivalry, see, above all, M. Keen, *Chivalry* (New Haven, 1984), but also S. Painter, *French Chivalry* (Baltimore, 1940); R.W. Barber, *The Knight and Chivalry* (London, 1970); J. Flori, *L'Essor de Chevalerie* (Geneva, 1986); R.W. Kaeuper, *Chivalry and Violence in Medieval Europe* (Oxford, 1999). For the complications in the concept, see D. Crouch, 'Courtliness and chivalry: colliding constructs', in *Soldiers, Nobles and Gentlemen: Essays in Honour of Maurice Keen*, ed. P.R. Coss and C. Tyerman (Woodbridge, 2009), pp. 32–48. For the tournament of that age, see N. Denholm-Young, 'The tournament in the thirteenth century', *Studies Presented to F.M. Powicke*, ed. R.W. Hunt and others (Oxford, 1948), pp. 204–68; J.R.V. Barker, *The Tournament in England, 1100–1400* (Woodbridge, 1986); D. Crouch, *Tournament* (London, 2005); E. Oksanen, *Flanders and the Anglo-Norman World, 1066–1216* (Cambridge, 2012), ch. 4.

Chapter 9

For warfare, there are a variety of available studies, P. Contamine, *War in the Middle Ages* (Oxford, 1984); K. DeVries, *Medieval Military Technology* (Peterborough, ON, 1992); M. Prestwich, *Armies and Warfare in the Middle Ages* (New Haven, 1996); J. France, *Western Warfare in the Age of the Crusades, 1000–1300* (Ithaca, NY, 1999); *Medieval Warfare: A History*, ed. M. Keen (Oxford, 1999). For the Marshal's period, M. Strickland, *War and Chivalry: The Conduct and Perception of War in England*

and Normandy, 1066–1217 (Cambridge, 1996), and for some revisionist comments J. Gillingham, 'Richard I and the science of war in the Middle Ages', in *War and Government in the Middle Ages: Essays in Honour of J. O. Prestwich* (Woodbridge, 1984), pp. 78–91.

Chapter 10

A useful overview of twelfth-century social structures is, D. Crouch, 'From Stenton to McFarlane: models of societies in the twelfth and thirteenth centuries', *Transactions of the Royal Historical Society*, 6th ser., no. 5 (1995), pp. 179–200, developed extensively as D. Crouch, *The English Aristocracy, 1070–1272: A Social Transformation* (New Haven, 2011). A useful study for the generation of John Marshal is, J.A. Green, *The Aristocracy of Norman England* (Cambridge, 1997). For contemporary France, there is C.B. Bouchard, *Strong of Body, Brave and Noble: Chivalry and Society in Medieval France* (Ithaca, NY, 1998). For a series of essays on daily life in the late twelfth and thirteenth centuries based on its correspondence, see, *Lost Letters of Medieval Life: English Society, 1200–1250*, ed. M. Carlin and D. Crouch (Philadelphia, 2013).

Chapter 11

For the status of the knight in twelfth- and thirteenth-century society, see generally, G. Duby, *The Three Orders: Feudal Society Imagined*, trans. A. Goldhammer (Chicago, 1980); F. Gies, *The Knight in History* (New York, 1987); D. Crouch, *The Image of Aristocracy in Britain, 1000–1300* (London, 1992), ch. 4; P.R. Coss, *The Knight in Medieval England* (Stroud, 1993), D. Barthélemy, *La chevalerie: de la Germanie antique à la France du xiie siècle* (Paris, 2007). For the clerical household, the nearest approach to a general study remains C.R. Cheney, *English Bishops' Chanceries, 1150–1250* (Manchester, 1950). For contemporary baronial administration, see N. Denholm-Young, *Seignorial Administration in England* (London, 1937). But for the class of secular clergy that Marshal employed, there are two fresh and comprehensive studies, H.M. Thomas, *The Secular Clergy in England, 1066–1216* (Oxford, 2014); J. Barrow, *The Clergy in the Medieval World: Secular Clerics, their Families and Careers in North-Western Europe, c.800–c.1200* (Cambridge, 2015).

Chapter 12

On the monastic orders generally: D. Knowles, *The Monastic Order in England* (Cambridge, 1949); J. Burton, *Monastic and Religious Orders in Britain, 1000–1300* (Cambridge, 1994). On the subject of monastic patronage at the time of the Marshal, see: E.M. Thompson, *The Carthusian Order in England* (London, 1930); J.C. Dickinson, *The Origins of the Austin Canons and their Introduction into England* (London, 1950); E. Jamroziak, *The Cistercian Order in Medieval Europe, 1090–1500* (London, 2013); E.M. Hallam, 'Henry II as a founder of monasteries', *Journal of*

Ecclesiastical History, 28 (1977), pp. 113–32; D. Crouch, *The Image of Aristocracy in Britain, 1000–1300* (London, 1992), ch. 10. For the Marshal's Irish abbeys, see A.H. Thompson and others, 'The Cistercian order in Ireland', *Archaeological Journal*, 88 (1931), pp. 1–36; R. Stalley, *The Cistercian Monasteries of Ireland* (London, 1987). For the twelfth- and thirteenth-century deathbed and its rites, D. Crouch, 'The culture of death in the Anglo-Norman world', in *Anglo-Norman Political Culture*, ed. C. Warren Hollister (Boydell, 1996), pp. 157–80; S.L. Waugh, 'Royal deathbed scenes in medieval England', in *Death at Court*, ed. K.-H. Spieß and I. Warntjes (Wiesbaden, 2012), pp. 117–34; S.D. Church, 'King John's testament and the last days of his reign', *English Historical Review*, 125 (2010), pp. 505–28.

MAPS

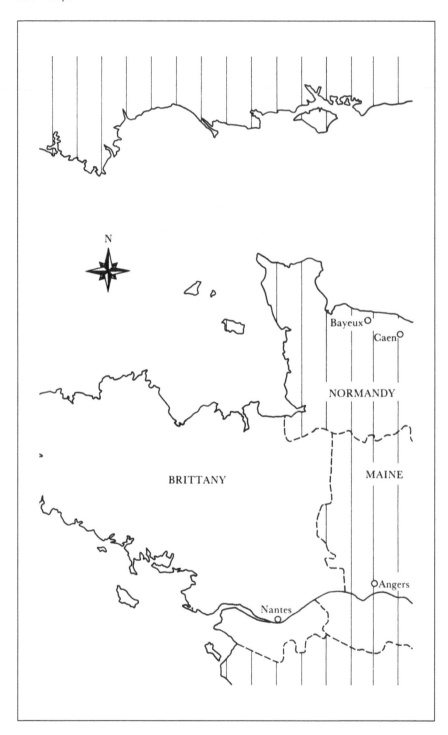

MAP 1 Northern France *c.*1200

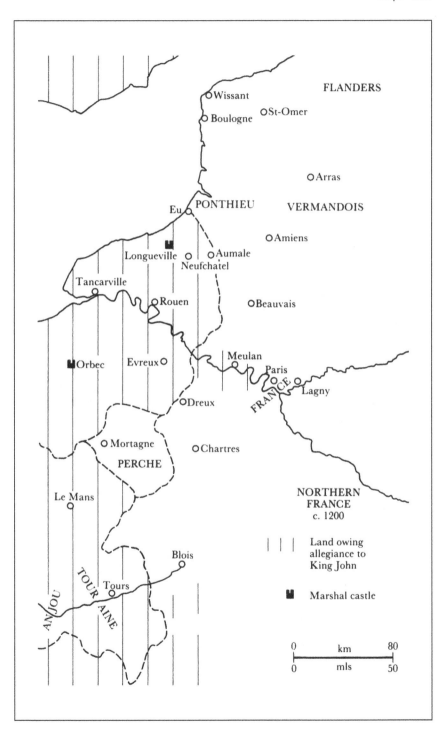

MAP 1 Northern France *c.*1200

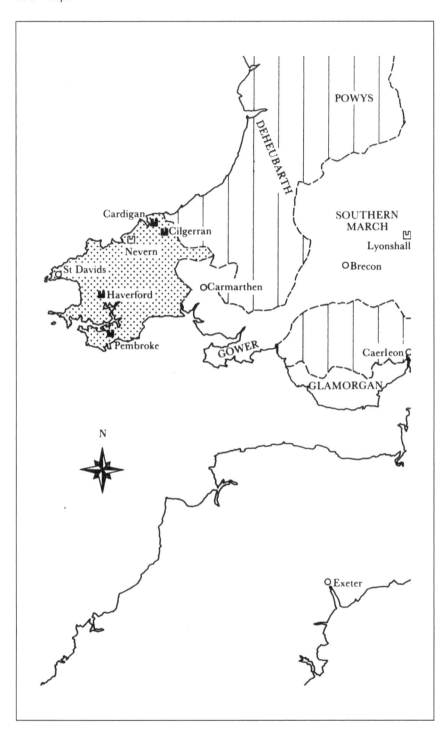

MAP 2 South–west England *c*.1204

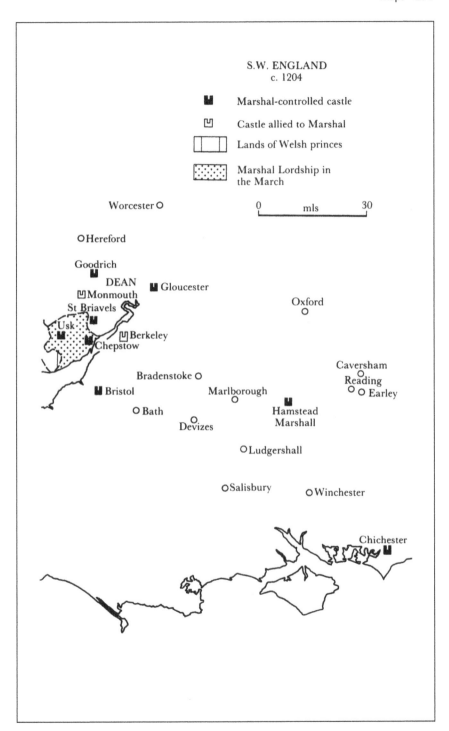

MAP 2 South–west England *c.*1204

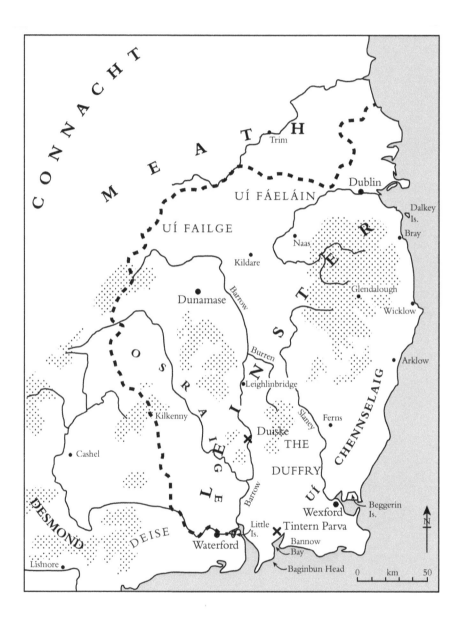

MAP 3 Leinster (Lagenia) *c.*1208

INDEX

Taylor & Francis eBooks

Helping you to choose the right eBooks for your Library

Add Routledge titles to your library's digital collection today. Taylor and Francis ebooks contains over 50,000 titles in the Humanities, Social Sciences, Behavioural Sciences, Built Environment and Law.

Choose from a range of subject packages or create your own!

Benefits for you

» Free MARC records
» COUNTER-compliant usage statistics
» Flexible purchase and pricing options
» All titles DRM-free.

Benefits for your user

» Off-site, anytime access via Athens or referring URL
» Print or copy pages or chapters
» Full content search
» Bookmark, highlight and annotate text
» Access to thousands of pages of quality research at the click of a button.

REQUEST YOUR **FREE** INSTITUTIONAL TRIAL TODAY

Free Trials Available
We offer free trials to qualifying academic, corporate and government customers.

eCollections – Choose from over 30 subject eCollections, including:

Archaeology	Language Learning
Architecture	Law
Asian Studies	Literature
Business & Management	Media & Communication
Classical Studies	Middle East Studies
Construction	Music
Creative & Media Arts	Philosophy
Criminology & Criminal Justice	Planning
Economics	Politics
Education	Psychology & Mental Health
Energy	Religion
Engineering	Security
English Language & Linguistics	Social Work
Environment & Sustainability	Sociology
Geography	Sport
Health Studies	Theatre & Performance
History	Tourism, Hospitality & Events

For more information, pricing enquiries or to order a free trial, please contact your local sales team:
www.tandfebooks.com/page/sales

Routledge
Taylor & Francis Group

The home of
Routledge books

www.tandfebooks.com